THE SPARTAN TRADITION
IN EUROPEAN THOUGHT

THE
SPARTAN TRADITION
IN
EUROPEAN THOUGHT

◨

ELIZABETH RAWSON

CLARENDON PRESS · OXFORD

1969

Oxford University Press, Ely House, London W.1

GLASGOW NEW YORK TORONTO MELBOURNE WELLINGTON
CAPE TOWN SALISBURY IBADAN NAIROBI LUSAKA ADDIS ABABA
BOMBAY CALCUTTA MADRAS KARACHI LAHORE DACCA
KUALA LUMPUR SINGAPORE HONG KONG TOKYO

PRINTED IN GREAT BRITAIN BY
ALDEN & MOWBRAY LTD
AT THE ALDEN PRESS, OXFORD

PREFACE

CLASSICAL scholars are aware of the long and remarkable tale of
the idealization of Sparta in antiquity, and a good deal of work
has been done on the subject. But when I attempted to carry on
the story, in outline, down to the present day—for a lecture,
and also for my own interest—I was surprised to find that almost
no part of it had been explicitly treated. Furthermore, such
recognition of Sparta's attractiveness in certain periods and contexts as I have found tends to be either so vague as to be useless
(it means precisely nothing to say that 'So-and-so admired
Sparta') or else actually exaggerated. I was left, therefore, to my
own resources: and the subject, though often of minor importance, is a vast one. I am very much aware of my incompetence
adequately to deal with the twenty-seven or so centuries involved,
as of the frequent superficialities and probable inaccuracies of my
rash attempt. But it seems to me that what is so fascinating is the
whole tale in all its length and variety, and therefore that a
first sketch was worth making and might encourage others to
amend it.

The following chapters cover, I believe, the most important
shifts and reversals of attitude towards Sparta in Western thought.
I have given a good deal of space to eighteenth-century France,
since it is here that Sparta's rôle is of some importance, and seems
to have been generally misunderstood. I should have liked to be
able to explore recent developments in Russia (although it seems
that socialists there as elsewhere now prefer Athens to Sparta),
and I suspect that Spain, Holland, Switzerland and Poland have
more to offer for certain earlier periods than here appears. But
the book is more than long enough, especially since I hope that
some of the subject's attraction may be felt by readers without
expert knowledge in any of the fields concerned. For this reason
I have tried to avoid scholarly controversy, particularly in the
first part of the book: the more willingly since E. N. Tigerstedt's
first volume of his as yet uncompleted work *The Legend of Sparta*

in Classical Antiquity, published in 1965 in Sweden (which I read when my corresponding chapters were well advanced, but which enabled me to fill several minor gaps), deals at great length with, and provides an immense bibliography for, the period down to the end of the fourth century B.C. I am naturally also indebted to the two volumes of P. Ollier's *Le Mirage Spartiate*, a first attempt to collect the ancient material on the subject.

It remains for me to add that I have not thought it necessary to provide translations of the passages in other languages. Greek is confined to the footnotes, while such other quotations, apart from those in French, as remain in the text, are almost all illustrative of rather than integral to the argument.

The book was conceived and partly written while I was a Leverhulme Research Fellow at New Hall, Cambridge. I am grateful to various friends and acquaintances, among whom I should like to mention the late Felix Raab, for the interest they have taken in my work; in addition, Michael Crawford helped me over the selection of coins for Plate 1; R. F. Tannenbaum read the typescript and gave me useful advice in preparing it for the press; and it has owed more, at every stage, to one who in no way resembles a Spartan Mother, save in her dislike of unnecessary verbiage.

E.D.R.

New Hall
April 1969

ACKNOWLEDGEMENTS

Illustrations: I am indebted to the following for courteous assistance and permission to reproduce: the Fitzwilliam Museum, Cambridge (Plate 1); the British Museum (Plates 2, 3, and 6); the Royal Academy of Arts, and the National Trust, Stourhead (Plate 4); and in particular, Monsieur Laclotte, Director of the Département de Peinture, Musée du Louvre, and Giraudon, Paris (Plate 5).

CONTENTS

LIST OF PLATES

I

INTRODUCTION

ANCIENT SPARTA: a militaristic and totalitarian state, holding down an enslaved population, the helots, by terror and violence, educating its young by a system incorporating all the worst features of the traditional English public school, and deliberately turning its back on the intellectual and artistic life of the rest of Greece. Such, at least, is the picture, if any, which mention of the name consciously or unconsciously conjures up in the minds of most people in this country today. The liberal democratic tradition that dominates modern English thought has very naturally tended to idealize Sparta's great rival, democratic Athens; and its consequent distrust of Sparta was reinforced by reaction against a very different set of political ideas, particularly prominent in Germany, where admiration for Sparta reached a fantastic conclusion under the Nazis; to some writers, at that time, Sparta was the most purely Nordic state in Greece, and an exemplar of National Socialist virtues. Two hundred years ago, however, an ordinary educated Englishman would most probably have viewed the Spartan constitution as a prototype of the British limited monarchy in all its perfection; his French contemporary might have been one of those who revered her, with Rousseau and others, primarily as an egalitarian, often more or less communistic, republic. Two hundred years before that she appeared in still other guises; as the ideal aristocratic republic, for example, practically indistinguishable from Venice. And so we might go on.

For over two and a half millennia politicians and philosophers, in the light of their own needs and convictions, have regarded now one aspect and now another of Sparta as significant. From almost the dawn of Greek history enormous prestige surrounded her, and this was exploited to recommend the most disparate virtues and institutions; the occasional reactions are correspondingly obsessive. Only Rome, sometimes as republic and sometimes as empire, has exerted greater attraction; influence cannot be measured, and is a word to avoid.

With the history of attitudes to ancient Rome scholars have to some extent occupied themselves. They have largely neglected the longer and even more Protean history of laconism, as the Greeks called it, though classical scholars have paid considerable attention to the first part of the story, that of Sparta's reputation in ancient Greece itself. But if Sparta has not dominated the stage as much as Rome, she has usually played a more prominent role than Athens. The reputation of one of the two great city-states of Greece necessarily involves that of its rival in practice as well as theory; indeed, most of our ideas about Sparta can be traced ultimately to Athenian critics, occupied above all with self-criticism. But between the end of the fifth century B.C. and the eighteenth century A.D. Athens, or at least Athenian democracy, was as a political ideal in almost permanent eclipse. It is the fortunes of Sparta that make up a continuous and comprehensible story, interesting and at times amusing in itself, and above all apt to throw light on the political and moral ideas of antiquity, and on the reflection of these ideas in more recent times.

What Sparta in fact was is of less importance to us than what she was thought to be; indeed scholars have always found it all but impossible to disentangle the one from the other, partly because so many of the ancient sources are strikingly lacking in objectivity. Let us, however, briefly recall her main features, as they appeared in the fifth century B.C. The state with which we are concerned was seemingly founded by some of the 'Dorian' Greeks, who entered the peninsula after the first flowering of Greek civilization in the Bronze Age, and it replaced an important kingdom of Mycenean Greece. It was officially known, like its forerunner, as Lacedaemon, rather than by the name of its new capital Sparta, as is usual today—though it was the citizens of Sparta alone, properly to be described as Spartiates, who controlled the whole southern area of the Peloponnese, an area which we now generally call by its Roman or at least late-classical name Laconia. This, like *laconic*, comes from the conveniently shortened forms of the adjective Lacedaemonian which were in common use in Greece.

The most striking, perhaps, of all the new Lacedaemon's striking features was the double kingship. Two kings from distinct and frequently hostile houses but both supposedly descended from the hero Heracles reigned simultaneously and with equal powers. But these powers had been progressively so circum-scribed (though not to the extent suffered by the monarchy in Athens and elsewhere) that by the fifth or fourth century the Spartan kings might be regarded as little more than hereditary commanders-in-chief, with various other privileges mostly reli-gious and ceremonial. The assembly of Spartiates decided which of the two kings was to lead a particular campaign; once in the field, the king could normally conduct war and negotiate with allies or enemies at his own discretion, but might be tried on his return should his decisions prove unwelcome (we hear of special commissioners being sent out to oversee a king's actions abroad, but this appears to have been unusual). The kings married into leading families at Sparta, not into each other's or abroad. Herodotus, who was interested in their position, implies that they not only presided over the council but had two votes apiece in it. Thucydides roughly denied this last, no doubt rightly for his own time;[1] and the presidency may also have passed by then to the ephors.

These were a board of five magistrates elected each year by the Spartiates. The ephors or 'overseers' appear to have been instituted originally as watchdogs of the kings on behalf of the citizens. They received from the kings a monthly oath to observe the laws (which, on entering office, they also ordered the people to do) and even had the power to arrest them, for the kings were subject to trial and punishment. There are late and perhaps un-reliable tales implying that the ephors might even inflict summary fines on them for various misdemeanours. The ephorate was closely similar in many respects to the supreme executive magis-tracy in other Greek states. By the fifth century its members presided over the assembly, conducting its business and putting questions to the vote; they were responsible for raising the military levy; they received foreign envoys, and determined whether to refer their requests to the council and assembly; they had extensive judicial functions, each ephor being charged to hear a particular class of cases; they had considerable police powers, especially over the helots. They were able to take a strong initiative on many occasions, and theorists sometimes regarded them as the real rulers of the state, but it seems that when there was a popular and energetic king they could sink

---

[1] Herodotus vi. 57; Thucydides i. 20.

into insignificance. It is noteworthy that they were apparently often men of humble extraction and popular sympathies, as these went in Sparta.

Not so the members of the council or Gerousia, consisting of twenty-eight elders over the age of sixty who were elected for life and sat with the kings—though possibly, in classical times, under the ephors—to prepare business for the assembly, on the pattern usual in Greece (this gave them the sole initiative in all legislation). The council also acted as the highest court of justice; to it were reserved all cases involving the penalties of death, exile, or loss of civic rights. The small number, permanence, and high age-qualification made the council look very oligarchic to fifth-century eyes, in spite of its popular election. According to the precious early document known as the Great Rhetra and quoted by Plutarch, the kings and council together could even overrule the assembly. But it is uncertain if this was so in the fifth century, when the ephors had become so potent a factor in the state, and when the assembly appears in all our historical narratives as the ultimate authority.

This assembly of all male citizens met to elect officials by acclamation, to decide on peace or war, and for the little new legislation there was. The ordinary member, unlike the Athenian, could probably only listen to the speeches of notables. Again, this was doubtless the usual state of affairs in the archaic period. During the fifth century the number of citizens seems to have fallen to a very few thousand, and this too made it possible to regard the whole state as an oligarchy, though even so it rested on a broader base than most Greek oligarchies, and in the seventh and sixth centuries must have appeared remarkably liberal. But the assembly was also restricted, as we shall see, to those fulfilling a property qualification, and further excluded the *perioeci*, the inhabitants of the other cities of Laconia over which the Spartiates early extended their rule; but these possessed, with the name of Lacedaemonians, probably considerable local autonomy (Athens, by contrast, fully enfranchised the whole of Attica). Even more obviously, the helots were excluded. Presumably in origin the earlier rural population, pre-Dorian but not necessarily wholly pre-Greek, these had been reduced to a kind of state serfdom. Helots lived on and worked the lands of individual Spartiates; they were bound to the soil, having no freedom of movement, but were not bound to their masters, being legally servants of the state; they could be freed or moved only by state order. They were, however, required to give a fixed proportion or quantity of produce to the Spartiate who held the land, for the support of his household and the payment of his dues in the common mess. They were also required to serve in war when called up by the magistrates. They appear to have been subject to arbitrary arrest and execution, and there are dark hints of terroristic tactics against them: sudden murder raids, the unexplained disappearance of some 2,000 helots who had distinguished themselves in the Peloponnesian War. This unfree population, at least after Sparta conquered the neighbouring province of Messenia in the late eighth century B.C., enormously outnumbered its masters, a fact that not only explains the ruthlessness with which it was often treated but doubtless had the greatest influence on the whole Spartan way of life.

Such was the political constitution of Sparta. Most of it was usually attributed to the great lawgiver Lycurgus, supposed to have been a member of one of the royal houses about the ninth century B.C., who imposed his laws as regent for an infant nephew. The ephorate however was sometimes believed, probably rightly, to be rather later in its full development at least, while as all agreed the double kingship went far further back. But Lycurgus was thought to be responsible also for the social institutions that the rest of Greece grew to find so remarkable. These were, in essence, the communal and military way of life of the Spartiates, with an economic basis ultimately supposed to involve an egalitarian division of land and the absence of coinage as well as the eschewing of industry and commerce, and a moral basis stressing such virtues as obedience and courage. In reality many features of this life must go back to a very primitive period, though it is probable that the system was much altered and developed at some time.

In Sparta, as elsewhere for that matter, deformed or feeble children were exposed at birth. It is uncertain how reliable may be stories that infant toughness was tested by means of baths in wine or icy water, but it is perhaps true that the decision to rear or destroy a child lay not with the father but with the elders of his tribe. At the age, probably, of seven the boy who had survived these hazards entered a 'herd' or *agela*, under the supervision of an older boy (with the right to beat his juniors) and ultimately of a magistrate, the *paedonomus*, but also of any citizen who happened to be present. At twelve the boys were taken from home and kept in barracks until the age of eighteen, where they were trained, under twenty-year-old officers, to drill and to fight in mimic battles. They were expected at this stage to take grown male lovers, and learn the proper habits of a soldier and a citizen from them. (Ancient authors dispute endlessly the exact nature of these relations; a form of bundling seems to have been practised; Cicero has probability on his side when he cites the rule of physical chastity in these contacts, and doubts its efficacy.) In barracks the trainees were questioned constantly by their officers at meals; the boy who gave an inadequate answer was struck smartly on the thumb. Our sources lay stress on the physical toughness of the boys' training and its military object; they went without shoes and had inadequate clothing and food—the last eked out by secret marauding on private property, for which they were praised if successful but beaten where lack of skill led to detection. Courage was tested at a religious ceremony involving endurance of the lash. The boys probably learnt to read and write, and to know selected poets, including Homer and especially their own warlike Tyrtaeus (of whose work the Spartan character in Plato's *Laws* is expected to be sick to death); and they were trained to take part in the choral performances at the great Laconian festivals, in song and dances as well as gymnastic competitions, like their elders. This whole system of training was known as the *agoge*.

When he had passed through the various classes or age-groups the young Spartan seems to have spent a period of time in the *crypteia* or Secret Band, whose members lived off the countryside and according to one source sometimes descended in fury to massacre the helots. Originally this was doubtless a form of manhood initiation rite for which parallels can be found, but it was probably, like so much else, rationalized as time went on, and the *crypteia* became in the first instance a secret police in peace and an intelligence service in war.

The object of the Spartan education, the object of the Spartan way of life, was war. The Spartan soldier in the field wore scarlet, lest his fellows should lose heart to see him bleed; he marched in step to the music of the oboe, wearing, in battle, a crown of flowers. He fought in platoons of thirty-odd men, grouped in companies, battalions, and regiments, with subordinate commanders at each level, an arrangement apparently entirely unique for classical Greece. The whole formed a phalanx of infantry usually fighting in a single line, eight to twelve men deep. So organized, drilled to the strictest discipline that Greeks had ever known, bred up from infancy to privation and to pain, the Spartiate at war was for centuries virtually unbeatable.

If he had born himself creditably in all this, the adult Spartiate was accepted into a *syssition*, or mess, of about fifteen men—unless blackballed by a pellet of bread. On membership of such a mess, which must in origin at least have been a military unit, citizenship depended. With this mess the Spartiate took his frugal supper, notable for the famous black broth (from pork cooked in its blood) that the other Greeks found so repellent, for moderation in drinking, and for educative post-prandial conversations on war and politics, to which the boys were admitted. The primitive fear of public opinion, which treated all disobedience and cowardice in particular so severely that life became notoriously hardly worth living, persisted as a factor more powerful probably than the hope of honours and promotion, especially selection by the *hippagretae* into the royal guard of Three Hundred.

It is uncertain how much a man regularly slept away from home, though we are told that on marriage he was at first only allowed to visit his wife occasionally and by stealth. But his wife, whether she was left in complete control of the household for this reason or not, had received a certain amount of 'gymnastic' training herself, had taken part as a girl in races and very active dances, as well as personal and satirical songs, at the festivals, and furthermore had probably not been permitted to marry till she was fully grown; and thus she was unlike most other Greek women in strength of mind and body. According to later, possibly idealizing, Greek authors (contradicted, for the earlier period, by archaeology) she was also unusual in being allowed no cosmetics or jewellery or dyed clothing, and in having her hair close-cut, at least on marrying. Men who did not marry were compelled, at least at some period, to undergo ignominious penalties, whether for primitive religious reasons or because of the increasingly serious population problem.

From the produce of his land, which was cultivated by helots,

B

the Spartiate paid the dues to his mess, largely in kind. If he could not do so he lost his full citizenship. It is possible that on the conquest of Laconia or later of Messenia some territory was distributed, according to a common Greek custom, into comparatively equal lots; and it appears that until the early fourth century there was some land that was not yet alienable, but doubtless owned in common by a family—a stage that most other parts of Greece left behind earlier. There can be little doubt however that there was not much financial equality; we know there were rich families who bred racehorses, and dangerously poor ones. The Spartiates boasted no doubt of the name *homoioi* or 'Equals', but this must have referred to their (theoretical) political equality, and perhaps to the superficially egalitarian mode of life. There were also traces of—perhaps primitive—communism; in some circumstances it was allowable to help oneself to the produce of another man's estate or the aid of his slaves and livestock, and even women were occasionally lent about, or held in common within the family.

Freed by helots (and wife) from the care of his property, the Spartiate devoted his time to hunting, drilling, and political duties. The Spartan phalanx became the admiration of Greece, the one professional force among a crowd of inexpert militias. The city, till far into her decline, never deigned to fortify herself, and the helots and Messenians were generally kept cowed. Perhaps it was at first only lack of time and the contempt common among Greek aristocracies which prevented the Spartiate taking active part in trade or manufacturing, which were left to the *perioeci*. It was believed in the fourth century that Lycurgus, in order to banish money-making and luxury, had actually forbidden the use of money save in the form of awkward iron spits. But in fact these appear simply to have been a survival of an institution widespread in Greece before the introduction of coinage in the late seventh century, and some foreign money probably circulated in Sparta even before the influx caused by victory in the Peloponnesian War. Other supposedly ascetic practices seem either to be archaic usages, sometimes of a basically religious nature, that persisted here alone, or propagandist statements by late moralists without any basis in fact. Others may be the result of a special crisis, such as the years of pressure and isolation in the middle of the fifth century. Perhaps the *xenelasiai*, or orders for the expulsion of foreigners, which so annoyed the inquisitive Athenians, were one custom that only became common now. But it is easily understandable that close control was also kept over Spartiates wishing to travel abroad; their country needed them too much.

Now lawgivers of extensive influence certainly did emerge in the small cities of Greece. The Athenian Solon, with whose name that of Lycurgus is so often bracketed, is a fully historical figure of the early sixth century. But the very existence of the latter is now often doubted. Some of our earliest sources notoriously ignore him or suggest that his origin was thought of as divine not human. Antiquity, however, spent centuries elaborating the events of his life, and the result may be read in the detailed biography of Plutarch. In reality it seems likely that Sparta underwent a fundamental reform or series of reforms about the early seventh century B.C. rather than at any of the variable but earlier dates given us for Lycurgus. This was a period of rapid development and thus of unrest in Greece, marked by the rising prosperity and assertion of classes outside the old nobility but rich enough to fight in the new fashion, with the heavy armour of the 'hoplite' foot-soldier. In Sparta's case, the conquest and division of Messenia may have enlarged or strengthened this hoplite class as well as suggesting the need to tighten up military training and make sure of moral unity among all Spartiates. The earlier seventh century is, at any rate, the age of the poet Tyrtaeus, whose fragments show part of the political constitution of Sparta as we know it in operation, attributing it to the kings Theopompus and Polydorus in whose time Messenia was conquered; and also—it can hardly be earlier—of the Great Rhetra, whose provisions seem closely related to those in Tyrtaeus. There were certainly later changes, particularly in the organization of the army, but the long-continued success of the system, and the cast of mind it induced, meant that by the fifth century Sparta was in many respects old-fashioned and indeed anxious to stop the clock. It was partly this fact that made her now seem strange to the rest of Greece.

It was observed, nevertheless, that she was not quite unique. Certain resemblances in Crete prompted the idea, already found by Herodotus in Sparta itself, that Lycurgus had taken hints from this source. The Dorian cities of Crete also had a large semi-serf population; they also had public messes for the men, and some sort of organization by age-groups for the boys, though beginning apparently only after adolescence and centred on the great families rather than the state. Their magistrates, the *cosmoi*, were compared to the ephors, and the country, being out of the main stream of Greek life at this time, was poor and old-fashioned. And finally Crete had a grand though semi-mythical lawgiver, King Minos, believed to be of far remoter date than Lycurgus but often said like him to have been directly inspired by a god.

The amazing vitality of Sparta as a political ideal springs in part from the complexity and even ambiguity of the system just outlined. Furthermore, she herself altered more than was always realized, while the outside world, and so the issues in which her name was involved, changed as well. The bewilderingly contradictory attitudes taken to Sparta in post-classical times can only be understood when it is seen how contradictory the ancient sources are too; necessarily so, for they are deeply rooted in the political and intellectual history of the ancient world.

As the only one of the leading states of classical Greece in which the king, or rather kings, preserved some at least of their powers, Sparta made some contribution to the ancient theory of kingship, and from the late Middle Ages she was in the forefront of the debate about absolute and limited monarchy. In the fifth century B.C. she acted as Greece's leading oligarchy; in the next, as in many later centuries, she seemed the embodiment of the mixed constitution, that combination of two or more types, most classically of monarchy, oligarchy, and democracy. The fourth century sometimes stressed her democratic and egalitarian side instead; and so Lycurgus became a patron saint of the Utopian tradition.

Distrust of commerce, and proposals for currency reform; belief in communism, or the vital importance of property rights, especially in land; militarism and pacifism; female emancipation; racialism and cosmopolitanism; education by the state and for the state, education of the whole man, anti-intellectualism; the most divergent ideas have been formulated or recommended with Spartan aid. There is no single thread running through the whole story; at most there are certain themes involving freedom, the rule of law, and the state's powers, to shape and educate in particular, which recur again and again in different forms. And there are also some wholly eccentric episodes.

There is one political ideal that Sparta cannot be made to reflect—the radical belief in individual liberty, issuing in liberal democracy. Here, if only stammeringly and by some distortion, Athens can speak—with the result that in most quarters today the long-established order of priority between the two perpetual rivals has been reversed. So deeply, however, have both impressed themselves on the European consciousness, that even in an age when classical antiquity is less familiar, and wields less authority, than before, one may take leave to doubt whether the long story of their transformations has really come to a full stop.

2

THE GROWTH OF LACONISM

NEITHER mythology nor archaeology suggest that there was anything peculiar about Bronze-Age Lacedaemon. Certainly Homer depicts the country of Menelaus and Helen as much like other kingdoms, and the only hint of things to come lies in his charming picture of Artemis following the hunt on Mount Taygetus;[1] for the hounds and hunting of Sparta were famous to the end of antiquity and beyond. As for the first dark centuries of the new Dorian state, all we have to throw light on its reputation are some lines of oracular verse, so old that they single out a people which was obscure after the eighth century as the first warriors in Greece. Sparta is allowed, perhaps only in compliment to Helen, to claim the fairest women.[2]

It was probably, as we saw, in the late eighth or the seventh century that Sparta's institutions reached more or less their final form in a reform or series of reforms designed to cope with problems common to much of Greece. At any rate, while other states in the seventh and sixth centuries were often torn by factious nobles or succumbed to tyrants, who sometimes profited from social unrest, Sparta prospered under her comparatively broadly based and firmly organized system, and developed a reputation not only for military prowess, but for political wisdom and the rule of law rather than of individuals; and even as a centre of the arts, especially the choral arts of singing and dancing, to which poets and musicians from the islands of the Aegean, the coast of Asia Minor, and even as far afield as Sicily were attracted (some of the philosophers of Ionia are said to have come on visits too). It is these three aspects that are celebrated by our only contemporary witnesses, the poets of the archaic age, both from Lacedaemon and elsewhere. Of the former, Tyrtaeus became famous all over Greece for his elegies, which, while Sparta was struggling against a Messenian revolt, preached courage in war and readiness to die for one's city—a relatively new ideal for

[1] *Odyssey* vi. 102.   [2] *Anthologia Palatina* xiv. 73.-

Greece, for Homer's heroes cared only for individual glory—and also the virtues of the political settlement; while the lyric poet Alcman, a little later, wrote of and for the choral competitions at the festivals. From (probably) the latter comes a fragment of verse speaking of Sparta as a place where the young men's spear and the clear-voiced Muse prosper, together with justice, who dwells in the open streets and defends virtuous deeds.[1]

And very similar is the language of Pindar, who can fairly be called the last poet of the archaic age, early in the fifth century.[2] By that time, however, Sparta, beset with political troubles and bypassed by economic and intellectual developments elsewhere, was falling behind in the arts. The city was a mere group of villages, as Thucydides notes, contrasting the architectural glories of Periclean Athens. But even in the last years of the century her great festivals, such as the Gymnopaedia, kept their fame and attracted visitors, and Aristophanes at the end of the *Lysistrata* can invoke the Laconian Muse to describe for him the girls dancing on the banks of the Eurotas.[3] As the belief hardened, however, that puritanism and distrust of the intellect had inspired Lycurgus' original regulations, the idea of Sparta as a city of art and poetry disappeared almost entirely until in modern times papyrus discoveries came to fill out our knowledge of Alcman and other early poets, and excavation in Sparta and elsewhere revealed the achievements of archaic Laconians (though hardly of the Spartiate citizens themselves) in vase-painting and architecture; revealing also the rich jewellery, the sculpture in ivory, bone, and bronze that was there in fashion. All show how open the country was to influence from the Greek cities of Ionia across the Aegean and from the Orient in general. Such a vision makes an ironical prelude to a history of the reputation of 'museless and unbookish' Lacedaemon.

But on the other elements of which the early poets speak, military prowess and political wisdom, her fame was to rest for

---

[1] Attributed to Terpander of Lesbos by Plutarch, *Life of Lycurgus* 21;
ἔνθ' αἰχμά τε νέων θάλλει καὶ Μῶσα λίγεια
καὶ Δίκα εὐρυάγυια, καλῶν ἐπιτάρροθος ἔργων.
[2] Particularly in fr. 199 (also quoted by Plutarch, *Lyc.* 21), ed. B. Snell.
ἔνθα βουλαὶ μὲν γερόντων
καὶ νέων ἀνδρῶν ἀριστεύοισιν αἰχμαί
καὶ χοροὶ καὶ Μοῖσα καὶ Ἀγλαΐα.
[3] Aristophanes, *Lysistrata* 1296 ff.

centuries. The Spartan phalanx had a great reputation long before the Persian wars. As for her political system, there is plenty of evidence from the poets, and from Herodotus, that Sparta regarded herself, and was regarded, as an embodiment of *eunomia*, which seems to mean both obedience to *nomos*, law or custom, and still more the possession of good laws and customs. It can almost be translated 'justice'; and indeed with the idea of *nomos* was indissolubly linked that of justice, *dike*. From the time of Hesiod, and later Solon, these to many Greeks, threatened with the violence and oppression of squabbling nobles on the one hand and the arbitrary, if sometimes more orderly, rule of a tyrant on the other, seemed supremely desirable. It had not yet struck them that they might be hard to define. Both were divine, and had divine sanction. *Dike* was a goddess from Hesiod on, and to Pindar *nomos* was king of gods and men. The Spartans were proud of their piety; they represented much of their history, to judge from Herodotus, as determined by their obedience to the oracle of Apollo at Delphi.

Somewhere about 550 Sparta began, with striking success, to build up a system of alliances into what is usually known as the Peloponnesian League, though at this time her ambitions were by no means bounded by the Isthmus of Corinth. In this process she gave practical expression to her preference for legal government. However uncertain the evidence for most of the supposed cases of action, except for the famous expulsion of the Peisistratids from Athens, and however complicated and interested her motives may have been, Sparta acquired, as both Herodotus and Thucydides bear witness, a glorious reputation for tyrant-slaying.[1] The world is upside-down, cries one of the former's speakers, when the Spartans fleetingly propose to restore the tyrant to Athens.

This stand for law against tyranny was seen as culminating in 480 when Sparta assumed the leadership of the Greek states against the monarchy of Persia—foreign as well as absolute, and the protector of several Greek tyrants. The ideals that Sparta exemplified were not hers alone; Athens was equally proud of being able to resist invasion without a despotic ruler commanding 'slaves' to obey him. And Herodotus makes the exiled Spartan King Demaratus warn Xerxes that his countrymen are but the

[1] Herodotus v. 92; cf. Thucydides i. 18.

best, or the bravest (for virtue to the Greek of this period still means primarily valour), of the Dorians of the Peloponnese, so schooled by wisdom and strict *nomos* that their natural poverty and their small numbers are outweighed. He lectures Xerxes on the freedom of the Spartans, 'which is not complete freedom, for they obey law and fear it more than your men fear you. And it orders them never to flee but to conquer or die in battle'.[1] These ideals, and their unwavering hatred of slavery, were put into practice in the defence of Thermopylae by King Leonidas and his three hundred Spartiates. 'Go tell the city, stranger, that here we lie, obedient to her decrees'—so runs the famous epitaph written for their grave by Simonides.[2] Obedience to the city was the duty of the highest; Pausanias, who succeeded Leonidas as regent for his son, is represented as declaring that his sole desire is to please his city by avoiding impiety in word and deed (not a conception he lived up to for long).[3]

Though Athens was the heroine of the naval victory at Salamis, the final defeat of the Persian army at Plataea in 479 was the work of the 'Dorian spear'[4]—of an army commanded by Pausanias in which the men of Lacedaemon and other Dorian states of the Peloponnese distinguished themselves. Before this nobody seems to have laid great stress on the Dorian origin of Sparta. Her ruling families traced their descent from Heracles, regarded as a pre-Dorian hero, and insisted that they were in some sense the heirs of the early rulers of Lacedaemon, Menelaus or even his brother Agamemnon who led all the Greeks against an earlier Asiatic foe. There was a cult of Helen at Sparta and, notably, of her twin brothers Castor and Pollux, the Dioscuri. Political alignments in the sixth century seem uninfluenced by racial considerations. But now a largely Dorian confederacy had defeated Persia where the recent attempt of the Ionian cities of Asia Minor to throw off the yoke had failed. The Ionians, in decline and partly orientalized, acquired a reputation for softness and probably for political instability; Herodotus, himself from

[1] Herodotus vii. 102–4.
[2] Id. vii. 228, ῥήμασι πειθόμενοι: it may in this context have a precise legal meaning, Spartan laws, or decrees, being called ῥήτραι. Later sources quote the line-ending as πειθόμενοι νομίμοις.
[3] Id. ix. 79.
[4] Aeschylus, *Persians* 817 (but some believe that he uses the word simply to mean Greek, cf.183).

a Dorian city in Asia, says that everyone, even the men of Athens, which claimed to be the metropolis of the Ionian cities, was ashamed of the name.[1] Conversely, Pindar likes to dwell where he can on the Dorian origin of cities he is hymning, and associates the freedom and *eunomia* of Sparta, like that of Aegina, with King Aegimius, the legendary ancestor of the Dorians.[2]

When, as we shall see, the political and social divergencies of Athens and Sparta became extreme, and it also became clear that the former's sphere of influence was to be predominantly maritime and Ionian, and the latter's largely Peloponnesian and Dorian, the idea that the Dorians had a particular character, especially as fine foot-soldiers averse to political extremes either of tyranny or democracy, and that Sparta was the Dorian city *par excellence*, was probably fairly common, though it is hard to trace. Several of Thucydides' speakers, Spartan, Corinthian, and Syracusan—all Dorians therefore—try to exploit the theme of racial solidarity.[3] But he himself probably rejected it; he certainly makes it clear that the ideological split of the time, between democracy and oligarchy, did not coincide neatly with the racial one, and he once notes a paradoxical superiority of Ionian troops. We may remember that, after all, like most historians he regarded Sparta's peculiarities as the comparatively recent inventions of Lycurgus, while he had before his eyes the very diverse institutions and characteristics of the other Dorian cities—commercial Corinth, naval Aegina, democratic Syracuse. The several branches of the Greek people were undoubtedly closely related and culturally interdependent; most modern scholars, in reaction from a revived racial interpretation stronger than any ancient one, find them hard to distinguish except in terms of dialect, a tribe-organization usually obsolete by classical times, and a few religious cults and customs.

The years after Plataea saw more important developments than a tendency to describe Sparta as Dorian. During this period the city turned in upon herself. Alarmed by the tyrant-like intrigues and ambitions of Pausanias, she recalled him and allowed the navy (which she could not afford) to decline. Athens was left to

---

[1] Herodotus i. 143; cf. vii. 99.

[2] Pindar, *Pythian* i. 64; v. 72; *Isthmian* ix. 2; and see below, p. 57.

[3] Thucydides i. 124; v. 9; vi. 62, and 82 (where an Athenian speaker in Sicily does use the distinction), viii. 25.

carry on the war against Persia at the head of a large body of allies, while Sparta struggled with dissension at home, disaffection in her League, and increasing desperation among the helots, who finally broke into revolt after the earthquake of 464. Her population seems to have declined dramatically. Meanwhile at Athens about 460 there triumphed that radical and imperialistic policy whose greatest representative was Pericles. He and his friends were ready to provoke a conflict with Sparta by detaching or crushing any of her allies who stood in the way of Athenian ambitions, while they believed that the man who rowed the trireme deserved political power as well as the man who could afford hoplite armour, and should thus be enabled by the reception of a salary to hold office as well as vote in the assembly. Further, the executive magistracies and the council should be closely controlled by the assembly; administrative boards should usually be large, and brief in tenure, while if special qualifications were not required the lot rather than election was used as the method of appointment, thus ensuring that the ordinary man was in control at most levels. In consequence the Spartan constitution, which in archaic times had been in the forefront of progress, now appeared essentially conservative, and its conservatism was a leading element in the attraction it had for members of the upper class even in Athens.

But if Sparta was the head of a league of oligarchies and the recipient of various vain appeals from dissatisfied allies of Athens, the little we know of oligarchic thought at this time suggests that her system was too anomalous to serve as a model. For example, the constitution of Boeotia, probably worked out in this period, with sections of a restricted citizen body acting in rotation as a council, has links with oligarchic ideas in Athens as late as 411, but none with Sparta, though the two states were allies. Instead, Sparta is praised for general qualities—for austerity and the ability to take prompt action on good decisions, with no words wasted. The former is connected with the great economic development of, in particular, Athens; the latter has a political aspect, in that democracy, which thrashed all important matters out in the assembly, was an argumentative form of government, but it also reflects the new intellectual developments in Greece, and above all the appearance of the sophists. These men were primarily concerned with education. Their curricula for the ambitious politician, however they might differ, were strongly intellectual and concerned above all with developing the power of speech and thought. It is perhaps surprising, given their interest in political education, that none seem to have thought that it should be organized by the state. But their own habit of wandering freely from city to city to teach may help to explain the fact. Few wandered to Sparta, however,[1] and they do not seem to have taken much interest in her. And one at least of the marks of that development of political thought associated with them might seem calculated to alarm the Spartans. This was the rejection of the archaic concept of divine and absolute *nomos* and *dike* in favour of an evolutionary view of human history in which law and justice are regarded as late developments, to be welcomed as useful or rejected as artificial. The contrast between *nomos* and *physis*, Nature, went deep. Though Herodotus' Demaratus, as we saw, could give it a turn favourable to Sparta, in many later forms it could be subversive of Spartan ideals. For it could lead to a denial of obedience to law, or to an insistence that all men were naturally equal.

The first in the long line of Athenian admirers of Sparta, or laconizers, as they were called, of whom we can know anything was Cimon the son of Miltiades.[2] Like his father, the victor of Marathon, Cimon was a hero of the fight against Persia. He was also long an advocate of the friendship with Sparta that would leave Athens free to concentrate on that fight, and an opponent of Pericles and all he stood for. He appears to have been one of the first to think that there was room for two leaders of Greece, and when Sparta was in serious trouble after the earthquake he urged the Athenians 'not to let Greece go lame, or the city lose her yoke-fellow'.[3] He was Spartan diplomatic representative at Athens, and called one of his sons Lacedaemonius. And Plutarch[4]

---

[1] Prodicus perhaps, and Hippias certainly form exceptions; but if Plato's *Hippias Major* 285d is correct, the latter could only arouse interest by lecturing on mythological and historical traditions.

[2] Plutarch, *Aristides* 2 tells us that that notoriously just statesman admired Lycurgus above all other politicians and preferred 'aristocratic' government. He provides no evidence, and Aristides was adopted and written up by fourth-century conservatives who had a great interest in both Lycurgus and 'aristocracy', while around 480 no interest can be proved in either.

[3] Plutarch, *Cimon* 4, from Cimon's friend Ion of Chios.

[4] Ibid. 15, 16, 10.

quotes a (not very reliable) friend and contemporary, Stesimbrotus, for his habit of saying to the Athenians that they ordered almost everything better in Lacedaemon, for his 'Peloponnesian' simplicity of life, his un-Athenian lack of intellectual interests and brevity of speech, together with a frank and generous bearing. (It is also possible to wonder whether he had his eye on Spartan customs when in his struggle for popularity he allowed produce to be taken freely from his estates and gave the men of his deme or ward common dinners.)

A friend of Cimon, the tragic poet Ion of Chios,[1] has a fragment of some interest in this context. Sparta, someone remarks, is a city not fortified by words or speeches, *logoi*, but where, when war comes, the hand seconds the mind's counsel. This is the traditional language of the poets about Sparta, with a new contrast implied. Another fragment of Ion's contrasts Asian luxury with Peloponnesian simplicity. The other side of the coin can be seen elsewhere in tragedy. Sophocles, perhaps in the 440s, made Menelaus in his *Ajax* into an arrogant bully with no regard for allies or those who do not fight as hoplites and a belief that fear is essential both to the preservation of the laws in a city and to prudent discipline in a camp.[2] The city where one can 'do what one wants' is doomed to disaster. It is surely hard to suppose that this is not a hostile picture of a contemporary Spartiate. He argues by means of a simple parable, and his last remark is that it is shameful to use words against an opponent if force is available. That opponent, however, has accused him of underhand trickery, and indeed Herodotus makes his Athenians accuse the Spartans of hypocrisy (and incidentally depicts some oppressive and rapacious Spartans abroad).

Among the often dubious materials available to Herodotus were clearly already many examples of brief and pithy Spartan repartee—what came to be known as 'laconic apophthegms'. Several times he takes note of Spartan impatience with long

---

[1] Nauck, *Tragicorum Graecorum Fragmenta*, Ion of Chios, fr. 63 (cf. 24);
οὐ γὰρ λόγοις Λάκαινα πυργοῦται πόλις,
ἀλλ' εὖτ' ἂν Ἄρης νεοχμὸς ἐμπεσῇ στράτῳ
βουλὴ μὲν ἄρχει, χεὶρ δ' ἐπεξεργάζεται.

[2] Sophocles, *Ajax* esp. 1072 ff. There was a famous temple of Fear, *Phobos*, in Sparta, probably as a war-demon, not a political abstraction as later supposed.

speeches,[1] and he recounts how the Scythian Anacharsis was supposed to have said, after visiting Greece, that he had found all the Greeks busy studying all sorts of wisdom—except the Lacedaemonians, but that they alone could listen and talk prudently.[2] Such an anecdote clearly comes from a laconizing source, and indeed the word *sophrosyne*, prudence or moderation, is henceforth to be closely associated with Sparta. Properly meaning 'soundness of mind', it is a concept central to Greek morality, with its fear of any kind of excess and its tendency to merge moral and intellectual terms. In politics it is to become a watchword of anti-imperialist and anti-democratic thought.

Herodotus himself has a warm admiration for both the great Greek cities and their part in the Persian wars. His curiosity about Sparta, which he had visited, as something *sui generis* is probably significant of his date, as well as nourished by the ethnographic literary tradition upon which early historiography built. He remarks, for example, on the extreme rarity with which citizenship was granted to outsiders, on the way executions were always done at night, on the Spartans' long hair (going out of fashion elsewhere) and practice of ceremoniously combing it before battle; and upon occasion he will compare foreign and oriental with Lacedaemonian customs. His great work is, however, a compilation of various materials and attitudes, and in his last book he formulates, as we have seen, a political and moral contrast between Greeks and Persians in which Sparta stands, if only implicitly, for the most typically Greek of cities.

But what can hardly have escaped the Greeks at this time was the profound contrast between Athens and Sparta, especially when in 431 the outbreak of the Peloponnesian War focused the eyes of Greece on the two rivals, and when there are some signs that even in Athens, held together for some time by Pericles' authority and success, admirers of Sparta were vocal.

Thucydides gives us in the psychological and generalizing terms so typical of him the fullest exploration of this contrast.

[1] Herodotus iii. 64 in particular: the Samians beg for help, and the Spartans complain that they've forgotten the start of the speech before the end of it. The Samians learn their lesson—but the Spartans can still go one better.

[2] Id. iv. 77 ἀσχόλους εἶναι ἐς πᾶσαν σοφίην is often translated as 'too busy to attend to wisdom', but this makes no sense in the fifth-century context surely? Unless the implication is that the Spartans alone go in for real wisdom, *sophia*, as contrasted with what the sophists teach.

Under the stimulus of the antithetic fashion in style in his day it receives memorable, possibly even overstated, expression. Yet he is perhaps not really interested in Sparta. He sees the growth and problems of power through Athenian eyes, in terms of economic and naval resources, the foundation of colonies and construction of fortifications. In his sketch of early history he tosses off Sparta's rise in an inadequate parenthesis referring to her constitutional stability and avoidance of tyranny, so that it is not easy to see why the one state had become, as he declares, as powerful by land as the other by sea.[1] The subsequent analyses of Spartan character are thus perhaps largely there to illuminate that of the Athenians, and also the actual progress of the war. But it is true that Sparta's own relations to her allies, who paid no tribute and still had a voice in shaping policy, and her claim, based on this fact, to be freeing the rest of Greece from the 'tyrant city', were of a kind to touch on Thucydides' basic preoccupations, as indeed was Sparta's avoidance of internal strife, such as ultimately ruined other states involved in the war.

Thucydides sets his scene in the famous account of the debate held at Sparta before the outbreak of war. The Corinthians, anxious to move their allies to action, complain that the Spartans' good faith in public as well as private affairs—in their *politeia*, which means their whole way of life in their city or *polis*, rather than simply their constitution, as the word is inevitably often translated—not only gives them *sophrosyne* but makes them suspicious of others and ignorant of the outside world. They avoid committing injustice but also forestalling it in others, and so their reputation for being safe and reliable is unjustified. They are pessimistic, always on the defensive, slow to observe and understand and slow to act (this last must have seemed a paradox). These to the intellectual Thucydides must rank as damaging charges, though there are ominous touches also to the contrasted picture of the Athenians to which the speech proceeds. These are bold, even rash, quick to conceive and effect the ambitions abroad that are leading to the enslavement of Greece. In a famous phrase, they are born neither to be quiet themselves nor to let others be so. They risk their bodies carelessly, but rely on their minds; compared with the stay-at-home Spartans they are experienced, advanced, modern.[2]

[1] Thucydides i. 18. [2] Id. i. 68–71.

The Athenians reply, basing their claims significantly on their display of naval strength, intelligence, and energy in the Persian wars, and on the operation of honour, fear, and interest. In their place the Spartans would be as unpopular, and less reasonable and gentle, less ready to use the processes of law rather than violence, as their previous brief tenure of power showed. For their institutions are peculiarly unfriendly, and the behaviour of their officials abroad is un-Greek.[1] An important theme has here been stated.

Next King Archidamus admits but justifies the Corinthian charges. Slowness can be *sophrosyne*, he says (a quality which, says Thucydides, was regarded as his own). We Spartans alone, he maintains, neither become insolent in prosperity nor give way to misfortune. We cannot be threatened or cajoled into rash or unjust actions, we are not so educated as to despise the laws nor so clever at useless matters like criticizing our enemies that we lose all capacity to act ourselves. We do not think slightly of our neighbours' intelligence, or think intelligence itself all-powerful in a world that is largely ruled by chance. We are brave warriors and have good judgement, owing to the strict order and firm discipline of our ancestral institutions. Our city has been always free and always glorious.[2]

It is hard to suppose that this close analysis is not largely Thucydides' own in form, though we should take seriously his claim to have tried to discover 'what was actually said' in each case, and have seen that Archidamus is dealing with well-known ideas. A more 'laconic' speech is made by the ephor who comes forward to say he can't follow the Athenians' lengthy arguments and clamours for war. The assembly agrees, moved, as Thucydides repeats, by fear—fear of Athens' growing power.

It would seem that one of the functions of the paired digressions toward the end of Book I on the Athenian Themistocles and the Spartan Pausanias is to drive home some themes announced in the speeches. Themistocles was the prophet, if not wholly the architect, of Athenian imperialism, and the embodiment of Athenian foresight and rapidity. Pausanias is hardly typical of his countrymen as we have learnt to know them in the speeches. But his progress from the liberator of Greece, in the days which the speakers so frequently evoke, to its would-be tyrant, dependent on Persia, recalls to our mind the Athenians' warning and

[1] Id. i. 73–8.   [2] Id. i. 80–85.

throws ironic light on Sparta's present programme. It has even been suggested that the figure of Pausanias may foreshadow that of Lysander and the concluding stages of the Peloponnesian War.[1]

The contrast of Athens and Sparta has not been finished in Book I. Thucydides allows Pericles, in the famous Funeral Oration, to redress the balance drawn up by Archidamus. Once again an implied contrast gives depth to the patriotic claims. If Pericles really spoke in similar terms, he must have had an eye on Athenian laconizers. One may notice in this connection the insistence that Athens has not copied her *politeia* from any other source, and compare Euripides' objection to those who praise other cities excessively.

It is the Athenians, says Pericles, who are truly free, in private as in public life. They are not angry with neighbours who follow their own preferences, nor do they inflict unkind humiliations on them (the Spartans' love of playing practical jokes on each other and the helots is often attested later). They hate idleness; they believe ignorance, not frank discussion, the bar to effective action; they love art and learning without falling into luxury and weakness. In their military institutions Pericles makes a more open contrast, and stresses that the city is open to visitors and hides none of its preparations, believing as it does in courage, not tricks and stratagems. The courage of the Athenians is equal to that of their enemies, without being the result of toilsome training or enforced by severe laws.[2]

It is uncertain when Thucydides gave their final form to these speeches—perhaps late in, perhaps even after, the war. But it is essentially the fifth-century vision that he calls up. Even the Corinthian oligarchs believe that institutions should alter and progress 'like the arts' in unsettled circumstances, though in quiet times it is best to avoid change. Both they and Pericles single out the Athenians, not the Spartans, for their passionate devotion to their city and its greatness. The debate about effectiveness, to which both Archidamus and Pericles contribute, is prejudged by the Corinthian lament over Athens' unparalleled speed and energy. When rival systems of training or education, *paideia* (the word is a newish one), are involved in the argument, that of Sparta is briefly characterized as severe and compulsory, while

---

[1] Id. i. 128–38.　　　　[2] Id. ii. 35–40.

C

Pericles can claim that the Athenians are as good in war without it. And Athens herself is an education to the whole of Greece. Sparta's claims to moderation, finally, are seen largely in terms of foreign policy and as a contrast to Athens' imperial ambitions, her unceasing desire to 'have more'.

These claims allowed Sparta to go into the Peloponnesian War, as Thucydides assures us, with a decided reputation for moral superiority. But his narrative of the early years bears out in typically Thucydidean style the analyses given in the previous speeches. He frequently shows Spartan strategy as timid or mis-conceived, or gives examples of atrocity incompatible with the liberation programme. He also notes the cruelty and trickery with which the helots were treated, and indeed declares that fear of the helots determines the whole Spartan way of life. The shining exception to all this is Brasidas, a man of intelligence and 'not a bad speaker for a Spartan',[1] of splendid dash and enterprise, who detached many of Athens' allies by the real moderation with which he treated them. But on the whole some colour is given to the remarks of the Athenians in Book V to the effect that, if the Spartans are pre-eminently virtuous among themselves, they are nothing of the sort to others, and that they are more remark-able than anyone else for persuading themselves that justice is whatever their interest may be.[2] For they do not care to face the dangers inherent in just and honourable behaviour, or trust their own power.

It is understandable that once at least, in the early years of the war, Euripides should have embodied his hatred of violence and selfishness in Spartan figures. Both Menelaus and his daughter Hermione appear in the *Andromache* as heartless and uncontrolled creatures, puffed up with wealth and power, regardless of the gods, and prone to use both force and deceit when taking exces-sive retaliation on their enemies, especially if these are slaves or foreigners or otherwise helpless. The vile passions of Menelaus and Helen have caused all the suffering of the Trojan War and its aftermath. The Spartans are detestable to all mankind, cries Andromache, treacherous, crafty, and hypocritical, murderous

---

[1] Id. iv. 84.

[2] Id. v. 105, 107, 109. At viii. 96 Thucydides remarks that owing to their sup-ineness the Spartans made remarkably convenient enemies for the Athenians, and echoes the contrasts of Book I.

and greedy for base gain, and she exclaims against the injustice of their power in Greece. The play is full of discussion of true and false *sophia* and *sophrosyne*. Is this what you call wisdom by the Eurotas? asks Andromache, shamefully tricked by Menelaus. Both concepts to him mean merely the ability to see one's short-term advantage, while Hermione (and Helen her mother) exemplifies lack of *sophrosyne* in all its meanings—moderation, common sense, and chastity.[1] By contrast, in some of Euripides' earlier plays, Athens is the moderate state, regulating her dealings with foreigners by due form of law and extending generous protection to the weak who turn to her for refuge; or at least, her mythical past is described in these terms and held up as an ideal. But increasing disillusionment is to be seen in Euripides' later works; and it may be significant that the Spartan characters of legend, recurring again, are treated without special hostility.

Aristophanes, who was himself anxious to end the war, shows how the ordinary Athenians adduced their belief that the Spartans were not to be trusted, as a reason for not negotiating. Even the god Hermes in the *Peace* describes leading Spartans as bribeable and likely to mislead foreigners.[2] To a great extent, however, the comic poets simply treat all strangers as ridiculous. The Spartans, with their peculiar dialect, diet, and garb—long dirty hair, long dirty mantle, and a stick—seemed especially comic. Most of the surviving evidence dates from the last years of the century or later, but the jokes were doubtless traditional. Aristophanes in the *Lysistrata* in particular mimics the thick dialect, and mocks the lack of elegance, the grotesque dances, and the length of hair and beards in Lacedaemon.[3] As for the women, they filled the poets of Ionia and Athens, who kept their women in greater seclusion, with not only amusement but horror. Already in the

[1] Euripides, *Andromache* 445–52, ὦ πᾶσιν ἀνθρώποισιν ἐχθίστοι βροτῶν... Cf. 724–apart from military prowess, they are the worst of men. *Suppliants* 187, Σπάρτη μὲν ὠμὴ καὶ πεποίκιλται τρόπους, 'Sparta is savage and deceitful', is in the context a pretty gratuitous remark. *Heraclidae* 1030 ff. regard Spartan invasion of Attica as ingratitude for Athens' protection of the children of Heracles, (and doubtless more recent benefits).

[2] Aristophanes, *Acharnians* 308, οἷσιν οὔτε βωμὸς οὔτε πίστις οὔθ' ὅρκος μένει say the old peasants, Cf. Peace 1067–8 . . . ἀλωπεκιδεῦσι πέπεισθε ὧν δόλιαι ψυχαί, δόλιαι φρένες (the priest), 623 (Hermes). And, later, *Lysistrata* 629.

[3] Aristophanes, *Lysistrata* 1072 ff.

sixth century there had been comment on the amount of thigh Spartan girls showed (their straight *peplos* was open at one side), and Sophocles and Euripides echoed the theme.[1] Euripides in the *Andromache* even allows an angry character to declare that given her upbringing no Laconian woman could be chaste if she tried. Helen's reputation did not help. Aristophanes however draws a better-natured portrait of a Spartan woman. The appearance of his Lampito astounds the Athenian Lysistrata, who exclaims that she must be capable, with those muscles, of throttling an ox. 'By the Twin Gods', she replies in broad Laconian and with the favourite Laconian oath, 'I should hope so', and goes on to give a boastful account of her uncouth gymnastic achievements; but it is she alone who is ready to support Lysistrata's drastic methods of ending the war.[2]

It wasn't only the women; it was assumed that pederasty was rife in the herds or *agelai* and the *syssitia*, and we are told by later grammarians that the verb 'to laconize' actually bears this meaning in Aristophanes and elsewhere (while a crack by a comic poet about Cimon's habit of sleeping away from home in Lacedaemon may involve a *double entente*).[3]

But no one made fun of the Lacedaemonian soldier. And so it was, as Thucydides makes clear, a shock when the troops blockaded on the island of Sphacteria near Pylos preferred to surrender rather than die (an occasion that presents him with the only laconic apophthegm he deigns to record[4]). Sparta, war-weary and anxious to recover what was by now quite a proportion of her citizen body, finally made peace in 421. Some of her allies, holding they had been let down and fearing she would join Athens in 'enslaving' them, tried to break away. But Sparta succeeded in reconstituting her League and recovering her military reputation, while Athens, giving striking evidence that her reputation for meddlesomeness was justified, helped to drive Sparta's old adherents back into her arms. When war broke out again, Sparta was certain that the fault was not hers, and her claim to represent liberation persisted; but her hand was now

[1] Page, *Poetae Melici Graeci*, Ibycus, fr. 58; Euripides, *Andromache* 595–601, cf. *Hecuba* 932–6. Sophocles, TGF fr. 788.

[2] Aristophanes, ibid. 81 ff.

[3] Kock, *Comicorum Atticorum Fragmenta* I, Eupolis fr. 208.

[4] Thucydides iv. 40.

heavy, and her dependence on Persia soon clear. Yet her refusal to wipe Athens from the face of the earth in 404, however complicated its motives, could appear as a crowning act of moderation, and there was some celebration at this point of the liberation of Greece. Greece was soon undeceived.

As Thucydides knew too well, the war had succeeded in exacerbating the strife of political parties all over Greece. In Athens itself strains had begun to show almost at once. It was the urban poor who had most to gain from victory, and the rich on the whole who had most to lose from war, owing to extra taxes and the ravaging of their land, from which the peasant class also suffered. After Pericles' death the city fell into the hands of conflicting and inferior politicians, some from commercial or manufacturing backgrounds despised by the upper class, some probably thoroughly corrupt; and the pressures of war helped to make the assembly changeable and rancorous. The disastrous expedition to Sicily disillusioned many with the régime that had embarked on and then mishandled that ambitious enterprise. And when the war with Sparta was renewed, and Persian subsidies allowed Sparta at last to keep an effective fleet, the revenues of Athens became more precarious than ever—but the demagogues stuck to the system of salaries for political duty that the upper class considered so corrupting, and dared not make peace.

As a result, Athenian oligarchs begin to appear in the open—drawn to Sparta perhaps as much by her enmity to the Athenian democracy as by her intrinsic attractions. From the early years of the war probably comes the pamphlet of an author pleasingly known as the 'Old Oligarch',[1] who still expounds, though regretfully, the logical character, and the strength and effectiveness, of the Athenian democracy. He may have an eye on the foe in several of his assertions—for example that the choruses of a democracy will be inferior to those of an oligarchy. And he explicitly says that Sparta's slaves are much better managed than those of Athens, who are scandalously bold and prosperous. He describes *eunomia* frankly as a state where the noble (or nobles) make the laws in their own interest and reduce the base to slavery; ignorant and foolish men should have no voice in affairs, and the people are bound to be uncontrolled and disorderly in power.

It is doubtless among such men as this, among the younger

[1] Pseudo-Xenophon, *The Constitution of Athens*, esp. i. 13, i. 11.

bloods in particular, that we should look for those extravagances
of dress and behaviour that Aristophanes calls laconomania. In
his *Wasps*, in 422, a man who is accused of intriguing with the
enemy is described as wearing a beard and a tasselled cloak, both
perhaps on the Spartan model.[1] But in 414, according to the
Birds, the craze was general; people wore long hair, went hungry
and dirty, and 'behaved like Socrates'.[2]

Perhaps this is not, strictly, proof that Socrates himself was a
laconizer, and it is sometimes supposed that Plato and Xenophon
in their dialogues have put into his mouth their own interest in
Sparta, like so much else that must be theirs. But the climate of
opinion being what it was, could Socrates' preference for the
simple life, and the criticisms of democracy which he seems to
have made, and in particular of the assumption that political
wisdom could be expected in the mass of men, really have involved no invidious comparisons? Of course he was no party man,
and loyal in the extreme to Athens; but in Plato's *Crito* the laws
of Athens are imagined as asserting their claim to his obedience,
because he has preferred to live there when he could have left it
for 'Lacedaemon or Crete, whose *eunomia* you are always talking
about'.[3] And this very definite statement, written not many years
after and in a work dealing with Socrates' death, is perhaps the
best evidence for the nature and extent of his laconism. At any
rate, the fact remains that all his friends and pupils of whom we
know anything were to a greater or lesser degree admirers of
Sparta—not that we need lay much weight on the enthusiastic
but temporary espousal of Spartan habits by his ex-pupil Alcibiades when in exile there. It should be remembered that, apart
from the extreme oligarchs, there was in Athens an influential
body of moderates, who projected their ideal primarily on to
their own ancestral *politeia*. They desired to restrict the franchise
to those who fought as hoplites or who owned land; to elect all
magistrates instead of choosing them by lot. They called this a
'good' form of democracy, or perhaps, as Thucydides did in

[1] Aristophanes, *Wasps* 475.
[2] Id., *Birds* 1281–3:
　　　　ἐλακωνομάνουν ἅπαντες ἄνθρωποι τότε,
　　　　ἐκόμων, ἐπείνων, ἐρρύπων, ἐσωκράτουν,
　　　　σκυτάλι᾽ ἐφόρουν.
[3] Plato, *Crito* 52e.

praising the régime that briefly succeeded the abortive oligarchic revolution of 411 at Athens, a combination of the interests of both parties; or even aristocracy, since they believed that the 'best' would be elected to office. It is very possible that like their successors in the fourth century some of them also admired Sparta and interpreted her constitution in accordance with their views. Certainly the moderate leader Theramenes took a leading part in negotiations there at the end of the war. The speech that Thucydides puts into the mouth of Alcibiades on his arrival as an exile in Laconia is an exquisitely calculated apology assimilating his own views to those of his hosts and, possibly, the moderates; certainly in practice he was to get on as ill with Athenian oligarchs as with Athenian demagogues. In my family, says he, we have never been democrats, only opponents of tyranny; we have tried to preserve moderation, keep the state united, and maintain our ancestral constitution.[1] In an age increasingly prone to bloody revolution Sparta's success in these last respects at least stood out. Thucydides allows Brasidas to claim that it was not Sparta's ancestral policy to subordinate the many to the few or vice versa.[2] He himself rashly believed that her political institutions had not changed since the days of Lycurgus. As well as his admiration for the constitution of the Five Thousand in 411, we may notice that he never actually calls Sparta an oligarchy, though he shows how she supported, and used, oligarchies and oligarchs. He also draws a comparison between Chios and Sparta, perhaps indeed reflecting the ideas of some of the laconizers at Chios when she revolted from Athens.[3] If so, they claimed affinity on account of having a larger and more dangerous slave population than anyone else, and also as 'the only other city that had been moderate in prosperity'. Chios' policy had always been prudent, and even the revolt was not ill-considered, Thucydides says. But he was probably also thinking of her constitution, which he would seem not to have regarded as a pure oligarchy, since he speaks of her as abandoning it and falling into the power of the few under the stress of events after the revolt.

It was, however, the true oligarchs who were the most obvious laconizers. In Athens in 411 they were thought to be intending

---

[1] Thucydides vi. 89.
[2] Id. iv. 84 (cf. perhaps i. 6, Sparta assimilates the life of rich and poor).
[3] Id. viii. 24; cf. 38, 40.

to betray the city to the enemy, to whom indeed the most prominent fled on the collapse of the oligarchic government. On Athens' final defeat in 404 the party was active again. The committee of five *ephori* that appeared was probably a piece of their party machinery rather than a government organ; in name and size it was clearly a straight crib from Sparta. But Athens soon passed, with the backing of Sparta or of Sparta's great admiral, the ambitious and cunning Lysander, into the hands of the Thirty—a board chosen to propose a constitution, but which usurped supreme power. On it the extremists were strong and finally in complete control.[1]

The most notorious member, Critias, recently one of the 'ephors', was of noble birth and had been an associate of Socrates. He was described by a later Greek scholar as a 'flagrant laconizer'.[2] Xenophon brings out this trait in his account of the famous scene in which Critias struck his more moderate colleague Theramenes off the list of full citizens and had him dragged off to execution without trial. The speech he utters contains an appeal to what, he says, is agreed to be the best of all governments, Sparta. And if an ephor there criticized and opposed the decision of the whole board, would he not be thought by all to deserve the severest of punishments?[3]

Critias had probably by this time already written two works discussing the Lacedaemonian *politeia*—one in prose and one in verse. The tantalizing fragments suggest that the dominant ideas are still those of freedom, moderation, and efficiency, especially in war. The last few years might well be thought to have reversed the verdict of Thucydides and the Old Oligarch on Athenian efficiency.

In the elegiac poem with which we are concerned[4] Critias praised the feasts in the *syssitia*, where moderate drinking promotes cheerfulness, health, and '*Sophrosyne*, neighbour to Piety'; it was the Lydians of Asia who invented the circulation of large cups round the table and the drinking of toasts, whence came

[1] It has been suggested that the number was inspired by that of the Gerousia (with the kings). But the Thirty was not, in theory or practice, a council, and if Xenophon is to be trusted Critias compared it to the executive magistracy, the board of ephors.

[2] Philostratus, *Lives of the Sophists* i. 16, λαμπρῶς μὲν ἐλακώνισε.

[3] Xenophon, *Hellenica* ii. 3.34.

[4] Diels-Kranz, *Fragmente der Vorsokratiker*, ed. 6, vol. ii, no. 88. Critias, frs. 6–9.

shameless language, damage to body, mind, and property—not to mention impertinence in servants. (It is doubtless to be understood that the Athenians have taken over these un-Greek customs; the Old Oligarch thought they were half barbarized owing to the influx of strangers, but it is never explicitly said that the Spartans are more truly Greek than the Athenians, in surviving literature at least.) The balanced Lacedaemonian diet, food and drink alike, encourages both hard work and the power of thought. And Critias attributes the famous aphorism 'nothing too much' to the early ephor and sage Chilon. In his prose study[1] he recurred to the Spartans' drinking habits, and pointed out how convenient for use on campaign their cups were—easy to pack, and designed to conceal and catch any dirt in the water. And he seems to have gone into the virtues of all their other utensils, furniture, clothes, and shoes (in the next century one could wear Laconian shoes without being a laconizer).

But in his elegies he had said that more men were 'good' by training than nature, and this seems to have been the main theme of the prose *Politeia*. It opened with the birth of the Spartan child, praising the athletic training of women as well as men because it conduces to healthy offspring. It probably followed him to manhood, describing various aspects of his life; Spartan dance-steps were certainly analysed. Critias' approval of this form of education might throw light on his action in forbidding rhetoricians—and his own old master Socrates—to teach in Athens. The most striking fragment, however, is one to the effect that in Sparta the free are freest, and the slaves most slaves. It may be that we can trace here both a new philosophic interest in definition, perhaps particularly Socratic, and a willingness, shared with the Old Oligarch, to face the word 'slavery'. (Critias also gave a careful description of the unceasing precautions that the Spartans have to take against their helots—fastening their doors with special locks and looking continually to their weapons.)

If we may build on a long fragment of one of his plays—a rash thing to do—Critias accepted the artificiality of law. But like others of his embittered generation he regarded human nature as uncommonly nasty. Man's original state was beastlike, disorderly, violent; there was no distinction between the good and bad. (This is, in fact, also the oligarchic description of democracy.) If

[1] Ibid., frs. 32–7.

laws and religion were simply invented as a curb, as this speech proclaims, they were none the worse for that.

One can easily imagine Critias admiring Lycurgus for imposing such laws on a country which Herodotus and Thucydides declared had previously been 'most disorderly'; even perhaps for pretending they emanated from Apollo.

For law is punitive, justice must 'enslave' crime and violence, but they are not enough; religion works through fear to the same end. There is another dramatic fragment indicating that law alone is insecure—a good character is safer; and here perhaps, on Critias' own principles, we return to the power of education. This idea points forward in time. But Critias' brief rule in Athens, which proved itself as inefficient as it was immoderate and illegal, marks the end of an age in the history of laconism as in so much else.

3

THE FOURTH CENTURY IN GREECE

By 404 b.c. Sparta had brought Athens to her knees and succeeded to the hegemony of most of Greece. The impression made by this achievement was enormous, though to us Athens' mistakes and Persia's gold may seem to have had a good deal to do with it. There seems to have been a spate of literature, now almost entirely lost, describing Sparta's institutions from a crudely utilitarian viewpoint, even though Athens, and some of Sparta's former allies, were soon struggling not without success against her predominance. Aristotle complains that many laconizing works simply praise these institutions as conducive to victory and conquest (the idea of Spartan timidity and slowness has disappeared), and instances that of one Thibron,[1] probably the Spartan commander of that name active against Persia in the 390s. Plato's Laws[2] also suggests that the Spartans (and Cretans) themselves regarded their way of life as purely military in purpose: one of the interlocutors points out that the place looks more like a camp than a city.[3] But they were clearly not alone.

The one surviving work with the title, so common in antiquity, *The Lacedaemonian Constitution* (or *Politeia*) to some extent reflects this narrow viewpoint. Its attribution to Xenophon has occasionally been questioned since antiquity, but it was certainly written by an Athenian (and for an Athenian audience) early in the century. If it is Xenophon's, it must date from the period in his life when this probably well-born young acquaintance of Socrates was in close contact with the ruling power. After his famous adventures in Asia Minor he found himself fighting under the Spartan King Agesilaus against Persia, and then against his own city. Under-

---

[1] Aristotle, *Politics* 1333b, cf. Xenophon, *Hellenica* iii. 1 and iv. 8.
[2] Plato, *Laws* i. 626c etc.
[3] Isocrates in the *Archidamus* puts in that Spartan prince's mouth the claim that his state's superiority has always been due to its being run like an army.

standably exiled, he went probably first to Sparta and then to an estate given him by the Spartans just beyond the borders of Laconia; and his sons were admitted to the Spartan *agoge*.

At any rate, the aim of the little work is simply to explain why Sparta, in spite of her small population, has grown so powerful, and its method is to find a rational explanation for all her peculiarities. The author begins, like Critias, with the regulations about women and marriage, vital to the breeding of healthy soldiers. Everything in the Spartan system of education, from the encouragement of theft to the officially recognized friendships between men and boys which, the author insists, are without any sexual element but involve the elder training the younger in 'virtue' or manliness, has its purpose too. Individuals cannot make their city great; Sparta alone makes 'virtue' a public duty, and alone publicly punishes cowards. The author gives much space to an account of the army, every feature of which, down to the scarlet colour of its tunics, he attributes to the original genius of Lycurgus (there is no mention of Crete, and Delphi merely gives its sanction afterwards).

Xenophon, if it is he, complains that no other cities copy Sparta's institutions, though all join in praising them. Individuals however did their best, thinking at this time that it was largely a matter of regular physical training. Plato speaks contemptuously of 'the laconizers in the various cities, who go about with cauliflower ears and with boxing thongs on their hands, wear short cloaks and devote themselves to athletics, under the impression that this is what has made Lacedaemon a great power in Greece'— none of which, he adds, saves them from expulsion as foreigners if they visit Laconia.[1] His words are probably more applicable to the 390s, when the *Protagoras* was written, than to the period before the war in which it is set. Also in the 390s we meet a flute-player who practised throwing the discus, in company, very suitably, with Thibron, because 'as a laconizer he piqued himself on his physical strength'.[2]

It does appear however that certain features of the Lacedaemonian army may have been copied in other parts of Greece at this period; the growth of the professional mercenary force facilitated the adoption of the more complicated manoeuvres for

[1] Plato, *Protagoras* 342b.
[2] Xenophon, *Hellenica* iv. 8. 18—one Thersander.

which the Lacedaemonians had long been famous (technical military writers were to call one such the 'Laconian counter-march')[1] and of a hierarchy of officers of different grades such as seems normal to us. Many Spartiates in fact served in these mercenary armies, especially after, in 371 and the following years, their country had been deprived of her leadership, and even of much of her own territory, by the Theban victories of Leuctra and Mantinea. The Thebans were compared to small boys puffed up at beating their masters. But a heavy blow had been dealt to the belief that Spartan methods in all their severity were necessary for success in war. Indeed, military science was already taking a new turn; new weapons, new tactics were emerging, and even the Spartan phalanx was soon to be superseded by the Macedonian variety. And so the political and moral aspects of laconism become increasingly important—not that such distinctions can be more than matters of emphasis, in a world where the citizen's first duty is still to fight for his city, and virtue, *arete*, often still means little more than valour; where the laws and institutions of the city are regarded as forming the character of the citizen, and the community of citizens, in their turn, as making up the city.

Even the *Lacedaemonian Constitution* has political interests. The virtues inculcated in the Spartan go beyond what a soldier needs. Election to the Gerousia is described as a contest of virtuous souls. Xenophon praises the shy reserve of the young men, and how they are kept too busy to succumb to pleasures or temptations; he paints Spartan drinking habits (in terms reminiscent of Critias, but minus the discussion of impertinence in slaves); he shows the most distinguished men running to obey the magistrates as an example to others, instead of disdaining to take any notice of them. In order to encourage obedience to law the almost tyrannic power of the ephors, who can fine anyone on the spot, and depose magistrates and imprison them on capital charges, was set up; the power of the kings, however, is far from tyrannic, in peace at least. The reciprocal oaths of these authorities appear as the fundamental feature of the only constitution that continues just as it was originally established.

Now the history of the time indicates that pro-Spartan parties all over Greece continued generally to be more or less oligarchic,

---

[1] Asclepiodotus, *Tactics* x. 14. Λακωνικὸς ἐξελιγμός (the work dates from the Roman period).

and anti-Spartan ones democratic. In Athens, too, it was 'the fellows with the cauliflower ears' who suggested some of the criticisms of democracy in Plato's *Gorgias*.[1] Conversely the only literary attack on the Spartan *politeia* that we hear of is by a certain Polycrates of Athens, a professional rhetor and sophist active at the beginning of the century, and certainly a thorough democrat; it is significant that our sources speak slightingly both of his social and financial standing and of his literary ability, and also that his best known work was an attack on Socrates.[2] The Athenians continued, too, to judge by the comic poets, to laugh at Spartan clothes, food, and archaic manners;[3] to judge by a good-tempered exchange of jokes in Xenophon's *Anabasis*, at teaching the young to steal too.[4] And speakers before the assembly or the courts tend to feel it necessary to apologize for too much praise of Sparta.

But at Athens the extremes of oligarchy had been discredited by Critias and his fellows more thoroughly than those of democracy had ever been. At the same time, however, certain Spartan features seemed almost irresistibly attractive. To be assured of the urgent necessity of concord and stability as well as obedience to law it was only necessary to look at Athens' own recent past, or at the wildly uncertain present of much of Greece. How to prevent faction; how to understand why one form of government turns into another; these were among the problems facing political minds. And so we can find even the staunchly democratic speechwriter Lysias lauding Sparta for her unchanging constitution and the absence of faction, as well as her military prowess, natural and acquired. As a result he even hopes her freedom will be immortal.[5]

But such language is chiefly found in those who tended to take

[1] Plato, *Gorgias* 515e.

[2] Jacoby, *Fragmente der Griechischen Historiker* (henceforth *FGH*) iii b, no. 597, p. 667. Other scholars do not identify Socrates' accuser with the author of the ψόγος Λακεδαιμονίων or think this last only a part of the larger work.

[3] Appearance, Plato Comicus *CAF* i, fr. 124; food, Epilycus ibid., fr. 3; advice to a prospective visitor to do as the Spartans do, Antiphanes, ibid. ii, fr. 44, ending ἐν τοῖς δ' ἐκείνων ἔθεσιν ἴσθ' ἀρχαικός. One would like to know more of the hero of Stephanus' *Philolacon*, probably of the later fourth century. The sole fragment perhaps suggests that he was a politician or mercenary soldier connected with King Archidamus' expedition to Italy in 338; ibid. iii, Stephanus, fr. i.

[4] Xenophon, *Anabasis* iv. 6.

[5] Lysias, *Olympic Oration* 7 (not delivered to an Athenian audience).

a moderate line in Athenian politics. Such men were now ready to accept, though they could not admire, the restored democratic constitution. It functioned with reasonable efficiency during the next century, and there was comparative peace between the classes. The peasantry may not wholly have recovered from the great war, it is true, and trade and industry seem to have lost some of their overseas markets; while the loss of a regular income from tribute was severely felt when campaigns abroad needed to be financed. The growing individualism and specialization of the age perhaps also gave the politicians cause to lament a new unwillingness in rich and poor alike to make sacrifices for the state, especially by personal service in war. A new—or rather the old—spirit was needed. Law was not enough to ensure it, though law was usually given an absolute value again. Now education was more important than ever, for part or all of the city must be trained in 'virtue', not merely particular intellectual skills. To politicians and thinkers who shared, or started from, such ideas as this Athens owed much of the importance, political and intellectual, that she kept in this century. They remained Athenian patriots and Athenian intellectuals; but they turned to Sparta for some of their inspiration.

One of those whose ideas we can follow most closely is Isocrates, the teacher of rhetoric and political pamphleteer. In 380 he is inveighing against surviving sympathizers of the Thirty and similar régimes as criminals 'who claim to be laconizers but act in a totally un-Spartan way';[1] and still, forty years later, against those, undoubtedly oligarchs, who 'regard her past statesmen as demi-gods' instead of praising her 'to a moderate extent', as most people do. It is right, he thinks, to praise her *politeia*—but not her foreign policy.[2]

Recent history indeed had lent increasing plausibility to the old idea that the Spartans left justice at home when they went abroad. Beside the greed and violence with which many of them, notably Lysander, administered their new empire Athens' past excesses paled. It was now Sparta which was charged with 'enslaving the Greeks', and Athens which could claim to desire their freedom, afford to recall the struggle against Persia. Spartan-backed oligarchies—the backing might include a garrison and a governor from Lacedaemon—were described as tyrannies. Indeed Sparta

---

[1] Isocrates, *Panegyricus* 110.   [2] Id., *Panathenaicus* 41.

now made no bones about alliance with real tyrants, notably Dionysius of Syracuse and the Persian king. Dependent on the latter's subsidies in the later stages of the Peloponnesian War, Sparta was subsequently involved in a squabble which was sometimes represented as a crusade to free the Greek cities of Asia; but in 387 she negotiated a peace that left Greece little better than a Persian protectorate.

Events, these, over which the panegyrists of Thermopylae and Plataea have always drawn a veil. But Lysias for one gives them plenty of publicity in the speech already quoted: I wonder how the Lacedaemonians can give the Greeks up to tyrants, to Dionysius and Artaxerxes, he says, when they are deservedly themselves the leaders of Greece for their political and military qualities; one would hope that having saved Greece in past dangers they will provide for her against future ones.[1] Isocrates' language is rougher. He was one of those who saw the cure for many of Greece's social and political ills in a united campaign against Persia, and in his *Panegyricus* in 380 he sets out Athens' title to be at the head of such a campaign. He argues, against oligarchic attacks on Athens' behaviour when she was the most powerful state in Greece, that Sparta's crimes have been incomparably worse. Don't think, however, he says, that I'm attacking Sparta— I only want her to be reconciled with us. And he praises the ruling class of both cities at the time of the Persian wars for their kind and faithful treatment of the allies, as well as their success in training the people in courage and virtue.[2]

But scandals were continuing. In 381 a Spartan force seized the citadel in Thebes in time of peace and set up a 'tyrannical government', thus setting in train the events that led to her own defeat at Theban hands. At Thebes itself resentment was symbolized by a melodramatic tale of the rape and murder of two girls, for which their father could get no redress in Sparta; the battle of Leuctra, it was said, was fought by the very tomb of the victims.[3]

Instead of contrasting Spartans at home and Spartans abroad, it

---

[1] Lysias, *Olympic Oration* 7. Cf. Andocides, *On the Peace with Sparta* 2 (their untrustworthiness).

[2] *Panegyricus* 73. Isocrates' belief that it is better to enslave barbarians than one's own neighbours (*Panegyricus* 131) enables him to detach the word εἱλωτεύειν—make helots of—from its context.

[3] Xenophon, *Hellenica* vi. 407 and later sources, less sceptical than he.

could be argued that her *politeia* was not what it had once been.
Possibly the earliest surviving exposition of the theory is in a
chapter of the *Lacedaemonian Constitution*, certainly misplaced as it
stands and possibly a later addition: the Spartans do not now obey
either God or the laws of Lycurgus; they used to fear to be found
in possession of gold, now some boast of it; they used to be
forbidden to go abroad for fear of corruption, now prominent
citizens long to go out as governors; they intrigue for power
instead of studying, as of old, to deserve it. And the Greeks
instead of calling on Sparta to defend them against injustice are
combining against her rule.[1]

The theory of Sparta's decline was probably shared on the spot.
Here, recent developments, especially the influx of wealth,
created a serious crisis, social, economic, and political, of which we
know too little. But there were certainly both attacks on the
existing system and attempts to shore it up. King Pausanias (not
to be confused with the earlier regent of that name) who was
exiled in 395/4 wrote a pamphlet apparently directed against the
laws of Lycurgus (in favour no doubt of a more purely royal
constitution—certainly shorn of the ephorate).[2] He is known to
have quoted various oracles, and these may have included both a
warning that courage and concord together ensure freedom, and
that, later so famous, to the effect that wealth alone would cause
Sparta's fall.[3] Or this last might come from some source favourable to Lycurgus and possibly also elaborating the stories of his
positive regulations against money and luxury, in an attempt to
get Sparta to live up to them.

After Leuctra, decline might appear complete and proven.
Victory ruined Sparta, says Isocrates in the 350s, when he wished
Athens to adopt a pacific policy, as did Eubulus and other moderate politicians of the upper class: moderation and military discipline gave way to arrogance and led to disaster. Empire depraves
everyone.[4]

Isocrates' ideal *politeia*, like that of the moderates of the late

[1] Xenophon, op. cit. 14.
[2] Pausanias, *FGH* iii b, no. 582, with commentary. Jacoby, probably rightly,
sees the king as arguing that the Spartan constitution, or all that was good in it,
was brought from Delphi by early kings, and that Lycurgus used violence; and
he would like to see Thibron's work as part of the controversy.
[3] ἁ φιλοχρημᾰτία Σπάρταν ὀλεῖ, ἀλλὸ μὲν οὐδέν. Aristotle, fr. 544.
[4] Isocrates, *Areopagiticus* 7; cf. *Philip* (346 B.C.).

D

fifth century, is projected on to the early Athens of Solon and Cleisthenes. For him this was democracy, but democracy combined with the aristocratic principle. The people was free, not enslaved as it is in oligarchies; it had the power to elect and supervise magistrates. It elected the 'best' to rule in the interest of all as the chance of the lot could not do. This, the giving of each his due, is the best kind of equality or fairness, and is also justice.

Above all, the ex-magistrates who sat for life in the council of the Areopagus (largely bypassed by radical fifth-century legislation, but apparently recovering some of its importance now) represented the 'best'. They had been as devoted to the state as to their private affairs; they had cared nothing for money (there was of course no payment for office yet) but a great deal for their fame and reputation; they kept watch over the laws, but especially over the unwritten laws and the daily habits of life, since a city depends on the character of the citizens, not the passing of decrees (the democratic Athenians were thought to pass far too many, often contradictory ones). Their laws therefore were few, but they cherished justice in their souls, and they educated the citizens in courage and obedience. The young were sober, respected their elders, and avoided the market-place.[1] The poor were hardworking and honest; the rich were kept busy with horsemanship, athletics, hunting, and study—what Isocrates calls philosophy. Both sides helped and sympathized with each other. There was unity at home and peace abroad; order and moderation (*sophrosyne*) reigned. It was a profound contrast to the present régime, which calls itself 'mild and common to all' and is nothing of the sort; which supposes that licence is democracy and lawlessness freedom, that complete freedom of speech is equality and the ability to do whatever one wants is happiness.[2]

Still, even this is better than the rule of the Thirty; Isocrates is eager to deny that he is an oligarch, and since most of the description of ancient Athens serves for Sparta too, he cannot analyse the latter as an oligarchy either. Indeed in a piece of very special pleading in the *Areopagiticus* he calls her the best, because the most democratic, of states, owing to her care for fairness and equality in daily life, the election of magistrates, and so forth.[3] Aristotle

---

[1] According to Plutarch, *Lycurgus* 25, Spartans under thirty never went near it; friends or relations did all their shopping.

[2] See especially *Panegyricus* 73 ff.; *Areopagiticus* 20 ff., 37 ff.   [3] *Areopagiticus* 61.

bears out that she was often called a democracy. Isocrates talks loosely of both ancient Athens and Sparta as a mixture of democracy and aristocracy, but denies once that the latter is a separate type of constitution rather than a virtue any type can embody. Generally he gives his own city precedence. It was because Lycurgus took Athens as a model that both states had a democracy tempered with aristocracy—though the statement is perhaps meant as a myth of Athens' proper position in Greece rather than as strict historical truth. The story, found in Plato's *Laws* and a late fourth-century orator, that the poet Tyrtaeus was really an Athenian sent to help Sparta at the time of the Messenian War[1] doubtless took its rise in a similar context. It may be remarked in passing that where so many Athenians not only wanted their city to resemble, but thought that in essential points she had once resembled, Sparta, it is not surprising that the equation of Spartan and Dorian never took much hold.

Praise of Sparta and Athens together was facilitated, after 370, by a *rapprochement* caused by common fear of Thebes. Xenophon describes speakers in the Athenian assembly recalling ancient cases of co-operation and calling one state the leader of Greece by land as the other by sea.[2] A few years after Leuctra Isocrates could publish his *Archidamus*, an eloquent plea for continued resistance by Sparta against Thebes, put into the mouth of the son of Agesilaus. Both he and his country are treated with sympathy, if not with complete identification. Isocrates has to begin by making him apologize for breaking his country's custom by speaking on a political issue while still young, and, less convincingly, regret his former opinion that speechifying is incompatible with action. He also inserts a striking number of glorious examples from Athenian history, and a perhaps invidious reference to Sparta's denial of free speech to free men, probably among the allies.[3] But on the whole his sympathy for Sparta appears to be warm. Archidamus insists that her claim to Messenia is just, and nothing is so important as justice. In the long run Sparta must succeed, given her unequalled military experience and the only *politeia* which is as it ought to be and has never altered (elsewhere Sparta's

---

[1] Plato, *Laws* 624a; Lycurgus, *Against Leocrates* 106. Later sources particularize, describing Tyrtaeus as a lame Athenian schoolmaster.

[2] Xenophon, *Hellenica* vi. 5.33.

[3] Isocrates, *Archidamus* 1, 15, 83.

past successes are ascribed to her having a *politeia* modelled on an orderly and obedient camp).[1] Divine favour, the Spartans' famous willingness for toil, their temperate life, fear of their fellows' contempt, and readiness to fight to the death will be on their side. There will be support from outside, including that of all the rich, prominent, and those who support aristocracy—while even the Peloponnesian democrats have become disillusioned. Let us remember our fathers' reputation and our own—how courted every Spartiate used to be at Olympia and the other festivals; and let us show that our admirers are not liars, our harsh and proud behaviour not affectation, and that we have indeed been better educated than others in *arete*.[2]

To the changed situation between Athens and Sparta, and to the moderate politician Eubulus, Xenophon seems to have owed the reversal of his sentence of exile from Athens. If he did not actually return there he certainly showed an interest in what was going on. A chapter of his *Memorabilia*[3] seems to reflect this period. Socrates is made to encourage the Athenians against the Thebans, and exhorts them to recall their heritage of 'virtuous leadership' (this virtue remains largely military). They have lost obedience and order in the carelessness induced by success; they must return to the ways of their ancestors, or at least of the Lacedaemonians, and if they try hard enough they may even excel these last. But when, he is asked, will the Athenians, like the Lacedaemonians, reverence old age, stop laughing at physical training, and obey the magistrates instead of squabbling about politics? Socrates holds that there is a hope of it; he points out that in some fields— in training for a chorus and in the fleet—the Athenians can obey and show *sophrosyne*. The whole chapter, and in particular the praise of the Areopagus, strongly recalls Isocrates' *Areopagiticus*, which may in fact have influenced it.[4]

---

[1] Ibid. 22 ff., 48, 60, 63.

[2] Ibid. 71, 95, 98 (ταῖς δ' αὐθαδείαις καὶ ταῖς σεμνότησιν. Some laconizers prefer to describe the Spartans as cheerful and friendly; doubtless this is another side to the same coin); 102.

[3] Xenophon, *Memorabilia* iii. 5 (perhaps *c.* 355 B.C.). The Areopagus, composed of tested men (ex-magistrates, whose term of office, by Athenian law, had undergone investigation), a very just, lawful, dignified (σεμνὸς) institution. Cf. *Memorabilia* iv. 4. Lycurgus taught the Spartans to be superior to others because of obedience to the laws. Such a state is successful in war, and immovable in peace.   [4] *Areopagiticus* 74.

But it must be remembered that in many respects Isocrates put Athens, even modern Athens, above Sparta; in particular for her artistic and intellectual life. He is never weary of praising Athens for her mythical discovery of law, religion, and agriculture, and her more recent position as the metropolis and centre of art and letters—themes that as he admits to some extent echo the innumerable funeral orations, delivered at the public commemoration for those killed in war, and which are to provide the basis of praise of Athens to the end of antiquity and beyond. He himself was a professional teacher of rhetoric, profoundly convinced that, if interpreted in a broad and serious sense, as an aesthetic and intellectual discipline dealing with serious themes in a practical manner, rhetoric was the training that his age was so urgently seeking (over which he came into conflict with the Socratic school). This explains why the 'education' in Sparta that he praises can only be that which results from the general climate of opinion, common to early Athens as well; and it throws light on the tortuous contradictions of his last work, in which he summed up his reactions to both cities.

The *Panathenaicus*, published in 339, is another encomium on early Athens, and especially her foreign policy, peaceful, philhellenic, and friendly to 'equal' constitutions, contrasted with that of arrogant, selfish, and aggressive Sparta (it is hard to see any practical reason for this attack on a new impotent state, and the fundamental object of the work has been much disputed). But the rambling work, which a long illness interrupted, finally resolves itself into an account of an argument with an oligarchic pupil from outside Athens, who objects that Sparta did at least discover, and show Greece, what were the best institutions.[1] The all-but-centenarian author represents himself as routing this adversary: the Spartans certainly did not discover piety, justice, and prudence—nor, towards their neighbours, did they practise them. They discover nothing; they are less interested in searching for truth than many barbarians, and their education, marked most strikingly by its encouragement of theft, only teaches them how to harm the Hellenes (earlier he complained that they neglected agriculture as well as other arts). The pupil, obviously a conventional fellow, says what he meant to praise was the athletic and military training, and the Spartan courage and unity. Very well,

[1] *Panathenaicus* 202 ff.

retorts Isocrates, but the use they made of all these was appalling—it was to damage the rest of Greece. Their unity is that of pirates, brigands, and other criminals, or, if this is going too far, of the savage and warlike Triballians (a tribe in Thrace). Exit the oligarchic disputant. But then, says Isocrates, I wondered if I'd been carried away, and I asked my pupils if I should alter my speech.[1] And the oligarchic student reappears to suggest that Isocrates' treatment of the Spartans had been ironical; that the arrogance he accused them of is close to dignity, and that such men are more high-minded than the partisans of equality, while to be warlike—able to get what you want and keep what you have—is better than to be peaceable, for everyone really wants to 'get more'. Though Isocrates neither agrees nor disagrees, this last suggestion at least is hardly consonant with the policy he had long been urging on Athens; but the space he allows the (possibly quite fictional) pupil to expatiate on the Spartans' victories, their uninterrupted freedom from foreign domination, as from faction, violence, and constitutional change or revolutionary social measures (the abolition of debts and redistribution of land anathema to all well-to-do Greeks) can hardly be without significance.

A glance at some of the leading politicians of this time, around and just after Isocrates' death, will make clearer the extent and variety of Athenian laconism. Isocrates, as we saw, in his later years to some extent reflects the programme of financial retrenchment and peaceful foreign policy, sometimes leading to friendship with Macedon, that was popular with the well-to-do from the 350s and under Eubulus dominant for some time. It counted among its chief adherents Phocion, who served Athens in what was now an old-fashioned combination, both in the field and on the platform. This prudent and honourable man had been a pupil of Plato's. He lived an austere life (avoiding, it was said, the public baths and often going without shoes, or without a tunic beneath his mantle) and was never seen to show emotion. The anecdotes in Plutarch's *Life* are noteworthy if not to be vouched for.[2] Once, we are told, another speaker jokingly promised to support him in proposing to the assembly to adopt the 'laws of Sparta'; 'You, with that scent and in that elegant cloak, to be praising Lycurgus and his *syssitia*', replied Phocion scathingly. Again, he denounced a certain Archibiades, actually known as the

[1] Ibid. 241 ff. [2] Plutarch, *Life of Phocion* 4, 10, 20.

Laconist for his long hair, short cloak, and morose expression, as a fraud when the latter refused to support his political programme (this man, with two friends, was also accused by Demosthenes of acting the gloomy laconizer by day and indulging in abominable excesses by night).[1] Finally, he is said to have sent his dissipated son to Sparta to be put through the *agoge*; the only effect of which was to annoy Athenian opinion. We can be sure that most Athenian laconizers would have jibbed at extending the medicine to their daughters. But they did, Plutarch assures us,[2] and inscriptions perhaps bear him out, entrust their infants to Laconian nurses, who had something of the reputation that English nannies used to have on the Continent: they rejected swaddling clothes and taught their charges not to be fussy about food or afraid of the dark.

Phocion, ultimately, was ready to accede to the Macedonian demand for limitation of the franchise by a property qualification; but whether this really makes him more of an oligarch than Isocrates, in whose time such measures were not practical politics, is uncertain. But it is clear that on moral and educational matters he was a more extreme laconizer. He himself, significantly perhaps, has left the memory of his swift repartees and of a consciously laconic brevity of expression, but no speeches. But his ally Aeschines, the enemy of Demosthenes, is to be found remarking very unoriginally in one of his that only virtuous men have influence in Lacedaemon, and that members of the Gerousia are chosen for their life-long moderation and sobriety—and then turning to praise the Athenian past so that he shall not be taken for a 'flatterer of the Lacedaemonians'.[3]

Demosthenes, on the other hand, though almost exclusively concerned with foreign affairs, talks much more like a democrat. Even in an early speech of 355, when some think he was in contact with Eubulus and his friends and before his energetic and anti-Macedonian policy which required appeal to the great imperialist and democratic days of the fifth century had been thoroughly worked out, he deprecates those who argue for a proposal by using Spartan or Theban examples. They could not do the equivalent in Sparta, where one may not praise the laws of another city, but has to praise as well as obey one's own. Why,

---

[1] Demosthenes, *Against Conon* 34.   [2] Plutarch, *Life of Lycurgus* 16.
[3] Aeschines, *Against Timarchus* 180–2.

indeed, eulogize other people, he asks the Athenians, when you are in every respect better off yourselves—more united, even? Even if other systems were theoretically superior, you ought to stick to that which has brought you to greatness. And he contrasts the rewards for merit at Sparta—election to the Gerousia, that is to say a small share in despotic rule over the people—with those open to every individual at Athens in the shape of crowns and other honours, at the hands of the sovereign people. The Spartan system may make for concord as interpreted in an oligarchy.[1] But to Demosthenes, as other speeches show, oligarchy is simply slavery; the denial of the rule of law: a régime with which a free democracy can have no stable friendship.[2] Spartan foreign policy, he argues at one time, is untrustworthy; it is unjust (though nothing to Philip's). To him the glorious past of Athens is slightly more recent than it is to Isocrates, but it bears some resemblance to his vision of a time when the citizens were brave, disciplined, devoted to the state, and simple in their private lives. This Athens stands alone, however, and the public splendour of the city is praised, as Sparta's could never be. And with all their faults the Athenians of the present remain gentle and generous; they obey the laws through the exercise of reason—small wonder, Demosthenes once says, if Peloponnesians act unreasonably.

Lycurgus (his name, hereditary in his highly aristocratic family, is not significant)[3] was also a bulwark of the anti-Macedonian cause. But in his whole cast of mind and character at least he bore more resemblance to his opponent Phocion; he was, it is said, like him a pupil of Plato, and also of Isocrates. His one surviving speech prosecutes, with all the rigour for which he became proverbial, an unfortunate merchant who left Athens in panic after the Macedonian victory at Chaeronea. It is a sermon on patriotism, or rather on readiness to die for one's country, and on how to instil it into the young. It is as an example that Lycurgus wants to see the defendant condemned. And it is because of their success in producing this self-devotion that he praises the Athenians of the past. His language is not unlike that of

[1] Demosthenes, *Against Leptines* 106. The speech was written for a legal case, but traditionally spoken by Demosthenes himself.

[2] Id., *For the Liberty of the Rhodians* 18-19.

[3] It is also that of a mythical king of Thrace torn to pieces by Bacchants.

Demosthenes as well as Isocrates—except that with the Athenians he joins the Lacedaemonians, and in particular the heroes of Thermopylae. Among the poetic quotations he inflicts on his audience, as he was notorious for doing, is a huge chunk of Tyrtaeus (whom he accepts as an Athenian by origin). He regards Tyrtaeus' teaching as the foundation of the Spartan training in *arete* (courage in the cause of the state); the poets were indeed the ancient teachers of Greece, and continued to be popularly regarded as such. And he also has read out a Spartan law on cowardice, inflicting death on those unwilling to risk their lives for their country. He would like to see it adopted elsewhere; do not be angry with me, he says to the jury, if I often talk of this people, and take examples of justice from a well-ordered city.[1]

In the years after Chaeronea Lycurgus did great service to Athens, reorganizing her finances and her military resources, even it seems restricting female luxury and attempting to revive traditional religious practices, as well as pursuing malefactors. It is also probable that at this time the existing system of military training and service for the young men was reorganized and extended, and put under the supervision of new magistrates elected by the people, *cosmetes* and *sophronistae*, 'orderers' and 'moderators'. It has always been very tempting to believe that Lycurgus was behind this; even that he may have been, in this as in some of his other measures, thinking of the 'well-ordered city' he had praised in a narrower context.

Phocion and the hypocritical victims of his wit remind us that laconism could take an individualistic form. It is sometimes thought that Socrates' friend or pupil Antisthenes, whose interests were primarily in individual ethics, had some hand in this development. Various sayings laudatory of Sparta are attributed to him on more or less reliable evidence, and there can be no doubt that he admired energy and courage, typified for him, as for some earlier writers, in the figure of Heracles, who could be seen as the legendary ancestor of the Spartans. Xenophon may have been influenced by Antisthenes as well as by the ethical teaching of Socrates. Certainly his interest in Sparta often takes the form of interest in and admiration for individual Spartan leaders, many of whom he knew personally. Among his most vivid portraits are

[1] Lycurgus, *Against Leocrates*, esp. 106–7, 128–30.

those of the bluff admiral Callicratidas, who chafed at the dependence on Persian subsidies in the Peloponnesian War and refused to enslave Greek prisoners; Clearchus and the other Spartans who were prominent among the leaders of the famous Ten Thousand, devoted and efficient soldiers, though sometimes harsh disciplinarians and sometimes wily to the point of deceitfulness; and above all King Agesilaus, whose long military career is treated with much sympathy in Xenophon's general history. But in the little work entitled *Agesilaus*, an encomium written after the king's death in a genre which encourages exaggeration, Xenophon not only defends him against his enemies' charges but sets him up in so many words as a perfect man and an example to all wishing to practise 'virtue', for his endurance, strength, and wisdom. Honest and just, self-denying and simple in all his habits—Xenophon draws attention to the old-fashioned doors of his house—but cheerful and friendly; respectful to the gods, obedient to his country's laws and customs, terrible to his enemies, generous to his friends, and humane to the unfortunate, he is devoted to his country but also to the welfare of Greece as a whole. The work has probably contributed more to the development of the idea of the noble Spartan than Xenophon ever meant; for it does not appear that he considered the king entirely typical of his countrymen, or wanted to argue here that his virtues were entirely dependent on its institutions. Neither subject nor author were always in agreement with official Spartan policy.

The perfect man is also the perfect soldier and general, even the perfect ruler. It was perhaps by an analogous path that Antisthenes became interested in monarchy and the ideal king. But non-democratic thinkers in the fourth century had an increasing interest in monarchy, though no one tried to preach it to the Athenians. If the best are to rule, the best may turn out to be a single man. Search for the ideal *politeia* could lead in this direction on grounds of practical efficiency as well, and there were important single rulers in outlying parts of the Greek world whose position required analysis and whose outlook a thinker might hope to influence, thus gaining the chance to form or educate a whole state.

Kingship was strictly distinguished from tyranny, often regarded as its corrupt form. This was defined as selfish and arbitrary, and often accounted hostile to the rich (and by an easy transition to the 'best'). But the king should rule for the good of and by the agreement of his subjects, and especially the best of them. His relationship to the laws was much canvassed; it might be said that he must act if not under, yet at least in accordance with the laws. In this context the Spartan kings, who had always aroused interest, and who in the early fourth century were represented by the remarkable Agesilaus, took on some importance. They were called kings, so the fact that there were two of them could be ignored. So, to some extent, could their hereditary status, since the Greek theory, as distinguished from practice, of monarchy primarily involves ethical justifications (Lysander, it appears, actually wished to open the kingship in Sparta to all at least who could claim descent from Heracles, and to get himself elected king on merit).

Isocrates, in his advice to the Cypriote King Nicocles, describes monarchy as the rule of the best man and thus the justest form of government, while in practice it is the most efficient and professional, especially in war—as is shown by the fact that those admirable states, Sparta and Carthage (here first linked in surviving literature), are oligarchies in peace but kingdoms in war[1]— how his analyses vary with his object! Even to the Athenians he can recommend a metaphorical kingship, when he urges the city not to seek tyrannic or forcible control over her allies but to emulate the rule of the Spartan kings, who had less liberty to do ill than private citizens but a primacy based on honour and rewards.[2]

Xenophon's *Agesilaus* is as we saw primarily the study of a good man rather than a good king; it is only when Agesilaus is in untrammelled command abroad, in fact, that his acts (uniting cities and causing their prosperity and happiness) are described as specifically kingly. But a king has to be a supremely good man; and Isocrates' analysis of the royal virtues,[3] in which temperance and care for the laws together with *philanthropia* or love of one's subjects bulk large, suggests how easily Xenophon's work could be read as a treatise on monarchy. The contrast he drew between Agesilaus and the luxurious, inaccessible Persian king was especially influential; and the whole account of Agesilaus as a leader in war was little less relevant.

[1] Isocrates, *Nicocles* 14; 24.   [2] Isocrates, *Peace* 143.
[3] Isocrates, *To Nicocles, passim.*

In fact, the fullest picture of the ideal king surviving from the fourth century is indeed Xenophon's; it is his fancy picture of the founder of the Persian empire, the good father, the living and seeing Law, whose title comes from his superiority in all things over his subjects. The *Cyropaedia* is however more than this; it is also a treatise on education, primarily for a ruler but also for a whole upper class, and thus, as in Greece at least such a work was bound to be, it is a study of the ideal state. It begins with the usual lament on political instability and people's dislike of all authority. But Cyrus, owing to the fear and love his qualities inspired, was readily obeyed; how did this come about?

Cyrus himself may or may not have been endowed with certain qualities derived from Agesilaus (beauty, in which the latter was notoriously deficient, not included). But the ancient Persians, whose education he shares, are seen, no-one ever doubts, as the Spartans of Asia.[1] Their laws, says Xenophon, begin at a different point from those of other states; instead of letting children be brought up anyhow and then forbidding them to do certain things, they so form the young that they do not wish to do evil. Boys, youths, adults, and elders are all organized to varying extents by the state. The educational system is directed to moral rather than intellectual ends. The boys learn justice, self-control (*sophrosyne*), obedience, and moderation in food and drink; and to shoot and throw the spear. As youths they sleep in the public buildings, visiting their wives, if they have them, rarely; they are kept occupied, as is wise at this dangerous age, especially in hunting, which is good training for war, and in military competitions. They show their modesty by avoiding the market-place, from which trade is banished. All the Persians who have gone through these stages satisfactorily are known as *homotimoi*, Equals in Honour, a name strongly reminiscent of the Spartan *homoioi*; the old men among them try cases, elect officers or officials, and remove their privileges from any who fail in their duties. The Persian king is strictly subordinate to law.

There are however several points on which the ancient Persians are carefully distinguished from their models. The *homotimoi* are an open class compared with the Spartiates; everyone who can

[1] Arrian, *Anabasis* v. 4.5 explicitly compares the customs of the early Persians, who were poor and lived in a poor country, to the Spartan educational system.

afford to maintain his son without a trade may put him into the way of becoming one, and in the course of his story Xenophon exemplifies his belief that good men may be found, and should be encouraged, in any class. We are also told that the Persians have decided that it is a mistake to teach deceit (presumably theft in particular) to those who are too young to discriminate as to its purpose. The formal trials at which the boys practise justice seem an original provision, like the formal punishments for ingratitude.[1] And then there is no doubt that Cyrus' own education transcends this semi-Spartan context. He goes to Media, where he learns to resist luxury; he argues about everything like a good pupil of the Athenian Socrates. His great achievement is his gaining the willing obedience of army and subjects, an obedience once contrasted with the compulsory kind he knew at school. And Cyrus himself ends, of course, as something much more powerful and grander than a Spartan king, though as regards his Persians, now the élite of a vast empire, he covenants to preserve their rights as the Spartan king covenanted with the ephors.

The practical, soldierly Xenophon may have very different ideas from Isocrates on the sort of education that well-off youths require; and very different ideas from Plato, to whose *Republic* the *Cyropaedia* has sometimes been thought to be an answer, on the organization of the ideal state. But in the long run Xenophon's most serious attempt at political literature allows us to see that his attitude to Sparta was not unlike that of his fellow-Athenians. Sparta, even the 'Lycurgan' Sparta of the past, may provide a basis for, but is not an embodiment of, the ideal.

A word, finally, about the historians. It is typical both of the atmosphere at Sparta and of the kind of interest the rest of Greece took in her that among the spate of pamphlets and *politeias* there appears to have been no local chronicle, of the type so common in Greece, devoted to her in the fourth century.[2] But many historians inevitably had to do with her, and in the earlier years especially

---

[1] The ancient Persians are no doubt too busy for agriculture; elsewhere Xenophon leaves no doubt that he thinks it by no means wrong for a gentleman and a soldier to cultivate his own lands himself, and in *Oeconomicus* iv. 3 he contrasts (modern, real) Persians with Spartans on this point.

[2] A possible exception is Charon of Lampsacus' *Leaders of the Lacedaemonians* (late fifth century?), but this may have been a general history on a chronological framework of Spartan kings' and, conceivably, ephors' dates. See Jacoby, *FGH* iii a, no. 262.

doubtless others beside Ctesias (author of a romancing account of Persia) could have been described as *philolacon*.[1]

Xenophon's one strictly historical work, the *Hellenica* or *History of Greece*, is a gappy and composite affair, hardly to be described as covering the years 411 to 362, but in which after the first two books Sparta or Spartans do often take the centre of the stage, and Xenophon shows off his knowledge of the place. Treating the Spartans' campaigns early in the century, he seems to accept their claim to be 'freeing the cities' (from Persia, now, not Athens), though individual commanders are not beyond his criticism.[2] Agesilaus and his brother are given eulogistic treatment; the latter's graciousness and popularity ensured willing obedience from his men, a very Xenophontic theme. The historian also tends to suppose that opposition is fomented by interested parties; a Theban speech suggests that the allies could seriously consider themselves 'enslaved' by Sparta but may be a later insertion. Xenophon marks examples of Spartan piety, Spartan obedience, and Spartan justice; he reports Agesilaus' brother as claiming that the city's greatness is due to its readiness for dangers and for toil. An identification with the Spartan official line may be seen in his tendency to blame the king in charge for the defeat at Leuctra, while bringing out the steady courage with which the news was received at home:[3] the ephors forbore to interrupt the Gymnopaedia and forbade the women to mourn; next day the relations of those who had died in the battle went about rejoicing; the friends of those who had escaped were sad and ashamed. (Subsequently, however, he notes a female panic.)

But as time went on the ingenuous and honourable Xenophon was clearly put to some embarrassment by his friends. There is a long investigation of a case where Agesilaus allowed expediency to prevail over justice, though its exceptional nature is stressed. The seizure of Thebes is told without overt condemnation, and Agesilaus is reported to have endorsed that initiative, but a little later Xenophon declares that by it the oaths to preserve the freedom of all Greek cities were broken, and that divine punish-

---

[1] Plutarch, *Artaxerxes* 13.4. φιλολάκων καὶ φιλοκλέαρχος: : i.e. an admirer of Clearchus, first Spartan governor of Byzantium and then leader of the Ten Thousand in Asia.

[2] Xenophon, *Hellenica*, esp. iii. 1.3, 1.20, 2.12, 5.1, 5.8 ff.

[3] Ibid. iv. 4.15, 7.2; v. 1.6, 2.6; vi. 4.16.

ment inevitably followed.[1] The later books are less notable for praise of Sparta than for marked lack of sympathy with Thebes and Sparta's rebellious allies. The reconciliation of Sparta and Athens is apparently dwelt on with pleasure, as is, certainly, the loyalty of the little town of Phlius, generously rewarded by Sparta. But the record ends in gloom, with chaos in Greece caused by Thebes' incapacity to maintain her leadership.

The general history of Ephorus, who came from Cyme in Ionia and may have been a pupil of Isocrates, was a flat and detailed work that set a precedent for the moralistic and exemplary tendencies and somewhat uncritical scholarship of too much ancient historiography, and was so extensively followed by later writers that large parts of it can be reconstructed.[2] Ephorus, who began with the Dorian invasion or return of the Heracleidae, recounted the life of Lycurgus in considerable and dubious detail; he mentioned his visits to Crete and Egypt, his interest in Homer, and the episode of a recalcitrant young Spartan knocking out his eye. We also know what he thought of the social institutions of Crete and how he refuted at length a thesis that they were copied from rather than by Sparta. They assisted the growth of courage and concord and thus ensured freedom—which is the greatest of blessings, since without freedom property is insecure. We may apply this to Sparta too, since Polybius complains that Ephorus' language about both places was identical. He also implies that among the institutions of Sparta, if not Crete, Ephorus reckoned the equal division of land.[3] If so, this is the first time we come on this momentous doctrine (for Xenophon's *Lacedaemonian Politeia* only said that at Sparta it does not matter if you are rich or poor, and Isocrates that luxury did not exist, and rich and poor loved each other, in early Athens and thus no doubt in Sparta too). It is interesting that it should be put forward by one so keen on the interests of property-owners as Ephorus, whose formulas often recall Isocrates—though we should notice that the equation, courage plus concord equals freedom, appears in an oracle prob-

[1] Ibid. v. 2.28, 4.1, 4.24.

[2] *FGH* ii a, no. 70. See esp. frs. 118, 148, 149. Cf. 173–5. Diodorus Siculus' account of events in Greece in Books xi–xvi (and of the Athenian expeditions to Sicily) is agreed to be closely based on Ephorus.

[3] Fr. 148—Polybius' polemic is certainly directed at Ephorus. Isocrates *Paneg.* 259 is usually thought to prove that he did not know of any division of land in Sparta—though he might only mean *since* Lycurgus, strictly speaking.

ably quoted by Ephorus from King Pausanias. We learn in a different context that Ephorus believed *eunomia* to involve sticking to simple laws, not laying down numbers of over-complicated ones. How precisely he analysed the Spartan constitution we do not know, but he was certainly a conservative, as his account of Athenian history reveals. Writing in the confused aftermath of the Theban victories, he was particularly interested, however, in the reasons for the rise and fall of empires. He stated that Lycurgus' reforms gave his country five hundred years of hegemony, where previous writers had applied such exaggerated figures merely to the duration of her constitution; he recounted her great deeds, especially at Thermopylae, whose heroes are treated to the most tedious of eulogies, with much rhetorical exaggeration and amplification. But hegemony, Ephorus held, is preserved by fairness and humanity, *philanthropia*, to subject allies. He seems to have held that the Athenian's pride in these qualities was not always justified; he certainly emphasized that after the Peloponnesian War the Spartans threw their gains away by neglecting *philanthropia*, while a definite quotation attributes the brevity of Thebes' hegemony to the fact that her citizens lacked not only intellectual training but all ability to get on with others; they had nothing but military qualities. On the whole, however, Ephorus seems to have been content with simple moral lessons; Pausanias the regent was probably slated for neglecting the laconic *agoge* for Persian luxury and indiscipline; the virtuous Callicratidas was praised, and Clearchus rebuked for harshness.

As for the bitter-tongued Theopompus, traditionally also a pupil of Isocrates, he has left his mark on the tradition largely by his attacks on Athenian imperialism and Athenian demagoguery.[1] As the son of an oligarch allegedly expelled from Chios for laconism his views on Sparta would be worth having in full, though his continuation of Thucydides need have had little to say about Lycurgus. A surviving fragment does reflect what we suspected to be a preoccupation of Chiote laconizers—the slave problem. But the distinction made between the Chiote purchase of barbarians for slaves and the Lacedaemonian and Thessalian reduction of Greeks is probably heavily to the disadvantage of the latter, especially as Theopompus did animadvert on the savage treatment of the helots. Full-blooded oligarchic laconism on the

[1] *FGH* ii b, no. 115. See esp. frs. 122; 321 and 322; 233; 332; 24; 323.

fifth-century model was clearly impossible now, for many reasons (Theopompus, indeed, was to build his later history round Philip of Macedon). Surviving fragments on Sparta as on other topics suggest a strongly rhetorical and moralistic bias again, with a particular hatred of luxury. Agesilaus was declared the greatest man of his day because of his *arete*; the anecdote is told of his refusing to accept delicate food for his troops from an ally, and his apophthegm thereon. Lysander, who often emerges so badly, is praised for energy, *sophrosyne*, and contempt for money and pleasure, which suggests, though it cannot prove, that Theopompus also sympathized with the Spartan imperialism associated with Lysander. But certainly he castigated Spartan vices too. Crime as well as duplicity was attributed even to Agesilaus; his son abandoned the old ways and came to a bad end in distant Italy. And it was possible for a parody of Theopompus, Anaximenes' *Tricaranus*, to be a savage attack on all three of the leading cities.[1]

[1] The third important historian of this period, Aristotle's nephew Callisthenes, is usually called anti-Spartan. It was hard to be much else if you began your book at the Peace of Antalcidas. Callisthenes' connection with Macedon, and undoubted sympathy for Thebes, are however relevant here.

4

LACONISM IN THE WEST

OUR PICTURE of fourth-century laconism has concentrated heavily and inevitably on Athens. But there is an outlying part of the Greek world where there were meanwhile interesting developments probably not without influence on later Greek thought—the Italian and Sicilian colonies.

Laconism was generally, no doubt, strong in places that could claim historical connection with Sparta. At a very early date, Herodotus tells us, emigrants from Lacedaemon helped to settle the island of Thera in the Aegean,[1] which itself became the mother-state of Cyrene, the leading Greek city in north Africa; Cyrene made much of its Spartan connections. The island of Melos called itself a Spartan foundation in the fifth century,[2] and there were other such claims, as we shall see, perhaps mostly invented as admiration for Sparta and interest in local history developed. But there is no doubt at all that Taras, the Tarentum of the Romans, in the heel of Italy, was founded from Sparta, though probably not by full citizens, in the archaic age. It prospered and became rich, but maintained ties with its mother-city, a fact that doubtless stimulated the wider interest Sparta took from the later fifth century in southern Italy. It was probably after Sparta's triumphant victory over Athens at the latest that several Greek cities here with famous early lawgivers (and probably archaic institutions, surviving in this remote area) began to associate them with Lycurgus. Locri in particular, now a fast friend, produced stories of early links with or even foundation by Sparta, and was perhaps the place of origin of tales circulating in the fourth century that the Locrian legislator Zaleucus took Spartan and Cretan features, as well as Athens' Areopagus, as models,[3] or that describe the (wildly misdated) Orphic prophet Onomacritus as a Locrian and the earliest of all legislators, the ultimate master via a Cretan lawgiver of Lycurgus as well as other Italian figures.[4]

---

[1] Herodotus iv. 148. [2] Thucydides v. 85.
[3] Ephorus, *FGH* ii a, no. 70, fr. 139. [4] Aristotle, *Politics* 1274a.

Pythagorean interest in Sparta is probably a contemporary phenomenon. It is unlikely to be older, for during the fifth-century dispersion of the sect those who fled from Italy to Greece seem to have settled in Thebes or elsewhere. But in the early fourth century the leading Pythagorean school was that of Taras, now the dominant city of Magna Graecia, and it is likely that its members saw affinities with Sparta in their own way of life (though they must, like Plato, have found the Spartans deficient in mathematical interests). In politics the Pythagoreans probably believed in the rule of the élite, that is to say of the authority of their own close-knit and indeed communistic societies, to which women seem to have been admitted. They were religious and ascetic; their reverence for their founder and for the past was extreme.

The great Pythagorean figure of the period is Plato's friend Archytas, who appears to have exercised at Taras a constitutional primacy not unlike that which, in Syracuse, Plato and their common friend Dion seem to have associated with Sparta. But the whole question of influences is obscure, as anything to do with Pythagoreanism is. All that can certainly be asserted is that, as we shall see, after Plato and Aristotle surviving Pythagorean literature shows definite interest in Sparta.

Laconism in Sicily seems to have been rather different in character or origin. The rivalries of the Sicilian colonies tended to divide them according to racial origin to an extent unusual in the Greek world, with Syracuse, a Corinthian foundation, claiming the leadership of the Dorian cities. In 476 her great tyrant Hieron succeeded in expelling the non-Dorian inhabitants of Catane (now Catania) and replacing them with a settlement of immigrants from the Peloponnese ruled by his son, under the name of Aetna. Pindar's first *Pythian Ode* celebrates, among much else, this new foundation: Hieron has given it god-derived freedom and the laws of the Dorians. He immediately adds that the famous and warlike Spartans also live under the laws of Aegimius, the primeval Dorian king.[1] Pindar's references to freedom and the mutual respect of people and king suggest that Aetna's ruler was not a tyrant, but had restricted powers, perhaps primarily as a leader in war, and that the citizen body, maybe a very narrow one, had considerable privileges. This is possible, for the Syracusan tyrants

[1] Pindar, *Pythian Odes* i, esp. 60 ff.

were supported by the landowning classes, whereas in mainland Greece it was often the poor who benefited from tyranny. Aetna was short-lived; but the idea that a limited monarchy was Dorian and Spartan may have survived in Syracuse into the next century, rather than have been imported then, in Plato's day.

Two speeches of Siceliote politicians in Thucydides, and indeed the course of events in the late fifth century, show the persistence of the idea of racial division in the island.[1] Syracuse was a Corinthian foundation and now a democracy; but the decline of Corinth left the latter's ally Sparta her natural Dorian protector against the ambitions of Athens. The successful intervention of the Spartiate Gylippus with a few Laconian troops when Syracuse was besieged by the Athenians brought Sparta's military reputation home to the Sicilians, and in the next few years we find Spartiates holding high commands in Sicily apparently on the grounds of their origin alone. One of these, Dexippus in Acragas, showed some hesitation in supporting the new tyranny of Dionysius in Syracuse. But Sparta, under the influence of Lysander, was at this point more amenable to the tyranny than to the democracy which it replaced and which had finally parted from Gylippus not on the best of terms. To the rage and astonishment, it seems, of the Syracusan democrats, the Lacedaemonian envoys after a disingenuous start turned out supporters of Dionysius.[2] The alliance was of practical value to both parties, but, as we saw, it did Sparta's reputation no service in Greece—in particular in so far as Lysias, a resident in Athens but of Syracusan origin, could see to it.

The simple ideas that Sparta produced grand generals and ought to dislike tyrants were doubtless complicated in the fourth century by contemporary theory, of whatever precise origin. There were at this time Pythagoreans in Syracuse for one thing, and indeed it was members of the sect here and in Taras who acted as intermediaries in Plato's relations with the court of Dionysius and his son. What at least is clear is that Dion, uncle to the younger Dionysius and a pupil and admirer of Plato's from the latter's first visit, in reaction against the riches and luxury traditional in Syracuse and considered as particularly typical of a tyrant's court, affected a simple life and austere manners which as the seventh *Letter* attributed to Plato suggests was called in Sicily

[1] Thucydides, iv. 61 and 64, vi. 80. [2] Diodorus Siculus xiv. 10.

'the ancestral Dorian way of life'.[1] After Dion and Plato had failed in their plans to educate the younger Dionysius in political philosophy, the former, now in exile, received the unusual honour of citizenship at Sparta (in spite of the formal alliance with Dionysius still obtaining). Subsequently, with a train of hangers-on from the Academy, though Plato himself stood aside, he invaded Sicily as a liberator. The adventurers representing Sparta and trading on her reputation for providing generals showed signs of support. Dion's idea seems to have been to establish himself as a monarch ruling by law, in accordance with Plato's later political theory. Plutarch tells us that he intended to set up a constitution 'of the Spartan or Cretan type, a mixture of democracy and royalty, with an aristocracy overseeing and administering the chief affairs',[2] while the favourable tradition of the Platonic school represents the philosopher as urging Dion's followers after his murder to set up no less than three kings, with powers like those of the Lacedaemonian royal houses or lesser, and a special concern with religious matters. Let them make a compromise between the claims of the tyrant's family and the democratic party by turning tyranny into kingship as the wise and good Lycurgus did: seeing what had happened to the kings in Argos and Messene, he established other magistracies to limit and protect the royal power, so that law was king over men, and not men tyrants over the laws. Let the Syracusans also adopt laws to discourage money-making and limit the power of wealth.[3] All this, as we shall see, is reminiscent of Plato's final political doctrine in the *Laws*, except for his proposal concerning actual kings.

The failure of Dion, and the subsequent behaviour of one of the Spartan adventurers, who set up as a particularly nasty independent tyrant, no doubt helped to weaken the influence of Sparta. Her power was now, years after Leuctra, insignificant. The Syracusans turned again to Corinth. The Corinthian Timoleon also abominated tyranny, but there was no vestige of monarchy in the constitution he set up, and he was a professed admirer of the Theban Epaminondas. There was a belated attempt, however, at

---

[1] Plato, *Letter VII* 336c Δωριστί ʒῆν κατὰ τὰ πάτρια. Many scholars still defend the authenticity of this work (sometimes that of *Letter VIII* too). At worst it is likely to be of early date and reasonable reliability.

[2] Plutarch, *Dion* 53.2.

[3] *Letter VIII* 355b–c; cf. *Laws* 692a (below, p. 68).

the end of the century to get a Spartan prince to oppose the new tyrant Agathocles—most unsuccessful, as the prince in question behaved abominably; while Taras kept up ties with the mother-city still, and hired impoverished Spartan royalties to fight the Italian tribes.

5

PLATO AND ARISTOTLE

AGAINST this rich and intricate background the figures of
Plato and Aristotle stand out, transcending but not alien to it. By
the measure of their greater genius, and in particular their profound faith in the intellect, they are more conscious of Sparta's
inadequacies, and more contemptuous of superficial laconism,
than even Isocrates could be. But their criticisms were destined to
have less effect than their approval, limited as it was, yet rooted in
the fact that their fundamental political beliefs had much in
common with those associated with Sparta.

Plato's youth, in the last years of the fifth century, was probably
passed in strongly laconizing circles; his family was noble, and
Critias a close relation. But his disillusionment with politics soon
embraced not only all shades of opinion in Athens, but all existing
states. Nowhere, he seems to have become convinced, did statesmen act out of real knowledge of what was best for a city. And
his whole career has sometimes been seen as a long investigation
of reality, and the methods of teaching the knowledge of reality
and therefore of virtue, with an aim which in the last resort may
be described as political.

Not that Plato positively turned against Sparta. Several of his
earlier dialogues mention her fairly favourably *en passant*. The
Apology[1] praises, indirectly, one important form of 'prudent
slowness' there—in matters of capital punishment. In the *Crito*,[2]
as we saw, Socrates is shown as an admirer of Spartan and Cretan
eunomia. Laches,[3] in the dialogue called after him, is portrayed,

---

[1] *Apology* 37b.   [2] *Crito* 52e.

[3] *Laches* 182e–183a, 188d. In fact Laches, a rich man and a competent commander, supported the peace party in the years before 421. In the dialogue he
admits he is not 'musical', i.e. intellectual (and he does not get far in defining
courage). But he likes, he says, to hear good men speak on such subjects as
virtue; such agreement of words and deeds is the real 'Dorian harmony', the
only truly Greek harmony. This play on the names of the musical harmonies or
modes may depend on a theory that these modes reflected racial characteristics
and also that the Spartans were not only the truest Dorians, but the Dorians the

probably correctly, as a bit of a laconizer—a good fellow, not very clever, and an admirer of Spartan expertise in war. The *Protagoras*,[1] which also ridicules the laconizers more severely, touches on a vital issue. It is a vulgar error to suppose that Sparta's soldiers, not her 'sophists', are her true glory; philosophy flourishes there better than anywhere else: these remarks, though obviously paradoxical, do rest on a serious criticism of the type of education in political virtue provided by the real sophists, and on a serious belief in Spartan good sense. The Seven Sages, whose wisdom was enshrined in pithy sayings, are represented by Plato as admirers of Sparta—one, Chilon, was a Spartiate himself. And there are women in Sparta, Plato observes, who share in this intellectual life of hers. Finally, Diotima in the *Symposium*,[2] teaching Socrates the mysteries of love, assumes that such off-spring as those of Lycurgus' mind, which ultimately saved Greece (that is, from the Persians), are more desirable than children of the flesh; though it is possible to go beyond such love of political wisdom or prudence to the love of science or true knowledge, and at last to the knowledge of pure beauty.

Several of the earlier dialogues are investigations into the standard virtues. The *Republic*, as the work entitled *Politeia* is traditionally called in English, is an investigation into justice. Socrates decides that it is easier to study this in a city than in an individual soul, to which it is on a larger scale analogous, and so he proceeds to construct something approximating to the eternal Idea or Form of the just city. He is convinced that there must be specialization of function and that the function of ruling must go to the best; this is the core of his definition of justice, which therefore involves not absolute but proportional equality. But the 'best' is here no easy equivalent for the existing upper class, however reformed or idealized, as the regulations for the choice

[1] *Protagoras* 342a–343b.   [2] *Symposium* 209d.

---

truest Greeks. Spartans in many anecdotes (including Plato, *Phaedrus* 260) do demand that words and facts, or deeds, should be consonant. But Plato does not share any belief in a racial base for the modes; he never in fact connects the Dorian mode, so dignified and energetic, with Dorians or Spartans, and he admits into the city of his *Republic* the Phrygian mode as well—and he cannot have imagined that the Phrygians, like the mode called after them, typified *sophrosyne* or 'good men engaging voluntarily in works of peace'. See also *infra*, p. 82n. 1.

and education of the guards or protectors show. These guards are to be trained from childhood by the state to combine ferocity to their foes (cowardice being severely punished) with gentleness to their fellow citizens (a quality dear to Isocrates and often claimed as a specially Athenian virtue). Suitable women are eligible and are treated just like their male colleagues, even to the point of exercising naked, as Greek men did. From within this group is selected a smaller body of persons over fifty years of age, who have been through a yet more rigorous training designed to develop still further their intelligence and love of wisdom; their position *vis-à-vis* the inferior guards and the ordinary citizens is similar to that of reason in the soul, which rules over both the spirited, ambitious feelings and the vulgar desires. The guards or guardians as a whole are to be preserved from ambition and greed by an entirely communist régime. They may possess neither property nor family. The state organizes the propagation of the species among them on fiercely eugenic principles, while the unworthy offspring of guardians are demoted and the occasional remarkable child of common birth taken up. To be properly run such a city must be small. And concord is further ensured by the careful inculcation of common beliefs, while all innovation, since it could only be for the worse, is forbidden. Age and tradition are honoured in all things. Poetry, notoriously, is banished entirely except for hymns and eulogies.

So much for an outline, very generally familiar. It would undoubtedly be wrong to say that the just city was based on Sparta. If we must find models, the *Timaeus*, which follows on from the *Republic*, makes mention of the caste system of Egypt, while Plato probably knew of Pythagorean communism and the radical ideal states of Hippodamus and Phaleas. In certain respects he was probably influenced by the medical thought of his day. Anyway, Aristophanes shows that communism and sexual equality were ideas in the air at Athens without any reference to Sparta. But the fact is that where justice was defined as the rule of the best, where the idea of the 'best' was still associated with those best able to fight for their city as well as to give it advice and with contempt for trades and manual labour, and where concord and permanence were believed on practical and theoretical grounds to be vital to a state, then one with some resemblance to Sparta was likely to emerge. Whatever the origin of the ideas in the *Republic*, one result was indubitably to draw attention to Sparta's hierarchical class system (for it is possible crudely to equate the Gerousia to the guardians proper, the *homoioi* to the auxiliaries, and the *perioeci* and helots to Plato's artisans), to the hints of communism and of feminine emancipation to be found there, and to particular features, such as the checks on trade, industry, and travel, and the conservative censorship of the arts.

Plato was well aware of the relationship himself. In Book VIII he comes to describe the progressive corruption to which his aristocracy like everything in the world of 'becoming' must at long last fall victim.[1] The first transformation is into a timocracy or timarchy, a form of which, he says, the much praised states of Sparta and Crete are examples. (Though he tends to talk in chronological terms, he cannot have thought that either had ever been identical with his perfect city.)

Timocracy is the state in which the ruling principle is ambition; reason and 'music' are neglected. (The latter covers the whole life of the mind, though beginning with what we call music, poetry, and dancing, all of which, with their strong mimetic and dramatic elements, were in Greece closely associated with morals.) Private property has been distributed among the guardians; the lowest class has been reduced to slavery and is harshly treated. Reverence for the rulers, the abstention from farming and lucrative trades by the fighting class, common meals, and care for military training survive. But force rather than persuasion is now employed in education, and the state will prefer warlike, spirited, and comparatively unintellectual leaders, will value tricks and stratagems, and be rarely at peace. The citizens will be secretly avaricious (a vice more typical still of oligarchies) and squander their wealth within their own four walls on their womenfolk, bending and at last breaking the laws for this purpose. This is hardly an over-flattering picture; and we may observe that it must be meant to apply to Lycurgan, as well as contemporary, perhaps just pre-Leuctra, Sparta. But timocracy remains superior to oligarchy, democracy, and tyranny, each more corrupt than the last. And so Sparta and Crete come nearest of existing states to the ideal.

Corresponding to the timocratic state is an individual, the contentious or ambitious man. He is not very 'musical'—he has

[1] *Republic* viii. 544c–548d.

some powers of appreciation, but is no speaker himself. He is obedient to the authorities, polite to free men, and cruel to slaves. He is eager for honour and influence, but associates them with military achievement alone. He loves physical activity, especially hunting; as he gets older he becomes fond of money. He is in fact obviously recognizable as a Spartiate or, occurring in another state, as a laconizer.[1]

The timocratic state drops out of political theory, and Plato himself never repeats this idiosyncratic analysis. But though he develops and elaborates both his praise and criticism of Sparta, his fundamental attitude alters little. Ultimately he came to feel that human beings were rarely to be trusted with absolute power, and he fell back on the idea of law—of which not much is said in the *Republic*—interpreted as the instrument and reflection of reason and true knowledge. The rule of law remained a second best to the rule of all-wise men—or one man: the *Republic* conceded that there might be only one guardian available, and if the just city were ever to appear on earth it would probably be by the agency of a single philosopher–ruler. In the *Statesman*, where Plato distinguishes six types of state—monarchy, aristocracy, and democracy, which respect law and tradition and are willingly obeyed, and their three respective corruptions—he says that the monarch who rules in accordance with law provides the best government available in this imperfect world (democracy is the worst of the legal, but the best of the illegal, governments).[2] But in his huge last work, the *Laws*, published after his death in 347, he regards even such monarchy as too great a temptation, and how far his attempt to plan a more realistic constitutional state brought him back to Sparta we must now consider. The *Laws*, too, was not without influence, especially on Aristotle, though its length and lack of unity and of literary attraction, together with its less dramatic conclusions, have always made it less popular than the *Republic*. Not many of us have read it, said Plutarch in the second century A.D.; and the same could have been said in many periods.

The *Laws* takes the form of a dialogue, set in a rather vaguely delineated Crete, between three old men, a Cretan, a Spartan, and an Athenian visitor, who plunge into a political discussion on the purpose of the state. It soon appears that Plato still feels that

[1] *Republic* viii. 548e–550c.　　[2] *Politicus* 291d, 300e–301a.

Sparta and Crete are on the right lines but too obsessed with war. Their representatives, both very limited, ordinary men, think that all their institutions are directed to success in war, which is the basic fact of political life. But the Athenian shows that it is better to receive willing obedience as the best and most just of men than to dominate opponents, while best of all is complete concord and general virtue. Without and within peace and harmony should be the aim of the state; while the sort of soldier Tyrtaeus praises is not so brave as the man who shows courage in the political struggle, where he must display also justice, temperance, and above all wisdom, qualities all superior to courage and with it making up (according to an old theory) 'virtue in its entirety'. Such complete virtue, or complete justice, is the lawgiver's object. The Athenian argues that this was in fact the object of Lycurgus and Minos, who were both divinely inspired; they tried to introduce every kind of good, human and divine (or bodily and mental), wisdom first and rational temperance second, among these last. They concerned themselves with every aspect of life—marriage, the rearing of children, and so on—putting them under the supervision of the laws with their punishments and rewards. And these laws they entrusted to wardens, some with true insight and some with right opinions only, but all made by *nous* or reason servants not of wealth or ambition, but of temperance and justice.

But this eulogy seems designed principally just to introduce the idea of the divine lawgiver; for Lycurgus and Minos promptly come in for criticism even on the score of the institutions fostering courage. Plato praised the law, however, whereby young men in Sparta must regard the laws as divinely ordained, and old men only criticize them in private. We, his Athenian says, are old enough to permit ourselves the liberty.

Endurance of pain, then, as taught at Lacedaemon, is not enough; courage is also resisting pleasure. It is illogical to shun pleasures, the Athenian tells the other two, as you alone do; if these can defeat you, you are not wholly free, but liable to become slaves (a nasty cut for a Spartiate). Temperance? The *syssitia* and *gymnasia* encourage that too, says the Spartan confidently. They can also encourage political intrigues and unnatural love, retorts the Athenian. Plato has here abandoned the laconizing defence of Spartan lovers, with its obvious affinities to his own earlier doctrine of love, in accordance with the tendency of the time to look on homosexual relations more suspiciously, or his own increasing disbelief in human self-restraint. He also abandons the laconizing admiration for Spartan drinking habits. For he thinks it a pity that there are no drinking parties, which properly organized and run form an admirable test of moderation or temperance, a part of 'music' and of education as a whole. It is useless to force men into virtue, and the Spartan admits for this reason the truth of the saying that when an Athenian *is* good, he is very good; and the lack of real self-control at Sparta is further proved by the looseness of the women. This too seems a strong shift, in emphasis at least, from Plato's earlier view of Spartan women. Finally, he reminds us that victory in war is not a reliable test of the institutions of a state.

In the second book Plato embarks on a consideration of education, which begins in infancy and teaches one to love and hate the right things before one can truly know what these are. He is mainly concerned with 'music'. Music, as the portrayal, by means of noble movements, harmonies, and words, of just men and virtuous deeds, is something that only exists these days in Crete and Sparta, so the Cretan claims; elsewhere corrupting innovations—so severely forbidden in Egypt—are always being introduced. But the Athenian objects that the morality thus learnt even in Crete and Sparta is commonplace and materialistic. He accepts and builds on the Spartan custom (at the festival of the Gymnopaedia it seems) of dividing the citizens into three choirs of different ages. But the songs of the oldest and wisest men, inspired by the judicious use of wine, ought not to be the choral lyrics which are all the Spartans and Cretans are trained to perform (perhaps sometimes they are only to be songs in a metaphorical sense; though certainly Plato has shown that he prefers epic to choral or dramatic poetry). You never attained the noblest form of song, the Spartan is told, for your state is a mere camp, not the home of true city-dwellers; and you never pick out an individual for special training in 'the whole of virtue'. This training all those over fifty who are fit for 'music' should have. With gymnastic, the other element in education, the Athenian promises to deal later, admitting that Cretans and Spartans do know all about that.

But in Book III Plato approaches his subject by a different road, in the course of which such attacks on Sparta's inadequacies are forgotten. He explores the origin and development of government, and the causes of its instability. He postulates a period of primitive simplicity after the last Flood, when men were neither rich nor poor and had no temptations to jealousy and injustice, but lived virtuously without formal laws. Then, as separate clans coalesced, legislation became necessary and aristocracies and monarchies emerged. At the end of his journey Plato considers Argos, Messene, and Lacedaemon, 'for what better or more famous states could we investigate?' These are the three states set up in the Peloponnese by the Dorians—whom Plato regards, oddly, as scattered exiles from other areas led by one Dorieus, so his praise has no racial basis. In each of the three, kings and people agreed not to wrong each other and overstep their powers; the arrangement was guaranteed by the other two. As conquerors, without old debts and able to divide up the land, the Dorians established equality, and laws which were accepted willingly, or nearly so. Under this system the three confederate states trusted to be able to defend all Greece against the east. But the powerful inevitably fall into folly and abandon moderation and justice. Only in Lacedaemon, where some god saw to it that the kingship was checked by its division between two houses, where a lawgiver with divine power counterbalanced it with a strong council of prudent elders, and a third saviour (probably Plato means King Theopompus, as in the version subsequently well known) curbed it yet further by the near-democratic ephorate, did the original institutions survive, to save others as well as the Lacedaemonians themselves.[1]

This is a passage rich in implications—it even foreshadows laconizing primitivism by attributing the same virtues to Sparta and a primeval Golden Age. More important is Plato's insistence on economic equality as vital to justice; and the assumption, it is hardly an assertion, that Sparta on its foundation like the other two states divided its land in equal lots is parallel to Ephorus' perhaps almost contemporary account of the Lycurgan (and therefore necessarily later) distribution.

Since unlimited and unrestrained powers, continues Plato, lead to excess and violence, a mean will result in freedom, concord, and wisdom. The two 'mother-types' of government are

[1] *Laws* iii, esp. 683c ff.

democracy and monarchy. When Persia, once a tempered monarchy, lapsed into the pure form, the people lost their good will towards their rulers and all desire to help them in war or with counsel. Athens, once a tempered democracy, marked by concord, modesty, and respect for law, degenerated into lawlessness when everyone was seized with a confidence in his own wisdom. But Sparta and Crete are still well mixed; and Sparta must be praised for this at least, that she differentiates between rich and poor, royal and private, only so far as the original oracle ordained. (Here too, we see Plato's refusal to distinguish between ancient and modern Sparta.)

This theory of the mean between monarchy and democracy; the description of the executive power in Sparta, if hardly the whole state, as 'mixed and measured' from three organs counterbalancing each other and thus themselves 'not unmixed', for each rules and is ruled; and the later remark, by the Spartan interlocutor, that it is really very hard to describe Sparta—the ephors make it look like tyranny, some features resemble a democracy, it is undeniably an aristocracy and, as everyone calls it, the most ancient of kingdoms: all these passages seem to have been of influence on later writers, from Aristotle onwards, working out the various theories of the mixed constitution.

At last the Athenian begins to construct, in great detail, the laws for a proposed new colony in Crete. The theory of the mixed constitution has here receded, but the theme of mixture and measure persists in various forms, and the new state can be seen as a mean between authority and liberty, and thus, in accordance with the requirements in Book III, between monarchy and democracy. In practice, Aristotle objected, it looks much more like a mixture of oligarchy and democracy, as the combination, for example, of choice and the lot in elections would imply. Plato is writing primarily for his countrymen, and the new state is to a considerable extent an improved Athens, harking back to the early fifth century. This is obviously true of the political and legal superstructure; the four property classes among the citizens recall those of Solon, there is a large council of 360 members, made up of smaller panels sitting in rotation, there are complicated procedures for choosing and investigating the numerous magistrates who are headed as in Athens by a board of generals. Much, further, is Plato's own invention, for example the board of *nomophylakes*, or

Guardians of the Law, though it partly recalls the Areopagus, which also coexisted with a larger council.

But the social and economic organization of the city is less Athenian. The new town is to be placed inland and have a poor but varied territory, so that a simple but adequate standard of life can be maintained without much foreign trade. Its citizens are carefully selected on eugenic grounds to form a body of a few thousand supported by a large population of slaves and resident aliens acting as merchants and artisans. Each citizen has an equal allotment of land (divided into two properties of different type and location) which he may not sell and of which the inheritance is governed by strict laws; there is a limit also on moveable property. Plato has given up communism, but he regulates the circumstances in which the use of other people's property is allowable. The citizen may not trade or possess gold or silver; a sort of small change, without value elsewhere, circulates. Marriage is arranged by the state, to which the child belongs; it educates him to have at least a decent knowledge of war and agriculture. The chief public official is the overseer of education, but every one may take it on himself to reprove or punish a child. On reaching manhood he may be selected for a tour of duty in the countryside. Even after his wedding he lives with his *syssition* and is occupied with training and drilling. His wife brings no dowry, so he is expected to choose her on public-spirited grounds, and is treated with ignominy if he does not marry (public opinion is indeed the lawgiver's favourite weapon).

A great many details here are certainly not Spartan—for example, the limitations on moveable property, the mass of resident foreigners, even various features of the army and the (thoroughly military) gymnastic training and public games— which last fact, so late in the fourth century, is only a sign of practical awareness unexpected in Plato. His citizens, further, are probably to help till their fields; and, *pace* late sources, women had dowries in Sparta. And Plato may or may not seriously have believed that the land had ever been equally divided there. Other features can be paralleled elsewhere in the Greek world beside Crete and Sparta; *syssitia* above all existed or had existed in many places, and Plato probably knew that land had originally not been fully alienable in Athens and elsewhere. A city's small change was often pretty valueless outside its territory, and there is no indication that Plato wants his to be as bulky as Sparta's. But the frequency of references, critical or otherwise, to Sparta, and usually to Sparta alone (occasionally to Crete alone, but rarely to any other state), speaks for itself.

The lawgiver ought not to aim at laconic brevity, for his laws must persuade as well as command.[1] It is best, like Sparta, to do without walls.[2] The members of the country patrol are tentatively called *cryptoi*, though the institution is hardly identical with the Spartan *crypteia*.[3] Sparta's treatment of women is half-hearted: they exercise, and neglect spinning and weaving, but in the new city they shall be properly educated and supervised to keep them free from luxury and extravagance, to which they are even more prone than men. They are to have some military training but (*pace* the *Republic*) only girls under the age of puberty shall race naked. They shall eat in *syssitia* like—but now apart from— the men.[4] *Syssitia* are to be organized on the Cretan or Spartan or some other model, it matters little.[5] (Aristotle was to think it did.) But 'though Sparta and Crete help us in many fields', the Athenian says, we shall go against them, in forbidding homosexual love.[6] The position of the helots he declares extremely debatable; it is doubtless wiser not to have slaves of a single race, who easily unite in revolt, and wiser also to treat them properly.[7] *Xenelasiai* are unnecessarily savage and inhospitable, but visitors must be carefully controlled and isolated.[8]

On other aspects of the *Laws* we need not here enlarge, for example on the famous nocturnal council introduced suddenly towards the end of the work to be the repository of wisdom and as such alone able to emend, though its first task is to preserve, the legislator's enactments. We will leave Plato with the reminder that law, still extending to custom in the old sense, and preventing, persuading, and educating as well as punishing, is now the direct expression of reason and of the supreme deity. The state ruled by law is a theocracy, not only set up by a divinely inspired lawgiver but put under the close supervision of Delphi (the reader may think of Sparta's relationship to the oracle). The citizen is persuaded rather than forced to obey, but all adults are taught to think, nay all children to play, in the same way. Every

[1] *Laws* iv. 721c. [2] Ibid. vi. 778d. [3] Ibid. vi. 763b.
[4] Ibid. vii. 806a. [5] Ibid. viii. 842b. [6] Ibid. viii. 836b.
[7] Ibid. vi. 776c. [8] Ibid. xii. 950b.

F

group has by definition a leader, and the leader must always be obeyed. Curiously enough, at the end of the vast work Plato connects this with military necessity, falling back, it seems, into the way of thinking for which he criticized Sparta at the start. But, in spite of all minor changes, he seems never to have wavered in his belief that, while all legislation hitherto had been the 'doctoring of slaves by slaves'[1]—by mere ignorant empirics—the legislator of Sparta has had a better inkling of the truth than any of his fellows.

Aristotle did not know the great age of Sparta himself; he came south as a youth to study with Plato only after Leuctra. But he is profoundly conscious of the Sparta of the theorists—of the numerous writers whom he refers to usually in general terms, but above all of Plato.[2] Like others perhaps, he refuses to bother with the fancy terminology of the *Republic*, and simply calls the first corruption of the just city 'the laconic government';[3] he quotes (and to some extent adopts) the views of the *Laws* on Sparta, and throughout his criticisms of Plato keeps Sparta in mind. But from Plato's ambiguous belief that she was the best of existing states Aristotle, in spite of an ability to formulate more devastating criticisms, and not only of the decadent present, never detached himself, any more than from many other typical Greek ideas as to the best form of state.

Any attempt to trace the development of Aristotle's thought is problematical; many works are lost, including the *Constitution (Politeia) of the Lacedaemonians* compiled by Aristotle late in life, or by his pupils, as part of the great Peripatetic research programme. (The fragments are mostly historical, but Lycurgus is praised with surprisingly unrestrained enthusiasm; and it is noteworthy that the work described his rise to power by a *coup d'état*, argued that he helped to establish the truce which all Greece observed at the time of the Olympic Games, detailed his sumptuary legislation against female elegance, and quoted the early poets and the archaic constitutional document known as the Great Rhetra.) And though the *Politics* is indubitably a composite work of his middle and later years, no attempt at disentangling it

---

[1] Ibid. ix. 857c.
[2] Contempt for superficial laconizers, as well as or rather than Spartans, is perhaps expressed in *Nicomachean Ethics* iv. 1276—the mock humility of Spartan dress is really boastfulness.　　　　　　　　　　[3] *Politics* v. 1316a.

has met with complete agreement. However, as far as Sparta is concerned, there are no major contradictions in it, though there are differences of emphasis enough to have made the work a mine for laconophils and laconophobes of various complexions.

It seems that in the early *Protrepticus* Aristotle argued, in Platonic fashion, that lawgivers or politicians who simply copy the policies or system of Lacedaemon or Crete or any other place, instead of acquiring theoretical insight and knowledge of nature, cannot rank as serious.[1] And in Book II of the *Politics* he sets out to clear the ground by demolishing the perfect states of previous writers, whether ideal or actually existent. He begins by refuting the *Republic*; here he is ready to use Sparta as a stick to beat Plato with. To communism he prefers private property, generously modified by a degree of common use. This exists in well-run states; for example, in respect to slaves, horses, dogs, and produce in Lacedaemon. There, as in Crete, common meals also help to create the unity that Plato is trying to achieve by mistaken means. All his rules will only come to an attempt to prevent citizens taking part in agriculture, as in Sparta (this is a first hint of Aristotle's awareness of contemporary affairs there); and Plato's lower classes, as he declares, would be in fact more unruly than the helots and other such groups.[2] Next he deals with the *Laws* (with one or two errors hard to explain), complaining especially that a mixture of democracy and oligarchy, or theoretically tyranny, is not very desirable. Many people would prefer Sparta or some other more aristocratic state, or else a triple mixture, which some indeed find Sparta to be, seeing monarchy in the kings, oligarchy in the Gerousia, and democracy in the ephors— or in the common meals and other regulations, with the ephorate representing tyranny.[3]

But when, after dealing with one or two other theorists especially concerned with equalizing property, Aristotle moves on to the real states, and first and foremost to Sparta, his intention is of course primarily critical; and he writes a series of damning chapters which have sometimes been the most influential of his pronouncements on the subject.[4]

With an echo, perhaps, of Book I of the *Laws*, he announces that his objections will fall into two classes: laws must be judged

[1] I. Düring, *Aristotle's Protrepticus* (1961), fr. B 49, p. 69.
[2] *Politics* ii. 1263a–1264b.   [3] Ibid. ii. 1265b.   [4] Ibid. ii. 1269a.

both by the lawgiver's intentions and by an absolute standard. His first complaint concerns the helots. The creation of such a class is not the safest way to ensure leisure for the citizens: in Sparta alarms have been frequent (Aristotle does not here refer to the doctrine of *Politics* I, that only 'natural' slaves, and never Greeks, should be reduced to servile condition). Next he remarks that, where the women are badly managed, half the city is without laws (a nicely malicious remark; in this context we may notice that he does not use that cliché, *eunomia*, in connection with Sparta). Unlike their own menfolk, they received no training whatever in endurance.[1] And hence the overvaluation of wealth in Sparta, especially since the women rule their husbands; in the days of the empire many affairs were in their hands. Military races, the Stagirite observes, are often henpecked—except those who prefer homosexual relations. But, interestingly, he does not suggest that the Spartiates fall into that class, and indeed the theme is henceforth much less prominent in discussion of them. The vaunted Spartan courage, Aristotle repeats, is a quality only partly or sometimes valuable to the state; but even here the women have had a bad influence. Unlike those of other cities, they were quite useless in the Theban invasion and caused more confusion than the enemy. And all this unseemly behaviour, far from being a new development, goes back to the most ancient times.

Next, the property system: Aristotle, accurately no doubt, but probably by now paradoxically to many readers, picks out the extreme inequality that has come about—because land, though it cannot be sold, can be given or bequeathed. Owing to the number of heiresses and the practice of large dowries two-fifths of the land is held by women. Attempts to encourage a high birth-rate only lead, under the existing system, to many Spartiates losing their rights through poverty. And the result of the decline in citizen numbers to under a thousand was that the single defeat of Leuctra was final and irreversible.

Turning to the constitution, Aristotle complains that the ephors, who are elected from the whole people, are thus apt to be poor and therefore venal—there have been many instances of corrup-

---

[1] Cf. *Rhetoric* 1361a: the object of the state is to secure good qualities in both sexes; in women height, beauty, self-control, and love of work without servility. Where, as in Lacedaemon, the women are badly managed, the city is barely half-happy.

tion. And their power has become so tyrannical that even the kings have to compete for the people's favour, and from an aristocracy Sparta has become a democracy. Yet it is true that by satisfying the people the ephorate holds the state together; and indeed all elements at Sparta are satisfied with their position. (Consent is an important conception to Aristotle, as Books IV–VI especially show.) But the mode of election—not described, but doubtless acclamation—is childish and should be reformed; while unqualified men with vast judicial powers ought not to be left unbound by regulations. Their free and luxurious way of life is not in conformity with the character of the country; that of their fellow citizens on the other hand is intolerably hard and leads to a secret 'flight from the law'. Before leaving the democratic aspects of the state, Aristotle objects that in practice the *syssitia*, supposed by many to be the most democratic element, do not work that way at all.

As for the Gerousia, Aristotle at one point seems to imply that election is the prize of virtue, in the traditional manner. But his ironic awareness of previous laconizers emerges, surely, very strongly in a later passage: if its members were superior people properly trained in manly virtue then it might be a useful institution, but in fact their education is such that even the legislator does not trust them. Senility, corruption, and favouritism are common among them; they are responsible to no one (control by the ephors is not the answer). The mode of their election is puerile,[1] and canvassing an improper practice. Although the legislator obviously intended, here as elsewhere, to encourage ambition, this, like avarice, is a dangerous source of crime.

The advantages or otherwise of monarchy are left open for the moment; but Aristotle assumes that a rational monarchy should be elective, and that Lycurgus obviously realized that the kings would not be superior men, since they are treated with suspicion and their quarrels are considered a safeguard. He also observes that writers have complained of the powerful office of admiral, equivalent to a third king, as another source of discord. (Doubtless they had the history of Lysander in mind.)

Finally, Aristotle comes to fundamental criticisms. He agrees explicitly with Plato in the *Laws* that the Spartans only aim at

---

[1] Cf. *Politics* v. 1306a where this election is also described as 'dynastic', i.e. typical of a very narrow oligarchy of a few families.

military virtue. As a result victory and power were fatal to them, for they knew nothing of the arts of peace. And he briefly expresses opposition, repeated elsewhere, to the vulgar idea of virtue, as a mere means to wealth and honour, that the Spartans hold. He appends a last complaint about their economic organization: the state revenues are ill-managed, there is no money in the treasury and a great unwillingness to pay taxes, all of which is folly in a military state. Lycurgus' institutions have resulted in public poverty and private avarice. Aristotle's comment, as so often, rests on empirical observation.

Crete, on which he is well informed, is dismissed briefly, as Sparta's model, older, simpler, more narrowly oligarchic and in most respects inferior, except in the organization of the common meals. For where the state finances these the poorer citizens are not in danger of losing their standing. (If some of the information here may come from Ephorus, the contrast with Sparta and the generally harsh judgements will hardly do so.) With Sparta and Crete is grouped the Phoenician colony, Carthage, the strong constitutional and social similarities of which had plainly been remarked before. Aristotle sees even occasional superiorities; elections are by merit, and the 'kings' (*suffetes*) are not hereditary. Carthage is, however, too commercial in spirit, and of her other faults some take her too far towards oligarchy and some towards democracy, away from aristocracy and 'what they call *politeia*'. But in spite of all, Aristotle accepts that these three states are 'rightly famous'.[1]

Book II has not made Aristotle's views on the way the Spartan constitution should be classified entirely clear. Book III, which lists, like Plato's *Politicus*, three good and three corrupt constitutions (kingship, aristocracy, and good democracy or *politeia*, against tyranny, oligarchy, and bad democracy, on the modern Athenian model), at least shows why Aristotle does not usually bother much about the royal element in Sparta. This here appears as forming the most extreme type of kingship in accordance with *nomos*.[2] At the other end of the scale is the absolute king, and in between are other forms, including that of Homeric or 'heroic' times, rather less strictly fettered than the Spartan which descended from it. Aristotle takes most interest in the two ends of the scale; but since he has defined the position of the Spartan king

---

[1] *Politics* ii. 1273b. [2] Ibid. iii. 1285a.

simply as that of a perpetual general, he soon moves away with the observation that an evaluation of it is hardly relevant to a discussion of kingship, as it is compatible with any form of government; and he turns instead to absolute monarchy and the old question of the all-wise man versus the rule of law. In Book V, however, where Aristotle remarks that kings rarely arise these days because men will not endure them, and thus they become by definition tyrants, he points out that the more restricted kingship is, therefore, the better it lasts. Witness the Spartan kingship—always divided, and further limited, yet paradoxically strengthened, by King Theopompus' establishment of the ephorate. And here we meet the famous anecdote to which so many constitutional monarchists of the future are to turn. To his wife, who asked him if he were not ashamed to leave his son less power than his father left him, Theopompus replied 'it will be more lasting'.[1]

Books IV–VI form an attempt to treat politics in an empirical spirit inspired by biology and medicine (they have sometimes been thought for this reason to be one of the latest parts of the work). Some people, Aristotle begins, are only interested in the perfect constitution; others fix their eyes on a real one, especially Sparta's.[2] But one can only introduce reforms agreeable to and suitable for the city one is dealing with. Laconism here, then, is regarded as hardly better than Utopianism; but Sparta, as one observable state among many, is regarded with considerable favour. Aristotle's framework is now very complicated: there are many kinds of oligarchy and democracy, dependent on the different combinations of different sorts of distinction and equality between citizens. (The best democracy is agrarian, where the busy peasants leave the laws and magistrates to operate unhindered.) There is also an inferior type of aristocracy, in which merit is one criterion for election, though not the only one.[3] Thus Carthage combines aristocracy and oligarchy, Sparta aristocracy and democracy. Aristotle continues to call the latter an aristocracy (explaining by this concept her opposition to tyranny, or the conspiracies that occurred when her people thought themselves equal in virtue to the ruling élite); but he also speaks of her as a *politeia*—constitutional government *par excellence*, a mixture of oligarchy and democracy usually described by one or other of these names. Polities shade off into secondary aristocracies and constitute the

[1] Ibid. v. 1313d.   [2] Ibid. iv. 1289a.   [3] Ibid. iv. 1294b.

best practicable form. For the middle course is best, and states where the balance is held by the middle class are soundest and stablest. Both absolute equality and the identification of power with wealth precipitate class struggles. From the middle class all great lawgivers sprang—including Lycurgus, 'as he was not king'.[1] (Aristotle at least, unlike Plato, belonged to it.)

The unfinished sketch of the ideal state, in Books VII and VIII, which now ends the work, is often thought to have originated separately and perhaps comparatively early. There is no reference to Sparta as a polity or an aristocracy here, though there are resemblances to what is said of her in the first books. The resemblance of Aristotle's vision to that of the *Laws* ensures an underlying attitude to her not unlike that in Plato's work, if a little more detached. Aristotle does not doubt that the end of the state is the happiness—which means, for him, the virtuous activity—of the citizens;[2] nor that this is best attained within the traditional small city-state and its leisured class of full citizens, formed by those who serve as hoplites and, when older, as councillors. These should own the land (divided in a complicated way), though friendly common use is recommended. Slaves of diverse origin, or failing these a non-Greek native population, cultivate it for them. There are common meals, 'which all agree are useful for well-organized states.'[3]

Crete and Egypt are mentioned, but it is Sparta which is most often in the author's mind. Those who advocate doing without city walls (Plato obviously included) are old-fashioned; experience has refuted this form of vanity, made ridiculous by mere numbers, and especially by modern military inventions. And more basic criticisms can be levelled at 'those Greeks of today who are considered to have the best constitutions'.[4] Their lawgivers, instead of aiming at all the virtues, vulgarly confined themselves to the useful ones; just as many modern writers, such as Thibron, praise Sparta for making conquest her sole aim. They are wrong in theory and practice: such imperialism is analogous to tyranny, while the Spartans, who have lost their empire, are not happy. Only those who deserve to be slaves may be conquered. Imperial-

[1] Ibid. iv. 1296a.
[2] Cf. *Nicomachean Ethics* 1102e: true statesmen aim at making the citizens good and law-abiding—like the lawgivers of Crete, Sparta, and other cities.
[3] *Politics* vi. 1330a.   [4] Ibid. 1330b.

ist states tend anyway to fall; the legislator has not taught them to live in peace.[1] This attack goes further than Plato's belief that courage is inadequate and peace superior to war; so does the passage, unfortunately corrupt, which probably formulates the charge we have met before, that the Spartans only regard even their limited sort of virtue as a means to the good things of life.[2]

No one, says Aristotle firmly, will doubt that the legislator must be concerned above all else with education.[3] For the citizen must be made to fit his government (and vice versa), and virtue is achieved by long practice. As the city has a single end, education must be the same for all and organized by the state; 'in this Lacedaemon is to be praised.' But what Aristotle then proposes is not very Spartan; for one thing he has already laid down that *nous*, the rational principle, is the end to which every nature strives, and so every educational provision must be directed to that end. Intellectual education is preceded, certainly, by physical and moral education. But precisely here a fierce attack is mounted on Sparta. Although her education does not deform the body, like some athletic training these days, it brutalizes children with the over-laborious exercises designed to render them courageous (which should not be the sole or main object anyway).[4] Real courage is associated with gentleness; wolves, cannibals, thieves are not brave. And in fact the Lacedaemonians do not excel in war any more; if they used to, it was not because of any special virtue in their training, but because they were the only people to train at all. We should judge the Lacedaemonians on this point by what they are today, says Aristotle, hinting perhaps at Plato's surprising unconcern with Leuctra.[5]

He passes on to the discussion of music in education, and here above all we feel his distance from old traditions still alive to Plato. 'Music', to Aristotle, has a more restricted significance now; much argument is required to justify giving it any place at all in the curriculum. It is individual and not choral, so Sparta cannot stand as the most musical of cities. Aristotle's chief references to her are deprecatory. He remarks that simply to learn to judge music

---

[1] *Politics* vii. 1333b.   [2] Ibid. vii. 1334b.
[3] Ibid. viii. 1337a, cf. *Nicomachean Ethics* x. 1179b: Sparta is almost the only state where the lawgiver has attended to education and daily life; elsewhere people live 'as they please'.
[4] *Politics* viii. 1338b.   [5] Ibid. viii. 1339a.

as a listener, without being able to play, as the Spartans say they do, is not good enough. And laying down the types of music he favours, he rejects the *aulos* (flute or oboe) as an unintellectual instrument (partly because you cannot sing as you play), 'though at one time it was popular in Lacedaemon as well as elsewhere'.

6

LACONISM IN THE HELLENISTIC AGE

THE GREAT figures of the fourth century continued to a remarkable extent to dominate Greek intellectual history, whether in rhetoric, historiography, or political theory. One proof of this is the astonishing persistence of interest in Sparta; for the place itself, deprived of territory by Philip and defeated again under Alexander, was henceforth of no importance beyond the Peloponnese.

It is true, no doubt, that the time for practical laconism was past; among the characters described by Aristotle's pupil and successor, Theophrastus, the laconomaniac has no place, and the 'oligarchic man' does not resemble him. But, though the once very influential political literature of the Academy and Peripatos is lost, the pupils both of Plato and Aristotle seem if anything to have had fewer reserves than their masters in admiration for Sparta. Perhaps more practical and less idealistic, they lay less stress on her intellectual and moral shortcomings. No longer a menacing rival of Athens (to which most of them did not belong by birth), Sparta, for them, takes off almost wholly into the realm of fantasy.

Plato's immediate pupils included a crop of practical lawgivers, apart from Dion, and some of them more successful than he; it seems to have been a common jibe that they liked to imagine themselves as Solons and Lycurguses. Law, justice, and the problem of expert knowledge are still preoccupying the author of the *Minos*, who here gives Crete pride of place over Sparta. Other pseudo-Platonic dialogues concentrate on the ethical side of laconism. *Alcibiades I* praises the descent, wealth, affability, and general greatness of Spartan kings in a wholesale if fairly light-hearted way. In *Alcibiades II*[1] the best form of prayer is said to be

---

[1] The dialogues mentioned probably range in date from the later fourth to the third century.

that of the just and pious Spartans—a simple request for what is good and right—and the best sacrifices their simple offerings.[1]

Among the Peripatetics too there were numbers who interested themselves in political theory or practice, or, like Demetrius of Phaleron, in both. Demetrius certainly regarded himself as Athens' newest lawgiver;[2] originally a partisan of Phocion, he ruled Athens for ten years with Macedonian support, maintaining a mildish limitation on the franchise, and various sumptuary regulations, in obedience, probably, to Aristotelian theory as much as practical requirements. He wrote much on Athenian history, among other subjects; but probably saw himself as Lycurgus as well as Solon, since in contrast to most earlier sources he declared that Lycurgus had nothing to do with military matters, and, unlike Aristotle, that he introduced his legislation without employing force.[3] For Demetrius himself was a man of peace, and his policy for an Athens dependent on Macedon was necessarily pacific; his conception however foreshadows that of other Hellenistic and imperial authors.

It may be that the most important for us among Aristotle's pupils ought to be the tantalizing figure of Dicaearchus of Messene, so admired by Cicero. Dicaearchus is known to have disagreed with his master and the contemporary Peripatetics in seeing the essence of man in practical not intellectual ability and in setting the active above the contemplative life; the intellectualistic ethics of Plato, and even Aristotle, had regarded them as interdependent. From such a kernel may have sprung a thoroughgoing admiration of Sparta. At any rate, a treatise of his on the *Lacedaemonian Politeia* is said to have been so highly regarded at Sparta itself that it was by law read out once a year to the young.[4]

---

[1] It may be mentioned that Heraclides of Pontus developed (or inherited) the theory connecting the characteristics of musical modes—Dorian, Aeolian, and Ionian—with those of the peoples whose names they bore; thus the Dorians were manly, sublime, gloomy, and so on, and the Spartans maintained this character better than others. The idea, however, was developed in a technical work on music and seems to have had a minimal effect on later antiquity (Wehrli, *Die Schule des Aristoteles*, vol. vii, fr. 163; note that the tragic Ionian harmony only fits the archaic Milesians). See also *supra*, p. 61n.

[2] Possibly he even took the title while giving Athens a new legal code.

[3] Wehrli, op. cit., vol. iv, fr. 89; such behaviour, he adds, was only likely in the creator of the Olympic truce.

[4] Wehrli, op. cit., vol. i, fr. 1. Perhaps, it has been suggested, in the archaizing Roman period?

It seems likely, too, that in stressing the importance of the discoveries of practical men and politicians, Dicaearchus insisted that the philosophers had learnt from Lycurgus; that he retailed the story that Pythagoras visited Crete and Sparta to study their laws,[1] and declared that Plato was a combination of Socrates with Pythagoras and Lycurgus[2]—perhaps because, as the source telling us this goes on to say, Lycurgus like Plato preferred 'geometric' proportion to the 'arithmetical' equality of democracy. One is also entitled to wonder if Dicaearchus' primitivism is relevant; in his famous *Greek Life* he represented the Golden Age as a time when men enjoyed health, concord, and leisure owing to their lack of arts and possessions and the moderation of their wants. Did he see Sparta as attempting to prolong this state?[3] For as we shall see, the Noble Savage and the Spartan were being compared at this time. It is much disputed whether Dicaearchus either in the *Tripoliticus* (which certainly had a description of Spartan common meals and has sometimes been identified with the special work on her *politeia* mentioned above) or elsewhere expounded the view known to but not adopted by Aristotle, that the best constitution was the triple mixture of monarchy, aristocracy, and democracy, and this was to be found in Sparta;[4] and whether, if so, the hold this version of the theory had in later antiquity, and especially on Cicero, was due to his formulation of it.

It was, at least, a popular Peripatetic view—at least if we may trust a source that possibly goes back to Theophrastus, and also shows another development of the time.[5] Aristotle's terminology in the *Politics* had been confusing, and contradicted the tendency of fourth-century conservatives to annex the word democracy. And so Aristotle's good 'polity' and corrupt 'democracy' came to be replaced respectively by 'democracy' and 'ochlocracy', rule of the mob. Thus democracy can be used of almost any constitutional government.

Dicaearchus, and perhaps more particularly his friend Aristoxenus, were probably the people responsible for bringing

[1] Cf. frs. 33–5, the certain fragments about Pythagoras.

[2] Fr. 41 (with Osann's emendation).

[3] Fr. 49. It may be significant that the source, Porphyry, goes straight on to talk of Sparta.

[4] Fr. 71. A Byzantine source used by Photius calls this form of constitution Dicaearchic; but it is often thought that this could merely mean 'the justly ruled' state.   [5] *Apud* Stobaeus ii. 147. 26 ff.

Pythagoreanism and laconism into a more definite relationship, especially through their interest in the political aspect of the former. Aristoxenus, who was primarily a musician, was the author of various works on Pythagoras and Pythagoreans, whom he exalted above Socrates and his school. But, though born in Tarentum, he lived in mainland Greece and studied under Aristotle, and it is uncertain how far the political philosophy of his *Pythagorean Maxims* reflects the master's *ipse dixit*. It is certainly compatible with admiration for Sparta, for it stresses the horrors of anarchy, the advantages of keeping to one's own customs whatever their shortcomings, and the need for magistrates to take great account of education and oversee all ages and classes. Aristoxenus probably also represented the various early Italian lawgivers, such as Zaleucus, as Pythagoreans.[1]

At any rate, after this not only do we find members of the sect in Laconia, but expressed admiration for Sparta in works claiming to be Pythagorean; above all, in the treatise *On Law and Justice*, ascribed to Archytas of Tarentum, but really of Hellenistic date, as the echoes of Plato and Aristotle show. This demands an eccentric quadripartite mixed constitution, and proffers Sparta as an example, with the kings representing monarchy, the *gerontes* aristocracy, the ephors oligarchy—which is unusual—and the *hippagretae* and *koroi* (commanders of the bodyguard and, presumably, the young men forming it) democracy—which is even more unusual. Her *eunomia* is due to the fact that these powers are counterbalanced, each 'rules and is ruled' (as Plato had put it in the *Laws*), and the greed of each is thus subdued. Laws should be engraved not on buildings but in the character of the citizens, as in Lacedaemon, most *eunomos* of cities. Dishonour should be the punishment law inflicts, not fines, which only teach people to regard money as important. Law, pseudo-Archytas declares, should be natural, practical, and beneficial; it copies natural justice, is easy to carry out, and aims at the advantage of the ruled not the ruler. Thus the best and most rational ruler sticks closest to law; the true king is a living law. Law ensures the subject's freedom and the state's happiness; it is to man's soul and life as harmony is to hearing and sound.[2]

---

[1] Wehrli, op. cit., vol. ii, Aristoxenus, esp. frs. 33–5.

[2] *Pythagorean Texts of the Hellenistic Period*, coll. and ed. Holger Thesleff, pp. 33 ff. (esp. fr. 4, p. 34). He dates the work to the late fourth century.

With the advent of Alexander and the great monarchies of his successors the problems of the city-state fell into the background, and with them to some extent even such analyses of Sparta as this; certainly explanations, like Aristotle's, of her political successes and failures. Numerous studies of her institutions and, after a time, of her history did appear;[1] but it is likely that they either formed part of the rich crop of antiquarian investigations that mark the great age of Hellenistic scholarship, or re-echoed conventional analyses, particularly the theory that luxury is the cause of political discord. For it was the ethical aspect of the laconizing tradition that had most relevance in the new world, a world much concerned with the way in which the individual might protect himself from the blows of fate, including the temptations of unprecedented wealth and extreme poverty.

One of the most interesting movements of the time, it is true, seems to have escaped the infection of laconism. It is noteworthy that Epicurus represents a conscious reaction against Plato and Aristotle, and as such was long a target for abuse. To him the function of government was simply the protection of the individual and his property in order that he might live a free life. Justice and law, though not rejected as unnatural, were only means to this end; the free man, said Epicurus, would not be a slave to laws. Such liberalism was undemocratic; only a minority could achieve freedom, and public activity in a popular state implied servitude to the mob, as bad as that to a monarch. But it was even more un-Spartan. Nor can Lycurgus' oracle-juggling and piety have appealed to the school that denied the possibility of prophecy and prided itself on freeing mankind from religious terrors; while its concept of virtue was not rudely ascetic nor contemptuous of private emotions and affections. It is not surprising, then, that Metrodorus, Epicurus' closest pupil, was one of those who scoffed at philosophers who thought themselves Solons and Lycurguses,[2] or that the scandalous sect was said to be banned in Crete and the Peloponnese.[3] Ironically, however,

---

[1] Fragments, (mostly, since they come from Athenaeus, about festivals, dialect, etc.) in *FGH* iii b, nos. 586 ff. The writers include Laconians and one Spartiate, Sosibius—his country's first true historian?

[2] Plutarch, *Moralia: Adversus Colotem* 1127b–c.

[3] Id. ibid., *Non posse suaviter vivi secundum Epicurum* 1100 d; cf. Athenaeus 547a.

a prominent late Hellenistic Epicurean actually hailed from Laconia.[1]

Cynicism, however, combined the sophistic rejection of law with the Socratic ethical tradition, and thus with one kind of laconism. Though Antisthenes was sometimes regarded as the founder, and Xenophon was much read by both Cynics and Stoics, Cynicism proper, which was a way of life rather than a formal philosophy, takes its origin and its name from Diogenes 'the Dog' in the later fourth century. The true Cynic was identifiable by his life as a wandering beggar, his assault on all superstitions, conventions, and laws, and his appeal to beasts and primitive men for evidence about the natural life. Possibly Diogenes himself knew Sparta; at any rate the saying of his with the best claim to be genuine is to the effect that the taverns are the mess-tables of Attica—a plain criticism of Athenian in the light of Spartan life.[2] A less probably authentic remark (also given to Antisthenes) is that to go from Sparta to Athens is to go from the men's to the women's rooms in a house. Later sources, including the letters in his name, put many other references to Sparta in Diogenes' mouth;[3] and Lucian, in one of the *Dialogues of the Dead*, makes him try to send up a message from Hades ticking the Spartans off for relaxing their severity.[4] Diogenes' *Politeia*, if a genuine work, seems to have advocated a valueless currency and the community of women, who were to dress like men and exercise naked 'as at Sparta'; Plutarch praises Lycurgus for carrying out what Plato and Diogenes after him only wrote about.

A pupil of Diogenes, Onesicritus, went to India with Alexander and wrote a highly embroidered account of his adventures. Not only do his fakirs—'gymnosophists' or naked sages—emerge as perfect Cynics, but in dilating on the simplicity and *eunomia* of the 'country of Musicanus' in India he apparently explicitly compared its common meals, of simple food largely the product of the hunt, with Sparta's *syssitia*; and the absence of slaves, though young men acted as servants, with the use of helots in Sparta and Crete. And he may have expected other features of his Utopia, such as the refusal to use gold or silver or study the sciences, to

---

[1] Demetrius of Laconia, no. 89 of the name in Pauly-Wissowa's *Real-Encyclopaedie*.   [2] Aristotle, *Rhetoric* 1411a 24–25.
[3] Diogenes Laertius vi. 2.59 (cf. Theon, *Progymnasmata* iv. 45).
[4] Lucian, *Dialogues of the Dead* i. 4.

recall Sparta too.[1] Here is the first certain forerunner of all those post-Renaissance authors who compare Indians, though American Indians now, to Spartans in simplicity and virtue.

Nevertheless, the natural life was not to be achieved without training. Perhaps this is why Diogenes is represented as praising Spartan boys; and when the story of his enslavement and consequent employment as a tutor at Corinth was elaborated, he was said to have introduced a curriculum with somewhat Spartan features.[2] Though the Cynics rejected intellectual disciplines as useless, they were deeply interested in the teaching of practical virtue, and to this end relied greatly on the anecdotes and examples of which some of them are known to have made collections. 'Laconic apophthegms' were already recognized as a useful type of maxim in Aristotle's *Rhetoric* (which also recognized the orator's tendency to turn for illustrations to famous events in Spartan history);[3] possibly special collections had even been made by then. But the apophthegms were more popular than ever in the Hellenistic period, and many were certainly used by, if they did not originate with, the Cynics, while enough are put indifferently into the mouths of Spartan heroes or Cynic sages to show how alike the Spartan and Cynic outlook must have been considered.

Quantities of these stories survive in the literature of later antiquity, and above all in the several collections of laconic and other apophthegms and *exempla* made for the use of writers and orators that have come down to us under the name of Plutarch.[4] There are a few hostile illustrations of Spartan deceit (especially Lysander's) or naïveté; but far commoner are examples of Spartan wit at the expense of useless learning or luxury, and also of superstition. Their lack of walls and of written laws are admiringly held up to us. There are also many anecdotes of endurance and courage; but the Spartans are often made to put justice or wisdom even higher. (Sparta's reputation for courage and love of freedom,

---

[1] *FGH* ii b, no. 134, frs. 24, 25 (cf. 17). Compare Arrian, *Indica* 10.8: all Indians, like all Lacedaemonians, are free—though the latter have helots. (From Megasthenes, rather than a comment of Arrian's own, and thus suggesting that Onesicritus' ideas were not unique in his day?)

[2] Diogenes Laertius vi. 27; 30–2.   [3] *Rhetoric* ii. 1394b.

[4] In Plutarch's *Moralia*: *Apophthegmata Laconica* 208k; *Instituta Laconica* 236f; *Lacaenarum Apophthegmata* 240c; and many of the sayings in *Apophthegmata Regum et Imperatorum* 172b are attributed to Spartans.

G

it may be remarked, was kept up by such episodes as her resistance to Macedon and to Pyrrhus of Epirus—unless our tradition is itself only evidence for that reputation; but some of her other peculiarities were in fact disappearing—walls were added to the town in the third century, and Hellenistic luxury and court ceremonial crept in.)

Almost eighty of the more than four hundred Plutarchian *Apophthegmata Laconica* are given to Agesilaus, who is always the most popular figure (Lycurgus running him second). Apart from exemplifying all possible relevant virtues, he gives good advice on education (let boys learn 'to rule and be ruled', or 'what they will use as men'), and on kingship. In this last he is joined by Theopompus (recommending the king to allow free speech to his friends and prevent his subjects being treated unjustly) and by other royal Spartans. In this booklet, too, we may meet the notorious Spartan boy who concealed a stolen fox beneath his tunic till it gnawed him to death, and various compeers of his; and a variety of excessively Spartan mothers, notably one who tells her son to return from battle 'with his shield or on it', (that is to say, either as a victor or as a corpse) and one who stabs with her own hand the son who comes home having flung his away in flight. The fifth century had thought of Spartan women as immoral hoydens; but in the fourth we enter the age of the Spartan heroine, obedient to Lycurgus' command to eschew elegance, chaste, a great housewife, but as devoted to the state as her menfolk, and as liable to apophthegm. Ephorus probably adorned his history with some Spartan mothers;[1] a Cynic source produced several, one a typically coarse variant;[2] and whether slaughtering one son or burying eight without a tear she is a favourite with the epigrammatic poets. These indeed established several Spartan themes as favourites in the genre. Some of the epigrams may have been composed for sculptures or paintings (though in what we have of ancient art, subjects from Spartan history, and to some extent Greek history in general, are hard to find). Thermopylae is inevitably a favourite subject; even more

[1] See Diodorus xi. 45 and xii. 74 on the mother of Pausanias and the mother of Brasidas.

[2] Stobaeus iv. 51, going back to Teles (third century B.C.), '*On Apathy*' or impassivity (that Cynic and Stoic virtue) and ultimately to Bion of Borysthenes, one of the earliest and most famous authors of Cynic diatribes. Pulling up her skirts she asked her fugitive son 'Are you trying to get back into my womb?'

popular is the sixth-century battle fought near Thyrea between Sparta and Argos with three hundred picked men on each side. The Spartiate Othryadas remained as sole survivor on the field, but killed himself rather than return home—thus Herodotus: in a variant much favoured now, he inscribes a trophy with his blood before dying. Most of the surviving epigrams affect the Doric dialect; and some show that the idea of Spartan could still be subsumed under that of Dorian valour.[1]

To return to the philosophers. There can be no doubt that the often satiric literature of the Cynics was very widely diffused. Cynicism has been called the philosophy of the proletariat. At any rate it was doubtless instrumental in extending laconism beyond the limited if influential circles in which it had hitherto been at home; while the old democratic ideals that might have worked against such an extension seem to have been passing away even in Athens. Nor was Sparta associated any longer with exclusiveness of class or race, for the Cynics like the Stoics even managed to see in her a reflection of their cosmopolitan ideal. All men are equal by nature; nature and training together make the good man. We are informed by a Cynic source that the foreigner or helot's son accepted for the *agoge* is regarded as the equal of the best in the land, while an unworthy scion of the royal house may be degraded to helot status.[2] Or, as a later Stoicizing writer[3] puts it, among the things for which Sparta is to be praised is the understanding that citizenship is a matter of virtue and training, not of birth, and the habit of allowing 'Scythians, Triballians, Paphlagonians or barbarians without a name' to become Lacedaemonians.[4]

[1] Gow and Page, *The Greek Anthology: Hellenistic Epigrams* (i.e. from the death of Alexander to about 100 B.C.). Asclepiades v and Tymnes vi on the murderous mother; Dioscorides xxxii (cf. xxx for a paternal version) on the tearless one. Hegemon and Phaennus i on Thermopylae; and Nicander ii (cf. i), Chaeremon ii, iii, Damagetus iii, Dioscorides xxxi, 'Simonides' v all on Thyrea or Othryadas; cf. also Damagetus xi on the statue of a Spartan boy wrestler. Most of these, with later versions of the same subjects, come to us from Book vii of the *Anthologia Palatina*.

[2] Stobaeus xl. 8, going back to Teles (and Bion) again.

[3] Bernays, *Die Heraklitische Briefe*, no. ix, p. 90. The author(s) of these rhetorical letters ascribed to the archaic philosopher Heracleitus date from the first century A.D.

[4] Foreigners were, as we saw, occasionally, and helots, or more probably the sons of Spartiates by helot women, could probably (at some periods at least) be put through the *agoge*; but that complete equality followed is more than dubious.

Popular as Epicureanism long was, the dominant philosophy of later antiquity was one that, uniting Cynic and Platonic elements, ensured the survival of sympathy for Sparta. At many stages in its history Stoicism admitted the affinity of its ethics with those of Cynicism, by which its founder Zeno was much influenced. Zeno's *Politeia*, apparently a work of his youth and written 'hanging onto the tail of the Dog,'[1] is, like Diogenes' work of that name, compared by Plutarch with the real *Politeia* of Lycurgus, and we hear of his advocating sexual equality and communism, and the abolition of money, attacking conventional education as useless, and cultivating a laconic style. Though most Stoics abominated Cynic extravagances of behaviour they were doubtless already willing to find examples of rigid and austere virtue, of the untroubled acceptance of all-powerful fate and of insensibility to emotion, in Spartan history or pseudo-history, and, like the Cynics, to use such examples in the task, increasingly vital to their conception of philosophy, of inspiring mankind to virtue.

The Stoics of the earlier period at least did not share the anti-intellectualism of the Cynics, and in their physics and theology operated a final reconciliation between those frequent enemies, law and nature. Law was for them dependent on the divine reason or providence that rules the cosmos, a conception that lies at the root of many more modern theories of natural law. Law, therefore, is divine and absolute, identical for all and co-extensive with virtue, as on different grounds it had been for Plato. Man is primarily a citizen of the universe, a cosmopolitan. But though, for this reason, one could even deny that Lycurgus and other lawgivers were able to make laws at all,[2] yet the way was open for Sparta to regain her place as the city most obedient to law.

Zeno, (like Chrysippus, the leading Stoic of the later third century, who refused to have anything to do with kings) is said to have been a devotee of the mixed constitution.[3] But in practice Stoics often supported or became advisers to kings, and the Greek theory of royalty could hardly be alien to those who held on the one hand that the universe was ruled by a single principle, and on the other liked to say that the wise man and he alone was not only truly free but a king. Of Zeno's immediate pupils, Persaeus of Citium combined being a pillar of the Macedonian court with

---

[1] Diogenes Laertius vii. 4; 32–3.   [2] Cicero, *Academica* ii. 136.
[3] Diogenes Laertius vii. 131.

writing a *Laconic Politeia*,[1] and Sphaerus of Borysthenes, also a courtier and writer on kingship, produced yet another of these tracts as well as a work on, perhaps a comparison of, Lycurgus and Socrates.[2] He also taught philosophy to King Cleomenes III of Sparta himself, and is thus closely connected with the most important events in later Spartan history; events that probably provoked more laconizing writing than we can identify today.

But the extent of Sphaerus' influence on the far-reaching reforms of Cleomenes is highly uncertain. Most of them were taken over from the recent programme of King Agis IV, and were a pretty direct attempt to solve the social and military problems of the time by increasing the numbers of citizens able to afford heavy armour, under the name of a return to Lycurgan ways and with the usual barrage of oracles in support. Young King Agis' abolition of debt and his attempt to redivide the land, most of which was now in the hands of a minute group of rich owners, into 4,500 equal 'Lycurgan' lots (also to call in all wealth in coined money?), together with his reintroduction of strict discipline, ran him into trouble with the wealthy, led by his colleague Leonidas II.[3] At first Agis had the best of it and deposed Leonidas for the more co-operative Cleombrotus (by means of an ancient law, perhaps specially resurrected, that once every nine years the ephors might watch for the omen of a shooting star, which would permit them to suspend a king). But a reversal of fortune led to the execution of Agis, and his mother and grandmother, in 241. Cleomenes was the son of Leonidas, but after a *coup* in 227 and the exile of most of the richest citizens he succeeded in forcing through radical measures—appealing, if we may trust Plutarch's source, to Lycurgus' own use of violence. Indeed, he had, in effect, to usurp tyrannic power, sweeping away not only the ephorate, which he could and did argue to be post-Lycurgan (and in origin subordinate to the kings),[4] but the second royal house. Cleomenes was a talented general, and the recovery of Sparta's old hegemony was undoubtedly the main object of his and Agis' policies. But his career too ended in failure, and he died in a riot in Alexandria,

---

[1] *FGH* iii b, no. 584. But as Macedon was on bad terms with Sparta, perhaps not a eulogy?   [2] Ibid., no. 585.

[3] The land of the *perioeci* was also to be redivided, into 15,000 lots.

[4] Plutarch, *Life of Cleomenes* x. 2 ff. (Cf. *Agis* xii. 2; he held that the kings together were supreme over the ephors.)

where he had been living in exile at the friendly, because anti-Macedonian, Ptolemaic court.

Apart from the probably strict insistence on economic as well as political equality between citizens—far greater, it seems certain, than had ever really existed before—the revolution, which frightened the rich all over the Peloponnese, had a good deal in common with ordinary social unrest in Greece, where the cry for abolition of debts and redistribution of land was frequently taken up by a leader ambitious of supreme power. Certainly here for the first time the Spartan legend was enlisted on the side of the have-nots against the haves, though it must be remembered that the helots were not intended to benefit. The citizen body was to be enlarged by selected *perioeci* and foreigners (probably ex-mercenary soldiers). Even this Leonidas tried to represent as un-Lycurgan, but Sphaerus as a Stoic might have approved. He is only attested as taking an interest (as we would expect him to do) in Cleomenes' reform of the *agoge*.[1] A Stoic tinge has also been detected in the historian Phylarchus, Plutarch's source for his *Lives* of Agis and Cleomenes (and for that part of the *Life* of Pyrrhus describing the heroic resistance of the Spartans, and especially the Spartan women, to his invasion some years earlier). These all suggest a probably much romanticized and moralized account, in which Phylarchus interwove reflections on virtue, fortune, and suicide, and laid the exotic local colour on thick; and in which he contrasted the previous luxury and inequality in Sparta (for which, echoing Aristotle, he largely blamed the women and their power), not to mention the yet worse luxury to which the wicked Leonidas' years abroad at the Seleucid court in Syria inclined him, with the reformers' simplicity and virtue, their gallant struggles and heroic deaths. Also those of their mothers and wives; among whom must be recalled, for the parts they were to play nearly two thousand years later on the tragic stage, Chilonis, daughter to Leonidas and wife to his usurping successor Cleombrotus but displaying an exemplary devotion to both; Agiatis, the rich, high-born, and affectionate wife of Agis first and Cleomenes after; Agesistrata, the mother of Agis, who gave up all her wealth on his demand; and Cratesiclea, the mother of Cleomenes, who endured and died with him in Egypt.

After Cleomenes' death, successive (and after a time single)

[1] Plutarch, *Cleomenes* xi. 2.

Spartan kings contended with varying success against the power of Macedon and, nearer at hand, the Achaean League; and also against rival claimants to the throne. The most notorious was Nabis, depicted perhaps unjustly by Polybius as a sadistic tyrant as well as an extreme demagogue, still appealing to Lycurgus as the founder of a military democracy.[1] But this was not the interpretation of Lycurgus adopted by the Romans, whose intervention had by now entirely changed the balance of power; and who were finally to restore to Sparta, which had suffered a brief period of incorporation in the Achaean League, a now nominal and futile liberty.

[1] Livy xxxiv. 30.1.

7

LACONISM EXPORTED

IT IS time to look beyond the confines of the Greek world. The first country to arrest our attention is Egypt, the history of whose supposed connections with Sparta forms a pretty climax. Herodotus points out one or two features—respect for age, the hereditary nature of certain callings—common to Sparta and that country that appeared so remarkable to the Greeks.[1] Later we find Isocrates declaring that the Lacedaemonians have copied from Egypt their common meals, physical training, exclusive dedication to arms, restriction on travel, and supreme devotion to the state; in this not very serious panegyric of Egypt he even claims to find the copy inferior to the model.[2] Next Ephorus explicitly states that Lycurgus paid her a visit (as Solon had genuinely done);[3] while at the end of the fourth century Hecataeus of Abdera, in a philosophic romance about Egypt, pretended that this visit like those of other famous Greeks was attested by the priestly documents there.[4]

Only after Alexander, however, was it possible to send Lycurgus off on a Grand Tour ultimately including not only study with Indian gymnosophists but trips to Libya and Spain.[5] We can discover some sort of background for even these last. In Libya the oracle of Ammon had been an object of Spartan reverence for some time, and the Dorian colony at Cyrene had, according to Herodotus, a tenuous original connection, which later historians much improved, and certainly a good deal of practical contact with Sparta; she stuck obstinately to Dorian dialect and cults, and the ephors found here as elsewhere may have been copied from Sparta. As for Spain, let us remember that foreign countries had

[1] Herodotus ii. 80; vi. 60.
[2] Isocrates, *Busiris* 17–19.
[3] Ephorus, fr. 149 (*FGH* ii b, no. 70).
[4] Hecataeus, fr. 96 (*FGH* iii a, no. 264).
[5] Aristocrates the Spartiate, fr. 2 (*FGH* iii b, no. 591; late Hellenistic or Roman date?).

increasingly to be fitted into the framework of Greek myth or history. And so, on the basis, usually, of some dubious resemblance of place-names or customs, distant towns or tribes were said to have been founded by Greek peoples or heroes of Greek legend. Thus some ethnographers said that Lacedaemonians had reached Cantabria, in north-west Spain;[1] doubtless because, as in neighbouring Lusitania, some of the inhabitants could be described as living 'in the Laconian manner'.[2]

What is important is that the barbarians were often highly sensible of such honours, and took over or even themselves invented such theories. Thus a number of native cities of inland Asia Minor, mostly, it seems, noted for warlike valour or primitive republican constitutions, claimed, implausibly, to be Lacedaemonian colonies (some may have had some Dorian Greek settlers at some point).[3] But two of the states near the head of the long procession of those eager to compare or even connect themselves with Sparta were less obscure; were indeed perfectly chosen to keep her fame alive through the centuries. For they were, in the East, the Jews, and in the West, the Romans.

What appears on the face of it to be the first evidence concerning the Jews is dramatic enough: a letter in the name of Arieus, an ambitious Spartan king of the late fourth to early third century, to the high priest Onias, which appears in the First Book of Maccabees and in Josephus' *Jewish Antiquities*, calmly proclaims that, as literary evidence shows, the Spartans are of the race of Abraham, and offers community of goods between the two peoples.[4] The letter is patently a forgery, but it may have been concocted as early as the second century B.C.—to give inquisitive Christian scholars of later ages an inordinate amount of trouble. Before that time certain Greeks had already been struck by the 'philosophic' character of the God of the Jews, and by their remarkable system of law. A pupil of Aristotle put down their endurance and

---

[1] Asclepiades of Myrlea 'and others', Strabo iii. 4.3.

[2] Strabo iii. 3.6 (owing to their bathing and eating habits).

[3] Especially Selge in Pisidia (always free, warlike, and ruled by law: Polybius v. 76b, the earliest evidence for any of these tales; cf. Strabo xii. 7.3), Cibyra (which became powerful owing to *eunomia*, even though under tyrants: Strabo xiii. 4.17), Nysa (Strabo xiv. 1.46).

[4] 1 Maccabees xii. 5–23; Josephus, *Antiqu. Jud.* xii. 225–7. The manuscripts of Maccabees misspell the Spartan king; Josephus has him correctly. Onias I was high priest 309–300 B.C.

sophrosyne to their derivation from Indian gymnosophists,[1] and among the original homes suggested for them was Crete[2] as well as Egypt. Probably it was a hellenized Jewish source, perhaps in Alexandria, which had both a large Jewish population and contacts with Sparta, that picked out the country favoured above all others by philosophers, and reversed the form of connection with it preferred by Greeks. However, also in Alexandria, the Peripatetic Hermippus had indicated that Pythagoras was influenced by Jewish (and Thracian) ideas. The thesis that Greek poets and philosophers had been pupils of Judaism was enthusiastically developed by hellenizing Jewish writers.

If the idea of a link between Sparta and Judaea was literary in origin, it appears to have been made practical use of. In 168 the hellenizing ex-high priest Jason ultimately set off from Egypt to Sparta, 'expecting protection on account of his kinship', if we may trust the Second Book of Maccabees;[3] it is not clear that he got there. About twenty-five years later the high priest Jonathan sent an embassy to Sparta, perhaps alone among the cities of mainland Greece, as well as to Rome. His (possibly genuine) letter, which is inserted in the text of 1 Maccabees, together with the more than dubious epistle of Arieus to which it appeals, claims that the two peoples have long known they are brothers and that the Jews regularly pray for the Spartans. He proposes to renew the friendship. A friendly but possibly rather surprised reply from the Spartan authorities is later recorded and further diplomatic contact indicated.[4] It appears certain that there was a Jewish community in Sparta not very much later; and the traditional connection doubtless counted for something in Herod's generous benefactions to the city and, as Josephus indeed observes, in his friendship for Eurycles, the *de facto* ruler of Sparta in Augustus' day.[5]

---

[1] Clearchus, fr. 6 (Wehrli, *Die Schule des Aristoteles* iii). Cf. Megasthenes, fr. 3 (*FGH* iii c, no. 715).

[2] Tacitus, *Histories* v. 2: Idaei become Iudaei. A connection with Sparta might have been worked out via the story that the founder of the Jewish race was Oudaeos, one of the Sparti or Sown Men, sprung of the dragon's teeth at Thebes (Stephanus of Byzantium s.v. *Ioudaea*). For Timagoras (*FGH* iii b, no. 381, fr. 3 = Stephanus s.v. *Sparta*) derived the Spartans from the Sparti.

[3] 2 Maccabees v. 9: the work is based on the history written by Jason of Cyrene, a Jew, in Greek and in a style typical of Hellenistic historiography, probably late in the second century B.C.

[4] 1 Maccabees loc. cit.; xiii. 166–70.   [5] Josephus, *Bellum Judaicum* i. 515.

The use to which a comparison, if not a connection, could be put is shown by two surviving Jewish apologists of the first century A.D. The philosopher Philo of Alexandria was concerned in his *Moses* to make the lawgiver of the Jews and his system better known to the outside world. He clearly has the model states of Greek thinkers in mind as he describes the creation of the sole lawgiver to attain the virtues necessary to his task, the sole whose laws came direct from God, the sole to be himself at the same time philosopher–king, high priest, and prophet. He taught, rather than commanded. Other legislations, Philo says, have been over-turned in troubles or subverted by luxury, but Moses' have never altered, and, while nature exists, may be immortal. People generally despise foreign laws, the Athenians have no opinion of the Lacedaemonians, and vice versa; but everyone takes an interest in ours.[1]

Philo does not here insist that the other lawgivers are dependent on Moses, though he elsewhere shows his acquaintance with such theories—and, it may be added, describes the best constitution as a democracy (in the newer, conservative, sense). His idea of natural, which is also divine, law is related to, though, given the nature of the Jewish God, it cannot be identical with, that of the Stoics; and naturally his belief in the moral and religious function of the state is even stronger than Plato's.

A little later Josephus, primarily known as a historian, was writing his two books *Against Apion* to defend his countrymen against one of the most virulent of Alexandrian Jew-baiters, and the charge that they were a misanthropic and upstart race un-known to civilized literature. Josephus retorts with frequent quotations from Greek writers favourably mentioning the Jews, and with the claim that Pythagoras, Plato, and all the philosophers took their religious ideas from Judaism. It is much the same with politics. Beside Moses, of course, Lycurgus, Solon, and Zaleucus were born yesterday. The political weakness of the Jews does not prove that their laws are bad, for all peoples, including the Athenians and Lacedaemonians, have had misfortunes. The cities of the Jews are inland, and they take more interest in agriculture and education than in commerce.[2] Their state is a theocracy, as such superior to the usual forms; its law, based on religion,

---

[1] Philo, *Moses* ii. 2–4 esp.
[2] Josephus, *Against Apion* i. 162 ff., 168; ii. 257, 280 ff.

inculcates every virtue. It does not simply give practical training, like Lacedaemon and Crete, or lay down regulations that are not enforced, as Athens and other cities. Moses began at the beginning, with infant diet and private life, and left nothing to caprice. No one, continues Josephus, knows their laws as we do—they are graven on our souls; no one has such concord as our common beliefs and habits give us. Change is undesired, impossible. Josephus proceeds to give a detailed account, with simplicity and sobriety as the keynotes, and an insistence that parents and elders are honoured and strangers well treated.

A future life is the only reward held out to the obedient Jew. If they did not know us well, Josephus asks, would the Greeks believe such a people existed?[1] Many of them call Plato, whose laws are easier and nearer to common practice, an impractical dreamer; some therefore reserve their admiration for Lycurgus, and all praise the Spartans for remaining faithful so long to their laws. But we Jews have obeyed ours for over two thousand years; and while the Lacedaemonians abandoned most of their way of life when they lost their independence, the Jews have maintained their far severer one through the greatest calamities. The Spartans, unlike the Jews, lived a life of leisure, training only for war— and in that they were unsuccessful. Often they forgot their laws and gave themselves up to the enemy. But how many Jews have been constrained by torture itself to betray their laws?

Against the charge of exclusiveness, Josephus appeals to Plato's desire to keep his citizens' blood pure, and to the common Greek refusal to associate with people of an alien way of life. He concedes that Lacedaemonians' fear of corruption did perhaps make them unfriendly; but the Jews, in contrast, welcome anyone who is ready to share their customs. Any people naturally tries to preserve its own habits and religion—usually in vain. And Josephus points to the inevitable collapse of the 'unsociable' Spartan way of life. What shocks him most about it, however, is its lax view of marriage.

Older, stricter, more permanent, in every respect better than, but fundamentally resembling (possibly for very good reasons) the best, accredited Greek models: that is the view taken by certain Jews of their way of life; and it was to be inherited by some of the Christian Fathers and applied to their own.

[1] Josephus, *Against Apion* ii. 220.

The roots of laconism in Rome were old and various. It has been suspected that the phenomenon owed its first impulse among the natives of Italy to Tarentum, anxious in the fourth and third centuries to assert her influence over the partly hellenized local tribes, and to the Tarentine Pythagoreans who drew disciples from the whole south and centre of the peninsula. One ancient scholar explicitly accused the Tarentines of inventing a partly Lacedaemonian foundation-myth for their neighbours, the warlike Samnites.[1] After the third century, however, Tarentine interest in Sparta probably declined; the city certainly did not attempt to preserve her ways.[2]

To come yet nearer to Rome, several towns on the coast of Latium claimed, pretty implausibly, to have been founded by Spartans or even 'Spartan Pythagoreans'.[3] And the Sabines, we are told, believed themselves to be descended from a band of wandering Lacedaemonians.[4] It is almost certain that the elder Cato, himself of Sabine descent, in his *Origines* told the story of Sabus, who left home in the time of Lycurgus with his followers, and that Cato was followed by other historians of the second century B.C.[5] The Romans expressed by this tale their admiration for Sabine austerity and courage. It was also pointed out that both peoples dwelt in unwalled towns. The story may also have helped them actually to trace some of their institutions to Sparta, as we shall see they did; for many Roman customs were thought, by Cato and others, to be of Sabine origin. A good many Roman families, too, could have claimed Spartan descent in this roundabout way, though we cannot be sure that they did so.[6]

---

[1] Strabo v. 4, p. 250. Aristoxenus' hand has been suspected.

[2] 'Tarentinis quid ex Spartana dura illa et horrida disciplina mansit?', Livy xxxviii. 17.

[3] Strabo v. 33, p. 233.

[4] Plutarch, *Numa* i. 1; Dionysius of Halicarnassus ii. 49.

[5] Cato, *Origines*, fr. 51; cf. Cn. Gellius, fr. 10 (both in Peter, *Historicorum Romanorum Reliquiae*).

[6] Notably the patrician Valerii and Claudii; the latter became in the later republic hereditary *patroni*, patrons and protectors, of Sparta as of many other Greek communities. Silius Italicus (*Punica* viii. 412; iii. 8) speaks of a Claudius as 'Therapnaeo a sanguine Clausi', and a Valerius as 'ingentis Volusi Spartana propago'; neat references to both Sabine and Spartan ancestry, but poets had to show obscure learning. Thus Ovid (*Fasti* i. 260; iii. 230) calls the raped Sabine women, and other Sabines, Oebalian, i.e. Laconian, after the legendary King Oebalus.

It would be a mistake to try to isolate too precisely the various streams of influence that went to make up Roman laconism. Xenophon had a great vogue in the second century B.C., and from its later years Stoicism gained ground in the governing class. Cicero, joking about the younger Cato's exaggeratedly Stoic way of life, calls the Lacedaemonians his models;[1] we know from Plutarch how often Cato practised, among other austerities, going barefoot and tunicless. Marcus Brutus, too, had a cult of Sparta that was perhaps Stoic in essence; he affected a laconic style when writing Greek, and after the fashion of his day for foreign associations he called a stream on his country estate Eurotas, and a portico after the Stoa Persica in Sparta.[2] But by this time the graver Romans had a wide knowledge of the history and literature of the glorious past of Greece, which they contrasted with a degenerate present, and its political philosophy had deeply affected their own. Most would have been able to echo such a panegyric as Cicero in the *pro Flacco* gives to Sparta, and especially to her virtue, the result of both nature and training, and to the unique permanence of her laws and customs, unchanged for seven hundred years.[3] It is true that to Cicero here Athens remains the first city in Greece, but it is for her learning and her legendary gifts to humanity alone.

But we can look more closely than this. With Rome's rise to power, political analysis of the city-state again became a relevant occupation. It was probably an unknown Greek thinker of the third century, whether Peripatetic or Pythagorean, who first forced Rome's institutions into the Procrustean bed of the mixed constitution, thinking perhaps, like Polybius after him, thereby to explain her success. Such an analysis is implied when the great scholar Eratosthenes links Rome and Carthage together, not later than the early second century, as amazingly well-run states. The two consuls, of course, represented the regal element; the two kings at Sparta, the fact that the (two?) *suffetes* at Carthage were usually called kings in Greek, and the belief that the annually elected consuls had succeeded directly to many of the powers and privileges, especially the military ones, of the expelled kings of Rome, made this easy. The senate provided the dose of aristocracy,

---

[1] Cicero, *pro Murena* 74.
[2] Plutarch, *M. Brutus* 2; Cicero, *ad Atticum* xv. 4.
[3] Cicero, *pro Flacco* 62.

and the people, meeting in its various assemblies or *comitia*, that of democracy.[1]

It is likely that the elder Cato for one was at least superficially acquainted with such theories. He certainly spoke of the Carthaginian constitution as mixed, and Cicero reports him as comparing Rome with Crete, Athens, and Sparta in one respect at least: with what is sometimes thought of as typical Roman empiricism, Cato considered it to his city's advantage not to have been established, like these, by a single lawgiver. How could one man solve every problem and foresee every need? The wisdom of many and the experience of centuries had gone to the making of Rome.[2]

Polybius, when in spite of his admiration for Rome he differed from this judgement, was perhaps consciously opposing Cato. The Greek historian had been a prominent figure in the Achaean League, and he gives a very unsympathetic picture of the League's hereditary enemy and her recent policy since she fell into the hands of 'tyrants', among whom he includes Cleomenes. But the Lycurgan system and the glorious past of Sparta are a different matter, as becomes clear when Polybius makes a slightly uneasy incursion into political theory in order to explain Rome and Rome's success to his fellow Greeks. From whatever immediate source, he briefly expounds the common theory of the three pure constitutions and their corruptions, and argues that the inevitable cycle of change through all six could only be delayed in a state where the three good ones are combined. Lycurgus was the first to understand this, and to balance the various principles, each with their tendency to perversion, against each other, so that the state should resemble a well-trimmed boat; and thus liberty survived at Lacedaemon for the longest period ever known. The

---

[1] There was surely laconism at Carthage too, where from the fourth century Greek, especially Siceliote, cultural influence was strong. A Spartan commander, Xanthippus, was hired in the first Punic War to fight the Romans and had all the effect that the Carthaginians, doubtless familiar with the history of their old foe Syracuse, could have hoped; and a Lacedaemonian historian, Sosylus, was in Hannibal's train and wrote an account of the second Punic War (which included debates in the senate, and possibly even a story about the prudence of the Roman young—see *FGH* ii b, no. 176, fr. 2: prompt admiration for Rome in Laconia?). He was also described as Hannibal's teacher—which is perhaps the basis for the story, in a late Roman source (Vegetius, *Epitoma Rei Militaris* iii, *praef.*) that Hannibal had a Lacedaemonian *doctor . . . armorum*.

[2] Cato, *Origines* fr. 8 (Peter, op. cit.); Cicero, *de Republica* ii. 1.

Romans, however, reached the same result (we are told) not by reason and foresight like Lycurgus, but through the experience of many struggles and misfortunes (doubtless an inferior route). Describing the Roman republican system, Polybius points out that neither consuls, senate, nor assembly can act at all without the assistance of the others.[1]

Afterwards Polybius compares Rome with all the states his readers may be expected to admire. Thebes, he thinks, and the quarrelsome and fickle Athenian democracy, are not worth discussion. Crete, *pace* the great authorities of the past, and most immediately Ephorus, is no good and not the least like Sparta— the Cretans' greed for land and money is not restrained by law, their intestine squabbles contrast with Spartan concord, and their rulers are all elected annually and in a quite democratic way. Plato's *Republic* is disqualified as fiction. This leaves Sparta and Carthage. To take the latter first, Polybius holds that her mixed constitution has now verged too far towards democracy; Rome is also superior in the military valour, piety, and contempt for riches shown by her citizens. As for Sparta, as far as concord, self-defence, and the preservation of liberty are concerned, Lycurgus showed superhuman foresight. By the equal division of land and the simple meals in common he produced temperance and concord; by the training in danger and hardship, courage. But he totally neglected foreign policy, and left his people ambitious, domineering, and greedy towards the rest of the Greeks. In this criticism, directed as it is against the whole of Spartan history, not merely a period of decadence, Polybius probably goes beyond Ephorus, whose formulae he otherwise reflects. He particularly complains that Sparta's economic institutions were incompatible with a large empire, and had to be supplemented by dependence on Persia and exactions from the Greeks. But to an imperial policy as such Polybius does not object, and this is why Rome, whom he saw as uniting the known world and, in the end, as benefiting her allies, is to him ultimately a greater and more glorious state.[2]

This was probably a frequent conclusion. It is certainly that of Cicero's *de Republica*, where comparisons are entirely to Rome's advantage. This famous work, long influential, but subsequently lost almost in its entirety, to be rediscovered in a still fragmentary

[1] Polybius vi. 3, 4, 10.   [2] Id. vi. 43.

condition early in the nineteenth century, is a discussion of the ideal state, embodied in Rome—as she had supposedly once been, not as she now was. Cicero primarily depends on, but frequently argues against, Plato's *Republic*—a merely imaginary state, he objects, and largely unacceptable to human feelings; but all his great knowledge of Greek political thought is adapted to the service of the Roman tradition.

Book II, agreeing with Cato's views on the advantages of gradual development, traces Rome's growth from Romulus' first choice of site (inland, according to the best notions, of course). Romulus soon discovered, as Lycurgus a little earlier had done, that royal power should be tempered by the authority of the best citizens, and set up a senate. And on his death the rustic senators found out a principle that had escaped Lycurgus: an elected king is likely to be better than a hereditary one. However, until the expulsion of the Tarquins, Rome like Sparta and Crete, though a mixed, was not a well-mixed state. Monarchy was still predominant, and thus revolution, following on its corruption into tyranny, a likely danger. Lycurgus' Gerousia, too, another fragment tells us, was too small; and both he and Romulus, by giving a bare taste of liberty to the people, provoked the struggles for the establishment of the ephors and the tribunes (who are linked elsewhere in Cicero; it was perhaps an established comparison). Cicero in fine praises the constitution of three equal ingredients with an unusually positive enthusiasm. It is not to him just a barrier against human ambition or fated decay; it is the stablest form because the most just to all, the ideal balance between rights and duties, the perfect combination of executive power, deliberative authority, and popular liberty, ensuring the harmony of all citizens.[1]

It is a pity that Book IV is almost entirely lost. For here Cicero defended the old social and educational institutions of Rome against those of the Greek political philosophers. Uniform public education, he remarks, is a subject on which the Greeks have wasted a lot of time. He reveals that Polybius, in a passage lost to us, had regretted Rome's neglect of it (similarly, Plutarch was to remark that her King Numa, supposed to be the author of many social and religious institutions, had proved himself a common-

---

[1] Cicero, *de Republica* ii. 9, 12, 23, 28, 50, 38 (cf. *de Legibus* iii. 16). Cf. iii. 9: treating the poor as slaves is paradoxical in a just state.

place lawgiver by ignoring it).[1] Cicero in return apparently mounted a violent attack on Greek education. How absurd the exercises in the gymnasium! How inadequate the military training! (a Roman could afford to jeer). One fragment recalls that in Sparta boys were taught to steal. Several others deal with homosexuality: some Greek cities admitted this without restriction, and Sparta herself with hardly any.

A speaker complains that Scipio, Cicero's mouth-piece, prefers that such *populi nobilissimi* should be attacked, not his beloved Plato. But Cicero obviously refuted the property regulations not only of Lycurgus but also the more radical Plato. And in his discussion of family life, women (who should be controlled by their husbands, not magistrates), the arts (often dangerous), and other subjects, it is more than probable that the errors of both authorities were made to contribute to the glorification of the Roman *maiores*.[2]

Cicero once seems to suggest that Romulus actually copied Lycurgus' Gerousia and translated the name to make the Latin *senatus*.[3] The theme of Rome's intelligent borrowings from various sources was a popular one at this time. Posidonius of Rhodes, the Stoic philosopher, savant, and historian of Rome probably helped to develop it; he may have said that the Romans imitated the Spartan *politeia* in all points but maintained it better.[4] Varro, the most learned of Roman scholars, found foreign origins for various customs; he certainly said that the Romans' old habit of sitting rather than reclining to eat came from Sparta and Crete,[5] and probably also that it was from Spartan respect for age that the Roman youth learnt to escort their seniors home in the evening.[6] It was also perhaps through Varro that Plutarch knew of a story in some historian that a Spartan called Pythagoras had been a friend of King Numa and taught him many Lacedaemonian customs—a tale probably dating from the late second century B.C., when the Romans discovered that Numa could not for chronological reasons have been, as they had long believed, a pupil of the philosopher Pythagoras.[7]

---

[1] Plutarch, *Comparison of Lycurgus and Numa*.   [2] Cicero, *de Republica* iv. 3–6.
[3] Ibid. ii. 27.   [4] Posidonius, fr. 59, *FGH* ii, no. 87.
[5] Varro, *de Gente Populi Romani*, fr. 37, ed. Fraccaro.
[6] Aulus Gellius ii. 15 ('ut scriptum in antiquitatibus est').
[7] Plutarch, *Numa* 1.

Dionysius of Halicarnassus, who wrote a strongly loyal history of early Rome in the time of Augustus, was eager to prove that his subject was a Hellenic not a barbarian city and to bring out the superior greatness and durability of her empire over all those of the past. In his description of the legislation of Romulus[1] he draws attention to various features of this constitution, so self-sufficient and admirable both in peace and war, claiming that they are copied from Sparta (or once at least from Athens) and sometimes improved in the process. For example, Romulus based his body-guard of three hundred, the *celeres*, on the Spartan royal guard of the same size; to encourage frugality and comradeship in war he introduced communal feeding on the Spartan model, if on holidays only, in each of the *curiae*. The senate or Gerousia was a Greek institution too. Above all, Romulus' decision to share his power with it was inspired by Sparta, where the Gerousia had extensive control. (If Dionysius hardly seems interested in the full triple mixture, this may reflect either the actual Augustan situation or the narrow outlook of his pro-senatorial source.) The description of the Roman king's privileges, as now laid down, recalls the set-up so familiar to us; but, Dionysius observes, by their generous gifts of the citizenship the Roman kings far surpassed the Spartans. (This, too, was a common theme; among others the pedantic Emperor Claudius, according to Tacitus, commented on Rome's method of strengthening her empire by treating the vanquished as brothers, a course in striking contrast to Spartan and Athenian policy.)[2] Finally, says Dionysius, Romulus' legislation on marriage and women was better than that of any other state, including Sparta, which quite neglected the subject. Such, probably, had been Cicero's view too.

Dionysius later reports that according to certain rationalizing historians Numa invented the story of his converse with Egeria in emulation of Minos and Lycurgus, who had both ensured obedience to their laws by attributing them to a god. On the expulsion of the Tarquins he makes the first Brutus advise dividing the regal power on the Lacedaemonian model; and this was the cause of the two consuls being set up. Finally, a fragment from

---

[1] Dionysius of Halicarnassus ii. 13–27. His special source for these chapters, according to the most recent study, dates from the Sullan period. Though the references to Greece are mostly, they need not be all, Dionysius' own insertions.

[2] Tacitus, *Annals* xi. 24.

his last book shows him still hammering home Roman superiority, on the grounds that neither Athens nor Sparta went so far as to subject strictly private and domestic matters to the moral oversight of the state, as Rome did by means of the powers given to the censors.[1]

[1] Dionysius ii. 61 (cf. Polybius x. 2 on Scipio Africanus exploiting popular superstitions just like Lycurgus); iv. 73, xx. 13.

8

UNDER THE EMPIRE

UNDER the empire it became hard to suppose that Rome was exactly like Sparta only better, though it might still be said of the past, especially in a moral sense: the Spartans came closer than others to the *gravitas* of early Romans.[1] Though at the start of the period we find one understandable regret that Roman generals have shown themselves less obedient to the civil authorities than Agesilaus did,[2] and though Tacitus illustrates his argument that great oratory and political corruption go hand in hand by pointing out that Crete and Sparta had neither,[3] interest in Sparta becomes generally less political. If Nero when in Greece refused to visit Athens and Sparta, the first, according to a hostile source, because the matricide Orestes had been tried there and the second 'on account of the laws of Lycurgus, which were inconsistent with his own policy', this is as likely to be a charge of luxury and debauchery as of tyranny.[4] Although Roman Stoicism was for a time in the later first century A.D. identified with a republican opposition, it is only in an ethical context that Stoic references to Sparta survive. Seneca (who was of course no republican) when recommending suicide or contempt for death quotes the tale of the captive Spartan boy who dashed out his brains rather than be a slave, as well as citing the Three Hundred at Thermopylae. (These last, as his father's *Suasoriae* show, provided a favourite set piece for the rhetorical declamations.) Or, recommending the good man never to give up, he adduces the Spartan refusal to take part in games involving a formal admission of defeat; and so on.[5] Spartan austerity was warmly praised by Musonius Rufus, in violent reaction against the excesses of his own day.[6]

As for the ordinary Roman, he would seem to have thought,

---

[1] Valerius Maximus ii. 6.   [2] Cornelius Nepos, *Agesilaus* iv. 2–3.
[3] Tacitus, *Dialogus* 40.   [4] Cassius Dio, lxii. 14.3.
[5] Seneca, *Epistulae Morales* lxxvii. 14; lxxxii. 20; *de Beneficiis* v. 3.1. cf. Seneca Rhetor, *Suasoriae* ii.
[6] Musonius Rufus, ed. Hense, pp. 112–13. Cf. 3, 97, 125.

when he heard the word Laconia, primarily of the hunting hounds, fine marble, and purple dye that she exported; and perhaps also of the hot-air chamber in the baths called the *laconicum*. Meanwhile the poets made piquant use of her eccentric treatment of women. Virgil, with his

> virginibus bacchata Lacaenis
> Taygeta

was not the first Roman poet to evoke the dances of the Lacedae-monian maidens.[1] After him Ovid painted mythical Lacedaemon in the colours of a later day, as *Dorica castra*, a Dorian camp, and made Helen wrestle naked in the palaestra;[2] while Propertius expresses a desire for Spartan freedom of contact between the sexes—though it is peculiarly hard to envisage his Cynthia as a sporting and unsophisticated Spartan girl.[3] Perhaps this common literary fashion, based probably more on classical than on Hellen-istic Greek prototypes, helps to explain why there is little inter-action between the not wholly dissimilar ideals of the Spartan heroine and the Roman matron. The latter was emphatically not expected to dance in public, at any period in her life.

We ought not to leave the early empire, however, without mentioning the first author to write a universal history in Latin, the Gaul Pompeius Trogus, largely because the later epitome of this work by Justin was much read in post-classical times, being conveniently brief and not in Greek. Sparta, in his moralistic and inaccurate account, has equal lots and no dowries for women and apparently no money at all to supplement the use of barter. The young are made to spend their time in the country, not in the market-place (a euphemistic account of the *crypteia*?). Lycurgus only *fingit*—pretended—to have the authority of Apollo for his laws.[4]

Meanwhile Sparta herself, nominally still independent, was engaged in an antiquarian revival, with favourable effects on the tourist trade. Rome had 'restored' the laws of Lycurgus in the second century B.C. The two kings had gone for good, however, though the ephors reappear, beside various new or comparatively

---

[1] Virgil, *Georgics* ii. 487 (cf. the early dramatist quoted by Cicero, *Tusculan Disputations* ii. 15).

[2] Ovid, *Heroides* xvi. 370 (the *Letter of Paris*, sometimes thought not to be by Ovid).

[3] Propertius iv. 14.

[4] Justin iii. 2–3.

new boards of magistrates. The Controllers of Women and Guardians of the Laws suggest the influence of philosophy here as in other states. The Gerousia, now elected annually, seems usually to have been in ultimate control. There were plenty of foreign settlers, the helots had been abolished by now, and most of the perioecic territory made independent. But, chiefly from the late first to the mid third centuries A.D., there are numerous inscriptions, full of archaic and dialect terms, recording winners in the musical or athletic contests of the *agoge*. A special 'contest in virtuous citizenship' is also attested; likewise special 'interpreters' and 'teachers of the Lycurgan customs.'[1] Spartan coins, which had existed for several centuries, had recently begun to sport a handsome head of the lawgiver. And it is from this period that we have vivid accounts of the boys' mock battles on the island Platanistas, between sides named after Lycurgus and Heracles, and, more horrific still, of the flogging ceremony with its not uncommon fatalities, both contests being considered Lycurgus' own creation. Cicero and Plutarch watched the latter; it is said to have attracted crowds of strangers to the theatre that now encircled the façade of the temple of Artemis.[2]

The cities in Asia Minor that had established historical connections with Sparta also proudly kept them up, as coins and inscriptions show.[3] So did Cyrene; the Cyreneans are often described as Lacedaemonians, though the population was mixed in the extreme and largely non-Greek. Hadrian's letter to the city shows anxiety to restore its 'Dorian and Lacedaemonian' traditions, and refers to 'Laconian order and moderation'.[4] Perhaps he and it were partly anxious to forget not only the recent Jewish revolt, but also the Cyrenaic school of philosophy, which had notoriously made pleasure the highest good.

In Greece as well as Rome, Cynicism and Stoicism, in a somewhat eclectic and primarily ethical form, were still going strong.

---

[1] *Inscriptiones Graecae* vi, esp. 65, 500, 554.

[2] Philostratus, *Life of Apollonius* vi. 20.

[3] See A. M. Woodward, *Sparta and Asia Minor under the Roman Empire* (*Studies presented to D. M. Robinson* ii p. 868) and A. H. M. Jones, *Cities of the Eastern Roman Provinces*, pp. 30, 49, 126, 131. Apart from those mentioned above, p. 95n.3, Sagalassus and Amblada in Pisidia; Alabanda in Caria; probably Synnada also.

[4] I am grateful to Miss J. Reynolds and Dr. P. M. Fraser for permission to quote these new readings.

It is significant of a new moral feeling that Lycurgus' magnanimous treatment of the young man who knocked out his eye
becomes a favourite *exemplum* of friendship and forgiveness—to
Epictetus for one, quoting his master Musonius Rufus.[1] Political
writing, Stoic or otherwise, consisted chiefly of treatises on the
good king, written with an eye to the Roman emperor. Dio
Chrysostom, who was converted to Stoicism in Rome by
Musonius Rufus, produced more than one of these. In one his
examples of the brave and virtuous king who loves his subjects
include beside Cyrus of Persia and others 'many of the Laconian
kings'. In another fragmentary piece the question is raised, what
makes the king? Are the Heracleidae, whose power was so
limited by that of the ephors, really kings? We may be sure that
the answer was a resounding yes. Elsewhere Dio links the endurance of Indians and Spartans, the educational qualities of Tyrtaeus
and Homer (who perhaps inspired Lycurgus with the idea of
syssitia), praises Agesilaus for refusing to allow any portrait to be
made of him, and calls Lycurgus and other radical lawgivers the
true philosophers. Sparta's self-control and regard for law were
the cause of her prosperity. But Dio is also ready to mention the
less glorious episodes in her history, and he sets the Stoic cosmo-
polis, in which all intelligent beings have a share, above the
Spartan polis, which excluded the helots altogether. Indeed, he
could argue that no method of enslaving others is just. The
Thebans were right to free the Messenians from Sparta.[2]

As for the neo-Pythagoreans, if certain surviving texts on
kingship fail to mention Sparta now, the old story of Pythagoras'
visit was repeated, and Spartan devotees, male and female, some
of unlikely antiquity, were listed.[3] And there is Apollonius of
Tyana. This famous sage and thaumaturge lived in the late first
century A.D., but his life was written, or written up, in the third.
The letters attributed to him are consciously laconic, and he is
supposed to have defended the Spartan way of life, notably
flogging and the expulsion of foreigners, in an argument with a
gymnosophist on the banks of the Nile; and also, when had up

---

[1] Epictetus, ed. Schenkl, fr. 5.
[2] Dio Chrysostom ii. 77; lvi. 5; cf. ii. 29, 44, 59; xxii; xxxvii. 43; xxxvi. 38;
xv.
[3] Iamblichus, *Life of Pythagoras* 25; 267—e.g. Chilonis, daughter of Chilon
the sixth-century sage.

PLATE 1

a

b   *c*

Lycurgus: Laconian coins of the Roman Period (bronze, twice actual size)

before the Emperor Domitian, to have claimed Dorian and Spartan precedent for his shaggy hairstyle. Not to mention effecting the complete restoration of Lycurgan discipline while visiting Sparta; or at least abolishing depilatories and persuading a descendant of Callicratidas, the hero of Xenophon and Ephorus, to give up the foreign trade that was getting him into trouble with the ephors. After all this, it is surprising to find an intelligent criticism of ancient Sparta for suppressing variety and competition put by his biographer into Apollonius' mouth.[1]

A fuller and to some extent a personal view of Sparta may be sought in those of Plutarch's *Lives* that deal with Spartans, and especially in that of Lycurgus. Plutarch more than once finds himself forced to blame his Spartans of the classical, and therefore perhaps already the degenerate, period for excessive harshness. But he is not anxious to believe Lycurgus responsible for the *crypteia*, *pace* Aristotle, or for the sort of treatment later meted out to the helots. The comparison with Numa shows that he really regretted the violence of Lycurgus' *coup d'état* too, like the tendency to the community of women, and the immodest nature of their education. But he likes to think of the lawgiver as founding the Olympic truce, as Aristotle believed he did; and of his people as rulers over a willing Hellas, crushing tyrannies and reconciling enemies 'often without moving a single shield'. From this school of decent and ordered private and public life other cities sought commanders and rulers; but Lycurgus was no imperialist. To Plutarch, as to Dio, he seemed a true philosopher, indeed the creator of the ideal state that Plato, Diogenes, and Zeno only wrote of.

The *Life* of Lycurgus is, as has been pointed out, in a sense also the last *Lacedaemonian Politeia* of antiquity, quoting or echoing the views of many writers and many periods. It does not only tell, though aware of its uncertainty, the story of Lycurgus as finally elaborated (his refusal to usurp the position of king from his infant nephew, his travels, his *coup*, his acquisition of Delphi's backing for his laws; then the brief revolt of the rich in which he lost an eye, and finally, after making the citizens swear to keep his laws till his return, his departure and his suicide). It also in-

---

[1] Philostratus, *Life of Apollonius* vi. 20; viii. 7; iv. 8, 27, 31–3. The inscriptions as we saw do suggest a new fever of Lycurgan enthusiasm in Sparta from the late first century.

cludes the fullest surviving account of the Lycurgan way of life. Plutarch, whose material mostly goes back to sources of the fourth and third centuries B.C., declares that the constitution was mixed, and stresses the part played by Lycurgus' newly created council, which acted as ballast to the ship or as a balance between kings and people. He thinks that the ephorate was introduced under Theopompus as a further curb on oligarchy (elsewhere Plutarch says it strengthened not democracy, but aristocracy, in Sparta). The equal division of land, the introduction of iron money, and the establishment of *syssitia* were aimed at eradicating envy and insolence, poverty and wealth, and leaving pre-eminence to virtue alone. (As the number of land-lots in his version is double the number proposed by King Agis for a Sparta deprived of Messenia, his sources would seem to include those popular in the revolutionary Sparta of the third century B.C.) There is no mention of any military origin or purpose for the *syssitia* or other features. Plutarch insists that, *pace* Aristotle again, Lycurgus did not neglect the women. Their physical education was regulated and by their public songs of mockery and praise they inspired the young men to valour (and marriage); their sentiments were modest and loftily patriotic. His account of the peculiar marriage institutions is admiring (dignified and decorous, while, at first at least, the rational lending about of wives for eugenic ends was destructive of base jealousy). So is that of the boys' training—and, brief and idealizing, of their relation to their lovers. And Spartan poetry and music are evoked especially as they appeared at the festivals (the three choirs of different ages are described). Everything, Plutarch believes, went well until Lysander, though himself uncorrupted, introduced wealth and the desire for it.

Together with the biographies of Agesilaus and Lysander, and of Agis and Cleomenes, this work was one of the chief sources of laconism for the Renaissance, when the *Parallel Lives* were the staple reading of schoolboys and statesmen. Plutarch's *Moralia*, too, a collection of essays much influenced by Stoic–Cynic ethical treatises, have many Spartan *exempla*; while the collections of Laconian apophthegms and political anecdotes included in it, which we have already met (they often come at least from the same sources Plutarch used), were also famous and influential in the fifteenth and sixteenth centuries and beyond.

On the whole there is very little that is not second-hand or superficial to be found in discussion of Sparta now, whether by those who claim to be philosophers or rhetoricians. The Greek literary renaissance of the period, the so-called Second Sophistic, brought with it much glorification of the great past. But Sparta was but one of many objects of interest; and indeed, in a primarily rhetorical and stylistically Atticizing movement Athens was bound to take pride of place. We have nothing to compare on Sparta's behalf with Aelius Aristides' *Panathenaicus*, an Isocratean panegyric of the mid second century. Rhetorical displays could be put nonetheless into Spartan mouths. Should Sparta be walled? Should the prisoners taken by the Athenians at Pylos be punished for cowardice on their return? Such questions were debated,[1] though rarely we may be sure with laconic brevity, or in a dialect considered not to be euphonious.[2] Leonidas and Othryadas cropped up, like the heroes of Marathon and Salamis, often enough to arouse the sarcasm of Lucian, who also mocked the flogging ceremony.[3] That, with the memory of *xenelasiae*, obviously took for this humane and cosmopolitan, if conventional, age the place of theft and homosexuality in the classical period as the most surprising and controversial facts about Sparta. But even they could be used for purely decorative purposes; a fictional love-letter will beg a lady not 'to laconize or imitate Lycurgus' by driving away a foreign suitor.[4]

Through the fourth century the sporadic references continue (and Libanius still went there to see 'the whips').[5] The emperor's position was by now almost as unlike that of the Augustan *princeps* as that of the Spartan king, but the latter might still be appealed to. Imperial panegyrics can set the virtuous concord of Maximian 'Herculius' and his colleague Diocletian above that of the royal pairs of descendants of Hercules in Sparta, or compare the hoped-for posterity of Constantine, who was also before his conversion under the patronage of Hercules, with the same Heraclid dynasty. But this is hardly what we have known as

[1] Philostratus, *Lives of the Sophists* 514, 528, 583.

[2] Pausanias iii. 15.2; it may be noted that the probably recent historical source he uses for this account of Laconia in his huge guide to Greece seems to have no political ideas, unless grouping events under reigns counts as one.

[3] Lucian, *Teacher of Rhetoric* 20, *Anacharsis* 920–1.

[4] Philostratus, *Love Letters* 28 (47).

[5] Libanius, *Orations* i. 23.

monarchic laconism.[1] The Emperor Julian himself, towards the
end of the fourth century, also strikes a new note in actually
complaining that, though the Spartans 'appear to have had the
best of governments, that of their kings', they neglected the
education of these kings, allowing it to be too familiar and
egalitarian; so that no wonder their subjects were sometimes
unruly. (The education of the kings at Carthage was worse.)[2]
But he praises his predecessor's Spartan austerity, though Cyrus
and Alexander are the monarchs he is particularly concerned to
see that he excels; and indeed in subsequent and probably more
sincere works, Julian, as we should expect of such a reactionary,
expresses very traditional views on the good king. And he
shocked his contemporaries by the extent to which he cut down
luxury and ceremony at court.

About 400 A.D. Synesius of Cyrene addressed a remarkably
frank treatise *On Kingship* to the feeble Emperor Arcadius. He
became persuaded, when in Constantinople as an envoy, that it
was unwise to hide an inaccessible emperor at the heart of a
formal and ceremonious court and to allow the empire to depend
on barbarian troops. And so, calling upon the names of Plato and
Aristotle, and on Roman tradition, he urges Arcadius to listen to
the promptings of philosophy; among other recommendations
he begs him to surround himself with friends, not flatterers, like
those most famous kings, Cyrus and Agesilaus, and to lead his
troops in person and share their deprivations, as some Roman
emperors have done. Was Agesilaus despised for acting thus?
Were kings in simple Laconian caps less fortunate than kings in
tragedy-robes? Barbarians, instead of doing the empire's fighting,
should till its soil, as the Messenians did for the Lacedaemonians—
or be banished beyond its frontiers.[3]

It was useless, as Gibbon remarked, for Synesius to 'address the
Emperor of the East in the language of Reason and Virtue which
he might have assumed to the Spartan monarch.' But Synesius
himself drew strength from the thought of Leonidas and his
own (supposed) Spartan forebears in the gallant struggle he
waged against the nomads ravaging Cyrenaica. Even though this
devoted pupil of Hypatia ultimately came to terms with Christian-

[1] *Panegyrici Latini* x. 94; iv. 36.　　　[2] Julian, *Orations* i. 13d, 16b.
[3] Synesius, *On Kingship*, esp. chs. 12, 16, 20, 26 (cf. 27, a Laconian apophthegm on war).

ity and indeed, though unwillingly, with a bishopric, he liked to claim that his ancient and noble family descended from Eurysthenes himself, who led the Dorians to Sparta (and sired one of the lines of kings). He also refers in his letters to the 'philosophic and Lacedaemonian' régime obtaining in his house—to the disgust of a slave, who ran away.[1] He makes an agreeable as well as significant figure to take farewell of as we leave the classical world.

[1] Synesius, *Letters* 57, § 197; 113; 144.

9

THE MIDDLE AGES

IT WAS inevitable that, given her place in Jewish apologetic literature and the Graeco-Roman ethical and rhetorical tradition, Sparta should occasionally attract the attention of the Fathers of the Church. During the great age of debate, when some Christians, in self-defence, were ready to assimilate a part of pagan culture, we find Tertullian describing Christian heroism as outdoing all precedents, including the Lacedaemonian endurance of *flagellatio*, and urging on the martyrs with the same examples. Here the famous and then still existing festival at Lacedaemon forms his climax: how slight such torments must be to those who will gain a divine reward, if they are so bravely borne for the sake of mere human glory![1]

The Christian writers of Alexandria, that centre of Greek scholarship and hellenizing Judaism, show their double ancestry clearly. St. Clement, accepting what is as we saw a Jewish thesis, like many others after him, not only supposes that Plato was following Moses in blaming Minos' and Lycurgus' concentration on physical courage, but also assumes that Moses was himself the archetype of all the Greek lawgivers. Clement regarded *exempla* as vital (for which reason he even approves of the Lacedaemonian way of teaching their children temperance by making their helots drunk). His works are full of classical learning. They remind his readers of how the Spartans excelled in simplicity and endurance, banished myrrh and purple dye, refused to allow respectable women to wear gold or flowered dresses (though in other passages he complains that their skirts were too short), and how it was not only Sparta that, as the oracle prophesied, love of riches would ruin. He contrasts the Spartan law, 'inscribed on the *scytalae* of the ephors', with the true, royal, living law, identical with reason.[2]

---

[1] Tertullian, *Apologeticus* 50; *ad Martyras* 4.
[2] Clement, *Stromateis* i. 25.151, 152; *Paedagogus* iii. 8; ii. 8.77; *Stromateis* i. 10.126; *Paedagogus* ii. 1088; *Stromateis* iv. 5.207; iii. 4.158.

Origen makes effective use of pagan precedent in the defence of the faith against Celsus. Do the Christians refuse to worship the emperor? Well, the Lacedaemonians refused to adore a human ruler, the Persian king (this has reference to a striking story in Herodotus), through fear of their sole lord, the law. Christian morality need not be seen as strange and repellent. Did not Lycurgus show wonderful forgiveness to the young man who knocked out his eye? Does not even the self-devotion of Socrates and Leonidas, who could have avoided their deaths, help one to understand that of Jesus?[1] But, says Origen, if the rewards awaiting the Christian are great, so is the penalty for backsliding. Punishments under the laws of Solon and Lycurgus were less harsh than those under the law of Moses, and what was breaking this last compared with neglecting the precepts of the Son of God? Opponents of the Christians, indeed, might use the same comparison for different purposes; the Emperor Julian, 'the Apostate', who argued that the 'Galilaeans' had adopted all the worst features of the Jewish creed, considered the God of the Old Testament shockingly cruel compared with Lycurgus, Solon, and the Romans—or the Spartan kings Agesilaus and Archidamus and other rulers. How superior to Moses our lawgivers are, he exclaimed.[2]

Against all their condescending approbation of Sparta the Christian apologists have not much to set in the way of outright condemnation. But her religion, of course, was indefensible. Eusebius once says there was human sacrifice there[3] (to the god of war). The whipping contests—in honour of a chaste and virgin goddess!—might make an example of scandalous pagan rites instead of admirable human fortitude; it is for such things as that, exclaimed St. Gregory of Nazianzus, that Julian despises the Christian martyrs.[4] Eusebius, following a Cynic source, pays some hostile attention to stories about oracles given to the Spartans, among other people; but here the gods' foolish and

---

[1] Origen, *Contra Celsum* viii. 6.747; 35.768; ii. 17.404. It is probable that some apocryphal Acts of St. Paul compared the self-sacrifice of the Athenian Codrus and the Spartan Lycurgus to Christ's; see John of Salisbury, *Policraticus* iv. 3, ed. C. C. I. Webb.

[2] *Apud* Cyril of Alexandria, *pro Christiana religione* 171d.

[3] Eusebius, *Praeparatio Evangelica* iv. 16.156 (from Apollodorus).

[4] Gregory Nazianzen, *Orationes* iv. 109; 134; *Poems* ii. 7.273–4 (cf. *Or.* xxxix. 679).

wicked advice comes out worse than do Lycurgus or his brave countrymen.[1]

In spite of Julian and those who sympathized with his attempted reaction, the fourth century saw the substantial triumph of Christianity. By now traditional philosophy and rhetoric were an accepted part of a full Christian education. Flippant references to Sparta can decorate the letters of Procopius of Gaza, a distinguished Christian sophist in the fifth century, just as they did those of his pagan predecessors. But the rise of the monastic movement, which was in some respects similar to and indeed under the influence of pagan, especially Cynic, asceticism, helped ensure that Sparta was usually depicted as even more puritanical than before. Thus St. Isidore Pelusiota (another Alexandrian by birth) ends with Lycurgus his list of pagan ascetics suspicious of the use of money; and like Clement mentions his restrictions on feminine elegance. He also repeats a Spartan proverb about the congruence of deeds and words or practising what you preach.[2] And it is even possible for communities of monks to be urged to copy those of the Greeks who live and eat in common—presumably in the first place the Spartans and Cretans.

But the Church, even in the eastern empire, was to turn away from classical learning (and especially from Plato), while the eastern empire prided itself on being Roman rather than Greek. The word Hellene came exclusively to mean, as it did in the Jewish tradition, pagan. Meanwhile, the cities of Greece proper had lost the last remnants of self-government and fallen into decay. Already in about 400 Synesius had complained that Athens was now better known for honey than philosophy, more than a century before Justinian shut the Academy or Paulus Silentiarius congratulated himself that his poem about S. Sophia would be judged by the learned and pious inhabitants of Constantinople, not by bean-eating Athenians.[3] As for Sparta, in 395 she was sacked by Alaric and his Goths, and afterwards little is heard of her. In the Slav invasions of the seventh and eighth centuries, most of Greece was temporarily lost to imperial control, and afterwards it appears that Sparta had to be rebuilt and re-settled, while in the tenth century the people of the surrounding country-side had to be evangelized by St. Nicon—especially the Maniotes,

---

[1] Eusebius, loc. cit. v. 24.218–28.233 (from Oenomaus, second century).
[2] Isidore Pelusiota, *Epistulae* ii. 146; v. 200; iii. 232.   [3] i.e. neo-Platonists.

even though they were probably not Slavs but descendants of the original population. Happy Lacedaemon, said his biographer some two centuries later, to find such a patron and be formed to virtue by more certain precepts and discipline than the vain laws of Lycurgus of old![1]

Though Greece was to remain a comparatively backward part of the empire, yet, as this comparison suggests, attitudes were changing again. It is true that, unless in the worst period of the Arab and Slav invasions, some knowledge of, and a tendency to excerpt and even imitate, Greek literature had persisted in Constantinople. The eleventh century, however, also saw a brief Platonic revival, and a beginning of laments on the fallen state of the ancient cities; in the twelfth a deeply disappointed metropolitan of Athens deplores the fact that her inhabitants are so changed that they cannot even understand his sermons, and the last age of Byzantine civilization, after the Fourth Crusade and the partial repulsion of the Latin invaders, saw further growth of an interest in the Greek past. The word Hellene was rehabilitated, and used by historians for the people of the empire, now reduced more or less to the historic areas of Greek settlement. While early chronographers (in Greek or Latin) had retained little Spartan history but a list of kings (of only one dynasty and truncated at an early point), and while even in the twelfth century Zonaras, though a close excerptor of classical historians, is only interested in the Spartans for their relationship to Jews and Romans, fourteenth-century historians in contrast often delight in references and comparisons, not always significant or accurate, to antiquity. Thus Nicephorus Gregoras is well aware of Lycurgus and Agesilaus as great men and statesmen, and can refer to the Spartan defeats at Haliartus and Leuctra.[2] Writers also had a

[1] *Life of St. Nicon* 130 (Sp. Lampros, Νέος Ἑλληνομνήμων iii, pp. 129 ff.). The Maniotes, in the mountainous peninsula of Taenarum or Cape Matapan, according to Constantine Porphyrogenitus (*de Imperio administrando* 50) in the tenth century; and the Tzacones, in the hills of eastern Laconia, according to the Chronicle of Monemvasia (ed. T. and K. Bees, pp. 64-5, i, p. 65), perhaps from a source of similar date; were ancient Laconians who had taken refuge in these fastnesses. The problem has been much discussed in modern times.

[2] Nicephorus Gregoras, *Historia Byzantina* x. 4.4 His correspondence (ed. R. Guilland) is studded with elegant classical references, like the rhetorical correspondence of late antiquity. E.g. no. 18, to the Great Domestic: please forgive the philosopher Joseph for appearing improperly clad—he was imitating the Spartans and their Gymnopaedia.

I

confusing habit of referring to modern towns by the name of their nearest ancient neighbour, and Mistra, newly founded on a foothill of Mt. Taygetus, is often called Sparta or Lacedaemon.

Serious analysis of the Spartan way of life is much less easy to find. But the great minister Theodore Metochites, meditating on political and other matters in the light vouchsafed by Thucydides, Plato, and Aristotle among other ancient authors, considers Athens and Sparta in some detail; especially the latter.[1] She seemed to him to be an aristocracy—a term that he does not distinguish very clearly from oligarchy. Though well aware of the praise she received and deserved, he is also aware of criticisms. He himself understandably prefers kingship (aided by wise councillors) to aristocracy; he is not tempted to make Sparta an example of the former. To democracy he is totally unsympathetic, and compares the disorders in Athens with those of another naval state, Genoa. Not wholly dissimilar is the language in one passage of Nicephorus Gregoras: speaking of Thessalonica during the rule of the Zealots, whom he considered a disreputable mob, and complaining that their constitution followed no respectable model at all, he explains that it was neither an aristocracy like that set up by Lycurgus, nor a democracy like that of Athens, nor anything else; not even a mixture such as the Cypriots (this must be a slip) or the Romans had.[2] (A Thessalonican historian, however, put his own city above Plato's *Republic* for equality and justice and above Athens for classical learning.)

Hitherto all these ancient states had appeared equally remote and alien. But Mistra, originally a Frankish stronghold, was reoccupied by the Byzantines in 1262 and from 1348 was the capital of the Despot of the Morea, who was often the heir to the imperial throne and in practice a fairly independent prince. Athens, meanwhile, was still in foreign hands, as were Thebes and other towns. No wonder then that the past history of the Peloponnese seemed to belong rather specially to the last Byzantine Greeks. In the fourteenth century the Emperor John Cantacuzene complained that the Peloponnesians neglected all the laws of Lycurgus, though they did observe one of Solon's—that

---

[1] Theodore Metochites, *Miscellanea*, chs. 99–100. Cf. 96–8 on the three forms of government and 103 on Carthage: the Carthaginian character, especially in war, is half-way between the Athenian and Spartan.

[2] Nicephorus Gregoras, op. cit. xv. 1.2.

of punishing any citizen who tried to keep aloof from the factions that rent the country.[1] His son Matthew, however, who at the end of his life was Despot of the Morea, was congratulated by the rhetor Demetrius Cydones on his victories over the barbarians and on the prosperity of Laconia, now governed by laws wiser and better than those of Lycurgus. The same writer attempts to inspire the next Despot Theodore Palaeologus with the thought of Sparta and Lycurgus: let him remember that he is ruling over the land of men who excelled in virtue, whose contempt of luxury and pleasure gave them command over all the Greeks. He complained that a letter from Theodore did show laconic brevity (so did those of a lot of Demetrius' other correspondents; it was a stock reproach among epistolographers of late antiquity), but not sufficient laconic obstinacy. Demetrius, a little earlier, also reproached one 'George the philosopher' for leaving his friends and settling in the Morea: he was told not to mistake the shadow of the Peloponnese for the Islands of the Blest. The cities, laws, and virtues of the Lacedaemonians were all gone, yet the philosopher, in his exaggerated love for all things Greek, was supposing that by the very sight of the soil he could call up Lycurgus, so as to converse with him and hear him dispensing his wise laws.[2]

All this is rhetoric; we cannot be sure what the philosopher George really felt about the Morea. But it was a place where classical studies were prosecuted, and of a later and greater philosopher George we know more. The great Platonist George Gemistus, also called Plethon, spent most of his life in Mistra (his views having made him understandably suspect to the Church in Constantinople) and even held high office there. Among his earliest works are two pamphlets, addressed one to the emperor Manuel Palaeologus in about 1418 and one to his son the young Despot Theodore.[3] In these, believing like the ancients that political success depends on political institutions, he advocates reforms that are markedly Platonic and Lycurgan in effect, if immediate in origin. The despotate, in spite of its indubitable vitality, faced a grave situation. Against external, especially increasing Turkish, pressure was arrayed a population highly

---

[1] John Cantacuzene, *Historiae* iv. 13.
[2] Demetrius Cydones, *Correspondence*, ed. Loenertz, no. 241, 251, 322, 32.
[3] A. Ellissen, *Analekten* iv. 2.

various in origin, oppressed by an extravagant and uncontrollable nobility, and burdened by unfair taxation. Plethon, who naturally accepts monarchy as the best of the forms of government (a king, assisted by skilled councillors, should rule and carry out the law) is chiefly alarmed by the fact that the peasantry, of whom the army now consists, make poor and unwilling soldiers. But mercenaries would be worse. The three classes making up a state should therefore be strictly divided. Those who protect or guard the state—soldiers and administrators—should be forbidden to trade or work the land, and these other two classes should also be kept distinct (though in some places, where large numbers of the population seem fit for military service, these should be called up in rotation). A third of the produce should go to the labourer, a third to the provider of his tools or means of work, a third to the state. In some districts a number of the farmers may be assigned to each member of the first class to pay their dues in kind directly to him. Inevitably these recall the helots, and Plethon would call them so, though insisting that they must be respected and protected from ill-usage. He also recalls the old reputation of the Peloponnese for economic self-sufficiency and urges a reduction in external trade and even the use of money (the currency was in a bad way at the time). He points out, too, that Byzantium itself was originally founded by Dorians,[1] while its second founders the Romans were actually themselves, through the Sabines, of Lacedaemonian as well as Trojan descent. In such words his enthusiasm for his adopted country, inhabited, as he holds, by the purest and most famous of all Greek peoples is made evident. In the letter to Theodore, Plethon also gives a reminder that a ruler should live simply, and betrays a prejudice nourished on ancient history against sea-power. And in the sketch of world history designed to prove that conquering races have always owed their power to good institutions, he gives due place to Sparta, while she obeyed the laws of Lycurgus, and omits Athens.

The references to Sparta in all this are much more than mere literary trimmings, as is borne out by the fragments of Plethon's vast treatise, the *Laws*, which undoubtedly embodied his deepest convictions. The *Laws* was burnt by Plethon's orthodox opponents after his death, and the part dealing with political questions is entirely lost. But the table of contents, usually thought to be the

[1] Megarians or Argives according to legend.

author's own, promises a constitution 'Spartan, but without the excessive severities that the majority of people are unwilling to accept' and with the philosophic education 'which is the principal virtue of Plato's rulers'.[1]

Plethon's suggested reforms for the Morea were taken up again by his pupil Bessarion, who, after he had become a cardinal of the Roman Church, wrote to Constantine Palaeologus, the last emperor of the east, then still Despot, about the affairs of the region.[2] Bessarion accepts his master's threefold class structure and, though himself anxious to revive certain arts and crafts, his opposition to luxury and trade. Remember Lycurgus' regulations about money, he says, and how the Lacedaemonians were successful as long as they did without it. He recalls the Hellenic heritage of the country; its people, given liberty and arms, will recover their ancient virtues as well. Let Constantine remember that he is ruling over Peloponnesians, and above all Lacedaemonians, who, disciplined from childhood by the institutions of Lycurgus, threw back the Persians at Plataea and later achieved the invasion of Asia. It will be his part to give his subjects rules of life and thus restore *eunomia* and the Spartan *politeia* and prove himself a true philosopher–king. Then he too will deliver Europe from the barbarian, and like his forerunners cross into Asia.

The Lacedaemon of Plethon and Bessarion was to remain a mirage. Most writers of the time, Italian now as well as Greek, confine themselves to lamenting the degeneracy of the country. When Ciriaco d'Ancona in 1447 came for the second time to Mistra, to visit Plethon and the antiquities of the neighbourhood, he found the ruin of its virtues even sadder than that of its cities—though he did meet one young man who had killed a boar and whose character and appearance made him trust that nature could still produce a Spartiate. As he approached the city, recal-

---

[1] Plethon, *Traité des Lois*, ed. C. Alexandre, p. 2. πολιτείαν δὲ Λακωνικὴν, ἀφῃρημένου μὲν αὐτῆς τοῦ ἄγαν τῆς σκληραγωγίας . . . προστιθεμένης δὲ τῆς ἐν τοῖς ἄρχουσι μάλιστα φιλοσοφίας. The brief history of Greece from the Theban to the Macedonian victories which Plethon put together largely from Plutarch and Diodorus gives rather more than their due share to the last campaigns of Agesilaus, other operations involving Sparta, and the events in Sicily with which Plato was concerned, including Dion's attempt to introduce 'Spartan kingship instead of monarchy' (*Hellenica* i. 22).

[2] Sp. Lampros, Νέος Ἑλληνομνήμων iii. 12.

ling her old pre-eminence in virtue and war, Calliope, as he explains, inspired him to verse:

> Alma Città Laconica Spartana,
>> Gloria di Greçia già, del mondo exemplo,
>> d'arme e di Castità Gymnasio e templo
>> E d'ogni alma virtu Specchio e fontana,
> Se politia, costumi e Legge humana
>> con l'altre tue moral Virtu contemplo
>> Poi te remiro,

then where, he is impelled to cry, is 'el tuo bon Lycurgo', where are the Dioscuri, Leonidas, Agesilaus, and a whole list of other Spartan warriors? Poor Constantine, though Ciriaco does call him *rex Spartanus*, would seem to come badly out of the comparison.[1] (The ode was soon translated into Greek, possibly by Plethon himself.)

And yet many of its inhabitants seem to have felt great loyalty to what was soon only the shadow of the shadow of the Peloponnese. The Turkish conquest scattered them over the Mediterranean, to earn a livelihood as teachers and copyists, or—the old trade of the dispossessed Spartiate—as mercenary soldiers. In contemporary accounts, on their tombstones, in the manuscripts they copied, they assume the proud name of Spartiates; which no doubt also recommended them to the humanists of Italy who often supported and employed them.[2] The Venetians meanwhile continued to instigate resistance in the Morea. And so contemporary events, as they were so signally to do two hundred years later, perhaps encouraged Western Europe to see the Spartans as the truest embodiment of Greek patriotism in the struggle against the east. (Already in the fourteenth century a proposed crusade had made Petrarch think of

> le mortali strette,
> Che difese il Leon con poca gente.)[3]

---

[1] For Ciriaco's full account, see R. Sabbadini's edition in *Miscellanea Ceriani* (1910), pp. 183 ff., or in *Saggi e Testi Umanistici* (1933), pp. 1 ff.

[2] For example it must be his memory of Spartan patriotism and even more of Tyrtaeus that makes Sannazaro write of 'Spartani musa Marulli' (*Elegies* ii. 2), though in fact Marullus, the Greek soldier and Latin poet who wrote such touching poems of exile, had no connection with Sparta and only a remote one with the Peloponnese.

[3] Petrarch, *Rime* xxviii. 100–1.

We must now retrace our steps for over a millennium. Sparta's appearances were understandably rarer among the Latin Fathers of the fourth and fifth centuries than among their Greek counterparts. St. Augustine's only reference is in a letter to a young man who is having trouble with a worldly mother; he regrets that she does not even resemble the Lacedaemonian mothers, who urged their sons on to fight for a country merely upon this earth.[1] St. Jerome speaks approvingly of Spartan *mensa frugalitasque*, and includes among pagan instances of respect for virginity some Spartan girls protected from dishonour by the leader of their Messenian captors.[2] Two Christian but secular works were of more significance. In the late fourth century the military writer Vegetius re-evoked Sparta's reputation in martial science, and contrasted her exclusive devotion to this with the Athenian dedication to letters;[3] and in the sixth century the two cities were contrasted again, this time by a great legal authority. Justinian's *Institutes* explained that civil law is of two kinds, written and unwritten, and is derived from two sources, the laws of Athens and Lacedaemon. The Athenians kept to what they found written down in their laws; what had the force of law to the Lacedaemonians was entrusted to memory.[4]

Law, warfare, and good morality therefore. But ideas of Greek history were becoming confused. Augustine's pupil Orosius made Byzantium a Spartan foundation, through mistaking the nature of the regent Pausanias' activity there.[5] In the sixth century Gregory of Tours produced a Lacedaemonian king, contemporary with Solomon, owning the impossible name of Festus;[6] he must come ultimately from the world chronicles, which preserve the names of a few important figures from Spartan history, including Lycurgus. (To other writers Menelaus might be the only Spartan king worth mentioning.) And even Isidore of Seville, whose *Etymologies*, written in the early seventh century, were long a quarry for knowledge of antiquity, does little for Sparta but include Lycurgus among lawgivers; an interpolator retailing the

---

[1] Augustine, *Epistulae* ccxliii. 6.
[2] Jerome, *Adversus Jovinianum* ii. 13; i. 41.
[3] Vegetius, *Epitoma Rei Militaris* iii, praef.
[4] Justinian, *Institutes* i. 2.10.
[5] Orosius, *Historia contra Paganos* iii. 13.
[6] Gregory of Tours, *Historia Francorum* i. 17.

ancient but heterodox identification of the Spartani with Cadmus' Sparti or Sown Men, sprung of the dragon's teeth, himself sows error.[1] (Athens did a little better, owing partly to her reputation for philosophy, St. Paul's visit, and the identification by the French of St. Denis with Dionysius the Areopagite, which gave them an appetite for fancy pictures of his home town.)

Even when the level of learning rose again there was little knowledge of Greek history, or feeling that it provided any sort of authority comparable to biblical or even Roman history (though Alexander provided something of an exception). And political thought, dominated by the belief that the ruler and his sanctions had only been made necessary by man's sin, did little but insist on the need for personal, and basically religious, virtues in both ruler and subjects. Thus still the *Policraticus* of John of Salisbury, one of the most learned men of the twelfth century and representative of a movement that has been called humanistic. He does fill his work with classical reminiscences, among them anecdotes and apophthegms of 'Ligurgus' (as he was often spelt) and other Spartans, from a variety, of course of exclusively Latin sources, some of which are now lost. But they simply illustrate such points as the ruler's duty to be economical, love his subjects, keep firm discipline, and so on. Where John does adumbrate some general idea, about the supremacy of a higher law or the right of tyrannicide (most personal of remedies for misgovernment), Sparta is not mentioned; indeed, later antiquity had detached her from serious political considerations.[2]

In the thirteenth century interest in philosophy, and especially the recently recovered Aristotle, largely overcame this promise of a new awareness of ancient history and literature. But it did mean the rapid development and partial emancipation of political thought, to fit the reality of a period in which urban and economic life were rapidly advancing. The *Politics* were not only read, they

[1] Isidore of Seville, *Etymologiae* ix. 2.2.

[2] John of Salisbury, *Policraticus* i. 5; iv. 3, 4, 5; vi. 11, 12, 14, 19; vii. 4, 24; viii. 2, 9, 10. In these passages John repeatedly quotes Valerius Maximus and Justin, and, for military matters Frontinus' *Stratagemata* and Vegetius. But no ancient source survives for the story of 'Caristolus', or of Chilon refusing to make an alliance with the dice-playing Corinthians (cf. hence, Chaucer's *Pardoner's Tale* 603 ff.); see also above, p. 117 n.1. One notes that the Spartans still are founders of Byzantium—almost their main claim to fame—and Hannibal's *doctor armorum* in Vegetius has grown to be *ductor armorum*.

were to a considerable extent understood. But historical interest in the states discussed in them was not much stimulated. Indeed these gave William of Moerbeke, who made the first translation in about 1260, considerable trouble. He does seem to have recognized, in the course of Book II, that his 'Lacosenses', Aristotle's *Lakones*, were identical with his *Lakedaemonioi* and with Spartans too; but neither he nor for a long time his readers grasped that the *Karchedonioi* were the familiar Carthaginians, and had nothing to do with Calchedon, where the Council of the Church had been held. And William's vague and inaccurate language was responsible for a persistent impression that Sparta's slaves were unruly because they were treated too gently, and that she not only had the normal number of kings (one), but had the right to elect as well as depose him.[1] (The chronicles, it will be remembered, had found one list of kings sufficient for dating purposes.)

The first commentaries on the *Politics* came rapidly, from Albertus Magnus and Thomas Aquinas. The former's treatment of Greek history and language was particularly cavalier. Both took Aristotle's reference to those who saw Sparta as a mixed state of three elements very seriously and imported it into their account of the chapters dealing with her. St. Thomas indeed ultimately stated in the *Summa*[2] that this was the best form of state; it may be recalled that while monarchy was usual in his world, absolutism was still foreign to its temper. For him, while one king is essential, two are very bad; and democracy only means that the aristocratic element in the *politia* is chosen from and by the whole people. It is the government of the Jews, before the time of the kings, that he is interested in showing to be an example of such a *politia*. Outside the commentary on the *Politics*, his references to Greek cities are few. But the Greek terminology and Greek ideas that, however adapted, got through him and others into the west European bloodstream obviously facilitated the later revival of interest and admiration.

Thomas' pupil Ptolemy of Lucca, who was responsible for completing the work known as *De Regimine Principum*, does however discuss the ancient states at some length, with the aid of

---

[1] Aristotle, *Politics*, ed. Susemihl, Book ii *passim*.
[2] St. Thomas Aquinas, *In libros Politicorum Aristotelis expositio*, esp. *lectio* xiii and xiv; *Summa Theologica* ii. 1.105.

Justin as well as the Latin Aristotle. He distinguishes between monarchic and 'political' or republican régimes, and sees that the latter appear in cities, as in Greece once and in his own Italy. Lacedaemon he analyses rather interestingly as a kingdom except as regards the capital, which is a *politia*; there are parallels to this in northern Europe. But he gives chief place to Aristotle's criticisms, some of them inevitably misunderstood. He regards the inadequacy of Spartan courage as meaning they were unwilling to die for their country; he deprecates the supposed popular election and deposition of the kings—all right for a 'political' leader, but not for a king, whom he had defined as hereditary and, in contrast with the former, above the law. He is also exceedingly severe on the luxury of the Spartan women, backing his disapproval up with quotations from the Bible and the Fathers.[1]

Ptolemy saw that Sparta resembled certain modern states; he did not hold her up as an example for his age. But if other writers discuss the Greek states of Aristotle more sporadically, they do also begin to show a pattern in their approval and reprobation. Most interesting as regards Sparta is the gradual emergence of King Theopompus. Aegidius Romanus (Colonna) was a papalist and one who preferred monarchy to other political forms. Discussing the qualities of the true king as opposed to the tyrant, and reposing on the ambiguity of the translation before him, he evokes the *rex quidam* who, according to the philosopher, with remarkable justice and modesty gave up a part of his kingdom (*not*, we note, of his powers) because it had been unjustly acquired, and told his wife that thus, though smaller, it would be longer-lasting. (He also approved the Spartans' generosity with private property, but followed the *Ethics* in reproving their affected humility of dress.)[2]

Marsilius of Padua, on the other hand, notoriously took up an extreme Ghibelline position and opposed all ecclesiastical interference with the state. Book I at least of the *Defensor Pacis* is also thoroughly imbued with a republican, Paduan spirit. A more or less popular legislature and an elected prince or board of magistrates, subject to positive not merely natural law and to popular

---

[1] Thomas Aquinas, *De regimine principum* ii. 13, iv. 9 and 14 ff. Ptolemy also used Vegetius, also quoted by St. Thomas as supporting evidence for the Lacedaemonians' exclusive interest in war.

[2] Aegidius Romanus, *De regimine principum* iii. 1.2; i. 2.26; iii. 2.9 ('decet verum regem per usurpationem et iniustitiam non dilatare suum dominium').

correction, constitute not simply a possible, but the only legitimate form of government. And so he treats to a regular eulogy 'a certain very prudent King Theopompus', who set up ephors (a fact Aegidius failed to mention) and thus lessened his own powers. What unique and admirable virtue, almost unheard of in any other man throughout the centuries! Having repeated the king's remark to his wife, he comments 'O vox heroica, ex inaudita prudentia Theopompi procedens': to be noted by all rulers desirous of exercising absolute power over their subjects. This may well be a cause of their fall as recent events (in France) have shown. (Later, discussing the damage bad priests do to the state, he declares they are frequently responsible for the corruption of women, which, as Aristotle explained with reference to Lacedaemon, is a serious matter.)[1] Theopompus, correctly interpreted, is henceforth a fairly familiar figure—to be met with, for example, in the work of Gerson, the great conciliar theorist who would extend the concept of the mixed constitution to the Church itself, and agreed that the king's authority derived from the community and ought to be restricted so as to avoid tyranny.[2]

Other aspects of Sparta, such as state control over education or marriage, were still inconceivable, and outside political theory she arouses little interest. In that fantastic ancient Greece, for example, peopled by dukes and knights, of which late medieval storytellers and poets have much to say, Athens, Thebes, and Corinth all appear on the map. But not Sparta—partly because she had been so briefly under Latin rule in the thirteenth century? On one occasion she even loses Helen, who is described in a Catalan chronicle as wife to the duke of Athens.[3] And an English poet, telling early in the fifteenth century what is recognizably the story of Lycurgus' end (and that in a political context), merely remarks 'ther was a knyght, I not what men hym call . . .'.[4]

---

[1] Marsilius of Padua, *Defensor Pacis* i. 11.8; ii. 17.12.
[2] Gerson, *Sermo ad Regem Franciae nomine Universitatis Parisiensis. Opera* (ed. 1606) iv, col. 802.
[3] Ramòn Muntaner, *Cronica*, ch. 214.
[4] T. Hoccleve, *The Regement of Princes*, l. 2950 (on the enforcement of law).

10

SPARTA REDIVIVA

IT IS not possible to recount here in any detail the well-known history of the recovery and diffusion of the main works of Greek literature; nor, clearly, to consider all Sparta's appearances in Renaissance writings, which would require profound knowledge of the period. It must suffice to indicate the main features of the interest she aroused, quoting some of the most famous (and often, in this respect, typical rather than original) works of the time, before turning to concentrate on certain specific political themes.

It is obvious that the Renaissance was fated to admire Sparta. Great though the authority of Plato, or the popularity of Xenophon, might be, this admiration was nourished above all on Plutarch. The *Lives* were translated soon and often, forming as they did the best full-length studies of ancient virtue, and among the Greek subjects—even if these tended to take second place to the Roman—Agesilaus, Lycurgus, Lysander, and Agis and Cleomenes were not the least known. The *Moralia* were considered a storehouse of ancient wisdom: for example, the work on education was hardly less influential in this field than were Cicero's and Quintilian's writings on the training of an orator; while the collections of apophthegms were held to possess remarkable educational qualities both in style and content. They were several times translated into Latin (first by Filelfo), usually in combination with sayings from other sources, especially *dicta philosophorum*, and, during the sixteenth century, of modern heroes too. In Erasmus' huge collection the laconic apophthegms fill the first quarter of the book. What more suitable work, he asked, to dedicate to a prince, who has little time for reading, and especially to a young one (he also thought the *Lives* and *Moralia* had a vital part to play in such a youth's education)? In the same way Henri Etienne, publishing an edition of apophthegms from Plutarch and Diogenes Laertius with facing Greek and Latin, regarded them as ideal both for students and busy statesmen. These were indeed the two groups thought to have most to learn from Sparta.

The humanistic ideal of education was of course far wider and deeper than that of Sparta. It showed little disposition to force all its subjects into a single mould or, at least in its best days, to use excessive severity. But in so far as its end was the formation of the whole man, in his moral and physical aspects as well as his intellectual, and this man was expected, now that the active as opposed to the contemplative life was again admired, to use his superior qualities in public life, it is understandable that a few references to Sparta should constantly recur in support of certain points.

Treatises on the ideal ruler were traditionally largely moral in content; they now lay more stress on education than ever. Indeed, no hard and fast line can be drawn between books on the training of a prince and of a gentleman. The most distinguished educationalists were often tutors of princes; the perfect prince, with his unparalleled opportunities for showing the virtues of liberality, benevolence, and so on, was also the perfect man. Thus a 'Mirror for Princes' was worth study by all aspirants to excellence as well as to any degree of responsibility. Furthermore, it was the ruler's duty to encourage right education in his realm; another reason, sometimes, for discussion of the subject in such works.

Above all, of course, Sparta proved the immense power of education for good or ill; exemplified in the story of Lycurgus and the two dogs, taken over from Plutarch's *de educandis liberis*.[1] As a demonstration to his countrymen the lawgiver, having trained two dogs on opposite lines, loosed them together with a hare in the assembly. One chased it energetically, the other turned lazily aside to a plate of food. After numerous literary appearances, the scene is engraved as an 'Educationis et consuetudinis typus' in one of the most famous emblem books of the early seventeenth century.[2]

The formation of the good man begins even before his birth; and this, too, had been understood in Sparta. In particular, a story that was to develop a political bearing might be invoked: that of Agesilaus, who, himself being small and lame, was rebuked by the

---

[1] Plutarch, *Moralia: de educandis liberis* 4. (See also *Apophthegmata Laconica*, 225f. in two versions; in the more extreme, the dog trained to hunt was a lapdog by nature.)

[2] Otho Vaenius, *Emblemata Horatiana* (1607), p. 57. As the German version of the accompanying verses puts it:

> Lycurgus weiset uns durch seine Hünde an
> Wie leicht sich die Natur ohn Zucht verderben kann.

ephors for taking a dwarfish wife likely to bear him 'not kings
but kinglets'. The reputation of Spartan nurses was recalled; and
a tendency to dispense with the mother's superintendence when her
son is six or seven may be strengthened by the thought of Sparta—
though education, especially in the sixteenth century and in the
north, often remains rooted in the home, as it was not to do at a
later period that also turned to Sparta for support.

The main lesson that Sparta had to teach was expounded in the
first truly Renaissance treatise on education, and one of the most
widely read. Vergerio, discussing the pupils, in particular the
scions of princely houses, who will combine the practice of arms
and letters, praises both the Cretans and more especially the
Lacedaemonians, as authorities on education, for training the
young from their first years to courage and endurance.[1] Even
mothers inculcated these. Subsequent generations are constantly,
if often rather more casually, urged on by the Spartan example to
exercise and privation. It was pointed out (from Justin, as much
as from Greek sources) that the Spartans thought children should
lead a country life; that they gave them simple clothes and plain
and barely sufficient food; and that they regarded hunting as a
manly and toughening sport. One author recommends, in verse,
the growing prince to take cold baths:

> frigoraque innocuis pati Spartana lavacri
> artubus,[2]

and a dip in the December Eurotas. Naturally enough, the teaching of theft is ignored; and Vergerio is one of the few even to
mention the savage whipping contests.

The Spartans were also commended for providing for cheerful
relaxation, jokes, and laughter; and at the same time for abhorr-
ing drunkenness (and dicing, as Platina and Sir Thomas Elyot,
drawing on the story in John of Salisbury, remind us).[3] Vergerio,
like others, recalls the story of Spartan boys being shown drunken
helots, but he at least hastens to point out with unclassical sensi-

---

[1] P. P. Vergerio, *De ingenuis moribus* (finished by 1402).

[2] M. Marullus, *Institutiones Principales* 15; ii. 138–9, 624.

[3] B. Platina, *Principis* Διατύπωσις (ded. to F. Gonzaga in 1471). Sir Thomas
Elyot, *The Boke named the Governour* (1531) i. 26. (there are other, sometimes
rather confused, sixteenth-century references to this). See also i. 10, 20; ii. 9;
iii. 3, 7, 14, 22.

bility that while it is good to know what to avoid, the vices and misfortunes of others must not be laughed at. Truthfulness and taciturnity were accepted as Spartan virtues especially worthy of youthful emulation (perhaps we should not pass over the frequently quoted maxims ascribed to Chilon, a Lacedaemonian as well as one of the Seven Sages, particularly those on controlling the tongue and the gestures). So, above all, was reverence for elders (taken over by Rome from this source). The Spartan ambassadors who, alone among the spectators in the Athenian theatre, rose to make room for an old man are trotted out *ad* (one would suppose) *nauseam*.

But there was certainly no desire to neglect the mind, and this means that any promising features in Sparta are picked out, while the rest are usually passed over. For a moment a dim phantasm of that forgotten early Sparta, devoted to music and poetry, rises before us. Leonidas' approval of Tyrtaeus' patriotic songs (as asserted by Plutarch's Cleomenes) recommends the learning by heart of poetry as an incentive to noble deeds. Some humanists were rather doubtful of the place of music in education; many are encouraged not only by the views of Plato and Aristotle, but by Lycurgus' belief that, far from being effeminate, it had a place in military training and even in war itself, and they recall the strict censorship it was found possible to exercise there (panegyrists of music, of whom there were many in the later Renaissance, confine themselves to Spartan enthusiasm and omit Spartan suspicion concerning it). On dancing, opinions differed sharply; some educationalists like the learned and pious Maffeo Vegio[1] in the earlier part of the fifteenth century, or, later, the Calvinists, reject it as immoral in spite of Lycurgus. Others accept it, sometimes under Spartan-type safeguards. Finally, Lycurgus' experiences (like those of Ulysses), rather than his laws, may be used to show the educational value of travel for budding statesmen.

Rarely do we hear of Sparta the foe of the intellect (though Platina preferred Roman education for that reason); but in the sixteenth century, when the new education had sometimes become rigid and narrow (and when, also, paradoxical literary exercises were popular), attacks on learning might be made,

---

[1] Mapheus Vegius, *De educatione liberorum.* Lucian, *De saltatione* 10 had appealed to Spartan precedent (of the mythical period).

either in the name of religion or of practical effectiveness.[1] Or even, as by Montaigne in his essay *Du Pedantisme*, in that of nature:[2] 'c'est chose digne de très-grande consideration que, en cette excellente police de Licurgus, et à la verité monstrueuse par sa perfection, si soigneuse pourtant de la nourriture des enfants comme de sa principale charge, et au giste même des Muses, il s'y fasse si peu de mention de la doctrine.' Spartan children learnt *à bien faire*, and a Stoic courage before fate. Praise of the virile but unintellectual Tamberlaine suggests that we need a pinch of salt.

If we pursue the prince into adult life and full responsibility, we find that the Roman emperors and generals remain, as they had been in the Middle Ages, his prime models, together with Alexander and, now, Cyrus of Persia. But several Spartans may now join the supporting cast, and Spartan kings be praised in general terms, for warlike interests and devotion to duty in particular. Among the numerous laconic apophthegms repeated for the ruler's benefit one of the commonest is that of the Spartan rebuking Alexander for incurring useless danger (by fighting a lion). Lycurgus, who having been regent for his nephew qualified as a ruler and appears as such in the *Apophthegmata*, shows temperance (of course) and benevolence, a stock royal virtue, by forgiving the man who put out his eye; he also sets an example to his subjects by demanding nothing from them, in his laws, that he was not himself willing to give; thus the influential *De regno* of Francesco Patrizi in the late fifteenth century[3] (a work stuffed with classical *exempla*), which held that the prince should obey his own laws simply as a precedent. The constitutional associations of Theopompus might have appeared a little dubious; but Plutarch had drawn the teeth of his most famous saying by interpreting it to mean only that the king should subordinate himself

---

[1] See especially Cornelius Agrippa, *De vanitate scientiarum* (1531). As an English instance, we may perhaps quote Fulke Greville, *A Treatise of Humane Learning* xlii:

> For which respects, Learning hath found distaste,
> In Governments, of great and glorious fame;
> In Lacedemon scorned and disgrac'd
> As idle, vain, effeminate and lame.
> > Engins that did unman the mindes of men
> > From action, to seek glory in a den.

[2] M. de Montaigne, *Essais* i. 25.

[3] F. Patrizi, *De regno et regis institutione* (1518, written in the 1480s). It was a chief source for Elyot's *Governour* (not a king but a member of the governing class). See for Spartan references esp. ii. 1, 3, 11; vi. 6; viii. 10, 20; ix. 1.

to virtue, and in this sense Erasmus can refer to it as a much-praised remark. There was nothing against a rival recipe for stability ascribed to Theopompus: that princes should cultivate their friends and protect their subjects; or against his advice that citizens should be obedient. Similarly, King Agesicles of Sparta (who might understandably be confused with King Agesilaus) said that the king who rules without guards can rule as a father.

The arrogant and deceitful Lysander can for the most part figure only as a dreadful warning (under the rubric *de ira* in Patrizi, for example), and Agis and Cleomenes are perhaps surprisingly little quoted, being good Plutarchian heroes whose revolutionary tendencies could be glossed over; they made, however, little show in the apophthegms. But Agesilaus is a triumphant example of temperance, affability, of military virtue, of magnanimity, of respect for fortune, and of kingly *brevitas loquendi* (though not perhaps of magnificence). His supposed remarks are produced again and again: that *astutia* is unworthy of a king, that flatterers are to be avoided like assassins, that it is more glorious to provide a subject for historians than sculptors, that justice is the essence of kingship—'how is the Great King (of Persia) greater than I if not in that?'—, that the crimes of the educated are less excusable than those of the ignorant (this last suitable in one who is also an adviser on education). It is not too much to say that he was the favourite Spartan of the time, summing up in himself all the Renaissance virtues (except beauty, as Patrizi regretfully concedes). As the eagle proclaims in an epigram,

> ipsa inter volucres quantum caput effero, tantum
> mortales omnes cedere Agesilao.[1]

Finally, there was considerable interest in the female of the species. Though much defence of the female sex is primarily rhetorical, humanists on the whole believed woman capable of the heroic virtues as well as of higher education, pointing out that Plato and Lycurgus had thought many qualities common to both sexes. The lists of female worthies include no Spartans, perhaps partly because the ladies of the apophthegms were obscure if not anonymous, and there were no queens in Sparta; but the courage

---

[1] M. Marullus, *Epigrammata* iii. 51 (no classical prototype). Agesilaus was not, however, often used as a personal name in the new age. The best-known example is perhaps that of Agesilao Marescotti, born in 1577 of a noble Bolognese family, and later chamberlain to Pope Paul V.

of Lacedaemonian women, illustrated by various episodes, is frequently referred to from Petrarch on.[1] It is the heroines of the Plutarchian tradition who are the main object of this sometimes rather appalled admiration (the naked wrestlers of the classical Greek, and the Roman, poets are suppressed, and so, for the most part, are the cowardly and luxurious Spartan females of Aristotle). Castiglione,[2] it appears, can take the Spartan mother; Ludovico Domenichi, in his *La Nobiltà delle Donne*,[3] is dubious about filicide and bellicosity—it is often stated that Lycurgus, like Plato, wanted women to undergo military training, an exaggeration that leads one to suspect that Spartan women are getting confused not only with Plato's but with the Amazons, with whom they are now often associated.[4] (Domenichi, having announced that he will say nothing of the bravery of Lacedaemonian women or Amazons 'percioche queste sono cose triviali e pubblicate fino alle barbarie', immediately piles up all the examples of faithful wives and courageous mothers from Sparta that he can find.)

Few men wanted to be saddled with a virago in the home. In serious works on female education in particular, a careful choice of *exempla* often ensures that the Spartan woman shall merely appear as a pattern housewife and Lycurgus as a pillar of marriage and the family. If Cornelius Agrippa[5] is sardonic in assuring his readers that Lycurgus' provision that husbands might lend out their wives was never made use of by the women, others, apparently, echo him in all good faith. A writer on marriage repeats the tale of Lycurgus' inability to envisage and therefore to enact penalties for adultery in Sparta; political writers may praise his rule against dowries, so that wives were chosen for virtue alone. Even Ludovico Dolce, one of the most conservative of sixteenth-century writers on female life, reminds us that Lycurgus encouraged marriage, and tells the story of the Spartan girl who, captured in war and asked what skills she had, replied proudly

---

[1] Petrarch, *Familiarum Rerum Liber* xxi. 8.10, 20.

[2] Baldesar Castiglione, *Il libro del Cortigiano* (1528) iii. 33.7.

[3] Ludovico Domenichi, *La Nobiltà delle Donne* (1549).

[4] But Lactantius, *Divin. Instit.* i. 20, had had a tale of Spartan women in arms putting to flight Messenian raiders—an aetiological legend designed to explain the Spartan cult of Aphrodite armed. The ancient epigrams on the statue of this goddess were well known in the sixteenth century and much imitated (see p. 203.n.1).

[5] Cornelius Agrippa, *De nobilitate et praeecellentia feminei sexus* (1527).

PLATE 2

The Spartan Mother slaying her Son

(Gilles Corrozet, *Hécatomgraphie*, 1540)

that she could govern a household.[1] The lawgiver's prohibition of paint and finery, as reported by the Fathers, was often recalled. His approval of dancing for girls, however, was matter for less censorious authors.

It is time to turn to more strictly political questions; and this, in Italy, for us means the tradition of republicanism. Where this still survived in the fourteenth and fifteenth centuries the increasing interest in classical history naturally benefited republican Rome more than any other state; the Romans were *nostri*. Not only did Cola di Rienzo try to resuscitate her on the spot; Florence soon rejected the medieval belief that she had been founded by Julius Caesar (whose death at the hand of Brutus was now, *pace* the authority of Dante, applauded) and claimed an earlier, republican origin. Venice, which could not pretend to go back so far, nonetheless insisted that she had been founded by Roman nobles and was the heir of Roman liberty, while the exaggerations involved in comparing her wars and conquests to those of Rome caused some irritation outside her frontiers.

The Greek republics take a secondary place, but they do take one. The first to be singled out is not Sparta. Florence from the end of the fourteenth century was both the centre of the new learning and the rallying point of republican sentiment against the expansionism of the Visconti of Milan and subsequently of the king of Naples. Behind the passionate identification with Roman tradition there emerged a growing interest in Athens. The comparison first made was perhaps the cultural one. But it was also recalled that Athens had been the champion of republican liberties in the wars against Persia (here indeed the medieval chronicles had tended to leave out Sparta) and against Macedon. Further affinities emerge in several of the works of Leonardo Bruni.[2] His *Laudatio Urbis Florentinae* is based on the *Panathenaicus* of Aelius Aristides. Admittedly this is the obvious model for a humanist city panegyric, and Rome still bears the largest part in comparisons. But Bruni can find striking points of contact with his model, whether describing Florence's geographical position, her autochthonous population, her role in the struggle against foreign tyrants, the harmoniously mixed nature of her govern-

---

[1] Ludovico Dolce, *Dialogo . . . della Institution delle Donne* (1545).

[2] For all these works, un- or inadequately published, see H. Baron, *Crisis of the Early Italian Renaissance.*

ment, or her cultural primacy and especially the fact that her language is a model for all Italy. And he picks up Athenian themes elsewhere, especially in the funeral oration for Nanni degli Strozzi, based on the Funeral Oration in Thucydides' work. Florence is a model for others, not an imitator. She is a school of Greek letters. Her laws aim at the liberty and equality of all citizens; all can win honours if they merit them, and opportunity stimulates ability. (It was accepted in Florence that artistic and intellectual achievement were dependent on liberty.) Here Bruni describes the Florentine government as an example of the *forma popularis*; in his special account of it written in Greek he returns to viewing it as mixed.

As the century wore on that part of the comparison, at least, founded on the arts, learning, and philosophy became ever more irresistible; 'appellataque tunc passim Florentinorum urbs ex conventu doctissimorum virorum Athenae alterae', as an early sixteenth-century writer said, looking back to the days of Lorenzo the Magnificent.[1] But the second Athens was not long to remain proud of her title.

When Dante wished to criticize the political instability of Florence he contrasted her in famous and ironic words with the two great Greek cities, the double fount of law:

> Atene e Lacedemona, che fenno
> Le antiche leggi, e furon si civili,
> Fecero al viver ben un picciol cenno
> Verso di te, che fai tanto sottili
> Provedimenti, ch'a mezzo novembre
> Non giugne quel che tu d'ottobre fili.[2]

But now it was about to appear that one of these states, and that the one with which Florence had come to compare herself, bore all too close a resemblance in this very respect. Meanwhile in other and less stable republics the 'optimates' began to develop an admiration for Venice and her long survival. Thus Francesco

[1] Giovanni Corsi, dedication to his life of Ficino. By the late sixteenth century Lorenzo and Pericles were being compared as *de facto* rulers of popular states; but the full comparison, resting also on their similar positions as patrons of the arts and friends of the leading thinkers of the day, probably depends on an appreciation of fifth-century B.C. art and thought not to be found in the Renaissance. But the idealization of Lorenzo developed by and for the Medici in the sixteenth century paved the way for it.

[2] Dante Alighieri, *Divina Commedia*: *Purgatorio* vi. 139 ff. (cf., as the commentaries do, Justinian, *Institutes* i. 2).

Patrizi, the Sienese author of a lengthy *de Institutione reipublicae*,[1] who, if himself showing some Florentine influence, does not discuss his city's great rival. Though his account of the mixed nature of the Venetian government is unclear and not very classical, the stage is plainly being set for a comparison between Venice and Sparta. The thousand years of the former's survival could also early in the sixteenth century be contrasted with Sparta's mere seven hundred.

In Florence, in the years of strain and crisis following the French invasion of 1494 and the departure of the Medici, there developed a newly realistic and critical approach to political theory, basing itself on history rather than philosophy and on Aristotle rather than Plato. As in Athens at a similar period of anxiety, the idea of stability was a primary preoccupation. Though Venice and her policies were not loved, her constitution was increasingly seen as a possible model. Even Savonarola and his friends, advocates of a so-called *governo popolare*, distrusted by the *grandi*, modelled their Consiglio Grande of all privileged citizens on that of Venice (the *popolo* in Florence forming only a minority of the inhabitants). In 1502, under pressure from the *grandi*, the constitution was modified by electing the Gonfalonier, like the Doge in Venice, for life. But this did not satisfy those intellectual Florentines, often from the most distinguished families and many of them instrumental in the return of the Medici in 1512, who met in the Orti Oricellari and continued to discuss the virtues of the Venetian and the ancient forms of government.

The relation, especially the chronological relation, of the Machiavelli of the *Principe* to the Machiavelli of the *Discorsi sopra la prima deca di Tito Livio* is still discussed; but certainly the latter, that infinitely influential attempt to sum up the political lessons of experience, ancient and to some extent modern, were largely if not entirely written between 1515 and 1518 when Machiavelli, now out of office, was a *habitué* of the Orti. They were indeed dedicated to two of its members. Machiavelli however was more sympathetic to the late régime than many of his friends, and certain that some form of republic was the only type of government suited to unfeudal Tuscany.

Rome, as his title shows, of course provides most of his material.

---

[1] F. Patrizi, *De institutione reipublicae*, published 1494, written before 1471 (well before his *De regno et regis institutione*).

But as a student of Polybius now, as well as of Plutarch and Aristotle, to whose approach in the middle books of the *Politics* his own bears some affinity, he can scarcely avoid Sparta. Basing himself on Polybius as well as on Aristotle and his commentators, he repeats that a mixed government, in which *re, ottimati,* and *popolo* have a share, is the best and stablest form. Like Polybius, he declares that Sparta was more fortunate than Rome, for Lycurgus set up such a government complete, to last for over eight hundred years without alteration or disorder. It is to be noted that he still speaks of Sparta as though he believes her to have only one king. But Machiavelli soon leaves the somewhat artificial theory of the mixed government behind him; although it is probably still implied when Venice and Sparta are both described as having, unlike Rome, given a preponderant share of power to the nobles. Both have entrusted to the nobility, and not to the people, the vital function of safeguarding liberty, and so preserved it longer than the Romans did; for the nobility was satisfied with its own position and not irritated at that of the people. Both states avoided the struggles between senate and people from which Rome suffered, though for different reasons (Sparta because, though she armed her people, the whole body of citizens was small and their way of life egalitarian, while the kings tended to be supporters and defenders of the popular party; Venice, because circumstances allowed her to close her citizen list without creating jealousy, and to use non-citizen forces in her defence). To such states as these growth is fatal, as the history of both Sparta and Venice shows (the latter's attempts at expansion on Terra Firma had recently been checked). Both resemble each other and differ from Rome also, as Machiavelli elsewhere says, by giving the supreme magistrate power for life, while strictly supervising his exercise of it. They are, for all these reasons, stable and admirably organized for survival; 'e sanza dubbio credo che, potendosi tenere la cosa bilanciata in questo modo, che e' sarebbe il vero vivere politico e la vera quiete d'una città ma . . . a molte cose che la ragione non t'induce, t'induce la necessità'. And if necessity forced such a state to expand, it would collapse, while peace (an old belief) is likely to mean effeminacy and discord. And so, as the desired balance cannot be preserved, 'bisogna nello ordinare la repubblica pensare alla parte più onorevole' and copy Rome, which by arming a large and energetic populace and giving easy admission to foreigners (and also by ruling through her allies, not directly as Athens and Sparta tried to do) conquered the world, though at the cost of perpetual internal disorders. The free German cities and the Swiss republics are regarded by Machiavelli as too exceptional in their circumstances to be compared with other unambitious republics. Athens, it should be noted, usually appears as a pure democracy, shortlived in comparison with Sparta in spite of frequent tinkering with the constitution, and scandalously ungrateful to her great men. No parallels are drawn between her and Florence.[1] And in his last great work, the *Florentine History*, explaining that the most useful lesson history can teach the politician is the cause of internal discord, Machiavelli remarks that the divisions in Florence were more notable, numerous, and complicated than those of Rome and Athens, where only two parties, or classes, contended for power.[2]

Machiavelli believed that a republic can only be set up, or reformed if it has become corrupt or lost its liberty entirely, by an individual with supreme power—though the people, he insists, is capable of preserving and enjoying its freedom, once gained. And so the great heroes of history are Moses, Romulus, Lycurgus; the great traitors men who, like Caesar (this in the best Florentine republican tradition), destroyed liberty instead of acting as *riordinatore*. It is vital that the *ordinatore* or *riordinatore* should be a single man. Romulus must be excused for the murder of Remus, and the less well-known cases of Agis and Cleomenes should be pondered; the latter succeeded where the former failed because he got rid of the ephors. Morally dubious means are often unavoidable. Force was employed by all the most famous legislators, and by Cleomenes as well, while Savonarola showed that he would not have been averse to it. Religion is a vital weapon; Lycurgus and Numa, and even Savonarola in enlightened modern Florence, succeeded in persuading the people they were directly inspired. In all this, Machiavelli's special interest in Cleomenes is unusual and interesting. He sees him as having achieved the almost impossible, the reform of an old, partly corrupt, and luxurious city, even if at the price of brutality; had it not been for Macedon, he would have

[1] N. Machiavelli, *Discorsi sopra la prima Deca di Tito Livio* (published 1531) i. 2, 5, 6, (note 'Sparta, come ho detto, essendo governata da uno Re e da uno stretto senato'). Cf. i. 35; ii. 4.

[2] Id., *Istorie Florentine: proemio*.

equalled Lycurgus in reputation. But the ordinary Spartan king, it will easily be understood, is to Machiavelli simply a good republican leader. Agesilaus lines up with Scipio, Timoleon, Dion, though Nabis appears among the absolute rulers or tyrants, with Phalaris and Dionysius. Consistently, therefore, when Machiavelli turns to consider the other form of government, in the *Principe*[1], he can repeat what he has said about Nabis, who had a firm foundation in popular support; but this is one Mirror for Princes in which the conventional virtues of Agesilaus can have no place.[2]

Sparta also contributes something now to that cause so close to the heart of Machiavelli (as of many Florentines since Bruni), the revival of a citizen militia on the medieval and classical, especially Roman, model. He insists that even though her limited numbers made her hegemony fragile, Sparta's successes especially in the Peloponnesian War show that money is not the sinews of war as everyone repeats; and that fortresses are not either—here a laconic apophthegm is unavoidable. What matters most is courage. And in the *Principe* he compared the 'armed and free republics' of the Spartans and the Swiss. In this context Sparta and Rome stand on the same side, as representatives of austere, warlike, and patriotic antiquity; though, in the introduction to the *Arte della Guerra*, Machiavelli makes one of his characters confess that in this corrupt age a man who educated his sons as the Spartans did would be considered a wild beast rather than a man (a theme that Rousseau took up, in more absolute condemnation of his own time than his predecessor seems here at least to have intended). But for our story it is more significant that Machiavelli carries further Polybius' distinction between Rome and Sparta, and, by linking the latter in several specific respects with Venice, gave her a place in the modern world that she had not yet had; and also that he gives a newly urgent evaluation to the figure of Lycurgus.

During the years in which Machiavelli was writing the Medici were attempting to turn their principate, with its republican façade, into an open monarchy (and thus provoking references, favourable and otherwise, to Augustus, and, thoroughly hostile, to various Greek tyrants). Finally the last Florentine republic, of 1527–30, after a brief aristocratic phase returned to the ideals of the

---

[1] Id., *Discorsi* i. 9, 10, 11. *Il Principe* ix. Cf. *Discorsi* i. 40.
[2] Id., *Discorsi* ii. 10, 24. *Il Principe* xii.

popular party, pressing them indeed to a more uncompromising extreme. In this last and desperate pass it appeared more clearly than ever that the spirit, even more than the constitution, of Rome or Sparta was the only safeguard of *libertà*. The militia, which had been revived some years earlier, was now reconstituted and considered a fundamental institution of the republic. Luigi Alamanni,[1] in his verses in memory of Zanobi Buondelmonti, speaks of his friend's inspiration at this time in

> Licurgo e Numa
> Ch'ebbe sempre al suo gir maestri e duci

and urges the youth of Florence to abandon its lucrative manufactures for arms:

> il braccio stenda
> A chi tanto onorò già Sparta e Roma.

Alamanni, like Buondelmonti, had been a friend of Machiavelli and a dedicatee of the *Vita di Castruccio Castracani*. 'Licurgo e Numa', 'Sparta e Roma', were potent phrases to him; both recur in his verse, as he evokes ancient sobriety and family discipline, or the simple, republican lives of the ancient destroyers of kings and tyrants. He longs for such reformers as Romulus, Numa, and Lycurgus in his own decadent century; though above all, in his bitter exile, he desires a Brutus. Athens he does not mention.

In 1530 many of the *grandi* acquiesced in or even welcomed the return of the Medici; the rest of the republicans went into exile. In 1531 Machiavelli's *Discorsi* were published in Rome. About this time the most distinguished of all his friends, the historian Francesco Guicciardini, put on paper some typically cautious *Considerazioni* upon the work, casting doubt on many of Machiavelli's ideas and exploding many of his parallels. He was even more dubious of the doctrine on the legislator than Machiavelli, who had confessed that it was hard to find good men ready to do evil or vice versa. Guicciardini thought such use of force a terrible example, to be adopted only in the very last resort. He found Lycurgus possibly the only example of a *riordinatore* who had employed it successfully and without being himself corrupted, for

---

[1] Luigi Alamanni, *Versi e Prose* (ed. 1859), vol. i: *Selva settima* and *Selva Ottava*, cf. Satire ii; vi; vii. He also wrote Italian epigrams on Leonidas and one on Spartan women (vol. ii, pp. 126, 134); also on Themistocles and Miltiades.

Romulus was a doubtful case. He also reiterated that of course money and fortresses were often vital in war. He was much less under the spell of antiquity than his friend, much less confident of the wisdom of the people, to whom he vastly preferred the 'optimates'; but, though ready to see advantages in the rule of a preferably elected prince, he admitted a *governo misto* to be the best and stablest form, and Rome, Sparta, and Venice to be examples of it. Guicciardini is anxious to ensure that the virtues of each simple type are combined. Speed, secrecy, and continuity are the traditional virtues of monarchy; and here he thought the Venetians had managed better than either the Romans or the Spartans, by making their 'king' elected, perpetual, and closely limited at the same time. (He at one time argued for just such a Gonfalonier in Florence; in practice during most of his life he was an adherent of the Medici family.) The Lacedaemonian senate might well have been larger; but because it was drawn from the whole body of the people (this is true in theory perhaps), it was superior at least to the Roman one, which was a source of strife and disturbance. On the whole, however, Guicciardini's remarks about Venice are not accompanied with classical references.[1]

Among the Florentine exiles was Donato Giannotti, a moderate and another graduate of the Orti Oricellari. Though he was one of the few who persisted in believing that Florence could yet return to a republican constitution, and though he lacked Guicciardini's scepticism of so much of the basic doctrine of the *Discorsi*, he shares his more optimate interpretation of the mixed constitution. He had begun his literary career with a work on the constitution of Venice. Here his Venetian interlocutor feels no need to envy the ancient republics of Rome or Lacedaemon, and compares his city with the former in everything but extent of empire; he then devotes himself to direct description and analysis.[2] But in the treatise *della Repubblica Fiorentina*,[3] written in exile in Venice and undoubtedly read by his friends there, though not published till the early eighteenth century, Giannotti considers the

---

[1] F. Guicciardini, *Considerazioni intorno ai discorsi di Machiavelli*, esp. ix, ii (not published till the nineteenth century; *Opere*, ed. Palmarocchi, vol. viii).

[2] Donato Giannotti, *Della Repubblica de' Viniziani*; completed 1526, published 1540.

[3] Id., *Della Repubblica Fiorentina* iv. 8, iii. 1. Cf. preface to *Discorso sopra il fermare il governo di Firenze* (1527); and *Discorso sopra il Riordinare la Repubblica di Siena* (all in *Opere Politiche e Letterarie*, 2 vols., 1850).

mistakes and *mutazioni* of the last few years and brings not only Venice and Sparta but Florence and Athens together. The framework is familiar to us. Like so many contemporaries, he is obsessed with *diuturnità* and *tranquillità*. His task, as he sees it, is to find for Florence an administration that only great external violence can alter. The answer is, as in almost all cases, a mixed constitution. Sparta according to Aristotle had had one; so had Rome. Florence till 1512 (when the Medici returned with limited powers) had too little of a *principato*; but Giannotti insists that all states, which necessarily incline to one of the pure forms (this seems to be a development and regularization of the ideas of Machiavelli's *Discorsi*), ought to lean towards the people, and not the prince. To give the latter too much power is very unsafe. Even Lycurgus the Lacedaemonian, who was praised above all others for having at one step introduced an all but perfect republic—*poco meno che perfetta*—, made an error here, and it was left to Theopompus to temper yet further the kings' authority. (And if Romulus and Lycurgus were guilty of oversights, says Giannotti modestly, doubtless I shall be too.)

Among the themes taken over from the *Discorsi* is the importance of the legislator or *riordinatore*, with Lycurgus one of the most familiar examples, especially of those who rely on force (as is so often necessary) or divine aid. The legislator has the double task of guarding against internal and external dangers, and must therefore introduce both a sound political system and a militia; this was realized by Lycurgus, when he set up his republic, which lasted for eight hundred years without any alteration and proved able to defend itself continuously, and by Romulus, those two statesmen wise above all others. Giannotti also explains that Lycurgus understood the great importance of *costumi* and of education; but he touches on these much more lightly than French eighteenth-century writers were to do. Where he most anticipates Rousseau is in his interest in public meals (which Patrizi for one had thought impossible in the modern world).[1] Festivities of some kind are natural and inevitable, he says, and so should be regulated. The German republics, he notes, like Sparta and Rome, have *feste* marked by *modestia e costumatezza civile*. And so he would introduce to Florence occasional *pasti pubblici* for the men of the militia, overseen by magistrates and followed

[1] F. Patrizi, *De institutione reipublicae* iv. 1.

by a magistrate speaking in praise of the custom. Or the principle might be introduced in a slightly different way, and he gives other suggestions.

But the main source for his new constitution is Venice, not only easier to know than Rome but smaller and more pacific; Giannotti is less ambitious for Florence than Machiavelli, or more hopeful of that balance which the latter had denied. The mixed constitution that he elaborates incorporates a series of checks and balances of a very Venetian cast, designed to prevent the 'tyrannic' magistracies from which Florence had suffered near the end. A Gonfalonier for life, but well controlled, at the head of the state will assist stability; and here, as Machiavelli had done, Giannotti links Sparta and Venice. Such a magistrate did not lead to tyranny in either of these well-mixed governments. The only attempts to seize supreme power were those of [Marino] Faliero and Pausanias, both easily frustrated. (Elsewhere both are adduced as evidence for the prevalence of ambition even in a state where the first magistrate is closely bound and limited by the republic.[1])

And now, looking back, Giannotti is ready to adduce Athens as a warning to Florence. He sees that it was because the republic of 1494, and even more that of 1527, had refused to give the *grandi* their share of power that these had twice combined with the Medici to bring it down. Those persecuting the *grandi* find no end to disorders; like the Athenians with their ill-mixed republic and their perpetual ostracisms of leading men.

But republican spirit in Florence was fast dying. So far as the classical states are concerned, what we soon find is an apologist of the Medici arguing at considerable length a thesis usual among defenders of princely rule, that Jews, Athenians, Spartans, Romans, and Swiss (even if their constitutions were well mixed, as Sparta's was) were all factious and miserable until they acquired a lord. Liberty, both external and internal, where it is identified with the rule of law, is only to be preserved and enjoyed under a prince.[2]

By now most of Italy was under the dominion of Spain, and elsewhere too in the peninsula absolutism was usual. It was now the Rome of the empire, not of the republic, to which men

---

[1] D. Giannotti, *Della Repubblica Fiorentina* iv. 6; iii. 12; iii. 3.

[2] G. B. Guarini, *Trattato della Politica Libertà* (1818; written 1599). Venice, in spite of appearances, is not a republic but a *signoria*.

looked back; this is the great age of commentaries on Tacitus, the historian who taught tyrants to rule and subjects to endure. The only major republics to survive were the narrow ones of Genoa and Venice, and this, with the final vicissitudes of the Florentine republic, seemed conclusive proof that a popular state was doomed to faction and ultimate loss of liberty. For all the Florentines' attempts to obey precepts such as those of Lycurgus, she and Athens were to be linked in obloquy for a long time to come.

In Genoese writers we find occasional praise of Sparta in various contexts; in Venice we find something more—the inheritance of Florentine ideas on this as on many other matters. Precisely, in fact, as had been the case with Sparta, Venice's reputation had reached its apogee when her lingering decline had already begun. The Venetians, stimulated to a previously unknown activity in the field of political literature by their position as leaders of the resistance to Spain and absolutism, began to produce a series of complacent eulogies of their system, which they sometimes went so far as to regard as perfect and probably eternal. An early and influential example of the genre was that of the Cardinal Gasparo Contarini.[1] It takes up the doctrine of the mixed constitution as reasserted by Machiavelli and Giannotti (whose description of Venice had just been published), introducing it with a reference to Sparta, and going on to explain, of course, that in Venice the Doge represents the regal element, the senate the optimate one, and the Consiglio Grande the popular. It later draws some rather strained parallels, several of which concern Sparta; and, as in antiquity, similarity is rapidly interpreted as imitation. Contarini suggests, as Giannotti had not himself done, that the feasts given by the Doge four times a year to selected citizens are a modified and improved copy of the public meals held in those illustrious states Lacedaemon and Crete, intended, as those had been, to foster friendship and unity, but far less disorderly and promiscuous. Our ancestors, he further says, set up the famous Council of Ten, the Consiglio de' Dieci, which had the function of preventing strife and conspiracy, in emulation of the ephorate, the Areopagus, and the decemvirs of Rome. But to Contarini Venice is of course vastly superior to all the ancient republics. Her mixed government is better balanced; he sees each part as mixed in itself, which has the particular advantage that the

---

[1] G. Contarini, *De Repubblica Venetorum libri V* (1543).

popular part is not all that popular. And all her citizens, not only
some, as in Sparta, Athens, or Rome, are devoted to virtue.
Venice, above all, is better adapted for peace than either Rome or
Sparta. It should be observed that her policy at this period was
inevitably cautious and unadventurous, while Italy as a whole
was sick of war.

Since war and conquest were deprecated, while stability and
survival were seen in Venice as the glory of the past and the task of
the present, and since Venetian writers without exception had a
horror of popular predominance, the old comparison with Rome,
which was now analysed in Machiavellian terms, presented its
problems. All that could be done was to cover her with praise
of a general kind, while pointing out how superior in longevity
and tranquillity Venice was, and compare minor points and
episodes. Rome still, indeed, receives more discussion than any
other ancient state, but Sparta certainly gets more than before.
Most of the Venetian panegyrists of the middle of the century, all
admirers of Aristotle and of the mixed constitution, either refer to
Sparta's admirable and not too democratic mixture, and the 800
years' survival she owed it, or explicitly compare her to Venice on
these points. Other features of the Venetian republic, especially
(what had been much stressed by Contarini at least) the rule of
law, the rarity of honours and monuments to individuals, and the
distinction paid to old age, especially in the bestowal of office,
must irresistibly have recalled Sparta now. Even attempts to
distinguish the two suggest that they did tend to come together in
the mind. Garimberto[1] explains that Venice managed her generals
differently, and that, though she too excluded foreigners from
political influence, she was more generous to them than the
Spartans were, letting them at least dwell in the city. Memmo[2]
thought the Doge was modelled on the Spartan king; he also
admired much in Lycurgus' educational system, especially the
training in endurance and abstinence (but better to travel than
star in villa), and wanted Venice to follow his example in abolishing dowries. We may notice that the Dieci sometimes appear,
pace Contarini, as part of the optimate element in the state. Also

---

[1] G. Garimberto, *De Regimenti publici de la Città* (1544), pp. 20b, 28b, 29.
Cf. 41—how wrongly Sparta and Athens treated the cities under their rule.

[2] G. M. Memmo, *Dialogo nel quale . . . si forma un perfetto prencipe e una
perfetta repubblica* (1563), pp. 91, 94, 96–7, 124–6, 134.

PLATE 3

Lycurgus and the Two Dogs
(Otho Vaenius, *Emblemata Horatiana*, 1607)

that that favourite figure with the Florentines, Lycurgus, drops into the background. Venice, like Rome, had had no single law-giver, nor did she now feel the need of one.

It was often accepted that many of the main European king-doms were mixed states with a predominant regal element. Thus Venetian republicanism and northern European ideas of consti-tutionalism, which as we shall see were developing an interest in the ephorate, could reinforce each other. The classical and Italian tradition could be adapted even more easily to the elective mon-archy of Poland with its powerful senate. Goslicki's *de Optimo Senatore*[1] was written in Italy and published in Venice in 1568 (and had more influence in western Europe than in Poland); although, of course, his interest in Roman matters is intense, he agrees that the long survival of Venice and Sparta proves the worth of their government, which he regards as mixed (as he does that of England too; but Elizabeth and James were to suppress a translation of his work). He compares the Polish (and Roman) senate to Theopompus' ephors, however, rather than the Gerou-sia; he refers to Lycurgus' obedience to his own laws, the Lacedae-monian state's care for education and, by instituting public meals, for the prevention of luxury (but proves the senator's need for wealth by the means test for public life at Sparta).

It is perhaps also significant that, while by no means all native writers do so, the Frenchman Audebert[2] picks up Contarini's comparison of ephors and Dieci:

> Non Ephores desunt speculantes omnia circum

he remarks in a poetic eulogy of Venice (also, in which he is not alone,

> Moenia nulla urbem cingunt Lacedemonis instar

though he has to admit that the reason for this absence of city walls is not the same).

Strict logic still demanded that the Venetians should openly put Sparta above Rome, and this was done by one of their best-known

---

[1] Laurentius Grimalius Goslickius, *De Optimo Senatore* (1568), pp. 9b–10, 14b, 16b, 35b, 23, 29, 73, 80.

[2] G. Audebert, *Venetiae* (1583). Cf. A. Medin, *Storia della Repubblica di Venezia nella poesia*, p. 40. But poets, and indeed all save strictly political writers, prefer to compare Venice with even Troy (pressed into service via Antenor the founder of Padua) or Athens with her naval and artistic glories.

writers of the later part of the century. Paolo Paruta indeed near
the end of his *Perfezione della Vita Politica*[1] calls her a 'vero essempio
di perfetto governo'. He thinks that one element in a mixed
constitution must be stronger than the others, but not by much.
The Gracchi and Pericles gave far too much power to the people;
but Sparta, when Theopompus had regulated the disproportion-
ate authority of the kings, was ideally tempered, with the optimates slightly preponderant. The citizens, barred from personal
power, strove only for that of their country; being satisfied with
the influence they had, they put the liberty and preservation of
their city above all other tasks—and peace and tranquillity are the
true end of government. 'A questa è la nostra repubblica molto
simile.' Paruta also admired much in the Spartan way of life:
particularly the military exercises, resembling the Roman ones,
the games, public feasts, and an education, like that in Persia,
aimed at civil virtues. For *consuetudini* are as important as laws;
'la consuetudine è madre di nostri costumi', and Agesilaus was
thus able to fix his laws in the souls of the citizens better than any
of those who left written legislation. Rome had an admirable
system of rewards; but Sparta took thought for both rewards and
punishments. Before we believe ourselves in eighteenth-century
France, however, we should remember that Paruta ends with the
need for education to be not only religious but Christian, and
that education in civil virtues is not strictly civic education; and
that in any case the matter is only touched on *en passant*.

His posthumously published *Discorsi Politici*[2] deal largely with
problems suggested by Roman or modern history; but it is made
clear again in the first *Discourse* that Sparta had the best of all
mixed governments—the word perfection still haunts Paruta as it
does so many other Venetians. Her superiority to Rome lies, as
usual, in the combined perpetuity and limitation of the royal
power, and the predominance of the senate, necessary if the usur-
pation of power by either king or people was to be prevented—
though he holds that the ephors made the state too popular, and
would have been unnecessary if the senate had been a little larger.
He also reiterates his praise of the *savissimo legislatore* who realized
that tranquillity was the true end of political life, though his own

---

[1] P. Paruta, *Perfezione della Vita Politica* (1579) iii. (*Opere Politiche* (1852),
pp. 396, 401).
[2] *Discorsi Politici* (1599) i. 1, 11, cf. 14.

use of force is accepted; and his praise of the habits and education that trained the Spartans to virtue and obedience to the laws. Considering this education, Plutarch had rightly set Lycurgus above Numa. In three vital respects therefore, so he concludes, Sparta was superior to Rome. Paruta brings out clearly that Venice in these respects recalls Sparta; but he does not press minor parallels in an artificial way or insist that there had been direct copying, and he points out the exceptional advantages and opportunities that Lycurgus had, for example to introduce equality of possessions; and, in contrast, the slow and gradual formation of the Venetian state. He also explains why the Spartan militia and the Spartan attitude to fortifications need be no model to Venice, which indeed ran her military affairs in a very un-classical manner.

But the influence of a very distinguished foreign author had, towards the end of the century, a disturbing effect on the Venetian myth in general and on the comparison with Sparta along with it. Jean Bodin was a jurist and student of history whose early training in Ramism had given him a pleasure in differing from Aristotle. He is best remembered for his newly precise doctrine of sover-eignty, which is, he insists, simple and indivisible. Consequently he denies the whole possibility of a mixed constitution (though a state in which sovereignty lay in one part might devolve the administration on to another, or on to several other parts). His first famous book, the *Methodus ad facilem historiarum cognitionem*,[1] makes short work of Machiavelli, Contarini, and the rest who held Sparta, Rome, and Venice all to be mixed. Bodin points out that as far as the first is concerned the doctrine is not even Aristotle's own, and rebukes Machiavelli for accepting the belief that she had only one king. Sovereignty here, he maintained, had originally lain with the kings. Lycurgus set up a popular state, but after the kings Theopompus and Polydorus made it possible for the senate to overrule the assembly, Sparta was an optimacy, as all the Greek historians and orators bear out. Plutarch, whom Bodin acclaims as his best guide, is here used to unusual but intelligent effect. Venice appears in the *Methodus* as a popular state, only the 'nobles' being real citizens, and as such is compared to the admittedly more extreme Rome and Athens; 'nihil enim cum

[1] J. Bodin, *Methodus ad facilem historiarum cognitionem* (1566; 2nd ed. 1572), cap. vi.

L

Lacedaemoniis commune habent.' (And of Carthage we know too little to judge.) He points out the traditionally democratic use of the lot among the Venetians, but not the Lacedaemonians, 'quorum Rempublicam suae similem facit Contarenus'; says that Athens and Venice are alike, and unlike Sparta, in having too many magistrates, and even obstinately omits the Spartans from his list of people encouraging friendly sentiments by public banquets, though they include Minos, Plato, Moses, the early Christians, the Athenians, Romans, and Venetians and the Swiss as well.

In other chapters however Bodin seems to repent of making Venice a democracy, and in his *Six livres de la République*[1] (which in his own Latin version and in the various translations that were rapidly made gained for a time a position in Europe rivalling that of the *Politics*, of which it could be seen as an up-to-date and corrected version) Venice is, more convincingly, an optimacy again, citizens being defined more broadly than by Aristotle. This does not however mean that she goes back to being associated with Sparta, on which Bodin essentially repeats his earlier doctrines; except in so far as he states openly that free states tend to be less fickle if they have somewhat stupid citizens. Sparta, Venice, and the Swiss have done better than the over-clever Athenians and Florentines. This was, or became, accepted doctrine. He also has a different but pregnant comparison; though refusing to differentiate fundamentally between 'virtuous' and less virtuous régimes, and rejecting the word aristocracy in favour of optimacy, understood in the ordinary sense as the rule of the few or the nobles, he granted that in both Sparta and Geneva worth did count in the gaining of office. His other remarks about Sparta, some critical, some admiring, will be considered later.

Reactions to all this in Italy varied. Some insisted hotly that Venice was mixed in spite of all; others that Sparta was, and that Aristotle had said so too, even if Venice might be an optimacy. Others admitted both to be such. It is still possible of course to speak of them both together as ideal aristocracies or, rather loosely, as aristocracies which are still in some way mixed in their governments (according to P. M. Contarini, Venice in this surpassed Sparta by being a quadruple combination; had he been

[1] Id., *Six livres de la République* (1576; *de Republica Libri Sex*, 1586, in some respects fuller), ii. 4; vi. 4, and ii. 6.

reading pseudo-Archytas?)[1] and to repeat the particular parallels. But the original root of the comparison has been cut away, and a certain lack of conviction is often traceable when Sparta is mentioned. It is true that Giovanni Botero, himself no Venetian, who devoted much of his influential *Ragion di Stato* to the methods by which states might be preserved, links Venice with Sparta (and Carthage) as examples of medium-sized states which, while they avoid conquest, can long endure; he also praises King Theopompus, though now rather for his care to maintain than his willingness to limit his power, a shift of stress in which, at this period, he is not alone.[2] And in his *Relatione della Republica Venetiana*, dedicated to the Doge and senate in 1605 as a supplement to his *Relatione Universali*, a description of the states of the world, he does in fact collect more points of similarity between Venice and that admirable republic, Sparta, than anyone else before him. He follows Contarini and the rest on the Doge's quarterly dinner parties; he says that the Venetian respect for old age is a Lacedaemonian idea that came first to Rome, as Aulus Gellius said, and thence to the lagoons; that the rule that gifts from foreigners to Venetian ambassadors must be sanctioned by the senate is perhaps copied, in modified form, from the Spartan practice of forbidding them entirely; and that there are further resemblances in the eager rivalry between citizens, in the moderate extent of private wealth, and in the cautious treatment of foreigners, with whom, as is well known, the *gentilhuomo* might have nothing to do.[3]

Nonetheless, Botero remains more interested in Rome, Venice's only equal in fame, even if his interest takes the form of pointing out how very different were both her means and her ends. And if (following Bodin) he thinks that, while Rome was an ill-ordered democracy, Venice and Sparta were optimacies, he abandons the Machiavellian tradition and gives our comparison a second severe shock by returning to the classical view that Sparta cared for war and war only, in contrast to Venice's devotion to peace and quiet.[4] And also to trade; at bottom Botero believes that Venice's prosperity and survival depend on her peculiar site, vast wealth, and

---

[1] P. M. Contarini, *Compendio Universal di republice* (1602). Caimo, see below, p. 155n.1, certainly knew this as other laudators of Sparta.

[2] G. Botero, *Ragion di Stato* (1589), pp. 8, 10; 6.

[3] Id., *Relatione della Republica Veneta* (1605) i. 39, 42, 44; ii. 90.

[4] Ibid. ii. 82.

on other factors having nothing to do with Sparta. One of the main tendencies of his later work was to draw attention to such factors, away from the classical belief that a good constitution is the main or even sole reason for success. In this light his comparisons with Sparta appear unimportant, if not purely ornamental.

Indeed Sparta is increasingly despised or ignored. The fact is noted with a satirical eye by Traiano Boccalini,[1] himself a lover of Venice, in an unfinished sketch for one of his famous *Ragguagli di Parnaso*. This makes the Venetian republic claim precedence on Parnassus over the Swiss and German republics. Her representative, with typical arrogance, disdains all possible ancient competitors as well, except Rome and Carthage; though his German opponent objects that the Venetian aristocracy has in fact copied numerous laws of the Spartans, Corinthians, and Athenians, and supports the contemporary Greeks—it is the Germans on the contrary who have inherited the Roman tradition. (For some time Carthage, which had at least been a commercial port as well as having had an exemplary mixed constitution, or optimacy if preferred, had rated occasional favourable mention.) As for the attacks on the Venetian ideal produced under Spanish or papal influence, they tend to ignore antiquity, though they attempt to show that the constitution had frequently been altered (the notorious *Squittinio della libertà Veneta* maintained that she had often not even been independent).

In the 1620s, true, one may still find such a remark as that early Rome, Venice, and Sparta (with France and some other modern states) were supreme examples of *ragion di stato*, because their laws and the interest of the government came near to coinciding, and to coinciding too with justice and honesty.[2] But times are changing, and the old Venetian belief in their own superiority to all other peoples has turned, in the hands of Pompeo Caimo, to

---

[1] Traiano Boccalini, *Ragguagli di Parnaso*; the first two centuries were published in 1612 and 1613, the year of the author's death; a few others in 1614. Our passage appears as no. 49 of a third century, edited by L. Firpo largely from MS. in 1948. Sparta proper is notably absent from the *Ragguagli*; for the unfortunate state of Laconia, described as having a senate and elective *duce* (as perhaps the medieval tradition of Lacedaemon suggested), is transparently the Papal State, as, among other features, the ubiquity of the various nephews of the *duci* shows.

[2] L. Zuccolo, *Della Ragione di Stato*, 1621 (*Politici e Moralisti del seicento*, ed. Croce and Caramella (1930), p. 35).

a newly strong insistence that the modern world has nothing to learn from the ancient, and that Venice is quite unique; and also to a newly harsh exposé of the shortcomings of all ancient states. Sparta, with help from the critical chapters of Aristotle, is attacked for economic inadequacy, obsessive militarism, and the tyranny of the ephors—though her obedience to law was good.[1] About the same time Baltasar Bonifazio, in two *Additamenta* to a new edition of Contarini,[2] complains that a story has got about that the Doge has two votes in council, like the Spartan king (according to Herodotus). Nothing of the sort; and his power could hardly be more different, since he has none in war and little in any other sphere (he was indeed rapidly losing what remained to him). He also makes the somewhat obvious point that Venice is a maritime power, whereas taking to the sea marked the beginning of downfall for the Queen of the Peloponnese.

Within and without Italy, however, Machiavelli and Giannotti, Contarini and Paruta and Botero were still being read; which explains certain facts about the *Histoire du gouvernement de Venise* (1676) by Amelot de la Houssaye, which provoked that government to complaints, since it found itself not regarded as wholly beyond criticism. Amelot remarks in his introduction, in what appears an old-fashioned manner, that he has occasionally compared the Venetian magistrates with those of Rome and Sparta 'pour montrer ce que la République de Venise a emprunté des deux autres, et le bon usage qu'elle en a su faire'; that he will do this briefly except for two comparisons, 'que peutêtre on ne laissera pas de trouver beau', between the Doge and the Spartan king and the Dieci and the ephors. He opens his first chapter with equally traditional words: 'J'écris l'Histoire du Gouvernement de Venise, qui est sans contredit le plus beau d'Europe en son genre, puisque c'est une fidèle copie des anciennes Républiques de la Grèce, et comme l'assemblage de toutes leurs plus excellentes Loix.'

But this is somewhat disingenuous. In fact a good many of his comparisons work to the disadvantage of Venice. For example he distinguishes her nobility of birth from the nobility of merit and election in Sparta; while Sparta encouraged rivalry and mock

---

[1] Pompeo Caimo, *Parallelo Politico delle republiche antiche e moderne* (1627), esp. pp. 25 ff.
[2] In 1628.

fights among the young men in order to increase warlike virtue, not as Venice does to divide and weaken the populace. The Venetian militia is so poor it should only be used as the helots were—'pour garder le baggage, et faire montrer aux Ennemis en la place des morts'.[1]

As for the set comparisons,[2] we begin by piling up old and new points of resemblance. The Doge's subjection to the laws, and to a college of magistrates in particular, his lack of a bodyguard, the (by now) private status of his wife, the privileges of his eldest son, his preservation of the ancient usage of public feasts if in a limited form, all these recall Sparta. But Amelot somewhat undermines his own case by explaining that there is no resemblance at all in the amount of power each had; for the Doge, these days, has absolutely none at all.

The long account of the Dieci or Dix is even more malicious. To Amelot this was a fearful institution, responsible for a situation really only to be compared with the Terror at Rome under Tiberius. To call it 'la Copie de ce temple fameux, que les Ephores de Sparte élevèrent à la Crainte' is not much more complimentary. Beside the main resemblance of function minor similarities are pressed again. Both ephors and Dieci were late arrivals who usurped the power of other magistrates; both were popular with the lowest classes. They differed in that the ephors could only condemn a king with the aid of his colleague and the senate, while the Dieci could deal with a Doge by themselves. On the other hand the ephors could put ordinary men to death without trial, for which reason Plato called them tyrannic; the Council of Ten has often shown it was equally absolute by condemning citizens upon mere suspicion.

Amelot ends his work by discussing the now obvious decline of Venice, which he ascribes largely to the expansion on to Terra Firma, already so often criticized. It was particularly foolish in a state with Sparta's example before it. But 'il semble que les Vénitiens ont voulu imiter les fautes de cette fameuse République, comme ils en ont imité les Maximes et les Ordonnances'. They are however even slower in deliberation. All republics have this

---

[1] A. N. Amelot de la Houssaye, *Histoire du gouvernement de Venise* (1676), p. 363 n.; pp. 56 ff. and 58; 76–7 (from Athenaeus); cf. 6, 24 for harmless comparisons.

[2] Ibid., pp. 199 ff. (212 esp.).

fault. True, the Venetians are not, like the Athenians and Florentines, over-clever; but the Lacedaemonians if slow in deliberation
were at least prompt in action. Like the Lacedaemonians however,
the Venetians know how to deceive. After all this a compliment
on the obedience of both as a reason for their long survival could
not be much comfort.[1] It may be added that Amelot also directed
devastating attention to the pedigrees by which Venetian nobles
connected themselves with ancient Romans, as for example the
Cornaro with the Cornelii.

The book was widely read and influential in weakening the
admiration for Venice (which, as we shall see, was strong in
England). But the almost obligatory stop on the Grand Tour
must have been enough to reveal to outsiders how increasingly
unsuited the sober mantle of Sparta was to the ever weaker and
more frivolous Serenissima.

[1] Ibid., pp. 313, 335, 358.

KINGS AND EPHORS

OUTSIDE Italy the issues were different. Men were mostly faced, not with the choice between despotism or a republic, but with settling the precise amount of power to be wielded either, in the newly centralized monarchies, by the king or, in the Empire, by the emperor over the princes or the princes over the cities. Furthermore, the Reformation exacerbated the old question of relations between Church and ruler and introduced the possibility of a difference of faith between ruler and subject. Must the Protestant obey his prince against his conscience or his Church? Was the Catholic justified in rebellion against a heretic?

Political discussion therefore turned largely on rights and duties, supremacy and allegiance; and it continued to be, or once more became, to a great extent theological as well as legal in outlook. But Greek history was now well known and provided evidence, authority, or ornament in varying measure. Sparta's significance of course continues to lie in her kings, limited by law and in particular by the power of the ephors. What is in origin little more than a casual comparison slides with some writers into a form of authorization; and at last becomes so regular as almost to constitute the veritable definition of the theory it indicates.

Luther finally advocated complete obedience to authority, which he regarded as of divine institution. Calvin also stressed the necessity of obedience, and if he intimated that where obedience to man involved disobedience to God its claim failed, he never permitted active resistance. Yet he was, unwittingly, the source of much anti-absolutist thought. He suggested in a famous passage of the *Institutes* that in those countries where special representatives of the people have been set up to protect its rights, these may even have a duty to check and control the chief magistrate. Such representatives had been the ephors in Sparta, the tribunes in Rome, the demarchs in Athens, and were, perhaps, in modern monarchies, the Orders or Estates.[1]

[1] J. Calvin, *Institutes* IV. 31.

Not that Calvin was the first to think of ephors,[1] though they seem more commonly to have been compared with the Parlements, rather than the Estates, in France. The idea that modern monarchies were or might be in some sense mixed governments was old by now; it was asserted of France in the early sixteenth century by various writers, including Machiavelli, and, in a vague sense, by Claude de Seyssel, who later settled for a mixture of monarchy with aristocracy, the latter residing primarily in the Parlements. He does not himself mention ephors; but others, it appears, did. By 1555 a political writer, one of the most absolutist authors of the increasingly absolutist period of François I and Henri II, was protesting that the Parlements were not to be compared with ephors, for it was the kings who could bridle them, and not vice versa.[2]

After the middle of the century it became a condition of survival for many Protestant communities to develop a theory of the right of revolt. In 1550 a Lutheran tract, the *Bekenntnis* of Magdeburg, proclaimed the right of lower magistracies to resist higher ones. The exiles from Mary Tudor's England soon followed a similar path. John Ponet, in that remarkable little work *A Shorte Treatise of Politicke Power*,[3] did not confine himself to strictly theological arguments, unlike his fellow Englishman Goodman or his Scottish contemporary Knox. Ponet, though in no sense a strict Calvinist, seems to be one of the first Protestant writers to pick up, perhaps from Calvin, the comparison of ephors, tribunes, and Parliament, as offices standing between prince and people—though, since the English Parliament, not to mention the minor magistracies in general, was pretty subservient to Mary, Ponet boldly extends the right of resistance to the whole people. Ponet holds, like other English constitutionalists, that the people has not

[1] Compare and contrast with Calvin Melanchthon, *Commentarium in lib. III politicorum Aristotelis*, 1530 (*Corpus Reformatorum* xvi. 440), who also admits the existence of a form of monarchy where kings not only govern according to the laws but special *custodes* have been set up. Such was Sparta: 'in Germania sunt electores, in Gallia certi principes curiae parlamenti tamquam ephori regum.' But these are ineffective, for kings can only be restrained by *religio*; bishops should be appointed 'tamquam ephori regum ad moderandum vim regiae potestatis'.

[2] G. de la Perrière, *Le Miroir politique* (1555), pp. 22–3. 'Aucuns ont voulu dire que le Royaume de France n'est seulement gouverné par monarchie d'un seul Roy, ains est aussi gouverné par l'Aristocratie de Parlemens lesquelz ils comparent aux Ephores des Lacédémoniens.'

[3] J. Ponet, *A Shorte Treatise of Politicke Power* (Strasburg, 1556).

given complete control to the ruler but reserved some political, especially legislative, power to itself, which it exercises through Parliament. He talks of the mixed state, though this, if logically pressed, would mean assimilating the Estates to the Spartan assembly, or Gerousia, or both, rather than to ephors; this ambiguity was to persist.

Ponet's radical arguments were not followed in England for a long time; it was in France that ephors were soon to become popular (tribunes, let alone the obscure demarchs—neither of whom had had real kings to cope with—take second place or drop out altogether). After the shock of the Massacre of St. Bartholomew in 1572 the Huguenots turned back to the old doctrine that it is the people that has put power, however divine its nature, into the hands of the king, and regulated it by a contract (not to be confused with the social contract made by individuals in a state of nature with each other, to which the ruler is not a party). Thus the *De Jure Magistratum in Subditos*,[1] published anonymously but now believed to be by Theodore Beza, Calvin's acknowledged successor, himself. To him the king is, like the Roman emperor, only the highest of the hierarchy of magistrates representing the people, and holding authority from them by a contract and under the laws. Just as the king may punish lower magistrates who break the contract, especially by acting against the true religion, so the magistrates, above all the Estates, may resist him, even by force of arms. Private persons may not do so, unless in an extremity, when the Estates are impotent and corrupt; in which case they may rally behind individual or associated minor magistrates, 'the healthiest part' of the nation. Beza's foremost example of the contract and popular control is of course Israel. But he also remarks that the 'three Estates of Rome could depose consuls', and points to the mutual oath sworn by kings and ephors in Sparta, and the ephors' power to depose the king who broke it. And he sees that this oath is not unlike those sworn by many modern kings to maintain their subjects' privileges.

Almost precisely contemporary was another famous work, Hotman's *Franco-Gallia*.[2] This was a eulogy of (disguised as an investigation into) what Hotman saw as the elective monarchy of early France closely controlled by a national council. But Hotman

---

[1] 1574; French version *Du droit des magistrats*—see esp. p. 51 for Sparta.
[2] F. Hotman, *Franco-Gallia* (1573), cap. x, xv; cf. xii.

does declare that this medieval government is identical with the mixed governments of the ancients, and he compares the council or the Estates with several classical institutions before going on to modern parallels such as the English Parliament and the officer known as the Justicia of Aragon. In particular he praises what he calls the ancient and famous law of the Lacedaemonians, which joined ephors to kings in order, as Plato said, to bridle them (this does not suggest very clear ideas as to the mixed constitution, however). Later, when attempting to show that the person and power of the king have always been distinguished, he recurs to the ephors and the oath they exacted from the kings. (He also compares Lysander to the early Mayors of the Palace who left the French king without power.)

Finally, again almost at the same time, ephors crop up, if very much *en passant*, in a similar role in that curious pamphlet the *Réveille-Matin*;[1] but its author is less insistent than Beza that opposition of any sort should be restricted to the Estates, since these are no longer powerful in France. They alone, however, may depose or kill. The work also praises Spartan military discipline. And the epistle to the Poles prefacing one edition warns them that they will discover the French king whom they have chosen to be nothing like so good as the Spartan and Roman ones; they should never trust kings.

The most classically minded of these radical works was the *Vindiciae Contra Tyrannos*,[2] as indeed its author's (or authors') pseudonym, Stephanus Junius Brutus, would suggest. It goes a step further than the *De Iure Magistratuum*, holding that the king has no power of life or death, no right to legislate or tax, without the consent of the Estates, and that any local magistrates and officers of the Crown and nobles may act 'comme Ephores et Controlleurs publics' and raise the standard of revolt. (It is plain that the clear meaning of the Greek word *ephorus*, overseer, is an element in its attraction.) The *Vindiciae* discusses all other relevant states from Israel to Aragon, and goes into greater detail about Sparta than its predecessors. It describes the limitations on the monarchy, which Aristotle nonetheless, it reminds us (not wholly correctly), called a true monarchy. The kings' chief power was in

---

[1] *Réveille-Matin des Français et de leurs voisins, composé par Eusèbe Philadelphe Cosmopolite en forme de dialogues* (1573) ii. Cf. Edinburgh edition, 1574.

[2] *Vindiciae Contra Tyrannos*, 1579 (by Duplessis Mornay and Languet).

the field, but even here the ephors were above them (true, at least for one period). It evokes, of course, the monthly oath of the kings to keep the laws, and the ephors' power to try the kings, as retailed by Aristotle, and to hear appeals from their judgement. Archidamus, Agesilaus, and even Pausanias are called on to bear witness to the royal duty of obedience to the law, which they saw as divine. Sometimes a Spartan *exemplum* was not so easy to find; the obvious examples of glorious tyrannicide were Athenian and Roman. But the *Vindiciae* contrives to clinch its argument by a Plutarchian story showing the Spartan senate formally exonerating subjects guilty of treachery to a tyrannous governor. It also repeats from Dionysius of Halicarnassus the tale that Rome copied Spartan customs, presumably to give the latter more authority. And, protesting that it is by no means opposed to monarchy as such, it proposes to give the French monarch sincere advice—to follow the precedent of King Theopompus.

The ideas in these works found fertile ground elsewhere in Europe, particularly in Scotland, where her subjects forced Queen Mary to abdicate, and in the Netherlands, where William the Silent, defending himself from the charges of Philip, reminded his Estates that the rights of vassals in Brabant were so great that their duty was in practice just to support their prince and keep him to his oath, like the ephors in Sparta.[1] But in France towards the end of the century the Huguenots found that they had the prospect of a co-religionist on the throne, and they began to argue hotly in favour of hereditary right, the Salic Law, and the rules of primogeniture. Hotman's volte-face was particularly notable; but he preserved his interest in the Spartan monarchy, since it was hereditary, and indeed his attempts to elucidate the laws of succession there[2] provide the only non-modern material in one of his essays on the subject. It was now the Catholic Ligueurs, anxious to change the succession, who took up the ideas of elective monarchy and popular sovereignty, based on man's natural liberty and equality, and associated with the Pope's power to depose rulers and free subjects from their allegiance. The fanatical Rossaeus,[3]

---

[1] *Apologie . . . contre le ban and edict publié par le Roy d'Espagne* (1581), p. 52.

[2] *Disputatio de controversia successionis regiae inter patruum et fratris praemortui lium* (1585), pp. 17, 40, 64.

[3] G. Rossaeus (? G. Rose, bishop of Senlis), *De iusta Reipublicae Christianae in Reges impios et haereticos authoritate* (1590), cap. i, iii. Cap. iv, hysterically proclaiming the old doctrine that pagans are superior to heretics, institutes a

although he tries to dissociate his ideas from those of heretics and Scots, is very willing to praise ephors and even tyrannicide, which he declares that Lycurgus like the other ancient legislators permitted; just as they all saw that the end of government is the virtue of the subjects—that is, the saving of their souls. Another Ligueur, Boucher,[1] also includes ephors among his precedents; while among his examples of tyrants who met with divine vengeance is Cleomenes, who slew those *custodes reipublicae*, showed shocking faithlessness, and met a peculiarly horrible death after being smitten with madness. This in fact conflates the story of Cleomenes III with Herodotus' account of the much earlier Spartan king of the name; but it is quite logical for monarchomachs, as Barclay was to call them, to regard Agis and Cleomenes as tyrants rather than glorious *riordinatori*.

Among adherents of limited monarchy open to direct classical or Italian influence praise of Sparta may be found unassociated with praise of the ephorate. The Huguenot monarchomachs were the first to publish La Boëtie's *Contr'Un*,[2] a humanist attack on tyranny written earlier in the century. It praises Lycurgus' institutions, which educated the Spartans to recognize law and reason alone, and repeats a tale of Herodotus' about the Spartans' devotion to liberty, setting this beside the spirit of Romans and Venetians. But a truer monarchomach was the great Scottish historian and humanist Buchanan, whose *De iure regni apud Scotos*,[3] justifying his countrymen's treatment of Mary, had a European readership. Buchanan protests that he cares nothing for names— king, doge, emperor or consul, all are mere magistrates in office to maintain the law, and the inferior party to the contract. King Theopompus knew such a form of government to be the stablest. And Leonidas, Agesilaus, and the rest are described in classical

---

[1] J. Boucher, *De iusta Henrici III abdicatione* (1589).
[2] E. de la Boëtie, *Discours sur la servitude volontaire ou le Contr'Un*, probably written in 1548.
[3] G. Buchanan, *De iure regni apud Scotos* (1579).

---

far-fetched contrast between the ancient lawgivers and the Reformers: the former did believe their laws were given them by God; Luther and Zwingli admitted to being on conversational terms with the Devil, while their private lives were most unlike those of, for example, Lycurgus and even Mahomet. (As for Calvin, he was in every way more unspeakable still.)

fashion as true kings, in contrast with luxurious modern monarchs.[1]

But on this point the authority of Bodin[2] was to weigh heavily against him. He, with his insistence on sovereignty as indivisible and closely associated with the power to make law as well as do justice, explained that Calvin's ephors, tribunes, and demarchs could only occur in states that were really popular or optimate, not in the monarchies that he himself most approved (while admitting one or two fundamental limitations on the king's power). Nonetheless, he is ready to defend hereditary kings against Aristotle by praising Lacedaemon (and Macedonia), and indeed discusses the rules of succession there at some length, to show the dangers of interfering with it. He did of course think that the country was originally a kingdom (as all the old states were, so he said, before they were corrupted). But it was hardly fair of him to annex Theopompus, using the story highly idiosyncratically, to show that the king, while reserving sovereignty to himself, should simultaneously take care not to appropriate the authority due to his council or senate and the subordinate magistrates.

Blackwood,[3] refuting Buchanan, denies there were kings in Sparta: 'inane regum nomen erat'. He does try to prove that even in Sparta the legislator was not bound by the laws, by showing that the heir to the throne was exempted from the regular education. However, Lycurgus and the rest, he said, including Plato and Aristotle, were all ignorant of politics. Contempt for antiquity is not uncommon now among the monarchists, who, in defence of papal claims in particular, develop further than ever before the traditional theory that royal power is given directly by God; and who triumphed with the final failure of the Estates and the general desire for order and peace. The Scot William Barclay, however,

---

[1] There was much neo-scholastic political theory in Spain. The Jesuit Mariana, like Buchanan a historian and humanist, is best remembered for the storm that his justification of tyrannicide rather unfairly caused, and his attempt to apply anti-absolutist beliefs to the government of the Company of Jesus. He has the substance though not the name of an ephorate; but mentions the limited monarchy of Sparta as described by Aristotle as a leading example of the type of state he preferred. J. de Mariana, S.J., *De Rege et Regis institutione* (1599), esp. i. 10. In ii Spartan virtue and education are conventionally lauded.

[2] J. Bodin, *Six livres de la République* (1576 and 1586) ii. 5; ii 3; vi 4; vi. 5; iv. 6.

[3] A. Blackwood, *Adversus Georgii Buchanani dialogum . . . pro regibus apologia* (1581).

for one, who dedicated his refutation of *Buchananum, Brutum, Boucherium* and other monarchomachs to Henri IV,[1] clearly finds pleasure in turning his enemies' weapons—taken from Israel or Sparta—against themselves. He illustrates the fatal effects of rebellion, even against a tyrannic king, by recounting the sad history of the Spartans after they deposed and made away with King Agis; though in fact, after the ephors were set up, he reminds us, the kings (as Nepos says) were not real kings, and the oath of the ephors is therefore irrelevant to discussions of monarchy. He illustrates the attractions of hereditary succession by pointing out that even Sparta had it; the need for some supreme authority by the position of the great magistrates of classical times, the dictators, tribunes, and ephors themselves; and the frightful *insolentia* of the ephors by the well-known story of the king punished for taking a short woman as his wife. He also demolishes the theory that Rome copied Sparta.

On one subject Sparta and antiquity in general could quite legitimately appear on the absolutist side, just as they had embarrassed, in this respect, the monarchomachs, fundamentally more genuine admirers of antiquity. Those who asserted the prince's rights over his subjects' religion, as opposed to the dangerous doctrine of rebellion for conscience' sake and ecclesiastical rights, were justified in observing that in Sparta, as in Rome, political and religious power were associated. Not only had Lycurgus persuaded the people that his laws were divinely inspired, with splendid results in the way of political stability, but the Spartan kings had also been the chief priests. The German Lutheran Henningus Arnisaeus[2] (a great opponent of ephors) explains apparently with regret that this last feature cannot be copied in a Christian country. His hatred of interfering Catholic clergy from Rome also leads him to commend Lycurgus for his distrust of foreigners. Not till the eighteenth century could now fundamentally secular political writers easily follow Machiavelli in taking the side of the classical states on both the constitutional and religious issues.

---

[1] W. Barclay, *De Regno et Regali Potestate* (1600), esp. pp. 61, 116, 139, 326.

[2] H. Arnisaeus, *De subiectione et exemtione clericorum* (1612) i. 4, ii. 1; cf. *De iure majestatis* (1610); and *De auctoritate principum . . . commentatio politica opposita seditiosis quorundam scriptis qui omnem principum Majestatem subiciunt censurae Ephororum et populi* (1612).

Ephors were to prove difficult to kill. The French Calvinists for a time combined hereditary with limited monarchy. Hotman revised his *Franco-Gallia* in this sense, and Daneau,[1] author of a lengthy systematizing work, united approval of hereditary succession (and mention of Sparta as one of the states that never admitted women rulers) with believing the oath of the ephors to be a *pulcherrimum exemplum* of the *foedus* or contract with the supreme magistrate. But by the time of Louis XIV the Huguenots were concentrating desperately on professions of complete loyalty. On the further side of the Channel however we shall see ephors cropping up occasionally till the Restoration; and in Germany, early in the century, they proliferated remarkably. Althusius[2] was a Calvinist, syndic of a German city and in close touch with Holland, facts that throw light on the basically republican frame of his thought. He has been called the philosopher of the monarchomachs, but his sources are more varied than this might suggest. Ignoring other aspects of his corporative theory, we may remark that he followed Bodin in regarding sovereignty as indivisible, but held, unlike him, that it could only reside in the community. With him the word 'ephor' takes the final step to becoming a common noun. It is no longer a case of comparing ephors to Estates; every community has ephors representing it, to set up and if necessary to remove, to defend the rights and to control the actions of, the *summus magistratus*. Tribunes were ephors, Estates are ephors, the Seven Electors of the Empire are ephors, there are general ephors and particular ephors, ecclesiastical and secular, hereditary and temporary ephors. Ephors may be appointed in any manner the people pleases, even, if it so pleases, by the *summus magistratus* himself. They should be of high rank and wealth, but few in number so as to avoid faction. Only as a college are they superior to the supreme magistrate; as individuals

---

[1] Lambertus Danaeus, *Politices Christianae libri VII* (1596), pp. 397, 414, 447–8. (Cf. *Politicorum Aphorismorum Silva* (1591), 'from the best Greek and Latin authors.' What the Greek historians have to teach him about Sparta is chiefly that its kings were hereditary and that the ephors could throw kings into prison and try them—as any *summa potestas* can be tried.)

[2] J. Althusius, *Politica methodice digesta* (1603; 3rd edition 1614). See especially xviii and xix. Althusius, like Danaeus and many sixteenth-century writers, also wants censors to supervise the morals, education, and law-abiding conduct of the citizens. They slightly confuse the two offices by calling ephors, in Sparta at least, censors—censors of the *summus magistratus*, of course. See vi. 4.

they are subject to his control. And in this general sense the word 'ephor' appears until Althusius' theories cease to arouse controversy and sink into the obscurity from which they were rescued in the late nineteenth century. The pages of the greatest political work of the first half of the seventeenth century, Grotius' *De iure Belli et Pacis*,[1] packed with historical quotations and references, attest that the position of Sparta's kings still formed a live issue. Grotius, while preferring absolute monarchy (though based on the contract as well as on natural law), did not deny that other régimes might legitimately exist, or that sovereignty could be divided. Sparta, which had kings subordinate to the people (especially after the introduction of the ephorate) and only doubtfully so called by many ancient writers, formed for him one example of one of these different types of state. More particularly, she stands alone to illustrate the first of seven cases in which Grotius permits rebellion; when such princes contravene the laws they may be resisted, or even executed, as Pausanias was. Grotius shows, too, like so many others before him, some interest in the laws of succession to the throne in Sparta. His followers and commentators, long dominant in much of northern Europe, continue to ventilate these questions from various points of the compass, well into the eighteenth century.

To trace in detail the history of scholarly studies of Sparta would be the task of another book than this (it would have grotesque episodes enough).[2] But the importance to political thought of both the Spartan and Jewish constitutions and the belief in their resemblance was perhaps relevant to the amount of ink expended by scholars especially in the seventeenth century on the 'enodatio perdifficilis et vexatissimae quaestionis', as the learned Huetius so rightly called it: how exactly had the two peoples been related?

The Middle Ages had been contented with speculation about

---

[1] H. Grotius, *De iure Belli et Pacis* (1625) i. 3, par. viii. 2; i. 4, par. viii. 1. 'Primum ergo, qui principes sub populo sunt, sive ab initio talem acceperunt potestatem, sive postea ita convenit, ut in Lacedaemone, si peccent in leges, ac rempublicam, non tantum vi repelli possunt, sed, si opus sit, puniri morte: quod Pausaniae regi Lacedaemoniorum contigit.'

[2] The first large-scale investigation—just as in antiquity, into the institutions rather than the history of the place—is that of the Dane N. Cragius, *De Republica Lacedaemoniorum libri IV* (1593). It has no political *parti pris*, but admires Spartan *virtus*, and ends curiously by wishing modern states would emulate Sparta in humanity (by burying the corpses of executed criminals), p. 269.

Abraham's end of the pedigree. The Jews were of course descended from Isaac, but the Spartans perhaps sprang from one of Abraham's sons by Hagar or Keturah. Or what of Eliezer of Damascus, sometimes said to be Abraham's son? Or would a less direct connection pass muster?

In the Renaissance it was realized that the Greek side of the story was even trickier. *Alii aliter*; explanations appear to have been legion. The ancient reference to 'Judaeus Sparto' or whatever the reading of Stephanus' text was thought to be was noticed, and various connections between Cadmus, his Sparti, and the Spartans worked out. Oebalus, a mythical king of Lacedaemon, might be identified with Ebal. That was *futilissimum*, said the great J. J. Scaliger: Ebal was only a cousin five times removed of Abraham and lived hundreds of years before Oebalus. He himself preferred to suspend judgement, as, after serious argument, did some other distinguished scholars.[1]

But attempts at *enodatio* went on. Grotius lent his authority to the theory that the Dorians were to be regarded as descendants of the Pelasgians (those conveniently mysterious blanks in early Greek history), and these came to Greece from Arabia.[2] Huet, the erudite bishop of Avranches, produced several ideas that were greeted with, in the circumstances, unnecessary derision; especially when he suggested a link via Crete, quoting Tacitus' statement that the Idaei of Mount Ida emigrated and became Iudaei. But he also, following the Jewish tradition of identifying many early lawgivers and prophets, thought Minos was Moses. Or, he also suggests, there is Hercules, ancestor of the Dorians, who had various oriental connections and should be identified with Joshua.[3] Another scholar preferred to make the Lacedaemonians offspring of the Thracian Odomantes and—misled like an ancient commentator on Aristophanes by a joke about circumcision—the Odomantes of the Idumaeans or Edomites, who were brothers of the Jews.[4]

In the eighteenth century the urgency of the problem was no longer felt, and scepticism of every kind was mounting. The

---

[1] J. J. Scaliger, *Isagogicorum Cronologiae Canonum Libri III* (1606), p. 332.

[2] H. Grotius, *Commentarii . . . ad Maccabaica* 16; xii. 21.

[3] P. D. Huetius, *Demonstratio Evangelica* (1679); Prop. iv, p. 93, 155, 196.

[4] Stephanus Morinus, *Dissertatio de cognatione Lacedaemoniorum et Ebraeorum* (1683) i. 13 (cf. Scholiast to Aristophanes, *Acharnians* 157).

famous letters were increasingly denounced as forgeries.[1] If the problem was still considered by learned ecclesiastics, editing Josephus or commenting on Maccabees, they hazarded no new theories. But the legend was only knocked on the head in the nineteenth century, with rational explanation of its invention.

[1] G. Wernsdorffius, *Commentarium de fide historica librorum Macchabaicorum* (1747), pp. 140 ff., gives a full account of the balance-sheet in his day.

12

IN UTOPIA AND AMONG
THE SAVAGES

No ONE today would think of taking Agesilaus as a model, either for himself or for his rulers. And ideas of constitutional government and its safeguards have been profoundly modified since the days of clamour for the mixed state or for the ephorate. But when we discuss rival patterns for society as a whole, we still find we have not quite forgotten Sparta; and the modern reader, who tends to be better acquainted with Plato than with Plutarch or Polybius, may find more interest in a brief consideration of Sparta's part in the Utopian tradition.

The imaginary states depicted by economic and social reformers from the sixteenth century on drew inspiration, from the start, from many sources. Theoretically, of course, from reason and nature; in practice, very often, from reaction against crying contemporary abuses, above all faction, war, and the unhappy effects of extreme social contrasts and rapid economic change; from the traditional belief that money was the root of all evil, from admiration for the humble and hardworking early Christian communities or the monastic orders, and, as time went on, from the strange peoples of the newly discovered continents. But Plato's *Republic* remained vitally important, above all because it had established the literary genre, and to many the authority of Aristotle continued to recommend the ideal state briefly sketched at the end of the *Politics*. The Renaissance was well aware that the ideal states of ancient and modern times bore a strong family resemblance (due, of course, to common and usually unconscious presuppositions even more than to direct imitation), and also that Sparta, not this time merely following, as so often, in the wake of Rome, headed the whole list and gave it the encouragement of her real existence. For one thing, Plutarch had explicitly praised Lycurgus for achieving, through his legislation, what Plato and the other philosophers had only dreamt of.

It would, of course, be folly to attempt to measure Sparta's influence, direct or indirect. But there can be little doubt that she contributed to the authority of such ideas as those of state restriction of, or control over, private property, the use of money, industry, commerce, and foreign contacts; a measure of equality between the sexes, with the regulation of sex and marriage in the service of the community, particularly by the laying down of minimum ages higher than was usual; public and primarily moral education, common meals, and simple uniform clothing—especially the restriction of the young to a single garment; regulations against luxury in building (Lycurgus was supposed to have insisted that only the saw and the axe should be used on a Spartan's house, but the Renaissance inevitably went on to see the ideal city in terms of town-planning); the insistence on few and simple laws—often a direct reaction against the present, as well; and the tendency to make the imaginary state a republic headed by variously elected magistrates and councils with members of great age and experience; to make it, too, for a long time, a citystate with a small territory—as might be natural in Italy, but even More's Utopia is a confederation of cities; and lastly, the view that susceptibility to change was a mark of imperfection.

If a Utopia is, in theory, an attempt to construct by the sole light of reason a society where man will be as good and happy as possible, in practice it might be defined as an imaginary society embodying a number of the above ideas. They are almost all found in some form in More's *Utopia* itself, which in 1516 was the first true ideal state of modern times, and became in its turn a work of enormous influence; although it should be remembered that to More and many of his successors a state created by reason without Revelation could not have the final word. What we must do, therefore, is very briefly to trace the development of the Utopian tradition and indicate where, and to some extent why, it departs from its classical origins; and whether, when it is still close to these, it appeals openly to them or not. Even where the classical states are not called up as precedents, the mere existence of their modern counterparts will increase the attention they receive and help to determine which aspects of them appear relevant to the present.

One important distinction soon emerges. The complete rejection of private property was in the air in the sixteenth century.

One can find some expression of it in the works of many human-ists, such as Colet and the great Greek scholar Budé, both friends of More's; and the most famous Utopias, More's own, with Cam-panella's *Civitas Solis*[1] and Andreae's *Christianopolis*[2] a century later, subscribe to it. So does More's eccentric Italian translator Doni[3] in his own imaginary state. Campanella even adopts Plato's sexual communism and warrior females (praising Spartan women in the process), though More's unit was the patriarchal family, and Andreae's the smaller group of immediate relatives. But there is a sub-species, or moderate Utopia, which contents itself with enforcing equality of possessions as well as leaving the family more or less intact. This may lean on Aristotle's ideal state, as briefly described in Book VII of the *Politics*, or the 'second-best state' of Plato's *Laws*. Both of these bore a very definite relation to Sparta; and everyone knew (or rather believed) that her land had been divided into equal lots.

An early example of this sub-species is the description of the country of the Garamanti, given to Alexander the Great in Guevara's work on the ideal prince.[4] These are a simple and peaceful people, laconic of speech, with equal inheritances, few laws, identical clothing (a single garment), and strict family plan-ning. All innovations are forbidden. There is also early euthanasia, a real novelty? Later, there are Italian Utopias reflecting a revived Aristotelianism. Francesco Patrizi's *Città Felice*[5] is closely based on the *Politics* and on Venice, whose myth undoubtedly had some Utopian features. A small citizen body, supported by a slave peasantry and by merchants and artisans, owns equal lots of land and devotes itself to war, government, and virtue. Ludovico Agostini, too, a pious gentleman of the Counter-Reformation, constructs an imaginary country with a class of nobles who own the land, although the state controls its use.[6] Trade is limited, and there is public education, religious and moral rather than intellec-

---

[1] T. Campanella, *Civitas Solis* (1623).

[2] J. V. A. Andreae, *Christianopolis* (1619).

[3] A. F. Doni, *Il mondo savio e pazzo* in *I Mondi* (1552).

[4] A. de Guevara, *Libro del emperador Marco Aurelio con el Relox de Principe* (1529); the Garamanti, naturally in such a work, are not republicans.

[5] 1553; this Francesco Patrizi is not to be confused with the fifteenth-century bishop, the Sienese author of the *de Institutione reipublicae* and *de regno*.

[6] Ludovico Agostini, *La Repubblica Immaginaria*, ed. L. Firpo, 1957 (extrac-ted from his dialogues *L'Infinito* ii. 2).

tual. Manners are ascetic and warlike. The citizens are united by ties of family and kinship, but also by occasional common meals. Not entirely dissimilar is the earliest French Utopia, the *Royaume d'Antangil*.[1] Bacon's fragment, the *Nova Atlantis*, is as it stands a hasty sketch of a moderate Utopia in its social, not political, aspects; there is no communism or even exact equality, but a patriarchal family, public education, eugenic features in the relation of the sexes, and little contact with the outside world.

Few works even in this class actually mention Sparta. Doni had said that, had he thought it worth while, he could have pointed out which features in the *Mondo Savio e Pazzo* came from Sparta, and which from Plato and other sources; but his failure to mention More, who certainly influenced him strongly, reminds us that anyway we should perhaps not lay too much weight on the classical citations that always looked so well.

In some respects most late Renaissance Utopias move away from Greek positions. Except for Patrizi and the French author, their creators were too horrified by the misery of the poor of their time, and the idleness as well as luxury of the rich, to tolerate a strictly hierarchical class structure or accept the Greek idealization of leisure. Work—for a reasonable number of hours—and natural equality are the rule for all, or all but a few priests or officials. A small number of slaves, however, and criminals under sentence (as in More), or foreigners, often survive for the most degraded tasks. This means, not so much that Sparta or Plato are overtly criticized, as that they seem to take, with the whole tradition, a rather egalitarian turn. Indeed, when democracy on the Athenian and Florentine model was regarded as a proven failure, the Utopian form of state was almost the only available vehicle for egalitarian ideas. It is no doubt to a horror of poverty that the relative lack of austerity should also be traced; comfort stops short, of course, of corrupting luxury. An un-Spartan, un-Greek pacifism is usual; the religious question is of new importance, states being either Christian or ready to abandon for Christianity their enlightened, rational religion, though not, in several instances, their principles of toleration. Un-Spartan, too, though not so un-Platonic, are the intellectual interests of the inhabitants. In the seventeenth century these become increasingly scientific and

[1] *Histoire du grand et admirable Royaume d'Antangil*, par I.D.M.G.T. (1616).

technological—in Campanella, Bacon, and to some extent
Andreae. (True, Agostini and Andreae still suspect the arts.) Thus
agriculture sometimes begins to be of less importance than industry and its organization, and in this Andreae, in particular, foreshadows later socialist thought. All this reflects, too, an increasing
independence of antiquity in intellectual life in general.

Finally, since most of our writers were desirous of establishing
what human reason could attain in shaping the perfect society,
rather than in pointing the way to reforms unlikely in the world
they lived in, and since many of them used the framework of the
imaginary voyage, which tends to mean the discovery of an
already flourishing state, the problems of founding such a state
are usually bypassed, and there is little interest in Lycurgus, the one
(supposedly) real and successful Utopian lawgiver, who so often
came to the fore when the possibility of creating a good society on
earth was genuinely entertained.

The reality of Sparta was certainly her strong point; wherever
Utopian ideas seemed to have come down to earth, she may be
found taking precedence over other objects of comparison. Even
Calvin can compare primitive monastic life to that of the Lacedaemonians;[1] and the military Orders, in particular the Knights
of Malta, could seem even more similar. In the early sixteenth
century, indeed before the real Utopias of that disturbed and
thoughtful age began, Antonio de Ferraris, known as Il Galateo,
spent his last years in the little Apulian town of Gallipoli, not far
from what every reader of Latin poetry knew as 'Lacedaemonian'
Tarentum, now Taranto. Il Galateo was a humanist, proud of the
Greek traditions of his province and his own family. In the en-
dearing description he gives of his life at Gallipoli he claims to feel
himself there in Sparta or Plato's *Republic*: 'sentio enim hic aliquid
Graecanicum.' There was no great wealth or poverty, the hum of
commerce was absent, and everyone was tranquil and happy. In
particular, the good doctor amuses himself with the fancy that the
chaste and charming women, who had proved their courage in the
recent Venetian siege, resemble Spartan girls (in spite of marrying
at twelve and never going out of doors). After all, he reflects, the
population is probably of Lacedaemonian stock.[2]

A century later, when the Utopian tradition was losing force in
Italy, Ludovico Zuccolo wrote a pleasant and unradical contribu-

[1] Calvin, *Institutes* iv. 12.8.   [2] *Descriptio de Urbe Gallipoli* (1513).

tion to the genre, and also put forward the republic of San Marino, which was long described in Utopian language, as a better candidate than the republic of San Marco for the title of the New Sparta.[1] Like the latter, he observes, San Marino could claim to have preserved republican liberty for over a thousand years—nay, even democracy, and that without being saved by stupidity, as the Swiss and Ragusans were, from the sad fate of Florence. She was far happier than Lacedaemon, for nature ensured her all that Lycurgus had aimed at by artificial and stringent regulations, maintained only with great effort. In San Marino, where prudence and nature worked hand in hand, he would have seen all his ambitions fulfilled. No foreigners, no merchants, bankers, craftsmen, or doctors dreamed of coming hither to corrupt the citizens' simple virtue. All were naturally equal in poverty, whereas Lycurgus' artificial and precise division of wealth could not be long sustained. Where poverty keeps the population down, infants need not be exposed, and in a naturally poor state a hardy education need not be forcibly imposed. The young devote themselves to hunting and military exercises (the San Marinesi had a reputation as mercenaries). And expansion, the cause of Sparta's downfall, is physically impossible.

General political writers recognized the Utopian state as a type; for a while they classified it rather than criticized it, though Platonic communism might come in for regular dismissal in the manner of Aristotle. But criticism was stimulated by an event that shocked respectable Europe—the appearance of the Anabaptists, and especially of their régime in Münster, suppressed in 1535. They themselves, of course, appealed only to Christian precedent, and their critics often hesitated to compare them with states which had a title to consideration. But Bodin for one was as ready to deal with the egalitarian Sparta of the Utopists as the mixed Sparta of the Venetians (it might also be observed that his sceptical rejection of two idealizing anecdotes about Sparta in Plutarch roused the indignation of Montaigne).

Bodin dismisses Plato's *Republic* and More's *Utopia* as impracticable, and even holds that complete communism would destroy the very essence of the *res publica*, which is only to be defined by contrast with *res privata* or private property. He admits that it is possible for a people to live, that is, chiefly to feed, in common,

[1] *La città felice* (in *Dialoghi*, 1625).

like the Spartans, Cretans, and Anabaptists of Münster—who
only succeeded in causing quarrels and destroying all family
affection. And for Bodin the family is the prototype and foundation of the commonwealth, its existence closely involved with
that of property, an institution in accordance with natural and
divine law.

Lycurgan Sparta, as we remember, was for Bodin a democracy;
indeed these states that equalize goods as well as honours and
rights are for him the only real democracies. But he did not, as we
also remember, think Sparta remained one long. No state has ever
for any great period maintained equality of rank (which is
against nature) or of goods (which is even more invidious).
Lycurgus' division was immediately subverted by the fact that, as
Bodin believed, Sparta adhered to the principle of primogeniture,
while the citizens produced different numbers of offspring. Finally,
when lots were allowed to be sold, even equality among those
who owned land disappeared.[1]

The Counter-Reformation had not at first stifled, though it had
modified, Utopian thought. But in the seventeenth century most
of Catholic Europe settled to the defence of traditional forms of
society. The Utopian stock continued to bear fruit, however, in
England,[2] and also in France, where critics of contemporary
society, at first usually unquiet spirits of no great literary or social
eminence, and often of Protestant or *libertin* affiliations, developed
the form of the exotic imaginary voyage.

More's Utopia was set in the framework of one of Amerigo
Vespucci's voyages, Bacon's New Atlantis was reached by a ship
off course in the Pacific, Andreae pretends to have been wrecked
on shores under the sway of Christianopolis (and there are classical
precedents, if not very famous ones, for philosophic travellers'
tales, for example those of Euhemerus and Iambulus, as preserved
in the historian Diodorus Siculus). But Campanella was perhaps
the only one of the earlier Utopists to be much influenced by
reports of newly discovered civilizations. There is possibly something of Peru in his City of the Sun, even if it is located in Tapro-

---

[1] J. Bodin, *Six livres de la République* i. 1, 2; v. 2, 4.

[2] Harrington's *Oceana* is in some ways a moderate Utopia with classical (and
Italian) sources, but owing to the place it took in the general political argument
of the time we will deal with it elsewhere. Other English Utopian publications
of the time are primarily religious in inspiration.

bane or Ceylon. As time goes on, then, more and more elements go to the making of Utopias; but it is worth pursuing the tradition a little further, particularly since the eighteenth-century return to directly classical inspiration is thus more comprehensible. There we will leave it; for nineteenth-century examples of the form, whether intoxicated by the scientific possibilities of the future, or rigidly agricultural, are even less interested in classical prototypes than those of the seventeenth century are. It may however be observed that the distrust of Sparta prevalent in liberal circles in the present century runs parallel to some extent with the new literary line of anti-Utopias.

It should be remembered that, while accounts of, in particular, the Inca state of Peru and the Chinese empire by missionaries and others were to have great influence on the Utopian tradition, such accounts were themselves influenced by it. Not merely were their authors often consciously or unconsciously recommending countries in which they often felt a proprietary interest in a way likely to appeal at home; they tended themselves to understand these alien civilizations in terms that were not alien, and to be impressed by what seemed to strike a familiar note. The swift and general realization of the corruption and ruin that contact with Europeans usually brought both 'civilized' and 'savage' societies doubtless reinforced one of the oldest (and most Spartan) features of Utopian states, the need for foreigners to be kept out. And the state socialism of Peru, a highly organized civilization that yet lacked money and certain familiar arts such as writing; China, with its philosopher-officials and its distrust of dealings with outsiders; how else but within the Utopian tradition were such things comprehensible, and what wonder if conventional Utopian features are exaggerated, or mistakenly introduced?

And there was a further reason for bringing exotic, or at least American, peoples into connection with both ancient and ideal states. The great dispute as to the nature and capacities of the American Indian and, in consequence, the way he should be treated split sixteenth-century Europe; above all Spain, where the controversy inevitably took shape in legal and Aristotelian terms. Against the theory that the Indians fell into Aristotle's category of barbarians who were slaves by nature, and could be used as such without injustice, there were many protests; but none so persistent and forceful as those of the famous Dominican, Bartolomé de

Las Casas. He composed his enormous *Historia de las Indias*[1] (begun in 1527) to prove that the Indians fulfilled every one of Aristotle's conditions for living the good life, and were indeed superior to any other pagan people and, in some respects, to a good many Christian ones, too. Any and every race known to Renaissance scholarship appears in the comparison; but in several contexts Las Casas is particularly concerned with resemblances to Sparta. There was, he argues, in effect human sacrifice in Sparta (the whipping contests) as in Mexico; there was polygamy. Burial customs were similar in both, and similar, also, to those of the Church. Mexican education was as careful as (and in encouraging toughness, hard work, obedience, and discipline, it equalled) that of Sparta, while in forbidding theft and in its treatment of girls it was far nearer reason and natural law (the pagan's sole guide). Finally, he insists that the laws and government of Mexico were just as good as those of Lycurgus and Plato; in particular, he repeats, as good as those of the three states placed highest by Aristotle: Crete, Sparta, and (still!) the *Calcedonios ó calcedonenses*. Almost the same words recur when he comes to deal with Peru. These are the three republics, according to the philosopher, 'que menos ó menores defectos tuvieron'; Peru, where rulers and governed go about their business in order and tranquillity, is better than any of them 'en buenas leyes y costumbres'.

The *Historia de las Indias* was not published till the present century. But Las Casas only made explicit and worked out in detail a line of thought that was likely to strike any defender of the Indians. The laws of Peru, in particular, are sometimes compared with those of the ancient legislators. Garcilaso de la Vega,[2] 'El Inca', as he had a right to call himself since his mother was of Inca blood, could in his famous if idealized account of his country of birth quote one learned ecclesiastic (himself also part-Indian) who put the Inca legislators beside and even above Numa, Solon, and Lycurgus; and another who thought that if Incas and Mexicans

---

[1] *Apologetica Historia de las Indias* (Madrid, 1909), pp. 512, 522, 565, 580–3, 603, 614, 668, 676, 681 (the last also has a vast list of peoples the Peruvians excel—'á los assyrios á los babilonios á los taxiles á los beoçios á los samites á los pheniçes y poenos', etc., etc.)

[2] Garcilaso de la Vega, 'el Inca', *Los Comentarios Reales de los Incas* (1606) ii. 27, v. 11, quoting P. Blas Valera, whose MS. is lost; and the Jesuit Joseph de Acosta's *Historia Natural y Moral de los Indios* (1590) vi. 1 (cf. vi. 26 Mexican care for education as the foundation of the state compared to Plato's).

had made some errors, so had Lycurgus and Plato. As for his description of these laws, various features stand out and speak for themselves; above all, the agrarian and sumptuary laws and those regulating labour in common and other forms of fellowship—all kept for over six hundred years—, not to mention the frequent communal meals.

Other writers adduce antiquity only to show its inferiority, now sometimes being asserted. Botero remarks that the Inca laws on the distribution of land far surpassed those of Lycurgus or the Romans. Somewhat later Sir William Temple allowed the legislators of China, Peru, Scythia, and Arabia an equal claim with those of Greece and Rome to Heroick Virtue, and regarded the institutions of the first, as in effect many came to do, as superior to the 'imaginary schemes of European wits'. On the other side of the question (arguing that the ancients' sources of information were as wide as ours) he revived the antique heresy that Lycurgus 'travelled into India and brought from thence also the chief principles of his laws and politics', which he learned from the 'Brachmans' (Temple regarded Sparta as not typically Greek).[1] It is a pity that we cannot also send Lycurgus off to China and Peru; but probably no modern was so bold.

The taste for tales of voyages, flourishing since the early sixteenth century, reached great heights, particularly in France, where in 1663 it was said to have ousted novel-reading. It is not surprising, therefore, that knowledge of ancient Greece itself might, for the general public, come wrapped up in accounts of travels in the Turkish empire—highly exotic, if comparatively close at hand. The main point of Guillet's lively *Lacedemone ancienne et nouvelle*[2] was the comparison between the manners of classical and modern times, with the purely natural virtue and reason of antiquity shining the more brightly for contrast. Unfortunately, like so many literary voyages, this one (supposedly by Guillet's brother) had never taken place at all, and the distinguished antiquarian and doctor Spon rated the author soundly for the fraud, without being able to prevent the work continuing on its very successful course right through the eighteenth century.

[1] Sir William Temple, *Essays: Of Heroic Virtue* and *Of Ancient and Modern Learning* (first published in *Miscellanea*, 1692).
[2] [G. Guillet de S. Georges] *Lacedemone ancienne et nouvelle* (1676); published under the name of his brother the Sieur de la Guilletière.

But the really famous travels in Greece are now starting, Spon's and Wheler's trip among them. It may be pointed out that for some time Sparta, in the interior, had been one of the more inaccessible parts of the country, and little visited. And henceforth genuine visitors tend, with a few exceptions, to be either severely topographical and archaeological in their interests, or, later, so overwhelmed with the beauty of the site in the fertile Eurotas valley with Taygetus towering above that they are unable to turn their minds from myth and poetry to social and political matters.

Let us return to our Utopias.[1] They had become, then, almost a recognized branch of travel literature, without having entirely broken the link with their Greek originals. This at least is very true of the chief French Utopia of the period, Denis de Veiras' *Histoire des Sévarambes* (1677), which was realistic enough to persuade some people it recorded genuine discoveries in the *Terre Australe*.[2] Veiras was of Protestant origin, and spent some years in England; his book, however, escaped condemnation in France, and it has been suggested that it reflects the reforming zeal of Colbert. Looking for the problems of Louis XIV's France in the exotic Utopia, we observe the importance of religious controversy. Not only toleration but purely rational religion now seem to be seriously advocated, and the Sévarambes positively reject Christianity. The close association of religion and the state, often broken by earlier writers who had to leave room for a Christian hierarchy, is reaffirmed, perhaps under the influence of Peru and China and the persistent religious disorders of France more than under that of the ancient world.

[1] It is impossible to analyse here the various attempts actually made in this century to set up model societies in new countries; often their founders had more religious than classical learning, but that is not altogether true either of the Jesuits or some of the founders of North American colonies, who were doubtless aware of any relation to Utopian ideas that their states may have had.

[2] Which was only an article of faith at this time and thus left more scope for invention than America. Slightly earlier than Veiras comes the *Terre Australe Connue* of Foigny, rather a satirical attack on European society than a serious attempt to show how it could be rebuilt, but though fantastic, still from a Utopian standpoint. His naked and vegetarian hermaphrodites are far more rational and healthy than what we know as man, and can do without most of the usual Utopian machinery of government, but their public education, great learning, etc. show they belong to this tradition rather than that of the Noble Savage.

Peru and China were also empires of vast extent, managed by means of well-organized censuses and regular subdivisions. In this they were far more obvious models for France, and the Sévarambes, than the ancient city-states. So were their absolute and divine emperors. Veiras however effects a compromise with old Utopian traditions by calling his ruler Viceroy of the Sun, this god being the true monarch and owner of all property. His fundamental laws may not be overthrown by the Viceroy, who is elected, and also has a strong council to keep him to his duty. He dwells however in splendour in an Australian Versailles, and sixteenth-century Utopias are recalled by the interest in town-planning, as in the stress on work for all, on comfort and abundance, and on the arts and sciences.

Most of the details can be, and have been, paralleled again and again both in earlier ideal states and in genuine travellers' tales. It is clear that nothing need come at first hand from Sparta, and also that the origins are not forgotten. It may be recorded that the legislator of the Sévarambes was a Persian, educated by a Venetian tutor in Greek letters, and that the two 'tirèrent tant des livres anciens que nouveaux, des observations qu'ils avoient faites dans leurs voyages, et des lumières qu'ils avaient naturellement, les Loix et les règles de bien vivre'. Indeed it is with the legislator, treated with unusual seriousness, that we come closest to Sparta. Hints for Sévarias' life may have been taken from Xenophon's Cyrus, the just conqueror and king, from Moses who led his persecuted co-religionists to a promised land as Sévarias led his Parsees, from Manco Capac the first Inca as described by Garcilaso de la Vega, not to mention Numa Pompilius, Diocletian, Calvin, the emperors of China, and even Oliver Cromwell and the author's own career (Sévarias is an anagram of Vairasse). But Lycurgus is indubitably present in him too. Alone of the band Lycurgus, like Sévarias, rebuilt a shattered society after preparing himself by extensive travels, and he was always seen as one of the chief legislators to use religious deceit for noble political ends.

The similarities in his achievements are exaggerated by the laconophil Montesquieu, when he wrote that 'quand vous voyez dans la vie de Lycurgue, les lois qu'il donna aux Lacédémoniens, vous croyez lire l'histoire des Sévarambes'.[1] But the ancient ideas still surviving in this work are many. There is complete equality

[1] Montesquieu, *De l'esprit des lois* iv. 6.

between citizens; the state owns the land and organizes the distribution of products (without using money) between the various communities; it gets rid of deformed infants (sending them humanely abroad), forbids marriage before a certain age, and then renders it compulsory, though cohabitation is still restricted. It educates the children from the usual age of seven, girls as well as, though apart from, boys, and trains both in patriotism and in warlike exercises—though war is regarded as an unlikely eventuality. It also prevents contact with corrupting strangers, although, by a practice Bacon began, it sends out spies to make sure that no scientific or other discoveries pass it by.

The ideas of Utopia and of the Noble Savage are very closely related. Reason and nature, those two ambiguous concepts, had been allied since the Stoics. It is only necessary to lay a little more stress on the latter than the former, and the all-powerful state, with its complicated economic regulations, its numerous and carefully elected magistrates, its highly organized education, dissolves into a community without laws or government, arts or sciences. The people who live according to natural law rather than Revelation also live, very often, in a state of nature.

Even in the Middle Ages and the early Renaissance certain primitivistic strains of thought have been traced. Thereupon came the accounts, not, this time, of the great civilizations of Mexico, Peru, and China, but of the simple Indians of the Caribbean, and later of Brazil and North America. The battle was soon joined between those who regarded the savages as beasts or little more and those who saw them through a golden haze. Indeed, at first it was the Golden Age of the ancient poets and mythographers, or their fanciful pictures of the Fortunate Isles, that were recalled by the Indians' idle life, in a tropical climate, where earth brought forth her fruits in abundance; by their ignorance of private property, of distinctions in rank, of organized religion and government—or at least what appeared to the untrained European observer to be such. The Indians' naked beauty gave a classical turn to the thoughts of Renaissance man, and the wildest ancient myths seemed to spring to life.

But comparisons soon became less poetical. Not that the linking of Spartan and savage is a rapid growth (or even so common as is sometimes supposed). For one thing, it must be remembered that the ancient, primarily Cynic, theory of the Natural Spartan (who, we recall, bore a resemblance to the simpler Indians of India) was hard to disengage from the eclectic pages of Plutarch. At first perhaps there is simply an insistence that even Lycurgus had nothing better than savage society to build upon—all peoples are capable of civilization to the highest degree. Thus Las Casas, on his wilder tribes.[1] Montaigne, one of the first and most influential men of letters to champion Indian society and criticize that of Europe in its light, goes somewhat further. He indicates the relation between the Utopian and primitive visions very neatly in his famous chapter *Des cannibales*.[2] This rests of course chiefly on the fact that the lack of money and private property was a feature of both; both involved some sort of egalitarianism, and Sparta, and some other Utopias, made a point of having few, if important, laws, and few arts and sciences. Liberty, however interpreted, was vital to both. Montaigne regrets that Lycurgus and Plato had no knowledge of nations that surpassed not only the Golden Age as depicted by poets, but also the conception and even desire of philosophy. 'Ils n'ont peu imaginer une nayfveté si pure et simple, comme nous la voyons par experience: ny n'ont peu croire que nostre societé se peut maintenir avec si peu d'artifice et de soudeure humaine.' The Indians, Montaigne points out, possess no institutions whatever; he lists all that they lack at great length. Discussing their punishment of false prophets, he adduces the ancient Scyths; and discussing their thirst for glory, unmixed with greed, and their warlike excellence, he is soon to be found diverging to Leonidas and another Lacedaemonian hero.

It was natural enough that, faced with the task of classifying and comprehending peoples so foreign to its own experience, the age should fall back on the ancient world for comparative material. For us, the next step is taken in Canada, whence French missionaries in the seventeenth century often sent back enthusiastic accounts of their charges, from real interest and affection or to prove, to those who supplied money, that the pagans were worth persevering with. The Jesuits were not surprisingly those most given to classical reminiscences.

Till now the northern tribes had been despised and little known.

[1] Op. cit., pp. 126–7. Even the Athenians were savage before they were taught; look at what the Cretan legislators did; 'dejo de traer à la memoria Licurgo', as all he did is so well known to those who read of history, politics and philosophy. [2] M. de Montaigne, *Essais* i. 31.

Their circumstances were emphatically not those of the Golden Age. Instead of careless inhabitants of the tropics, who had only to stretch out their hands for luxuriant fruits, and whose bodily delicacy had been stressed by Las Casas (because Aristotle's natural slaves were physically strong), here were hardy and virile peoples despising all occupations but war and the chase, trained to endure extremes of cold, hunger, and fatigue, living in fraternal affection and equality, their only political institutions a council of elders (for they greatly revered age) and sometimes a chief, elected and with limited powers. Like all respectable savages they were classically handsome, often eloquent, and they lacked money and, to any great extent, private property. No wonder they are often compared to Greeks and early Romans, and other nations of antiquity. Particularly full of such material is the widely read account of New France by Marc Lescarbot.[1] He jeers, indeed, at those who, 's'imaginans une république de Platon', ask if marriage exists there; but he describes the life of the Indian as 'à l'antique, sans appareil', and spends several hundred pages illustrating this with a flood of classical learning. The races which surface most often seem to be the ancient Gauls and Germans,[2] and it is wrong to assign the Spartans too prominent a place here.[3] But they certainly prove relevant when Lescarbot comes to describe the tests of valour which the Canadians set themselves, their dances, and their unwalled settlements.

Montaigne might criticize Europe as he studied his cannibals, but he had no desire to abandon his library for the forests of a *monde enfant*. The missionaries might seize opportunities to point out the shortcomings of their own countrymen, and a few even wondered, rashly, for a moment, whether the Indians, who went naked without shame and whose women brought forth painlessly, had fallen with Adam. But in the last resort they must condemn them as pagans, and most of them can see natural vices as well as natural virtues. As the seventeenth century went on, however, and French society became increasingly rigid, rebels of

---

[1] M. Lescarbot, *Histoire de la Nouvelle France* (1609); in the fuller 3rd edition, 1618, see esp. Book VI chap. 14.

[2] Grotius indeed argued that the North Americans were descended from ancestors of Tacitus' Germans, though this was not generally accepted.

[3] As does Gilbert Chinard, in *L'Amérique et la rêve exotique dans la litterature française au XVIIme et XVIIIme siecle* (1913) ii. 1.

all kinds—religious, social, and political—began to employ the old arguments with new ardour. Some took to the woods themselves; and, returning to a wandering life in Europe, published (usually in London or Amsterdam) accounts of their adventures which show the *bon sauvage* coming to full development. Such writers thirst increasingly for freedom—not only from absolute kings, but from all magistrates, laws, religious and sexual dogmas. Often the wild men are described as natural deists, perhaps combining this with worship of the sun as symbol or subordinate deity. (This differs from the religion of many Utopias only by the absence of an established priesthood.) It had to be admitted that marriage existed among the Indians; but divorce was easy and simple, and intercourse before marriage unrestricted.

In all this there is much that is unclassical, or that, like the extravagance of praising nomadism as proving a noble contempt of possessions, could only lead to peripheral classical peoples like the Scyths. But a consciousness of similarity did remain. Now that admiration for the savage was less condescending, it was more easily associated with admiration for antiquity; and vice versa, since the sixteenth century, the modern world had to some extent emancipated itself from its sense of inferiority, and even those who did not proclaim their hostility to the ancients were ready to admit that they were in some ways at least simpler, more primitive, than modern men.

13

THE REVOLUTIONARY PERIOD
IN ENGLAND

ELIZABETHAN England, with one eye on the needs of the country and another on rebellions abroad that provoked some sympathy, torn between the original teachings of the great reformers and traditional constitutionalist formulations, tended to touch with a long pair of tongs theories that anyone, even the Estates, might resist the monarch. Hooker, indeed, would not allow it; but before him some Anglican writers agreed, very noncommittally, that in some countries officers with such duties had been set up (they seem to have thought primarily of the Electors in Germany) —though it was often argued that, even if the king's civil power rested on a contract, his religious authority was direct from God and unchallengeable. The Puritans for their part found it necessary towards the end of the reign to deny that they followed the Scots or other recent Calvinist parties in allowing rebellion.[1] But it was only to the most classically-minded writers, it seems, like the Italian-travelled diplomat and courtier Charles Merbury, that such theories were most readily indicated by reference not to Electors but ephors; and he considered that unless the common belief that 'a Prince should be subject unto the States and Peares of his Realmes: as the kings of LACEDEMON were to the EPHORI' were 'well tempered and conveniently limited' it would be most 'prejudicial unto th'estate of a Monarchie'.[2]

But Merbury was perhaps unusual in refusing to advocate mixed government. It was very frequently stated that this was what England had—though what happened when the parts conflicted was fortunately not an urgent question and was not explored. The classical prototypes were not always adduced; but we

---

[1] Bancroft in his alarmist *Daungerous Positions* . . . (1593) refers on p. 29 to Buchanan and his praise of 'the discipline of Laconia where it was strange to have one man pull off another man's sockes, at his going to bed'.

[2] *A Briefe Discourse of Royall Monarchie* (1581), p. 43.

find, for example, Aylmer comparing his country with, and only with, 'Lacedemonia the noblest and best city governed that ever was', and its kings, senate, and *hippagretes* to king or queen with the two Houses of Parliament. In each case no element can act without the others, though in Sparta senate and ephors were more powerful than the king.[1] And Sir Thomas Smith, in his *Commonwealth of England*, describes England, though with some confusion of language, as in some degree mixed (which indeed he thought most states were). But he too perceived that in foreign affairs or diplomacy at least 'the Kingdome of England is farre more absolute than the Dukedom of Venice is, or the Kingdome of the Lacedemonians was'.[2]

Sparta indeed increasingly comes in tandem with Venice, or at least is seen through the eyes of the Italian writers.[3] Thus, to take two great names, Sir Walter Raleigh perhaps betrays his acquaintance with Machiavelli when he praises Sparta above Rome or Athens because her mixed government had kings and a preponderant nobility, which 'preserves liberty longer than the commons';[4] and Bacon when he remarks that 'the fabric of the state of Sparta was wholly (though not wisely) framed and composed' to military ends (like that of Spain), and that her chary admission of foreigners unfitted her for empire.[5] But if the Florentines and Venetians were much read, arguments over the mixed constitution and limited monarchy turned more often on England's own past and theories about the Saxon constitution, parallel to Hotman's about early France; and even more on biblical than native precedent. It might be claimed that the only original suggestion concerning Sparta made in these years was the query (involving an ignorance of the works of Athenaeus that cannot be sufficiently censured) whether that strange Turkish or Greek drink, coffee, 'blacke as soote, and tasting not much unlike it', might not be identical with 'that blacke broth which was in use amongst the

---

[1] *An Harborowe for Faithfull and Trewe Subiectes* (Strasburgh, 1559), H.3. He is arguing that it is not dangerous to have a woman ruling 'if it be under Law'.

[2] 1583, though written earlier; ii 3.

[3] Cf. Richard Beacon, *Solon his Follie* (1594), especially the consideration of Lycurgus (a lawgiver being required for Ireland).

[4] *The History of the World* is brief about the Spartans ('they liv'd Utopianlike') but, of course, severe on the Athenians.

[5] *Of the True Greatness of Kingdoms and Estates.*

Lacedemonians?'[1] And it was only owing to a horrid pun that a large tract of North America seemed likely to bear the name Laconia—'so called by reason of the great Lakes therein' wrote Sir Ferdinando Gorges. However, the company to which the Council for New England had granted the stretch of land west and north-west of Maine failed to pay and was dissolved in 1613, and Laconia disappeared from the map.

Milton in 1641 still placed the English constitution, with its 'free and untutor'd monarch', above those of Rome and Sparta so praised by Polybius (though he thought episcopacy incompatible with a proper temperament).[2] But as the political crisis developed and the spate of pamphlets grew the ephorate was swept if not too prominently into the controversy. The moderate political writer, Hunton, in 1643 popularized the term 'mixed monarchy' for a form in which the royal element predominates and gives unity to the whole. His opponent, the royalist Ferne, while admitting a partial and unenforceable limitation and mixture of power, took the opportunity to agree that the English monarchy was more powerful than the Spartan: it had no ephors. He could then safely quote Calvin. But Hunton retorted that Calvin had expressly stated that Estates were ephors; and his own doctrine, however formulated, did permit resistance, if not judgement over the king's person.[3] Henry Parker, an able and thoroughgoing Parliamentary writer, went further; he felt that ephors and tribunes had caused 'broyles', and were less fitted for the task of controlling the king than Parliament, which is not only created by, but *is*, the people.[4] And Milton, reviewing the controversy, insisted (not quite accurately) both that Aristotle considered the Lacedemonian form of monarchy the truest form, and that Lycur-

---

[1] G. Sandys, *A Relation of a Journey begun An. Dom.* 1610 (1615), p. 66. Was the idea his own? It reappears in the *Anatomy of Melancholy* and other of the more fanciful works of the period. See *Notes and Queries* i (1849) 124, 139, 155, etc., when a contributor suggested blood and coffee mixed would have been suitably nauseous—the new attitude to Sparta!

[2] *Of Reformation touching Church-Discipline in England*, 1641 (*Works*, Columbia U.P., 1931-8, vol. iii. 1, p. 63).

[3] Sir Philip Hunton, *A Treatise of Monarchy* (1643); Dr. Henry Ferne, *A Reply unto several Treatises pleading for the armes now taken up by subjects* (1643), pp. 59, 85; and Hunton, *A Vindication of the Treatise of Monarchy* (1644), p. 55.

[4] Henry Parker, *Some Few Observations upon his Majesty's late Answers and Expresses* (1642), p. 14 ff.

gus, *Spartanorum rex*, or Theopompus, whichever it was who was inspired by the sad fate of Argos and Messene to set senate and ephorate alongside the royal power, were admirable examples to all kings.[1]

The traditional theory of mixed government, even in its most monarchic form, shackled the royalists embarrassingly, since it did not permit the king to legislate alone. But Sir Robert Filmer was almost alone, before the Commonwealth, in abandoning it. He followed Bodin in holding the mixed state to be an impossibility and declaring that the classical republics had mostly been at bottom democracies. Thus he can lean heavily on traditional abuse of Athens, and to some degree of republican Rome, which, he argues, soon lapsed into out-and-out democracy. In *Patriarcha* he suppresses Sparta, which so conspicuously lacked the democratic vices of instability and factiousness.[2] But in a later work he pointed out that ephors, far from having the authority of antiquity, came late in the world's history, that Aristotle, who once made the Lacedemonian a type of kingship, elsewhere denied it was one at all, save in the field, where it was absolute; and that the best politicians (obviously Bodin in particular) made Sparta a democracy. Or if she were to be regarded as an aristocracy, well and good; for 'if a limited monarchy cannot be found in *Lacedemon*, I doubt our Observator will hardly find it anywhere else in the whole world'.[3]

And this was very much the opinion, too, of Hobbes, whose absolutist doctrines, however, could justify Cromwell as well as Charles; just as he agreed with Filmer (and other royalists, including James I himself) that classical influence was real and disastrous. Hobbes notoriously thought the very knowledge of Greek and Latin too dearly purchased, since it made men think that liberty only existed in a democracy. Those who live in one 'find no such matter'.[4]

But whatever had been the case hitherto, classical influence was about to gain strength. When the supremacy of the people and the sole legislative power of its representatives in the House of Com-

---

[1] *Defensio Prima*, 1651 (*Works*, vol. vii, ch. ii, p. 87, ch. iv, p. 215).

[2] *Patriarcha*, 1680 (but written before 1642), ed. P. Laslett, *Patriarcha and other Political Works* (1949); especially pp. 86–92.

[3] *The Anarchy of a Mixed and Limited Monarchy*, 1648 (Laslett, op. cit., pp. 301–3, 308).   [4] *Leviathan* (1651), especially ii. 19, ii. 29, iv. 46.

mons was proclaimed, and when Charles I by losing his head had removed the most obvious impediment to republican theory, those few who did look backwards looked more naturally to antiquity (and Venice) than to Saxons and Goths. One pamphleteer, an optimist, was persuaded that the new constitution would be as long-lived as Venice or Lacedaemon, and another in 1658 regretted that it had not been so.[1]

Milton for one still considered Sparta an admirable state.[2] From 1654 he supported the Protectorate, if not without misgivings. But he sometimes envisaged Cromwell less as a permanent ruler than as the great institutor frequently needed in times of transition to liberty. It is with the first Brutus that he explicitly compares him; but Lycurgus, whom he often mentions, must have contributed to his belief.

There is no doubt that the man who

> cast the Kingdom old
> Into another mould

caused the figure of Lycurgus, often openly under the escort of Machiavelli, to advance towards the forefront of men's minds. As early as 1649 a hostile pamphlet spoke of 'An Act (drawn up by the *Demy-Lycurgus*, Judge Oliver) directing them to govern the Kingdom according to the new model'd principles of old *Machivilianism*'.[3] To some the Machiavellian figure to whom Cromwell, not necessarily invidiously, was assimilated was not Lycurgus but *Il Principe*. James Harrington, however, whose *Oceana* (1656) made him far and away the most influential literary representative of the republican opposition to the Protector, hopefully pictured his Olphaus Megaletor, a transparent disguise for Oliver Cromwell, as inspired by the study of Machiavelli to imitate Lycurgus.[4] Cromwell, to whom the *Oceana* was dedicated, refused to be deflected by what he called 'a little paper shot' from keeping a power Harrington regarded as tyrannical, and so the British Lycurgus never materialized. There was even more need for him after Cromwell's death, and Lycurgus' is still the name that springs most easily to the urgent pens of those discussing the

---

[1] R.–H., *A Discourse on the natural Excellencies of England* (1658).

[2] *Defensio Secunda*, 1654 (*Works* viii. 49 'Spartana civitate optime instituta').

[3] *Mercurius Elencticus* (30 April to 7 May 1649).

[4] Harrington, *Works*, ed. Toland (1700), pp. 77–8.

origin and extent of the legislator's powers in 1659 and 1660, often to some degree under the impulsion of *Oceana*.[1]

But Harrington is important to us in more ways than this; indeed, he is one of the most important figures in this whole study. Fantastic as his description of a Utopianized England, historical names all disguised in semi-classical clothing, may be in form, he was a profoundly serious student of Machiavelli and Hobbes, an original thinker, and a writer whose influence, though great in his own time and land, was not confined to them. Harrington's belief that it is possible to found a scientific and certain study of politics upon history divides him from most of his predecessors, whose political thought was not yet fully secular; but also from both his great contemporaries, Hobbes and Locke, who despised the empirical study of history, and even from his adored Machiavelli, who was too pessimistic and aware of corrupting forces ever to suppose a perfect and permanent state could be created. It is the combination in Harrington of a Machiavellian view of antiquity with certain elements of the Utopian tradition, above all its connection of politics with economics, that gives Sparta a position in his work at least equal to that of Rome, if sometimes secondary to Venice; and which makes the picture of her far richer and more rounded (however extensively unhistorical) than that of any other post-classical writer before the eighteenth century in France.

Harrington extols 'Antient Prudence', which created mixed states and survived to reach new heights in Venice, whereas Modern Prudence issued either in monarchy or the unsatisfactory 'Gothick Ballance'—which was not a properly librated Commonwealth at all, but a wrestling match between king and nobility, and sometimes people too. Since, in England, this had crashed with the revolution, the way was open to turn back to Ancient Prudence. Like most of his contemporaries he says that the first mixed constitution was that of Israel, instituted by God. But the (possibly kindred) Lacedaemonians improved upon it by the light of nature and reason to form the best ancient example. Athens was less well balanced, but some of her features were echoed by Venice, which as Harrington later wrote 'either transcribed the whole and every part of her commonwealth out of Athens and Lacedaemon, or happened to be framed as if she had

---

[1] E.g. that of Harrington's opponent, the otherwise unclassical Presbyterian Baxter, in *A Holy Commonwealth* (1651); Theses 178, 186, 289.

done so'.[1] Venice however is better than either, and alone of all states hitherto is immune to decay.

Ancient Prudence is essentially the rule not of men but of laws —which alone are able to check man's tendency to corruption. A legislator can establish the rule of law at once, and this is why the Spartans could grow in virtue, while the Romans, though they struggled to improve their constitution, were got down at last by its original imperfections. (Laws should be few, of course, as Lycurgus and Solon knew.) Further, a state, to be perfectly balanced, must be equal both in its 'foundation' and its 'super-structure'. It will then be immortal.

Now Harrington was a firm believer in the leadership of the nobility and gentry. From the ranks of the leisured and virtuous all lawgivers, Moses, Lycurgus, and Olphaus Megaletor among them, had sprung; and how could 'mechanic' commonwealths compare with Rome, Sparta, and Venice 'plum'd with their Aristocracys'? But he disapproved of titles and of a legally privi-leged, closed class as mere invitations to jealousy and sedition. The fact that the Spartiates formed a single class only divided into senate and assembly by the process of election formed a point of superiority over Rome, with its patricians and plebeians. The reformed Oceana therefore possessed a limited but fairly wide body of citizens with whom, as the people, sovereignty rested. Harrington made great play with his discovery that dominion follows the balance of property (he held that the recent revolution was due at bottom to the fact that the constitution had not been changed to take account of changes in the ownership of land, away from king and nobles). And so, to ensure that the people should preserve its power, he proposed a limitation on landed property. Whatever he learnt from the history of his own and other countries, especially the unsuccessful attempts of the Gracchi to impose an 'Agrarian' in Rome, Sparta (with Israel, the only other state to possess one) was the most convincing proof to him of its feasibility. While she kept her 'Agrarian', he believed, she was 'immoveable'.

So much for the foundation. In the superstructure, or actual government, however, and above all in the arrangements for the rotation of office, which he regarded as the great safeguard of liberty, Israel, Sparta, Athens, and Rome all were far inferior to

[1] *The Prerogative of Popular Government*, 1658 (*Works*, p. 313).

Venice, the inventor of the ballot-box with which Harrington's name is so closely associated. Ephors and such-like devices were an inadequate substitute for proper rotation. In military matters, however, Harrington accepts the Polybian and Italian preference for Rome. He too considers Sparta a state for preservation, Rome a state for expansion. And, in accordance with England's active foreign policy in these years, he prefers expansion. But unlike Machiavelli he does not think it necessary to pay for this with instability. He agrees, too, that the Roman system of colonies, and leagues of allies, was superior to the Athenian and Spartan habit of subjugating the conquered; here even Venice is too 'unequal'.

In the other detailed and complicated new arrangements for Oceana, set up after nine imaginary legislators from nine famous states, including Laco de Scytale[1] of Sparta, have given Olphaus advice, there is little that is exclusively Spartan. Spartan, Roman, and biblical precedent is quoted for the new division of the people into tribes and smaller groups, on which everything rests. And Sparta and Rome reinforce the decision that the assembly (in so large a country necessarily a representative one) shall only decide and not debate; the senate of course can do the latter. Spartan public education, and her games and festivals, are also put under some degree of contribution (though not as the French were to put them); and the anti-intellectual nature of the former is excused by Sparta's peculiar circumstances. Travel is prescribed for the politician, and Lycurgus' practice is adduced (where his precept could not have been). And her state-controlled religion is recommended. So is her habit of relying on her citizens for arms in youth and for counsel in age.

Harrington had opened his work by saying that he proposed to describe Oceana in narrative just as Dicaearchus had described Lacedaemon. He ends with a parallel between Lycurgus' feelings and actions on completing his work and those which he ascribes to Olphaus Megaletor on the like occasion.

The significance of Harrington's treatment of Sparta is proved by the attacks it receives in two works that stand out among the flood of discussion the *Oceana* provoked. Matthew Wren (son of the bishop of Ely) was Harrington's chief critic from the royalist

---

[1] In reference to the Spartan custom of winding official despatches round a *scytale* or staff.

standpoint.[1] His comparative modernity of outlook, however, was shown by his objection to stress on the classical republics not as impious but as narrow. Not only were monarchies to be met with in Greek and Roman history, but what of Persia, Egypt, or China? But the main brunt of his argument is inevitably directed at Sparta, together with Venice. It was clearly no longer possible to concentrate fire on those easier targets, Athens and Rome. Sparta's stability had been too strongly urged as only second to that of Venice, and in any discussion of the dangerous doctrine of the 'Agrarian', which Wren saw would lead to 'downright levelling', she must take first place. This is perhaps the first time since Agis and Cleomenes that the Lycurgan land system has been a matter of even half-practical discussion.

Like his occasional predecessors in the task of deflation, Wren can list seditions at Sparta simply by turning from the pages of ancient philosophers to those of ancient historians. Harrington retorted that most of his examples dated from the time when Lysander and the spoils of the Peloponnesian War had destroyed the balance of wealth to power and thus unsteadied the constitution; and that many of the quarrels had been peaceably settled at the court of the ephors. But he was driven into a corner by the helot revolts, and reduced to admitting that if the helots are counted as part of the Lacedaemonian state, it is not an equal commonwealth—but if not then all is well, and there never was any real sedition. Wren argued, furthermore, that such stability as Sparta had was the result of her peculiar education and her poverty, not her 'Agrarian' or her constitution; while that of Venice, also much over-rated, was due to her geographical situation and her prudent fear of her neighbours (a view owing something to Bodin and Botero?). And he pointed out that the classical states always abandoned Harrington's beloved principle of rotation in a crisis; witness the re-elections of Marius in Rome and Lysander in Sparta.

As for the 'Agrarian', Wren had little trouble in proving that ancient authorities did not regard the allotment system in either

---

[1] *Considerations on Mr. Harrington's Commonwealth of Oceana* (1657), esp. pp. 58 ff., 78 ff. Harrington retorted in *The Prerogative of Popular Government*, 1658 (*Works*, p. 229), and Wren in *Monarchy Asserted*, Oxford, 1659 (see especially p. 65 f., 139 f., 168). Harrington had the last word with *Politicaster* (1659).

Israel or Sparta as established for Harringtonian ends (however dubious the belief in Lycurgus' purely moral intentions, to which of course he reverts). He was also right in accusing Harrington of underestimating the importance of property other than land, and saying that money would soon 'overballance' the 'Agrarian'. His opponent, who had only envisaged a limit on money in practically landless states like Holland, could but trust that, although such overbalancing might have occurred in small countries like Sparta and Israel, if the first had not limited currency and the other usury, it would not come to pass in a big one.

Anyway, like many another, Wren felt such legislation now impossible, whatever Lycurgus, with the backing of Delphi, had been able to do—though even in his case it was very odd that he should be able to persuade the Lacedaemonians to do without what makes obeying laws bearable. So 'let me not be choakt with the Example of *Lacedaemon* till Mr. *Harrington* has shown Us the power of his perswasion with the Nobility of *Oceana*.'

The other attack was even more scholarly and also issued from Oxford. But Henry Stubbe, a protégé of Sir Henry Vane, was no monarchist. In 1659 he was praising the *Oceana* but complaining that, since so many people were disloyal to the good old cause, its proposals were impracticable.[1] England's only safety lay in the denial of privileges to the disaffected and the creation of a strong 'co-ordinate senate' elected for life to protect the constitution. In 1660 he went further. Though in many ways less blind to reality around him than Harrington, it was perhaps the fact that he was a professional scholar that led him to pass over Venice and give his brief pamphlet *The Commonwealth of Oceana put into the Ballance and found too light* the form and subtitle *An Account of the Republick of Sparta with occasional Animadversions upon Mr. James Harrington and the Oceanistical Model*. He too wants to make Sparta out as a pattern for England; but his Sparta is a pure oligarchy. Apart from contradicting Harrington, who was 'neither acquainted in the *Greek* tongue, nor skilled in *History*, but trading with *Compendiums*' on numerous details, and sneering at the oddly-named 'Lord Laco de Scytale who [*sic*] never bare Peloponnesus', Stubbe argues that Lycurgus' reforms, far from being visionary like Harrington's, were a practical compromise—he left the monarchy, the tribes, and the unsociable nature of the people as he

[1] *An Essay in Defence of the Good Old Cause* (1659).

found them. Admirable as his senate was, it proved necessary within a hundred and thirty years to strengthen it by giving it a veto over the people's decisions, and all Greek history shows that thereafter what existed at Sparta was a simple oligarchy.[1] Thus the doctrine of the Balance is incidentally disproved, for the 'Agrarian' at Sparta did ensure a popular balance, and yet a government of a quite different complexion subsisted for a long time. It was ultimately brought down, says Stubbe, in the fourth century, not by any fault of king or senate but by the foolish measures and elections of the people.

A strong senate seemed the only answer, at this time, to others as well. Milton, in *The Readie and Easie Way*,[2] turned to General Monk to carry out his plans, proposed to replace Parliament by a senate or grand council elected for life, and appeals to Sanhedrim, Areopagus, elders of Sparta, and Consiglio Grande in support; though he brushes aside such checks (on the senate, here) as the ephors and tribunes as either useless or leading to unbridled democracy. He desired, too, to limit the franchise, and felt that an 'Agrarian' was 'never successful . . . save only where it began seasonably with first possession' (as, presumably, at Sparta).

But every possible theory of the period was in the air after the collapse of the Protectorate. In Ludlow's well-known words:

The great officers of state were for a select standing senate to be joined to the representative of the people; others laboured to have the supreme authority to consist of an assembly chosen by the Parliament, and a Council of State chosen by that Assembly to be vested with the executive power. Some were desirous to have a representative constantly sitting, but changed by perpetual rotation; others proposed that there might be joined to the popular assembly a select number of men in the nature of the Lacedaemonian Ephors, who should have a negative in things wherein the essentials of government should be concerned.[3]

What happened was the return of the Stuarts. Earlier that year a supporter of limited monarchy had written that our laws 'though

---

[1] One of the rare references to the Great Rhetra.

[2] *The Readie and Easie Way to establish a Free Commonwealth*, 1660 (*Works* vi. 111. See especially pp. 128, 130, 134).

[3] Edmund Ludlow, *Memoirs* (1698–9).

they have (God be thanked) forgot their Norman, yet they will hardly learn Greek, much less Utopian'.[1]

It was soon doubtful whether the laws had in fact forgot their Norman, and the debate began again. There were no strikingly new developments. On the one side there was a Filmer revival; on the other, pre-war theories of a mixed monarchy inherited from Saxon times were refurbished. Two at least of the most important opponents of absolutism, however, Henry Neville and Algernon Sidney, were covert republicans and carried on the classical and Italian tradition. They were not put off by assaults such as Wren's on classical precedents, nor by the argument that the histories of Athens and Sparta at least were too remote to be relied on, or that ancient declaimers 'never meant to give a true account of things'[2]—indications perhaps of the growing historical scepticism of the period; while as for Venice, in the 1670s interest in her reached greater heights than ever.

King Theopompus and the ephors naturally reappear soon after the king does, but Sparta gains less by this than she loses by the disappearance of all expectation of a new Lycurgus and the recognition that an 'Agrarian' is an Utopian measure. Algernon Sidney[3] acquiesced, openly at least, in the traditional English form of mixed monarchy, mentioning Theopompus and the admirable poverty of the Spartan kings (kings should not be 'glorious, powerful or abounding in riches'). But—and he was not alone in this[4]—he felt that the classical states had been much less ambiguous in their allocation of power within the mixture. He greatly admires Sparta and Rome—especially, on Machiavellian lines, the latter, which is a better model for an expanding and trading state like England. For him all blessings come from liberty; even stability—disorders in Rome and Sparta were slight and soon regretted. Certainly love of country: 'men would have

---

[1] Sir Roger L'Estrange (?), *A Plea for Limited Monarchy . . . to General Monk* (1660), *Harleian Miscellany* i. 14.

[2] G.S., *The Dignity of Kingship Asserted*, 1660 (against the *Readie and Easie Way*), p. 101.

[3] *Discourses Concerning Government*, 1698 (finished in 1680), esp. ii. 22, pp. 160–1; ii. 23, p. 170; ii. 24, p. 172; ii. 30, pp. 232–3; iii. 7, p. 276; iii. 10, p. 296; iii. 28, p. 378.

[4] John Nalson, *The King's Prerogative and the Subject's Privileges* (1684) puts ephors above tribunes because they knew and respected the limits of power on each side, pp. 57–8. Praise of Lycurgus, pp. 32–4, Theopompus, p. 57.

the same love to the publick as the *Spartans* and *Romans* had, if there was the same reason for it.' Sidney thought, however, like Machiavelli but unlike Harrington, that a perfect government is impossible and that frequent reorganization is necessary; and he saw this as the main task of the ephors (and senate, *pregadi*, or assemblies further north). He wisely doubts whether the peoples of Sparta and Israel were related, in spite of the similarity of their constitutions; or whether the Spartans and Germans were either (where did he get the idea that the latter thought so?). But he institutes a comparison between Saxon and Spartan (and to some extent Venetian) society, as divided into serf and citizen classes, the latter being at once the people and the nobility. It is surprisingly rare to find the Saxon and Gothic, and the classical and Italian, examples thus actually brought into connection.

In 1681, at the height of the succession crisis, Henry Neville, a close friend of Harrington, published his *Plato Redivivus*, a dialogue between a physician, an English gentleman, and a Venetian visitor that embodies modified Oceanic ideas in superficially monarchic dress.[1] Neville, who did not wish to exclude James II from the throne but so to limit the king's powers (as the existing balance in land demanded) as to assimilate them to the Doge's, expresses the hope that Charles II may be persuaded to imitate Theopompus. He produces, to encourage him, the favourite anecdote; the misfortunes of Argos and Messene showed that Theopompus was right in thinking that the ephorate would save the monarchy—it even saved the country's independence. But he wants Venetian-style committees to take over the powers abandoned by the king and hopes that these will be more satisfactory than either the justicia of Aragon or the ephors, since, being closely associated with the king, they will have less temptation to be 'sullen'. He also wants an elected and rotatory senate to replace the Lords. He even admires 'Lycurgus the greatest Politician that ever Founded any Government', for taking 'a sure way to fix Property, by Confounding it', and confirms the truth of the 'Agrarian' doctrine by intelligent reference to Agis

[1] As the satire *Oceana and Britannia* puts it (describing him as Politico/descended from the divine Nicolo);

> From his glib tongue torrents of words did flow,
> Propose, resolve, agrarian, forty-one,
> Lycurgus, Brutus, Solon, Harrington.

and Cleomenes; but he does not propose any limitation, even, on property in England.

It is Venice and Rome nonetheless that he refers to most often; Rome he admires to a Machiavellian extent, as more popular, and thus more powerful, than the other states. Indeed, he describes Sparta as an 'optimacy', like Venice, though a wise one.[1]

It will have been noticed that some of the writers quoted in this chapter neither avoid nor attack Athens. They had accepted ultimate popular sovereignty and complete republicanism; they tend to accept the belief of the fourth century B.C. that Athens was a mixed state, though they agree, if pressed, that she was not the stablest example of the form. Thus Harrington, who broke the invidious comparison with Florence by stating that the latter did not deserve the name of commonwealth at all. Sidney, too, complained that Filmer was too hard: 'and if I acknowledge that Athens was more subject to disorder, and had less stability than Sparta, I think it will be of little advantage to absolute monarchy.'[2]

Milton was not alone in finding the Areopagus one of the best examples of a senate. In 1660 he even combines with his senate some Athenian details and an 'Athenian' system of local government. And the Athenian *euthynae*, or investigation into the acts of magistrates at the end of their term, could be advocated as a practical method of controlling the now unruly executive.[3]

There was also the question of liberty of conscience, so dear to the independents. The very title of the *Areopagitica* (1644) shows where Milton had to turn for precedent. It is to Athenian practice he appeals as a private citizen anxious to advise the government; it is Athens' limitation of censorship to libel and atheism that he would imitate, and to which he gives first place in his history of censorship and its effects. Athens prosecuted the atheist Protagoras, but permitted Epicurus, who 'denied the divine providence', to teach. Milton's noble picture of a reawakened England freely examining every point of conscience surely owes something to the Athens whose intellectual achievements he praised so grandly in *Paradise Regain'd*. In this context Sparta is treated with contempt. 'It is to be wondered how museless and unbookish they were . . . there needed no licensing of Bookes

---

[1] *Plato Redivivus* (1680), especially pp. 52, 64, 221, 242, 248.
[2] Op. cit., sect. 18, p. 139.
[3] *Twenty five Queries* . . . (1659), *Harl. Misc.* ix. 424.

among them for they dislik'd all.' And Plato receives hard knocks for his 'ayrie Burgomasters' and for 'sequestering out of this world into Atlantick or Eutopian politicks'. Athens' importance in this connection is further shown by the fact that Stubbes claims to have written a 'discourse showing neither Rome nor Athens did allow liberty of conscience'.[1]

The movement towards Athens went no further than this. The extreme democratic groups, to whom 'people' did not really mean 'gentry', were unlikely, given their religious and social background, to seek much classical support; if they ever did, Sparta, in the Utopian tradition, was more likely to put in an appearance than Athens.[2] Their opponents, of course, might dilate with hostility on their Athenian character; though even the 'Athenian Levellers', it was claimed, never went so far as the Diggers. And soon even Neville goes back to regarding Athens, like Florence, as a corrupt democracy. For the mixed monarchy, which was now widely accepted as what was established in England, was more heavily weighted towards both monarchy and hereditary aristocracy than had previously often been hoped. Another favourite state fell out of favour when, during the eighties, the Tories mounted a really formidable attack on Venice, based on papal, Spanish, and French critics of the preceding decades. Rome, with which expanding England felt its affinity, kept its place. And Sparta could perhaps be said to be left as runner-up.

In neat illustration of this, Walter Moyle, a writer closely dependent on the republican tradition, wrote two tracts for the times under the title *An Essay on the Roman, and on the Lacedae-monian, Governments*.[3] In the latter Moyle in fact exaggerates the part played by Sparta in forming the thought of Harrington and Sidney. He claimed that there, as in Rome, 'the perfection of Government was aimed at in those early times'. Liberty consists in checks, balance, and the rule of law. 'It is an agreeable thought, to consider how many millions of people lived happily and died quietly under the Spartan government, in a succession of 700

---

[1] *The Commonwealth of Oceana put into the Ballance*, preface. He was a thorough champion of such liberty, however.

[2] *Tyranipocrit Discovered* (Rotterdam, 1649), a Utopian communist work, mentions Lycurgus, Agis and Cleomenes, and the Gracchi as well as religious authorities.   [3] 1698.

years.' He still felt that 'in Lacedaemon, the distinct function and different power of each branch of government was well known, and therefore it was as well known among them, when an encroachment and invasion was made by the one, upon the inherent rights and privileges of the other. I should be glad we could say the same of our own government here in England; but the boundaries and limits of the prerogative and liberty are not yet so well stated with us.' Sparta's only possible fault lay in the harshness of her education; but the virtue it nourished enabled her 'to right herself soon, if I may use a sea phrase' in a crisis. 'Such virtue we have once seen in England, upon the late happy Revolution; and I wish from my soul, that England may never want a like vigour upon a like occasion.'[1]

[1] Moyle reserved his views on the relation of Church and state to his equally tendentious *Essay on Rome*. He thought the connection between the two in all ancient states a very good thing. Like so many other people at this precise juncture, he also felt strongly about the advantages of a citizen militia as opposed to a standing army, and had earlier produced *An Argument showing that a Standing Army is inconsistent with free government* . . ., which quotes Machiavelli and all the classical states to this purpose.

14

SPARTANS ON THE STAGE

WHEN we turn from political theory to the arts we are reminded again how specialized was the interest that Sparta aroused. Hardly more than in antiquity do scenes from Spartan history make their way into the Renaissance or Baroque repertoire of the visual arts. And it is a commentary on Sparta's generally disappointing role in imaginative literature that the only poetic references at all generally familiar, in this country at least, are those of Shakespeare's Theseus, who describes his hounds

> bred out of the Spartan kind,

and hunting exploits

> in Crete, in Sparta and in Thessaly,[1]

or else the apostrophe to Iago:

> O Spartan Dog
> More fell than anguish, hunger or the sea!

(where the implications of the adjective seem curiously ambiguous, or even sinister, for an age that was only occasionally less than enthusiastic in its response to the idea of Sparta).[2]

To Shakespeare then, drawing no doubt on Ovid, Sparta seems to mean nothing but hounds and hunting. But more common in sixteenth and seventeenth-century verse than Spartan dogs are Spartan women, not the dancing girls of the classical or Roman poets so much as the Spartan heroines, especially the Spartan mothers, of the Greek epigrammatists. As soon as the Planudean anthology became known in Italy in the later fifteenth

---

[1] *A Midsummer Night's Dream* IV. i. 118, 125. Annotations to the effect that bloodhounds hunted silently, i.e. laconically, surely take Theseus' very English description of his Spartan hounds too seriously?

[2] *Othello* v. ii. 363. It is often suggested that Iago's final and obstinate silence may be relevant. But 'laconic' implies brief speech, not absolute silence. However, the boy with the fox was silent or at least secret enough, and doubtless known to Shakespeare. Nonetheless 'fierce' would seem to be the primary connotation of the adjective in this passage.

century it began to be used in the teaching of Greek, and translations and imitations of Greek epigrams, at first chiefly in Latin
and in the later sixteenth century in the various vernaculars,
come thick and fast. The moral and declamatory poems forming
the first book of Planudes' collection proved specially popular as
models, and those concerned with the Spartan mother who killed
her deserter son seem to have been great favourites. That known to
us as *Anthologia Palatina* IX. 61 comes high on the list of the
commonest models. Poliziano wrote a Greek variant, Marullus,
Casanova, and other poets Latin versions.[1] The half-dozen
closely similar epigrams found imitators too.[2] The other mother,
of 'with your shield or on it' fame, had only achieved a late
Latin epigram, by Ausonius. Poliziano translated it into Greek.

Outside Italy the picture seems similar. In England Sir Thomas
More and William Lily both made versions of the favourite
IX. 61, though both sound rather shocked at the lady.[3] The whole
group was well known in France, where the mother stabbing her
son got into one of the popular emblem books, which often
illustrate and moralize on Greek epigrams, as a symbol of patriotism.[4]

Once at least Spartan women and Spartan dogs are combined
to create a quite new type, the Spartan huntress. It will be remembered from Homer that Artemis hunted on Taygetus, but ordinary women never did so, or anywhere else in ancient times.

[1] Statistics in J. Hutton, *The Greek Anthology in Italy to the Year 1800* (1935).
The most popular theme of all seems to be the Statue of the Armed Venus in
Sparta. The mythological and amatory conceits this gave rise to do occasionally
mention the warlike nature of the Spartans or even their women.

[2] *Anth. Pal.* vii 230, 433 (cf. *Apophthegmata Lacaenarum* 240F–241A), ix.
397, 447. (As vii. 531 was not in Planudes' collection it was not known at this
time.) Among the rarer Italian versions is one by Luigi Groto (il Cieco d'Adria)
in sonnet form, *Rime* (1587), p. 153.

[3] Lily's 'horrida in exstinctum voce virago furens' is hardly a fair translation
of ἄρρενα ῥηξάμενη φθόγγον.

[4] Gilles Corrozet, *Hecatomgraphie* (1540), no. 5, one of the first French emblem
books. Alciati had been one of those translating the epigram, but he had not
used it in his famous *Emblemata* (1531 etc.)

See J. Hutton, *The Greek Anthology in France and in the Latin Writers of the
Netherlands to the year 1800* (1946). One notices how much less popular those
ancient favourites Othryadas and Leonidas are. Simonides' couplet on the
dead at Thermopylae, perhaps the best known of all Greek epigrams today, did
not reach this position till much later.

Perhaps there has been confusion with Amazons again. Anyway,
Herrick, describing the vision that gave him such a snub, declares
that

> her dress
> Was like a sprightly Spartanesse.
> A silver bow with green silk strung,
> Down from her comely shoulders hung . . .

He would however have been well in the classical tradition had he
referred to the Spartanesse, rather than Diana, when mentioning
the amount of leg the vision revealed.[1]

When we turn to the novels and romances of the sixteenth and
seventeenth centuries it is borne in on us as one of the ironies of
geography that Lacedaemon should lie on the borders of Arcadia
(and also hold sway over Venus' island of Cythera). It was inevitable, therefore, that a number of princes and princesses, carelessly
designated as Spartan, should appear in the tales set in a timeless
and unreal Greece. They are mostly butterflies not worth chasing.
But the unexpected propinquity of the two countries was not
inconvenient for those wishing to combine pastoral romance
with something more exciting or more serious. So we may pause
for a moment in Sidney's *Arcadia*, to find that Laconia, though it
has a single king at whose court the usages of chivalry appear to
prevail, is torn, unlike its happy neighbour, by a civil war between
the 'gentlemen' and the helots. One purpose of this is to involve
Sidney's two wandering princes, who have got separated and find
themselves on opposite sides, in feats of arms and a single combat
ending in a recognition scene. But the political situation is carefully worked out. The helots are not a mere mob but a once free
race now harshly enslaved. Their rebellion comes to a (temporarily)
happy conclusion, with the establishment by a single leader of a
mixed constitution.[2] To put these familiar ideas into a helot
setting is, I think, unparalleled. There are tragedies, it is true, on
stories of the conquest and rebellion of Messenia, where sympathy
does not lie with Sparta, though she is rarely attacked in any
detail. But the Messenians can be represented more easily than

---

[1] Robert Herrick, *Hesperides* (1648).

[2] *Arcadia*, Book i. In one passage of political analysis Sidney so far forgets his
King Amyclas (the name is genuinely that of a legendary pre-Dorian king) as
to say that Lacedaemon was ruled by its senate as Athens by its people.

the helots proper as a united people with traditions of independence.

Nor ought we to pass over a French novel of the next century, boldly entitled *Agiatis Reine de Sparte, ou les guerres civiles des Lacédémoniens*, by Ortigue de Vaumorière, who was an admirer of Scudéry and wrote a continuation of La Calprenède's *Pharamond*.[1] But in this, after a few pages of historical background out of Plutarch, we hastily leave Sparta for Corinth, in which much more suitable city Cleomenes, here still a very young prince, and Agiatis, whose parentage has inevitably become royal, both disguised under false names, pursue a much-crossed love-affair among 'the Waterworks, the Grotto's and Statues' of the public gardens of Timoleon, and at a delightful entertainment where tilting alternates with chariot racing and is followed by a ball (and a polite call next day). The author unfortunately was unable to sustain his work on this plane, however, and the almost historical denouement, in which Agiatis has to be married to Agis and the latter killed off before she can be united to Cleomenes, seems very perfunctory. As to the civil wars, they are almost purely dynastic affairs.

On the stage Sparta has played a much greater part—thanks largely to the peculiarities of a single ancient author. Polybius' charge that Phylarchus made his history read like tragedy receives striking posthumous justification in the number of tragedies that have been based on Plutarch's *Lives* of Agis and Cleomenes, which are indebted to Phylarchus for their abundance of pathetic scenes and prominent female characters. Few of the ideas we have recently met with, except for that of the Spartan heroine, and especially the Spartan mother, are to have more than a dim relevance in the theatre. In the hands of the various playwrights, and under the various influences dominating the state, most of our Spartans are to become first more strictly Stoic, and then more arrogantly individualistic, more absolutist in political philosophy, more sentimental in feeling, than any we have known elsewhere. On to traditional prototypes of Spartan virtue the poets impose distinct, if related, patterns of their own; the hybrid figures that result have in the best cases a certain fascination.[2]

---

[1] P. d'Ortigue de Vaumorière, *Agiatis Reine de Sparte* (Paris, 1685); English translation *Agiatis Queen of Sparta* (1686) alone available to me.

[2] Nobody is anti-Spartan, unless (see above) the authors of plays on Messenian

An inconspicuous Veronese, Paoli Bozzi, appears to have led the way, at the end of the sixteenth century, in turning to Plutarch's account of the death of Cleomenes for his tragedy *Cratasiclea*.[1] Bozzi was a conventional disciple of G. B. Giraldi Cinthio, by whom Italian tragedy was finally established as much on the Senecan as the Greek plan; static in form, often horrific in content, and full of Seneca's eclectic, but partly Stoic, sententiousness. There was, at this time, in conformity with ideas about the use of tragedy and the value of historical *exempla*, a liking for historical rather than mythological subjects. These were however for the most part, if not patriotically Roman, exotically Asiatic; so one may conjecture that Bozzi was attracted by the Egyptian setting of Cleomenes' troubles, as by the chance to moralise interminably on the court of the luxurious tyrant Ptolemy, whom he provided symmetrically with a good and a bad councillor. But the Spartan characters also gave him opportunities. Here is Cleomenes, driven from his country, who fails to get aid from Ptolemy and when he is falsely accused and in danger of ruin breaks out, with a band of companions, to wreak vengeance on Alexandria; and, their attempt failing, to die by their own hands. Here is his old mother Cratasiclea, who had long before come so bravely to Egypt as a hostage, now encouraging her household and at last going firmly to execution; with her die her precociously heroic grandson and her women, one of whom, the wife of Cleomenes' friend Pantheus, shows exceptional fortitude and generosity at the scaffold. All this is in Plutarch; Bozzi wraps it in the murkily supernatural atmosphere of dreams and prodigies that was *de rigueur* in Senecan tragedy (but newly associated with the people so idealized by the ancient philosophers). To him each of the Spartan characters is a grand *esempio di costanza*—of constancy, the Stoic virtue *par excellence*. Fortune and Virtue form the poles of his conventional tragic philosophy. There is no avoiding the blows of Fortune and the great are especially subject to her power; only Virtue, which consists primarily in courage, can resist her, banishing both hope and fear and thus remaining untouched. This is the burden of the

[1] P. Bozzi, *Cratasiclea* (Venice, 1591).

subjects. Hardy in his *Scédase*, on the Theban story referred to on p. 38, makes it clear that Sparta is only degenerating from her simple, warlike, glorious past (but there is a surprisingly unsympathetic Agesilaus).

chorus of Spartan women, and old Cratasiclea preaches regularly to the same text.

It is as a document of a deeper Stoicism, common in northern Europe, that we should read Antoine de Montchrestien's tragedy on the same subject, *Les Lacènes*.[1] If, to a chaotic world, the Spartan constitution was an example of political stability, Stoicism was often its moral refuge. It would seem that Phylarchus' probably rather Stoic Spartans reap a reward. Cratesiclea appears in no ancient collection of *exempla*; but she provides a model of *constantia* in the *Monita et Exempla Politica* of the great scholar and Stoic Justus Lipsius.[2] In Montchrestien's play there is indeed little but constancy. With deeper feeling and nobler language than Bozzi, to whom he plainly owed nothing, could command, he provides even less variety of plot or character. Cleomenes, and the audience with him, knows from the start that his doom is sealed; he, and we, are warned of it by the ghost of his friend Thericion, who killed himself rather than go into exile. And the king goes to meet this doom before the play is half over, leaving the women, and his young son, to their lamentations and their own exhibition of constancy. Here still is the defeat of Fate by Virtue: but now Virtue is rewarded by Life. Life and Death are the two words that re-echo through Montchrestien's grave choruses; the Spartans escape a life that is not worth living by a heroic death, to be rewarded by a life that is partly perhaps the pagan immortality of renown, but is also the life after death of the Christian faith that the poet, like others at this time, was anxious to reconcile with Stoicism.

Elegiac in tone and Renaissance in form, with its ghosts and portents, its choruses and long moralising harangues, the play was designed primarily for reading, not performance, and was already, for France, old-fashioned. Italian tragedy preserved many of its original characteristics longer, if it cut down the philosophy to make way for romantic and picturesque incident. Ansaldo Cebà's *Alcippo Spartano*,[3] however, which has an invented plot

---

[1] 1601; revised edition 1604. *Lacaenae*, or the Laconian Women, was the title of a lost play of Sophocles (set in Troy, with a chorus of Helen's women).

[2] J. Lipsius, *Monita et Exempla Politica* (1605), p. 51.

[3] A. Cebà, *Alcippo Spartano*, 1623 (dedicated to M. A. Doria). Cf. his treatise *Il cittadino di republica* (1617), which opens with approving discussion of the Spartans' claim to have learnt 'how to be free'. There are several subsequent

vaguely set in the fourth century B.C., also indulges in a little political laconism; its author, whose unusual interest in local colour in his plays has been observed, was a patriotic Genoese. However, after the hero has boasted his descent from King Theopompus and his obedience to the laws, the main features of which are detailed, and after a couple of choruses in honour of Lycurgus, interest is concentrated on Alcippo's wife, the portentous Damocrita who, to avenge her husband's unmerited condemnation for practising with Persia, poisons his accuser, tries to burn the wives of the 'tyrannic' ephors to death in a temple, and stabs herself and her children.

O di Greca virtù leggiadri esempi

cries the chorus, concerning the whole family. Alcippo is milder than his wife, and proud of his constancy in endurance; but the idealized Spartan of the apophthegms was ready to suffer his state to neglect or even wrong him. Plenty of terrible females, descendants of Clytemnestra and Medea, had raged through earlier Italian tragedies and received congratulation on their *virtù*; but it is a satisfaction to find a Spartan virago as the central figure of a revenge play.

A rather different lady appears in an English drama of the early seventeenth century. It is in the Greece of contemporary romance, with its royal courts, its oracles, and its obsession with love, that Ford's pathetic tragedy *The Broken Heart* is set.[1] But why more particularly in Sparta? Surely because Ford felt it to be a suitable setting for his heroine's constancy.[2] The princess Calantha, who during a solemn festivity and dance receives apparently unmoved the tidings of her father's, friend's, and lover's deaths and succumbs quietly to her broken heart only after disposing the fates of the remaining characters and the kingdom that is now hers, is a fantastic but not unmemorable figure (and one of the two Queens Regnant of Sparta known to fame,

---

[1] John Ford, *The Broken Heart* (1633). The influence of Sidney's *Arcadia* has often been remarked, especially in the name of the ruling King Amyelas.

[2] *Pace* certain commentators, there is really no attempt to characterize Sparta further, for example as anti-intellectual.

---

mentions of Lycurgus, but Cebà's perfect Genoese citizen is to be wealthy magnificent, trained in rhetoric, etc.

both English and theatrical); though the strictly orthodox Spartan female, ignorant of Renaissance physiology and careless of combining tenderness with her courage, had never let her heartstrings crack under any provocation. The theme of feeling suppressed for the sake of virtue is echoed in the other chief personages of *The Broken Heart*; in 'grieved Penthea', who, too, breaks under the strain, goes mad, and dies; in Penthea's old husband, who at last masters his jealousy; in her brother, dying bravely at her lover's hand; while that lover's own death, by opening his veins, is pattern-book Stoicism—Roman, not Spartan, however, and critics have sometimes made the connection with Sparta a trifle too easily. Most of these figures, created at a time when Stoic attitudes were common and primarily fed by non-Spartan sources, might be felt to fit, but hardly to demand, such a setting. Its explanation is surely to be found in the women—especially that proud creature of 'masculine temper' who protests her superiority to her sex. But the gentle Penthea too is admirable in her firmness; and it is perhaps relevant to remember that the later ancient sources do paint Spartan women as models of conjugal chastity, if scarcely as martyrs to frustrated love.[1]

In the later seventeenth century Sparta entered into one of the most barren patches of her posthumous history. This is true both of political thought (except as we have seen in England) and of general moral teaching; and thus true even of the stage. But she was never quite forgotten there, though sometimes strangely transformed. In France, tragedy was developing its strict conventions and, under the influence of the romance and contemporary aristocratic society, its interest in courtly love, while it neglected in comparison local and historical colour. Nonetheless, in its first flowering, contemporary with the early plays of Corneille, there was a vogue for subjects from ancient history, due partly to a fashion set by certain popular successes and partly to a lively interest in political questions. The hero of the time was not totally irreconcileable with the Spartan. Stoic self-reliance in the face of

[1] How far the English theatrical public's knowledge of the species was furthered by a lost comedy of Lodowick Carlell, *The Spartan Ladies*, entered in 1640 but apparently acted considerably earlier, it is hard to say. Massinger's *Virgin Martyr* (1620) had however wished to make us forget, by her Christian death,

> What the canonized Spartan ladies were
> Which lying Greece so boasts of.

misfortune survived, and the cult of constancy persisted (though the real Stoic could display his virtues as a slave as well as a prince). Being to a large extent the projection of the aristocratic, indeed still semi-feudal, society of the time, the hero is inevitably concerned, like the Spartan, with both war and politics; and in fact his unbounded pride in his own worth may lead him, in spite of the general acceptance of absolute monarchy, fiercely to criticize the king who treats him unjustly, and even to refuse him obedience. These years, ending with the Fronde, saw the final struggles of the nobility against the all-powerful monarchy; many of them were also years of war, and the militant patriotism of the time is reflected on the stage.

Thus, even if Sparta is hardly the perfect setting for lengthy even if unsuccessful struggles between love or family loyalty and the nobler passions, nor for the elegant rhetoric of contemporary verse, we may still regret that we have nothing from Corneille to set beside the first acts of *Horace*, where he showed how he could paint the victory of a warrior's farouche constancy over all other feelings, and its inspiration in a primitive and all-demanding patriotism. But while contemporary society apparently saw itself, not very plausibly in view of its untrammelled individualism, in the great ages of early Rome, it had less interest in Sparta. We have, however, two respectable Plutarchian tragedies from Guérin de Bouscal, the first of which, *Cleomene*,[1] dates from 1640, the very year of the far subtler *Horace*. As usual, the author has gone directly to Plutarch. Cratésiclée, thus illustrating the decline of formal Stoicism, has sunk to being little more than an encouraging confidante; the chief female role is given to Agiatis, Cleomene's devoted wife (really long since dead), with whom Ptolomée falls in love. For all her rock-like faith and her readiness to meet death, and even if necessary kill her children, at Honour's bidding, her fundamentally un-Spartan mainspring is Love. Nonetheless she strikes the Alexandrians as uncivilized:

> Elle est belle en effet, mais elle est bien sauvage.

This last her countrymen are also considered. But the struggle in Cleomene's soul takes a very seventeenth-century form. At first, giving way to his love for his family and his people (placed for most of the play on much the same level), he yields to his wife and

---

[1] G. Guérin de Bouscal, *Cleomene* (1640).

mother and implores the unworthy Ptolomée to give him aid—just as these feelings had led him to shun, on his defeat in Greece, the glorious death he so desired. Love, patriotism, and personal honour continue the struggle, under different shapes and in different alliances, within him. (Note the alliance of Love and Honour where Cleomene claims that all his deeds are inspired by, and aimed at making him worthy of, Agiatis.) At last, when every hope of safety is gone, all these impulses can be united, or rather the last-named can run riot; in his final bloody outbreak in Alexandria, Cleomene can find the glorious death he missed before.

The political framework of the play is also very much of its time. Open rebellion is not countenanced—Cleomene does not regard himself as subject to Ptolemy, though Ptolemy does, and Magas, the latter's brother, remains, though outspoken, ostentatiously loyal. But the king's unjust and suspicious treatment of these two, the greatest men in his realm, is strongly condemned. And much of the blame is put—as it was put in the France of Richelieu and Mazarin—on the evil councillor, who is sacked at the final curtain.

The companion piece, *La Mort d'Agis*,[1] breaks obviously tempting new ground by going back to the beginning of the whole story—the unsuccessful revolution of King Agis, ultimately frustrated by his colleague Leonidas IV. The author unifies the action by making Leonidas' daughter Chelonide (Plutarch's Chilonis) the wife of Agis himself, rather than of Agis' tool Cleombrotus; all too successfully, as the parallel between the first half of the play, with Leonidas at Agis' mercy, and the second, with the roles reversed, becomes artificially precise, and poor Chelonide, always interceding for the vanquished against the politicians' advice, and torn between husband and father, becomes a sad bore. However, Guérin de Bouscal, though no great artist, manages the political situation interestingly. Respect for Plutarch demanded that Agis should be the hero; but his egalitarian reforms must seem intolerable to the present generation. Yet these are not glossed over, as in later plays on the subject. Agis is drawn convincingly enough as a young idealist sighing for the age of Lycurgus, when Sparta lived in

L'innocence et la paix qu'on vit dans l'age d'or,

[1] Id., *La Mort d'Agis* (1642).

and so convinced of the rightness of his cause that he will not sully it with a political execution, however necessary:

> Léonidas est prince, et de plus mon beau-père

(and thus, one should point out, the perfect object for a real ancient tyrannicide, a Brutus or Timoleon). As a result, the *peuple ingrat*, which has already partly forced Agis' hand and got Léonidas banished, turns against its benefactor. Its behaviour is Agis' tragedy and the implicit justification of Léonidas' conservative convictions. But if Léonidas is wise, he is not innocent. Unappalled by the bloodshed he causes, tempted by personal revenge, finally shuffling off responsibility for his son-in-law's death on to senate and people, he comes to repentance too late. Agis dies nobly, Chelonide kills herself, and Léonidas is left to confess

> Droit sanglant de l'Estat, voilà vôtre victoire.
> Enfin vous triomphez au depens de ma gloire.

and to promise a speedy death from remorse. The fact that Honour and *Raison d'Etat* are never reconciled in this play is one more illustration of the profoundly un-Spartan morality of the age.

After the Fronde pure tragedy almost disappeared for a while, and when it returned was generally exotic in setting and melodramatic or sentimental in feeling. In the romance and its dramatic offshoots, especially tragicomedy, historical verisimilitude had never been a requirement; but for all that such works perhaps instinctively kept off Sparta. It forms, however, the scene of Philippe Quinault's otherwise highly typical tragicomedy *Le Feint Alcibiade*, of 1658. The plot is worth retailing for the entertainment it must give those with a knowledge of Greek history. They will learn that it was not Alcibiades, but a twin sister, Cléone, *sous le nom et l'habit de son frère*, who went off to Sparta, being in love with her brother's enemy Lysander. Here not only the wife of King Agis (Agis II, not of course the third century reformer Agis IV) but his sister too (promised to Lysander) fall in love with the supposed Alcibiades. After challenging Lysander to a duel and saving his life from a boar, not to mention rescuing Agis from conspiracy and assassination, Cléone is forced to discover her sex. Lysander transfers his affections back to her, Agis and his wife are reconciled, and Agis' sister is to be consoled with the real Alcibiades. Poor Lysander has been reduced to an inconstant lover, and there is nothing the least Spartan about the royal ladies; while King Agis, stated recently to have abolished the second kingship, is elevated to dizzily un-Lacedaemonian heights of absolutism. True, he is in a rage of jealousy and self-justification when he proclaims

Et croyez-vous un Roi capable d'une faute?
Pour rien faire de bas, il a l'âme trop haute.
Sur le trône l'erreur ne le peut assaillir,
Il est si près des dieux qu'il ne sauroit faillir,

still, what language for a fundamentally respectable Spartan monarch!

Quinault was, a little later, actually to write a tragedy with a Spartan protagonist. Under the influence of Racine's success with *Andromaque* he turned to a Greek setting and a comparatively sober style. In his *Pausanias* (1662) the contrast between the frank and passionate Spartan (represented as a real king, of course) and his wily Athenian opponent, Aristides, is well enough worked out; but the elaborate love-intrigue is the real subject, and the victor of Plataea, like so many conquerors, fades into a lover out of a romance. The fierce Spartan princess, Démarate, is modelled principally on Racine's Hermione rather than the traditional Spartan woman (though Hermione was of course a figure of Lacedaemonian legend, and Euripides had given her in his *Andromache* what he regarded as Spartan traits). The last act of the play sinks to the feeblest melodrama, notorious even at the time, though largely the fault of Ephorus; Pausanias is induced to stab his mistress in mistake for an assassin, and falls on his sword.

And now we find that Corneille did after all write a Spartan piece—the late and unsuccessful *Agésilas* of 1666. It is in effect a tragicomedy, and makes heavy concessions to the taste of the time that so favoured the sentimental Quinault. Lysander's two daughters emerge as perfect Frenchwomen. The troubles of the six marriageable characters, three Spartan and three Asiatic (not that one could guess), have never greatly engaged anyone's interest. But Corneille could still not avoid politics, and in Lysander's attempted plot against Agesilaus (perfectly historical), and in the latter's conquest (less so) both of his desire for vengeance against Lysander and of his love for the Persian Mandane, he embodied the lessons he loved to preach at this time, on the relations of kings with great subjects, and the demands of *Raison d'Etat*. Agésilas is thus at least a shadow of himself, unlike Quinault's characters.

There are a surprising number of references to the limits set by the constitution to the Spartan monarchy, though we need wonder less at the old contrast with Persia, where

> Le monarque, ou plutôt le tyran général
> N'y suit pour loi que sa caprice,

and treats merit and service as capital crimes. But Agésilas' final lesson is uncompromisingly absolutist. Lysander must remember

> Que les rois sont jaloux du souverain pouvoir.
> Qu'ils aiment qu'on leur doive, et ne peuvent devoir.
> Que rien à leurs sujets n'aquiert l'indépendance.
> Qu'ils réglent à leur choix l'emploi des plus grands coeurs.
> Qu'ils ont pour qui les sert, des grâces, des faveurs,
> Et qu'on n'a jamais droit sur leur reconnaissance.

After this, in spite of the partial return from exotic to classical settings, Sparta was not to appear again in France until, in the eighteenth century, the stage mirrored the great controversy in which she was involved. In England the first three tragedies with a Spartan setting to appear after the Restoration have little in common except that they, too, all sink the second king, and they are totally out of touch with what Whiggish political writers were saying about Sparta—understandably, as stage and court were closely associated. The first and worst, Otway's prentice attempt at an *Alcibiades* (1675), extravagantly pseudo-historical, is a crude mixture of the horrific and the romantic in abysmal heroic couplets. But the seventies, which saw the height of the rage for exotic heroic tragedy, were doubtless an unpropitious period.

Thomas Southerne, who began his career under the protection of James II, tells us that his *Spartan Dame* was 'begun by command of the Duke of Berwick'. Unfortunately the revolution of 1688 supervened and the play had to be suppressed, for the position of Celona (the Chilonis of the *Life of Agis*), whose husband usurped her father's throne, bore too great a resemblance

to that of Queen Mary, and her conduct, in following her father
to exile, too little. The play is full of significant references to
loyalty, and of jibes against the people and its claims, and against
reform, 'the canting name of all rebellion'. It is perhaps surprising
that it reached the stage in 1719. The work achieves the feat of
reversing Plutarch's political values entirely, thus going much
further than Guérin de Bouscal. The revolution is condemned out
of hand, and the dispossessed Leonidas is a blameless monarch.
Since Sparta has only one king, Agis can disappear entirely in
favour of Chilonis' true husband, the obscure and genuinely
usurping Cleombrotus, who is more easily vilified. The play is
still Baroque in style and spirit, and there is little that is Spartan
about the characters except for the fact that the Spartan Dame
herself is a rather more decisive creature than the other pathetic
heroines for whom Southerne was famous.

Meanwhile, Southerne had helped Dryden to finish his last
tragedy, *Cleomenes or the Spartan Heroe*, in 1692.[1] This also ran
into trouble with the new régime for its sympathetic picture of a
monarch in exile at a foreign court—though Dryden insisted that
it was innocently meant and that he had been meditating a play
on the subject for some years. It marks the furthest point of his
reaction towards classical form, eschewing a comic sub-plot and
only admitting a short 'rabble-scene', but in spirit it is a far from
consistent piece.

The fine soliloquy of Cleomenes with which the play opens
suggests that we may still expect for him Stoic treatment:

> Dejected! No, it never shall be said
> That Fate had power upon a Spartan Soul.
> My mind on its own Centre stands unmov'd
> And Stable; as the Fabrick of the World:
> Propt on itself; still I am Cleomenes.

'Cratisiclea', too, shows all her old firmness, and Dryden has
introduced not only a Spartan mother but a Spartan boy (Cleomenes' son had been prominent in Bozzi's play too). The fuss they
all make about their Spartan qualities is perhaps an indication of
strain. Cleomenes claims to be not only heroic but blunt and
laconic (less convincingly). When faced with a picture by Apelles
he shows himself a puritan and a philistine; but in other scenes his

---

[1] He clearly pronounced it Cleoménes.

behaviour, especially to women, is polite in the extreme. His Stoicism too is pretty intermittent; he is passionate, not patient, and quick to let fall 'a manly drop or two' or even question heaven's justice. For Dryden's professed object in the play was to move compassion; and one may wonder if his own sceptical temperament was not expressed in some passages, as in the arguments of the admittedly worthless Sosibius that

> Man is but man; inconstant still and various.
> There's no tomorrow in him like today.

or in the words of the boy Cleonidas, subjected to the pangs of hunger in the last act ('It pleas'd me to try how Spartans could endure it'):

> I find, that now my Body starves
> My Soul decays: I think not as I did.

There is some contradiction, too, between the royalist colouring to the picture of Cleomenes, essentially the princely hero and the man of honour, and his sudden decision to lead a revolt for liberty and against arbitrary power (though the contemptuous treatment of the mob which will not support him is unambiguous enough). But it should be remembered that the play was 'garbled' and 'gelded' for production by the cautious playhouse, and 'printed as it was acted', so Dryden may not be entirely to blame. Finally, Dryden says that the ladies complained that there were not enough tender scenes; and yet he has not only brought a wife for Cleomenes to Egypt, like Gúerin de Bouscal, but added an attempted seduction by Ptolemy's mistress. It is chiefly by her jealous machinations that Cleomenes is ruined. We may perhaps feel that such a fate is unworthy of a Spartan Heroe; especially if he resisted temptation largely because he was still in love with his young wife! But Dryden does not appear to be trying to suggest either that Spartan virtues are unattainable or that they conflict inevitably with the world around; he would be far in advance of his age if he were. Rather, surely, the subject simply did not suit either him or the audience he wrote for. The stage was in a state of transition at this time. Whig ideas were replacing Tory ones, and with the court less interested in the theatre plays begin to reflect the attitudes of a wider public. To the new age Cleomenes in his last days was probably too egotistic a figure to appeal. Dryden's is the last play on the subject (in any language, in fact), and references to the 'King of Sparta who was styled *ultimus heroum*' grow rare.[1]

Moral and patriotic tragedies with a classical—though not usually a Greek—setting became increasingly common, however. In 1696 the ever-obliging Southerne got an amateurish *Pausanias*[2] by a gentleman called Norton on to the boards. Here the dramatic and the political traditions are at last united. 'The author had his reasons' for the choice of subject, which is the treacherous attempt of Pausanias, shortly after Plataea, to impose absolutism at Sparta, breaking through the restrictions imposed by the ephors and the laws. In this he seeks support from the Persians, who are in reality using him as a mere tool in their schemes of expansion, and (horror of horrors) turns to stirring up the helots. So much is fairly historical. The appearance of faction in Sparta is deplored, and Pausanias' execution, in spite of his royal blood, is justified. The recent exploits of Leonidas in defence of freedom are glorified in contrast, and the chief mouthpiece of Whiggish sentiment is Pausanias' stern and patriotic mother (unknown to Thucydides, but not to Diodorus, in all probability using Ephorus). *Pausanias* is chiefly of interest in that it seems to be an early example of the identification of Xerxes' absolutism with that of the Bourbons and Stuarts, and of the Persian with the French threat—as the prologue is hardly needed to make clear.

Having come so far we shall hardly feel surprise at finding a few operas, by definition spectacular and romantic works which were usually produced for a court, upon Spartan stories; they form a further proof of the distance the seventeenth century could move from all serious treatment of such material. Nothing remains here of the old themes but much-prettified instances of feminine courage, and some patriotism, transmuted to dynastic loyalty. The imperial court at Vienna was treated to several such works. *Chilonida* is based on a romantic tale from early Spartan history; she rescues her husband King Theopompus from a foreign prison by swapping clothes *à la* Lady Nithsdale.[3] *La più generosa Spartana*,

---

[1] Roger North, *Memoirs of Musick*, p. 46 (written in the early eighteenth century, published in 1846). I do not know any classical warrant for this rather suitable appellation, nor who later may have styled him thus.

[2] Only remembered if at all for the incidental music of Purcell, who also wrote that for *Cleomenes*.   [3] Fullest ancient source Polyaenus viii. 3.

very patriotic, purports to deal with the defence of Sparta against Pyrrhus of Epirus, and for the gallant part taken by the women can claim some authority in the final chapters of Plutarch's *Life of Pyrrhus*—behind which again lurks the figure of Phylarchus. The early third century B.C. is however the period of Spartan history which it is least unfair to treat in dynastic and individualistic terms. One would like to have seen the warlike *balletto di damigelle Spartane* with which the work culminated, and the sets too. For 'L'Apparato fu bellissima Inventione de Signor Ludovico Burnacini'—an infallible indication of Baroque grandeur.[1]

Perhaps a chapter devoted to Spartans in fiction may end with a note on classical genealogies and foundation stories, still widely popular and taken with more or less seriousness. The one really true and ancient Spartan *origo* cut little ice at this period. Sixteenth- and seventeenth-century descriptions and histories of Taranto recount the foundation of the city by Lacedaemonian colonists under Taras or Phalanthus, but they draw no conclusions from it and often turn with relief to S. Cataldo—it was he, not Taras, who got an epic poem. (Still, as we have seen, the connection encouraged a neighbour of Taranto to believe himself in Utopia.) The Spaniards and Portuguese however clung pertinaciously, and sometimes into quite recent times, to the story that Greeks, including Lacedaemonians, had colonized northern Spain (and not only the well-known Greek cities of the Mediterranean coast). Scarcely seriously meant, however, is the *origo* ascribed to Ampurias in a Latin poem of 1612, the *Sparte* of the distinguished French historian J.A. de Thou, or Thuanus. We are told how in memory of the unfortunate Sparte, daughter to the leader of the Lacedaemonian settlers, Apollo improved and gave their name to the famous plains of Esparto grass in the neighbourhood. Cantabria, where Strabo located his Lacedaemonians, did stretch so far.[2] But

---

[1] Original versions 1676 and 1685, and both, like *Leonida in Tegea*, by the court poet Nicolo Minato. Among other libretto titles is a *Pausania* and an anonymous *Leonida in Sparta*. In the early eighteenth century there was more than one *Cleomene* (one at least utterly fictional), and an *Agide re di Sparta* by Luisa Bergalli (1725). Most of these, as was usual at the time, were set by more than one composer.

[2] Paris, 1612. See especially Apollo's words

> iamque fatetur
> Auctores generis Cantabria terra Lacones.
> Huic quoque, tantarum pereat ne gloria rerum,
> Formosae Spartes imponam nomina campo.

the sober and well-known truth (however tricked out by historians) was that Emporion, the 'trading post', was an early foundation of Ionian Greeks.

It is pleasant to find that we are even offered a Pope. In 1662 a volume of laudatory verse addressed to Prince Camillo Pamfili, the nephew of Innocent X, bore the title *Allori d'Eurota*.[1] This was justified in a ponderously learned preface, which traced the Roman family of the Pamfili (it needed to improve its pedigree) neatly back to the Spartan 'family or tribe' of the Pamphyloi, descendants of Hercules and of Pamphilus, son of the Dorian King Aegimius and founder of Sparta. The line reached the Pamfili via the Sabines, and the Sabine brought as king to Rome, Numa Pompilius. What could be more convincing? But only one of the copies of verses makes play with the notion, and it does not seem that the Pamfili took it up. There were rival stories that suited them better.

[1] *Degli Allori d'Eurota* (Venice, 1662). The *Discorso* by sig. Nicolò Angelo Caferri. (In fact, the Pamphyloi were one of the three tribes originally found in all Dorian states; in Sparta by fully historical times they had been replaced for most purposes by a tribe-system based on local divisions.)

Modern scholars, vice versa, do sometimes suggest that the word Sparta is derived from σπάρτον or Esparto grass.

15

FRANCE IN THE EIGHTEENTH CENTURY (I)

As THE reign of Louis XIV passed its peak, its critics increased in number and importance. Between the defenders of orthodoxy in Church and state on the one hand (who must at best, in the courtly words of Bossuet, doubt if Sparta's political ideas were 'aussi solides que spécieuses', and her virtues not too proud and arrogant)[1] and the discontented Utopian romancers, who had left antiquity far behind them on the other, there appeared a new kind of reformer. In one of the most famous can be traced a faint but definite tinge of laconism, both monarchic and, far more prophetic for the ensuing century, educational and social. Féne-lon, who brings many famous figures of antiquity on to the stage in his *Dialogues des Morts*, can paint his only Lacedaemonian, Leonidas, as the perfect king, in conversation and contrast with Xerxes. In language that is essential Fénelon, the former explains that 'j'étois roi à condition de mener une vie dure, sobre et laborieuse, comme mon peuple. Je n'étois roi que pour défendre ma patrie et pour faire régner les lois: ma royauté me donnoit le pouvoir de faire du bien sans me permettre de faire du mal'; and the second is told 'si tu n'avois pas été un roi trop puissant et trop heureux, tu aurois été un assez honnête homme'.[2]

Not that Fénelon wished his king to be less than absolute; but he was to be closely associated with law. He was to be strictly bound by the natural or divine law, which above all else demands the welfare, taken in the widest sense, of the people. And he was to be a careful observer of the earthly laws, that he alone ordains, but which reflect the higher law. He was, also, to be far more closely associated and acquainted with his people, both by con-stitutional devices and in his way of life, than the French monarch had become.

[1] *Discours sur l'histoire universelle* (1681) iii. 5.
[2] *Dialogue XL* (*Oeuvres complètes* (1851 etc.) vi. 248).

In *Télémaque* Fénelon's political views are expounded to his royal pupil in the course of a tale of voyage, with Utopian incidents. Its classical background is unusual, but Fénelon was doubtless following both his own tastes and his idea of the educationally suitable. Its Greece is the Greece of heroic legend before the coming of the Dorians; but Fénelon's Cretan states are so reminiscent not only of Plato's ideal cities, particularly of the proposed Cretan colony of the *Laws*, but of passages in Plutarch's *Lycurgus* that one suspects he is using the supposed connection between Sparta and Crete as a literary, if not a historical, justification for his descriptions. Cretan education, with bodily health and moral virtue as its primary aims, Cretan *cuisine*, with little wine or meat, and Cretan houses, plain in construction—all sound familiar. King Minos of course is described in very much the same language as Leonidas.[1]

The Cretan episode in Book V is as it were a first sketch for Salente, the ideal state of Book X. This Cretan colony in south Italy has fallen into decay, and is reformed by Mentor under the admiring gaze of Télémaque on closely Platonic lines. He revives Minos' laws on education, according to which *écoles publiques* teach piety, patriotism, and how to respect the laws and place honour above pleasure; 'il régla les habits, la nourriture, les meubles, la grandeur et l'ornement des maisons, pour toutes les conditions différentes. Il bannit tous les ornemens d'or et d'argent', and forbade the import of luxuries. He severely regulated artists, and 'retrancha ensuite la musique' (in this connection, Fénelon had mentioned Sparta as well as Plato with approval in *L'Éducation des filles*). He set up magistrates to watch over the *moeurs des particuliers*. The ownership of land is to be regulated by need, according to size of family and difference of rank—for in this the aristocratic Fénelon goes beyond ancient, let alone most modern, ideal states, admitting a hierarchy of seven classes, with slaves at the bottom.

Such background laconism, if one may call it so, found some echo. Open admiration for Spartan kings and Spartan simplicity of life is revealed in the *Voyages de Cyrus*, of Fénelon's faithful but tedious disciple the Chevalier Ramsey, who takes his prince on a

[1] *Les Aventures de Télémaque* (first published 1699), op. cit. vi. 426 ff., and 472 ff.

grand tour of ancient states;[1] it is also clearly visible in the enormously popular *Histoire ancienne* of Rollin, on which whole
generations were brought up.[2]

Télémaque visits a third happy community, that of Bétique in
Spain. But its virtuous primitives form a contrast to the civilized
Cretan states. For a time, however, comparisons of Spartan and
savage did persist. The learned Jesuit father Lafitau published his
*Moeurs des sauvages Amériquains comparées aux moeurs des premiers
temps*, with handsome plates, in 1724. His purpose was to defend
Christianity by its opponents' weapons, arguing that all races
showed, at an early stage of development, such similarity in
social and religious matters as to prove their origin from a common ancestor. Lafitau too had been in Canada, and had a high
opinion of its inhabitants' patriotism, love of glory, and contempt
for misfortune. If, among the innumerable parallels with antiquity
that he draws, that with the heroes of Homer was the newest and
in some ways the most pregnant, he does not neglect the Spartans.
Could the scarlet worn by these in battle really be war-paint? Like
them, the Americans have common meals for the men. Then, 'ils
se moquent dans leurs danses, mais Lycurgue avait fait une loy
de cette danse satyrique parmi les siens'. The war-chief, with limited and agreed powers, recalls the Spartan king, whose functions
were primarily military. 'Le père de famille, semblable au παιδο-
νόμος établi par Lycurgue, y harangue tous les matins la jeunesse,
et veille sur elle, et sur tous les exercices de ces jeunes gens, dont la
vie n'est pas moins dure que celle des Spartiates.' They escape
all education and grow up in the wildest freedom, it is true; but
Lafitau is convinced that this is only because American society
has suffered a recent decline. Nonetheless, it is clear that to him
the antiquity with which he is comparing America is not, as it
had so often appeared in the Renaissance, civilization's summit,
but a simple and early stage of its development.[3]

But in spite of Fénelon or the admirers of savagery, many of the
streams that went to make up the rising flood of opposition to
every kind of orthodoxy were likely to involve a certain contempt
for Sparta. The sceptical spirit learned to question the glories of
antiquity, either preferring to find matter for argument in more

[1] Sir Andrew Ramsey, *Voyages de Cyrus* (1727).

[2] Charles Rollin, *Histoire ancienne . . .* (1730–8).

[3] References to Sparta i. 56, 79, 273, 459, 509–10, 515, 576, 597, 604; ii. 2,
16, 28, 60, 240, 373, 397.

recent and more easily known periods, or believing ancient like modern historiography a tissue of lies and flattery; while the great debates on early chronology might bring the shaky historical position of Lycurgus to notice. And if one reaction to the economic and social state of France was a horror of extravagance and luxury, another was the desire to rationalize taxation and stimulate agriculture as well as trade, together with an attachment to property justifiable by the doctrines of Locke. The dynastic wars of Louis XIV had proved calamitous, and Fénelon was far from alone in his longing for peace; the persecution of the Protestants and quarrels within the Catholic Church had also visibly damaged the country. What the new age wanted was above all happiness—a sensible, moderate happiness with a firm base in the material pleasures of life as well as in a mind at peace with itself and free from the terrors of superstition. The ideal of the princely warrior was giving way to that of a more modest and socially responsible figure. Antiquity, it was sometimes observed, had its superstitions too, and modern follies could be more safely ridiculed under their guise. And ancient virtues, in an increasingly polished world, now often appeared as irrelevant and as uncomfortable to the merely humane as they did to the wholly Christian.

And so references to Sparta, until almost the middle of the eighteenth century, tend to be either hard to find, adverse, or purely frivolous. We may begin by looking up the leading Spartan heroes in Bayle's famous *Dictionnaire*.[1] We find that Agis IV is supposed to be motivated only by a 'raffinement de l'amour-propre' in his reforms, and the rôle of the omen of the shooting-star in Lacedaemonian politics is singled out for ridicule. Agesilaus' excessive love of war harmed his country. As for Lycurgus, 'Lycurgue, législateur de Lacédémone, vivait je ne sais quand'. He receives a few tempered compliments, particularly on his restriction of luxury, but it would be easy to criticize most of his laws, as Monsieur Dacier has done in his recent translation of Plutarch. Soon, with an assurance that the facts of his life may be found in the work of Bayle's predecessor and *bête-noire* Moréri, Bayle abandons politics to devote several exceedingly lengthy notes to a detailed exposition of the sexual *mores* of Spartan women, with comparative material from later times. And for some time to

[1] First published 1697.

come this aspect of Spartan life is to attract shocked or joyous attention from many writers; even, in 1742, a whole mildly pornographic novel.[1] Baroque Spartiates had been odd, but at these Rococo ones the mind rather boggles; and none seem to appear in the visual arts.

Even among those few who had, as we saw, an interest in Sparta there were strong reservations. Fénelon himself has harsh words for her cruelty (especially to the helots), her warlike ambitions, and idleness;[2] Ramsey adds her interference with private property; and the historian Rollin draws up two lists of 'choses louables' and 'choses blâmables dans les lois de Lycurgue', including in the latter the idealization of idleness, reminiscent of that of the French nobility of the day, and of course the immodesty of the women. And on the whole the political romances that continue to fall from the press in considerable numbers still show little interest in Sparta, whether they are the vehicles of aggressive deism, and often communism, recalling the *Histoire des Sévarambes*, or the more conservative sermons on virtuous monarchy and happy family life, to some extent the progeny of *Télémaque*. For most are fashionably gallant, thoroughly pacifist, and concerned with large kingdoms and their rational administrative and economic management. When the author of one of these exotic and communist romances, Morelly, came in the changed climate of 1755 to expound his ideas openly and analytically and with brief reference to the ancient lawgivers, he could only say that all, Lycurgus and Solon included, had created highly faulty codes.[3]

Even the great debate on *le luxe* went on its way without much reference to Sparta, though an occasional swipe at her was taken by those, increasing in number, who distinguished at least some types of luxury as beneficial.[4] But Voltaire at least has no place for her yet in this context, though he maltreats the Garden of

---

[1] *Les Dortoirs de Lacédémone*, by Meusnier de Querlon (1742)—in spite of its name, entirely heterosexual.

[2] *Dialogues des morts* vii, xvii.

[3] (Morelly), *Code de la nature*, 1755 (ed. G. Chinard, 1950).

[4] J. F. Melon, *Essai politique sur le commerce* (1734), ch. ix, 'du luxe', p. 139. In no way superior to Athens, Sparta had fewer great men, and Lycurgus' sumptuary laws 'ne méritent pas plus d'attention que ses autres lois qui révoltent tant la pudeur'. His communism was bound to produce lack of ambition and effort. Melon also prefers Lucullus to Cato!

Eden and Fénelon's Crete memorably.[1] And in his history of Charles XII of Sweden, a work that so clearly points the moral, as it adorns the tale, of exaggerated and destructive heroism, he more than once uses a phrase familiar as a Laconian aphorism to characterize the Swedes—but without making clear its origin.[2] A few decades later comparisons of Sweden and Sparta were out in the open. The comparison which Voltaire and others could not resist was a superficial but certainly unflattering one: with the frugal, anti-intellectual, militaristic Prussia of Frederick William. He was delighted that Frederick the Great on coming to the throne was undertaking to convert gloomy Sparta into brilliant Athens, and ultimately disappointed at the incompleteness of the transformation. There were still more bayonets than books in Berlin.[3]

It is true that education was still fundamentally classical, or rather Latin, for the ability to read Greek was not common, and also that admiration for the work of Plutarch, usually in translation, survived. But the Abbé de St. Pierre, for one, put his admiration for it simply down to its encouraging a desire to distinguish oneself 'par des talents utiles à sa patrie', so that it was valuable despite its faults. And he does not include a single Spartan in his list of the truly great, because virtuous and beneficent, men of antiquity (the Greeks are represented by Solon and Epaminondas), though he praises the place *en passant*.[4] And other prominent devotees of the classics also seem to avoid Sparta. But a somewhat unusual (and, doubtless fortunately, ill-documented) figure does rise before us in an early dialogue by Montesquieu, which he did not publish. Xanthippus, it may or may not be recalled, was the Spartan commander who saved Carthage from the Roman invasion in the first Punic War. Here he explains with affable modesty that he has only done what his education would make any Spartiate do, in intervening to protect a foreign city against a power pursuing its advantage beyond what justice or glory

---

[1] See esp. *Le Mondain*, 1736, and *La Défense du Mondain*, 1737 (*Oeuvres complètes*, ed. Moland, 1877, x. 83).

[2] *Histoire de Charles XII*, 1731 (op. cit. xvi).

[3] See P. Gay, *Voltaire's Politics* (1959), p. 150, n. 20 and 171, n. 70 for references to the *Correspondance* and elsewhere. London, so free and so respectful of talent, proved a more satisfactory Athens to Voltaire.

[4] *Annales politiques* (1735); 'Discours sur les différences du grand homme et de l'homme illustre.'

demand. Not so had Sparta acted, when she spared defeated Athens. 'Chaque Lacédémonien n'est-il pas né protecteur de la liberté commune', and trained by the severe discipline of Lycurgus to watch over the interests of all mankind? Xanthippus had at last left Carthage because his power there became too great; even in exile he remembers that he is 'enfant de Lycurgue, c'est-à-dire ennemi de la tyrannie'. He wants no honours; for while virtue unites us with our fellows, glory divides us from them. 'Nos lois, qui gênent toutes les passions, contraignent surtout celles des heros.' Honour in Sparta is not a chimera, lost and won capriciously, and associated as often with vice as with virtue: 'l'exacte obéissance aux lois est l'honneur parmi nous', and what Xanthippus is proudest of is of having been born to see his rivals preferred to him, and of loving the laws that drove him into exile.[1]

Here at last is the perfect early eighteenth-century Spartiate we had difficulty in finding; cosmopolitan, moderate, and reasonable, firmly rejecting extravagant seventeenth-century notions. The Spartiate was soon to become, even in Montesquieu's own hands, a narrower and harsher figure. Here also, as our quotations indicate, is a particular partiality for Lycurgus. Agesilaus has never recovered from the reaction against the princely warrior; his age, like that of the more political Theopompus, has closed for ever, while that of Leonidas is still to come, with the national wars at the end of the century and above all with philhellenism. But the age *par excellence* of Lycurgus is just opening. The hero of the time was the beneficent and constructive legislator, and whatever his specific provisions, Lycurgus undoubtedly was, or appeared to be, one of the most famous and most remarkable of all legislators. The creation of society almost from scratch by the genius of a single mind seemed proper—Descartes had earlier ascribed Sparta's success to this feature of her history[2]—and possible; had not Peter the Great done something of the sort? Lycurgus' name becomes part of the common coin of eulogy (if it is not improper to use so monetary a metaphor of him) even

[1] *Oeuvres complètes*, ed. A. Masson, 3 vols. (1950–5); iii. 119, *Dialogue de Xantippe et Xenocrate*. Cf. ii. 141, 'Pensées qui n'ont pu entrer dans mon dialogue de Xantippe', esp. no. 357, 'Sparte, une nation . . . chez qui les moindres citoyens sont ce que les seuls philosophes sont ailleurs.'

[2] *Discours de la méthode* (1637), Part ii: some of her laws were strange and even contrary to morality, but one man framed them all.

among those who in fact ignored or abominated his works. Frederick the Great employs it to Voltaire, and Voltaire to the Empress Catherine.

But there was perhaps only one of Lycurgus' actual—or rather supposed—enactments that received pretty wide approval. The education prescribed by Lycurgus might be faulty in itself and unsuited to a modern state, but at least it was thorough and it was public. The dominant psychological theory of the period was Locke's sensationalism, according to which man is simply the sum of his experiences. This might reinforce a patronising attitude to the less experienced ancient world, but it also meant that the importance of education, and of environment in general, seemed overwhelming; and to divorce politics from these impossible. Whether one was anxious to reconcile and re-identify king and people, government and governed; more concerned to spread enlightenment by taking teaching out of the hands of the obscurantist clergy and the ignorant parent; or simply disillusioned by the traditional education of the college, as a purely intellectual exercise directed to the memory rather than the judgement, and concerned with useless and irrelevant subjects—to put training into the hands of the state appeared to be the answer.[1]

And yet, as is generally known, the later eighteenth century in France is the great age of modern laconomania, gathering together the threads—moral, social, educational, and political—that had usually been separate since the Renaissance. The two main figures associated with this reversal of opinion are Montesquieu and Rousseau; in the next rank come Helvétius, Mably, and others. But while modern scholars are aware of the widespread occurrence of laconism in this period, it would seem that little attempt has been made to trace its development, nor to see how varied it was, and how strong the reaction against it.

---

[1] For an example between Fénelon and Montesquieu, see Lévêque de Pouilly, who ends his *Théorie des sentimens agréables* (revised version, 1747) thus:

'Les législateurs de Lacédémone et de la Chine, ont presque été les seuls qui n'ayent pas crû devoir se reposer sur l'ignorance des pères ou des maîtres, d'un soin qui leur a paru l'objet le plus important du pouvoir législatif. Ils ont fixé dans leurs loix le plan d'une éducation détaillée, qui pût instruire à fond les particuliers sur ce qui faisoit ici-bas leur bonheur, et ils ont exécuté ce que dans la théorie même, on croit encore impossible. L'histoire ne nous permet point de douter que ces deux États n'ayent été très féconds en hommes vertueux; ils l'eussent été apparemment encore davantage, si l'éducation et la morale y eussent été plus parfaites.'

Montesquieu begins *L'Esprit des lois* (published in 1748, after many years' labour) by dividing governments into three types, distinguished above all by the moral principles that sustain them: republics, which depend on virtue in the citizens; monarchies, in which the king governs through the law and the ruling principle is the sense of honour in the nobility, pride of class or profession, and the desire for advancement; and despotism, where fear is employed to crush and divide all subjects. Montesquieu's love and admiration for antiquity was unusually deep; the republics of the first books of *L'Esprit des lois* are almost exclusively the classical ones. 'On ne peut jamais quitter les Romains', he says apologetically.[1] He had already, in the *Considérations sur les causes de la grandeur des Romains et de leur décadence*, argued that republican government is only suited to a small country, in which everyone can partake in public life, and is incompatible with imperialism and extension.

Though less dear to him than Rome, Sparta and Athens also contribute a great deal to his system. Sparta's place is ambiguous, since at times she seems to be the chief representative, with Venice, of aristocracy, a subdivision of republic, where the virtue needed is more specifically moderation in the ruling class. But since Montesquieu says that the wider an aristocracy is, the better, and since in a democracy the people need by no means be equivalent to the whole body of inhabitants for him any more than for the ancients, it is understandable that elsewhere Sparta and Athens should be distinguished primarily as military and commercial republics, and the first should suggest quite as much as the second in the description of a popular state.[2]

Such a state depends, in the first place, on education in public virtue. 'On peut définir cette vertu, l'amour des lois et de la patrie' (but this is misleadingly narrow, as such love springs out of and causes a general *bonté des moeurs*). Lycurgus, with Crete which inspired him and Plato who improved on him, proved what could be done in a small state in antiquity to conquer passion and prejudice and teach self-renunciation. It is also dependent upon equality among the citizens. Equality, in a new or a revolutionary

[1] *Oeuvres complètes*, ed. A. Masson, vol. i (1950), xi. 13 (facsimile of the revised edition of 1758).

[2] xviii. 1, the country, more fertile than Attica, determined a government less equal; the ephorate founded to control the nobles, with parallels from Venice.

state, may sometimes be established by a division of land, as it was in Sparta and Rome; at other times it may only be possible to regulate and qualify inequality, as Solon did at Athens by setting up his four property-classes. Solon's remark, that he gave the Athenians not the best laws but the best they could bear, is a 'belle parole, qui devroit être entendue de tous les législateurs'. (Athens' later development illustrates the corruption of democracy, which comes about either by the loss of equality or its exaggeration—when the people refuses to be subordinate even to its own magistrates and undertakes all business itself.) Frugality is vital to the survival of equality. It may be added that Montesquieu holds that respect for age, as at Sparta and Rome, for paternal authority, and for the magistrates (here he quotes Sparta again) are necessary to maintain good *moeurs* in a democracy. So is a senate elected for life, as in Rome, Sparta, and early Athens, and so are censors on the Roman pattern; in Sparta all the old men acted as such. For change is usually for the worse, and Montesquieu holds the old view that constitutions tend to decline. In addition, he feels that virtue may be better preserved in a state not suffering from over-education, and is ready for the sake of equality to admit sumptuary legislation, restrictions on inheritance, and even the absence of money. He is much impressed by the achievements of the Society of Jesus in Paraguay.

The seeds of laconism are obviously here; and although Montesquieu never discusses Sparta alone at length, and although what he has to say of her is often purely descriptive or even hostile (helotism, which unites real with personal servitude, is 'contre la nature des choses', and Lycurgus, who mixed virtues with vices in his system, made his citizens harsh as well as virtuous), there can be no doubt that he set the stage for subsequent developments, above all for Rousseau. He ignored the recently dominant ideas of Sparta as a more or less limited monarchy or mixed state—he finds fault with Aristotle for failing to understand monarchy and not realizing that Sparta was a republic. He put her firmly in a remote, but not absolutely a primitive, context, making much of the Utopian themes of simplicity and equality. Thus he divorced her securely from England,[1] or for that matter

---

[1] Although the mixed constitution, with Sparta and England as the best examples of its monarchic version, was being expounded in French at this very time by the famous Genevan legist Burlamaqui (*Principes du droit politique,*

Venice, on the one hand, and from Red Indian savages on the other. By regarding her as a state ruled by *moeurs* rather than laws (or where Lycurgus had confused the two), and simultaneously defining monarchy partly as government by law, he pushed another old theme into the background. And in his insistence that a republican constitution rests on republican education he went beyond any of his predecessors, even Machiavelli, to whom he clearly owes much (perhaps not least the idea that Christianity is not suited to republics). His interest in federal republics, finally, opened a way for his successors to adapt to a large country ideas at first only considered suitable for small ones.[1]

By his nostalgia for 'ces vertus que nous trouvons dans les anciens et dont nous avons seulement entendu parler', and by allotting an inferior moral status to honour, the principle of monarchy, Montesquieu might seem in the last resort to lend his authority to semi-Utopian classical republicanism. But he insists that laws that fit the people they were made for will fit no one else; they must be adapted not only to the principle of government, but to climate, soil, area, the character and religion of the inhabitants, and so on. It goes without saying that the ancient republics are no model for modern, Christian states—even though the polished Athenians were not unlike the French in character. And modern states need not be deprecated. France used to have an almost perfect government in its monarchy, restrained by fundamental laws which secured civil liberty to the people, and supported by a nobility inspired by true honour;[2] though it is now falling into despotism (this is very much the thesis of the French aristocracy of the time, looking wistfully back to its great days). And in his chapters on England Montesquieu praises a country where 'la république se cache sous la forme de la monarchie', and the people retain at least a modicum of political virtue. He found in it various positive advantages; in such a large state assemblies must be representative, and this makes it hard for demagogues to stir up the people; and the famous doctrine of the separation of powers, not understood in antiquity, ensures liberty. But we need do no more than mention these parts of his doctrine.

[1] xi. 1–3.   [2] xi. 8.

1751, ii. 2, pp. 128–9). Here Athens is still associated with Florence and Genoa, as well.

After the middle of the century writers became bolder. Ideas formerly confined, more or less, to Utopian romances crept into general discussion. D'Argenson, horrified both by the corruption of the court and the misery in the provinces, joined issue with Montesquieu for supposing that equality and frugality could ever be out of place (later he welcomed Morelly's *Code*, though granting that communism was probably unworkable). But it was perhaps partly because Montesquieu had spoken of Sparta as he had that d'Argenson is to be found exclaiming in his private memoirs that 'l'égalité est le seul bien général et jamais législateur n'a eu plus de raison que Lycurgue sur ce point là'.[1] This equality, of course, is still mainly seen as a question of landed property; but sumptuary laws and a public education would contribute to it.

There can be little doubt that any real laconomania existing in the later eighteenth century owed much of its strength to Rousseau. What he felt for Sparta was more than mere admiration; it was a deep emotional attachment. There were few aspects of Spartan life that he did not ultimately find sympathetic (though after the early *Discours sur les sciences et les arts* he passes lightly over her military tendencies, while he holds that 'tout citoyen oisif est un fripon'). Rousseau's humble birth, his peculiar character and experiences, his reading, especially of Plato and Seneca, above all his Genevan and Calvinist inheritance, if only through its puritanical streak and its apprehension of the small republic as a living reality, all helped him to turn in his maturity at least as easily to Sparta as to Rome; certainly more easily than had Montesquieu, a lawyer rather than a moralist, an aristocrat born in a great kingdom, to whom his picture of both owed something and with whom he shared a hatred of despotism and a passionate admiration for antique virtue.

The *Confessions* suggest that it was primarily the Roman and Athenian heroes of Plutarch who filled Rousseau's boyhood imagination, and for examples of individual heroism he continued to turn first to Rome. But the *Discours sur les sciences et les arts* inevitably led him towards Sparta. Following in the wake of earlier variations on the theme of hostility to learning, particularly that of Montaigne, whom he both quotes and pillages,[2] he is bound to set her up as an ideal (along with early Persians, Romans,

---

[1] *Journal et mémoires du Marquis d'Argenson*, ed. E. J. B. Rathéry (1859 etc.), vi. 427 (21 June 1751).   [2] Especially *Du pédantisme*.

Q

Scyths, and Germans and his own Swiss in modern times). But there is a new accent of real if exaggerated sincerity: 'Oublierois-je que ce fut dans le sein même de la Grèce qu'on vit s'élever cette Cité aussi célèbre par son heureuse ignorance que par la sagesse de ses Loix, cette République de demi-Dieux plutôt que d'hommes? tant leurs vertus sembloient supérieures à l'humanité? O Sparte! opprobre éternel d'une vaine doctrine . . .'![1] He argues that learning obscures sincerity and disguises despotism, springs from and feeds our vices, makes states weak (observe Sparta's strength and durability); he argues that modern education omits to train the judgement and the moral sense (a note quotes Montaigne on Spartan and Persian education); and his last words are another echo of Montaigne, begging all but the most exceptional men to copy not that great people that knew how to *bien dire*, but its rival, that knew instead how to *bien faire*.

In the lively controversy that followed the appearance of the prize-winning *Discours*, Rousseau firmly side-stepped attempts to involve him in scholarly arguments[2] and continued to regard Sparta as a trump card. 'L'embarras de mes adversaires est visible toutes les fois qu'il faut parler de Sparte'; they would have given a lot for it never to have existed. 'C'est une terrible chose qu'au milieu de cette fameuse Grèce qui ne devoit sa vertu qu'à la Philosophie [as they argued] l'État où la vertu a été la plus pure et a duré le plus longtemps ait été précisément celui où il n'y avoit point de Philosophes.'[3] His old friend M. Bordes, who had argued that her laws had serious faults and were finally corrupted, and that if all the Greeks had resembled the Spartans in never writing their own history we should not remember them, gets short shrift.

Two fragmentary pieces, which bear witness to the moral value Rousseau always placed on a study of ancient as opposed to modern history, perhaps also bear witness to his increasing interest in Sparta at about this period.[4] The first consists of notes for a

[1] *Oeuvres complètes de Jean-Jacques Rousseau*, Pléiade ed. (1964), vol. iii. p. 12; cf. p. 20, 24 n.
[2] Especially with a professor of history (and mathematics) from Nancy, Gautier; *Lettre à M. Grimm*, ibid., p. 61; cf. p. 69.
[3] *Dernière réponse*, ibid., p. 83; cf. pp. 79, 90 n. (Spartan apophthegm on education).
[4] *Fragments politiques*, ibid. xii. 539 and xiii. 545. There are other references to Sparta in other fragments; see esp. iii. 488, confuting Montesquieu's preference

parallel between the republics of Rome and Sparta, considered as instructive and encouraging since both owed success to wisdom and showed that free institutions need not be unstable, and since their virtues, supplementing each other, enable us to draw the picture of a perfect state. They had similar *moeurs* and principles, especially an eager love of country; both fell in the end from expansion, though Rome, as so often, gets the better of the comparison of military policies.

The second fragment shows Rousseau actually sitting down to write a history of Lacedaemon, succumbing, he says, to a 'penchant presque invincible' that had long been tormenting him (and perhaps to the suggestion of some friend). The subject, he says, has been strangely neglected, but is 'propre à faire sentir ce que peuvent sur l'homme les loix et les moeurs, et ce que peut l'homme lui-même quand il aime sincèrement la vertu'. If the work reads like a panegyric it is the fault not of the author but of his subject, whose achievement was doubtless even greater than it appears through the medium of the foreign authorities; for the Spartans themselves, in their modesty, did nothing for immortality but merit it. Not that they committed no errors; but if they seem to us unnatural, it is perhaps because *we* are really so.

After this eloquent preface, with its splendidly typical climax, Rousseau has scarcely embarked on his narrative, and explained how the existence of two royal houses led to the end of despotism and finally to the rule of law, when he breaks off, in the midst, it seems, of a half-hearted attempt to excuse helotism. He undoubtedly had better things to do.

The *Discours sur l'origine de l'inégalité* (1755) is one of Rousseau's works that talks least of Sparta; but there are hints, both in his highly idealized dedicatory picture of Geneva, so reminiscent of Sparta (though there is only one actual reference to her), and in the text itself, that he is already working towards his final political conception of the Greek city. He saw this as an example of the kind of society that men had sometimes established in the beginning, or that might subsequently be established by rebuilding from the very foundations, as Lycurgus had done; a democ-

---

for paternal authority as found in Rome—wrong and unnecessary where laws are the source of *moeurs*; iv. 6, p. 492, people need know nothing but laws and those by heart, as Lycurgus showed; iv. 9, p. 494, a Spartan apophthegm; iv. 24, p. 498; vi. 8, p. 512; xiv. 2, p. 549.

racy that could still preserve the liberty and equality of the part-
ners in it, and also many of the natural and admirable features of
the 'Golden Age' (subsequent to and not identical with the pure
state of nature) such as reverence for age and a tough and healthy
education. His most significant remark is perhaps this: that while
our vices make society necessary, they also corrupt it—save in
Sparta, where education was under the charge of the law, and the
moeurs of Lycurgus made laws almost unnecessary.[1] But before
we pass on to consider Sparta's place in his mature political works,
we may turn aside to what may seem a special point. It is not
really so; the amusements and pastimes that make the citizens
known to each other, encouraging their corporate spirit and their
political judgement, and that form their physical and moral
abilities, are always of great political importance to Rousseau.
But there were certainly various personal and political reasons
leading him to fling himself into a new episode of the old story of
quarrels about the stage. In the *Lettre à d'Alembert sur les spectacles*
(1758)[2] Rousseau reproaches d'Alembert (behind whom stood
Voltaire) for suggesting in his article 'Genève' in the *Encyclopédie*
that that city might unite 'la sagesse de Lacédémone à la politesse
d'Athènes' if it would only admit a (severely controlled) theatre
to form its tastes. Rousseau grants that such pleasures may be
necessary in great towns, but in small ones, above all in small
republics, their results are disastrous. Changes are always dangerous; this would destroy republican austerity and equality, excite
the passions, distract the industrious, weaken female modesty
and reverence for age. Actors were doubtless more respectable in
Greece than they are now; but Greece, except for Sparta, was not
renowned for *bonnes moeurs*, and Sparta had no theatre.[3] At
Athens the effects of the stage were frightful; they included the
death of Socrates.

'Ne nous flattons pas de voir Sparte renaître au sein du commerce et de l'amour du gain'; only there were *moeurs* identical
with, not more powerful than, the laws. But Rousseau is increas-

[1] Ibid., esp. pp. 119, 180, 181 (apophthegm of Brasidas), 186, 187-8 esp.
[2] Ed. M. Fuchs (1948), esp. pp. 89, 103-5, 132 ff.
[3] It was pointed out to Rousseau that the remains of a theatre do exist in
Sparta. He could not know that it is of Roman date; he did suggest, rightly,
that it was not used primarily for the drama (*Correspondance générale*, iv. p. 106,
letter to M. Leroy).

ingly tempted to make comparisons. One of the disadvantages of a theatre in Geneva would be—'adieu les cercles'. In these small groups the citizens met, apart from their womenkind, and discussed political and moral questions; with their companions of the circles they enjoyed hunting and military exercises. This simple and innocent republican habit preserves some image of the *moeurs antiques*; it is fairly obvious whose in particular. And as Rousseau soars towards his peroration he leaves all hesitations behind. He describes the truly republican spectacles existing in Geneva: in the summer active, open-air reviews, military competitions, and so on, followed by public meals. 'Toutes les sociétés ne font qu'une, tout devient commun à tous', and though there is rather more harmless profusion, it is the very image of Lacedaemon. For the winter, why be afraid of balls? Dancing is natural, and a magistrate might preside over it. A city with such amusements would attract strangers, which is no advantage; but it would also draw home the citizens scattered, as they are from Geneva, over the face of the earth. 'Ainsi rappeloit ses citoyens, par des fêtes modestes et des jeux sans éclat, cette Sparte que je n'aurai jamais assez citée pour l'exemple que nous devrions en tirer; ainsi dans Athènes, parmi les beaux-arts, ainsi dans Suse, au sein du luxe et de la mollesse, le Spartiate ennuyé soupiroit après ses grossiers festins et ses fatigants exercices.' There, the hardest labours were considered recreations, and the slightest amusements were a part of public education. The citizens passed their life together in diversions, which were the great business of the state.

What, are we to have girls dancing naked? Rousseau anxiously anticipates the ribald question, answering bravely that we are not chaste enough for that. With all his regard for his compatriots, he knows too well the gulf separating them from the Spartans.[1]

---

[1] Distinguished Genevans told Rousseau that he knew nothing about the place and that it bore no resemblance to Sparta (e.g. Dr. Tronchin in *Correspondance générale* iv. p. 117). It is perhaps worth noting that Burlamaqui, also a member of the ruling caste there, had divided mixed constitutions into two sorts and considered Geneva an aristo-democracy, while Sparta (with England) was a limited monarchy. When the Genevan magistrates had condemned *Émile* and the *Contrat* for supporting the more popular party, and when Rousseau had renounced his citizenship, he was ready himself to regard comparisons with antiquity as inflated: 'vous n'êtes ni Romains ni Spartiates; vous n'êtes pas même Athéniens', only merchants and farmers concerned with nothing but

'Tout est dit en avouant que cet usage ne convient qu'aux élèves de Lycurgue.' And he ends with a description of these festivals and dances, as recounted by Plutarch, in all their simplicity and patriotic fervour: 'voilà, Monsieur, les spectacles qu'il faut à des Républiques.'[1]

We must not laugh; here is not only one of the first and fullest expositions of Rousseau's belief that *all* republics are or should be simple—*austérité républicaine* is genuinely a phrase of his—but of his closely connected conception of the republican festivity, on a Spartan or sometimes a more generally Greek model. And these were two ideas that haunted some Frenchmen well into the Revolutionary period.

Finally, a brief and incomplete sketch of Rousseau's mature political theory, as expounded chiefly in the *Contrat social* (1762), will suggest at how many other points his thought touched Sparta, and where he actually appealed to her example. This theory rests, of course, upon the basis of freedom and equality; in other words, upon the contract by which a number of men find it to their advantage to set up a society, but retain the inalienable sovereign power, which they exercise by meeting at stated intervals for legislation. Naturally therefore the legitimate society is likely to be a city-state, small enough for the members of the sovereign body to meet frequently and take a vital interest in public affairs. In such a state their love for their country will be more immediate, and the citizen's personal qualities better known and valued. For Rousseau was suspicious of the representative principle, thinking it likely to develop where the citizens have lost their interest in public affairs; and that the representatives themselves were all too easily corrupted, as now appeared to many Frenchmen (and not only to them) to be the case in England.

Brought up, as he had been, in familiarity with the Greek states and Geneva, where the number of full citizens was small, Rousseau was not seriously perturbed by the possible presence of a large number of inhabitants who had no part in this social contract. Indeed, though he was not a defender of slavery, he could even

[1] The manners and amusements of the patriarchal Wolmar household in *La Nouvelle Héloïse* (1761) are closely related; but since here it is only private life that Rousseau is reforming, there is no reference to ancient republics.

your private interests. *Lettres écrites de la montagne* ix, 1764 (*Oeuvres complètes* iii. 881, cf. 871).

describe helotism as necessary for the freedom of the Spartiates; in the traditional way, his citizens must be men of education and leisure.

They meet, then, to give expression to the General Will, which is by definition the advantage of the state as a whole. If, in a properly informed body, each member votes in accordance with his own belief as to what this is, particular interests should, Rousseau thinks, cancel out and the true General Will result. Thus intrigues, factions, and the interests of smaller, partial associations are the danger. While Solon and the Roman law-givers prudently assured that these last were many in number and fairly equal in power, under the unique and sublime system of Lycurgus there were none at all.[1]

It was largely this fear of particular sectional interests that made Rousseau so averse to commercial development and to an independent Church. He felt, however, that while enthusiastically occupied with public life the citizens would not turn their attention to commerce.

It is clear that the need for the individual to conform his will to the General Will means that the state requires the virtue and devotion of its citizens. It is for these qualities that Sparta is most often cited; it is to cultivate these that Rousseau is ready to give the state such great apparent power. It must make men *men*, as the ancient states did, and must enforce the relative economic equality that alone preserves liberty, by means of agrarian, sumptuary, and testamentary laws, and by control of exports and imports (ancient states were parsimonious and did not get into debt like modern ones). The state, too, must be responsible for the private *moeurs*, and the education, which will form the patriotic citizen. There is little direct discussion of education in the *Contrat social*; but the article for the *Encyclopédie* on 'Économie politique' holds that, education being of more importance to the state than to the father, whose power over his children will in any case lapse with time, the former should remove children from their parents at an early age, to be brought up in common and imbued with the laws and precepts of the General Will under the responsibility of elderly and carefully selected magistrates. Crete, Lacedaemon, and Persia had done this; Rome, miraculously, managed without, and the system is not suited to large states.

[1] *Du contrat social* ii. 3 (*Oeuvres complètes* iii. 372).

In *Émile* too, public education, as envisaged by Plato, or, more thoroughly, Lycurgus, who succeeded in 'denaturing' man by bringing him up to live entirely for others, is the only logical, though today quite unobtainable, alternative to the 'natural' and domestic education, for oneself alone, that the book proceeds to describe.[1] Education in the state, however, continues through life. For the censorship controls and guides, though it cannot altogether oppose, public opinion, and can thus do much at least to delay the decay of morals. In spite of the Latin origin of the word censorship, Lacedaemon, Rousseau holds, used public opinion even better than Rome.[2]

It must be remembered that Rousseau himself regarded all this state machinery as existing entirely for the sake of the individual. In the 'Économie politique' he insists that to wrong one man even for the sake of all is an execrable breach of the contract. The ancient states, he says, recognized the dignity of man; in Sparta, as in Macedon and Rome, the life of a citizen was the most serious of all considerations.

Religion, like education, had two faces for Rousseau, a personal and a public face. He believed that no state had ever been founded without a religious basis, and that religion was of the first importance in uniting and preserving a free state and its virtue. He hankered after the narrowly—he grants, too narrowly—patriotic religion of ancient peoples, Jews and Romans in particular. True Christianity, apart from introducing divisions into the state, is too unworldly; a Christian republic would quickly succumb to Rome or Sparta.[3] So we are offered a reformed civil religion, consisting of deism plus veneration for the contract and the laws, together with toleration for private beliefs. Montesquieu had believed that patriotism was an exclusively antique virtue; Rousseau in nothing more clearly shows his distinction from the usual Frenchman in his time and from the dominating cosmopolitanism of the Enlightenment than in his all-pervasive feeling for an exclusive love of country. He was not, of course, an advocate of aggressive imperialism, which involves disastrous expense, the risk of a tyrant seizing power, and so on. But the military and patriotic virtues are undoubtedly linked in his mind.

---

[1] *Émile* (1762), Book i.
[2] *Du contrat social* iv. 7 (*Oeuvres complètes* iii. 459).
[3] Ibid. iv. 8 (op. cit., p. 467).

Rousseau, like Bodin, distinguishes the seat of sovereignty from the form of government; but to him only popular sovereignty is legitimate. The logical corollary, he admits, would be democratic government too, where the whole people acts as executive as well as legislature. But democracy is a system for gods, not men. The General Will cannot deal with particular issues; if the government is identical with the sovereign, the latter will be corrupted by the necessary entrance of particular interests. This is the explicit criticism made of Athens. The further objection that democratic government is subject to faction and swift decay is however perhaps based largely on the traditional view of Athenian history.[1]

Such democracy, Rousseau also holds, might be possible in a very small, simple, egalitarian society; but since even Sparta did not achieve complete equality it must be out of place to seek it. As states grow larger, the government must become smaller and stronger. It is clear that Rousseau is attracted by the stage at which there is a strong elected senate. Mixed government is not impossible, but inferior to the simple forms and only exemplified by England and (worse) Poland.

Furthermore, the relations between sovereign and government have sometimes to be controlled by a special magistracy with primarily negative or protective powers. If too strong this may overturn the state; but for a long time the tribunes in Rome, whose chief function was to defend the people against the government, and the ephors, who held the balance between the two, did good service.[2] It is in such details that Rousseau's actual classical inspiration is clearest; in the same way, it is to the dictatorship in Rome and the suspension of the laws in Sparta that he appeals in seeking a way to cope with the occasional crisis.[3]

To these also he turns in his doctrine of the legislator. He still regards the good state as the creation of human reason. Thus, in the wake of the Greeks, and Machiavelli, whom he quotes, he makes use of the great lawgiver. 'He is the engineer who invents

---

[1] In the 'Économie politique' he called Athens not a democracy but a tyrannical aristocracy governed by philosophers and orators; not perhaps a considered pronouncement, but significant of its author's prejudice against contemporary *philosophes* (*Oeuvres complètes* iii. 246).

[2] *Du contrat social* iv. 5 (op. cit., p. 453).

[3] Ibid. iv. 6 (op. cit., p. 455).

the machine, the great prince only the mechanic who keeps it going.' How then could the simple, non-moral natural man set up a state? It was easier to postulate a single figure of rare and almost divine foresight, whose task it is to educate individuals to will the general good that they see and reject, and the public as a whole to know the general good it would will if it saw it, and to transform individuals into parts of a whole. Lycurgus, is, as ever, the chief example of such a figure. For example, the legislator's office should be outside the constitution; Lycurgus resigned his throne before beginning his work, and many modern cities have turned to foreigners, as Geneva to Calvin.[1] When Rousseau praises Machiavelli for seeing that the legislator would appeal to religious authority in his difficult task, Lycurgus must have been the first of those in his mind. But even they cannot create states to last for ever; even Sparta and Rome perished.[2]

Rousseau could not, however, confine the relevance of his ideas to the small republics for which he knew them to be best fitted. During his later years events in Corsica and Sweden, and above all Poland, awakened sympathy in all opponents of despotism. Rousseau, in the first and last cases, actually received invitations to be the *législateur*. How far could the ideal institutions be adapted to suit these already hardy and simple people? Rousseau prefaces his *Considérations sur le gouvernement de Pologne* (1772)[3] with a discussion of 'l'esprit des anciennes institutions', or the means employed by Moses, Lycurgus, and Numa to impress their laws on the hearts of previously savage or corrupt people by attaching these to each other and their country.[4] He praises the exclusive patriotism, the national peculiarities created in his citizen by Lycurgus, who 'lui montra sans cesse la patrie dans ses lois, dans ses jeux, dans ses amours, dans ses festins'. Poland is of modern countries the least unlike the ancient states; having no resources but its own courage against its powerful neighbours it can choose no other models. Prudently conservative as Rousseau shows him-

---

[1] Ibid. ii. 7 (op. cit., p. 381 f.), cf. ii. 8, on the sort of crisis in which a state may gain liberty; Sparta in the time of Lycurgus is an example, p. 385.

[2] Ibid. iii. 11 (op. cit., p. 424).

[3] The *Projet pour la Corse* (op. cit., p. 901), written in 1765, looks to Rome not Sparta (as the model for his restriction of private property: the state is to own much), and Switzerland. It involves many of the same ideas.

[4] Ibid., p. 953, esp. sect. ii, p. 956 ff. He has other comparisons of Moses to classical lawgivers.

self in sanctioning any kind of change, he advocates a tendency towards a federal system, with small and semi-independent provinces, a citizen army, of course, which like the Spartan disdains the construction of fortresses[1] (associated in his mind with oppression of the populace); equally of course, a patriotic (but not compulsory) education overseen by public men, not pedants; national religious festivals (reminiscent of Greece in general rather than Sparta in particular) where patriotism and virtue should be honoured; while the circulation of money should be discouraged by introducing taxes and rewards in kind; Lycurgus after all did not entirely abolish money, but kept his iron coinage.[2]

And there were other respects in which Rousseau permitted Spartan ideas to infiltrate into the alien modern world. Even Émile's solitary education has features either strongly reminiscent of Sparta, or for which she is actually cited. Her young men, Rousseau insists, did not grow up boors because their early training was not in book-learning—they were subsequently feared by the Athenians for their wit as well as their strength. And though Émile's bride, Sophie, the model of female education, who is playful but modest, submissive, entirely feminine and domestic, seems very un-Lacedaemonian at first sight, first sight is misleading. Rousseau's girls are not to dance naked, as we saw, nor to be trained in warlike exercises—'ce n'est pas là ce que j'approuve'. But at Sparta they were rightly brought up to be strong and healthy so that their sons might be so. The Greek custom of allowing bands of girls to appear in public, in dances and processions, was to their physical and moral advantage (and one suspects that Sophie's freedom of comment and judgement upon young men has its roots in Spartan festivals). After marriage their life was, equally rightly, purely domestic; the sole ambition of a woman should be 'celle de régner sur des âmes grandes et fortes, celle des femmes de Sparte, qui était de commander à des hommes'. Their power is to be able to send their menfolk to danger, death, or glory.

[1] Ibid. xii. 1012 f.   [2] Ibid. xi. 1003.

16

FRANCE IN THE EIGHTEENTH CENTURY (II)

So MUCH, then, for the arch-priest of laconism. But variations in the doctrine were made by other believers. Helvétius published his notorious *De l'esprit* in 1758 (before, it may be noted, the *Lettre à d'Alembert*). He was a strong adherent of sensationalist philosophy, taking to extreme lengths the belief in intellectual equality, and in the power of education, based upon it; and he linked this with the pleasure/pain principle of motivation that was to be so abhorrent to Mably. He is a complete utilitarian. If private interest alone moves man to action, virtuous action can only be what benefits the largest number of people—what is, in short, in the public interest.

This lands Helvétius in an exaltation of the power of the state. The moralist's preaching is all but valueless; but the legislator, himself the most virtuous because the most useful of men, is the true encourager of virtue, since by means of rewards and punishments he can cause public and private interest to coincide (to do this he may even have to 'briser tous les liens de la parenté' and 'sacrifier . . . jusqu'au sentiment même de l'humanité'). A despotism can never unite these two; and much in the way of commerce and *luxe* is bound to increase the strength of private interests.

And thus Helvétius is inevitably attracted to poor and egalitarian Sparta, and in particular to Lycurgus, perhaps his favourite example of a virtuous man. But his Sparta has some peculiar features. Firstly, he believed that strong passions are the root of great virtues as well as great vices; it is not reason, but interest, that must direct them. So he accepts and exalts the irrational enthusiasm sometimes attributed to the Spartans as necessary above all to soldiers and conquerors, whom he seems to admire. Their lawgiver shared this enthusiasm:

Lorsque Lycurgue voulut faire de Lacédémone une république de héros, on ne le vit point, selon la marche lente et dès-lors incertaine de ce qu'on appelle la sagesse, y procéder par des changements insensibles. Ce grand homme, échauffé de la passion de la vertu, sentoit que, par des harangues ou des oracles supposés, il pouvoit inspirer à ses concitoyens les sentiments dont lui-même étoit enflammé . . . C'est ainsi qu'il réussit dans un projet peut-être le plus hardi qui jamais ait été conçu, et dans l'exécution duquel échouerait tout homme sensé qui, ne devant ce titre de sensé qu'à l'incapacité où il est d'être mu par des passions fortes, ignorait toujours l'art de les inspirer.[1]

And he gives *bon sens* a thorough trouncing.

The rewards that encourage the useful passions are mostly sexual. Lycurgus obviously realized that women, elsewhere mere playthings, could be used to spur men on to glory. He made them dance half-naked at the festivals, taunting the cowardly and praising the brave; the young Spartiate became drunk with virtue. Had Lycurgus gone even further and formally presented the fairest as a prize for valour, 'quelque bizarre et quelqu'éloignée de nos moeurs que soit cette législation, il est certain qu'il eût encore rendu les Spartiates plus vertueux et plus vaillants, puisque la force de la vertu est toujours proportionnée au degré de plaisir qu'on lui assigne pour récompense'.[2] This is not much like the moral influence wielded by Rousseau's Spartan women!

In such a republic glory as well as love is the reward of virtue and of virtue alone; and thus 'la vertu éclairée et active . . . ne croit ou du moins ne parvient à un certain degré de hauteur, que dans les républiques guerrières'. The apparently rashest apophthegms of the Spartans were really prudent, since they encouraged the audacious obstinacy which made them invincible; and Helvétius even seems to regard the Spartan mother as an example of 'vertu éclairée et active'. We, of course, are too feeble properly to appreciate their heroism.[3] Since Helvétius believes the relations between individual peoples to be still those of the state of nature, he shows little indignation towards aggressive foreign policies.

The passion for glory is the root of art as well as virtue—so art, too, can only flourish in poor and warlike republics. 'Les Lacédémoniens, que certains auteurs ont pris plaisir à nous peindre comme des hommes vertueux, mais plus grossiers que spirituels [including, obviously, Rousseau] n'étoient pas moins sensibles que

---

[1] *De l'esprit*, essai iii, ch. vii (*Oeuvres complètes*, 1776, i. 401).
[2] Ibid. iii. xv (op. cit., p. 475).
[3] Ibid. iii. xx (op. cit., 522, 526).

les autres Grecs aux beautés des arts et des sciences'.[1] Helvétius produces the impressive list of poets bred or welcomed in Sparta; he quotes Plato on the intelligent conversation of the Spartans; he assures us that a bad argument was punished here as a bad action elsewhere, and thus the Spartans, free from superstitious, as from all other, terrors, even cited their religion before the tribunal of reason. Since to Helvétius a public education was on every count of vital importance, if he does not say much of Sparta in this context we can without doubt take his approval on trust.

Helvétius' political views received elaboration in his post-humously published *De l'homme* (1772). He now gives us, from his very different psychological standpoint, a clear vision of the happy and virtuous society not unlike that of Rousseau, whom he so often criticizes. It is plain now, as it perhaps was not before, that Sparta is rather more to him than one source among many for amusing illustrations (another had been China, admired by so many thinkers in the eighteenth century but not by Rousseau). Rome gets, as with Rousseau, as much general praise; but it is, usually, only general.

Antiquity, Helvétius believes, was superior in morals, politics, and legislation, though not in knowledge, to the present. In particular, its religion was subordinate to the state and not conducive to humility, and it realized the relation of education to virtue (from birth, as the fame of Spartan nurses shows).[2] Virtue and public felicity are of course on Helvétius' principles the same. Certainly the Spartans were happy. They were prosperous, for all possessed property (and thus were really part of their society), while their physical strength shows they were well fed and clothed. They were free from *ennui*, one of the worst of evils, since they were perpetually not only occupied but active. Helvétius repeats his praise of Lycurgus and other legislators, so far above Christian saints;[3] also his insistence that both he and the Spartans valued many sorts of skill and knowledge and were as enlightened as the Athenians[4] (but he does not repeat his rash remarks about family and sexual life). When he comes to his suggestions for a society

---

[1] Ibid., iii. xxx (op. cit., p. 608).
[2] *De l'homme*, Sect. i, ch. vi (*Oeuvres complètes* ii. 26).
[3] Ibid., Sect. i, ch. ix (op. cit., p. 25).
[4] Ibid., Sect. v, ch. xi (op. cit., pp. 65 ff.).

that shall make man perfectly happy,[1] his relation to an old, basically Utopian, tradition is clear (he refers to Machiavelli and to Hume's early sketch, based on Harrington, for a perfect republic). He asks whether the land should not be divided among families on the Spartan model; he wishes to prevent the growth of inequality, luxury, and finally despotism by doing, as Lycurgus did, without money or trade; this will facilitate the state's control of rewards and punishments, too. Elsewhere he remarks that a citizen militia, as at Sparta, is a safeguard against tyranny. He advocates, in the old manner (not entirely irrelevant to over-complicated, over-centralized France), few laws, small cities, and a federal system for large areas. He even asks, doubtfully, whether such a state might not last for ever. If Sparta fell, it was owing to adventitious causes only. But to introduce such legislation to France, he realized, could only result in depopulation and fatal weakness. Besides, by now he had given up hope of the reform of the French monarchy; it had become a despotism.

In the sixties another distinguished laconizer emerged.[2] Mably was, however, on many points a hearty enemy of Helvétius, and despite Rousseau's accusation of plagiarism seems to have developed political views somewhat similar to his independently. Though a much less original thinker than the latter, Mably's popularity in his own day and at the time of the Revolution was very great, partly on account of his surprising prophecies of the course of events and his championship of the States-General. To an admiration for Locke's psychological and political theory he joined a knowledge of Plato and Thucydides, of Xenophon and Cicero as well as Plutarch, rare for his time; he was reputed to know them almost by heart, and his devotion to the morals and politics of antiquity puts even Rousseau's into the shade; for him no Geneva provided a rival mirage.

Mably's first success came in 1763, with the *Entretiens de Phocion*. The Athenian statesman rejects with horror the apotheosis of the passions by 'sophists', and restates the old, Platonic

---

[1] Ibid., Sect. ix, esp. ch. ii (op. cit., p. 337 f.); cf. vi. xii (p. 134); xiii (p. 138); xiv (p. 142).

[2] After some conventional early works, his doctrines, and their connection with Sparta, appear fully formed in the *Droits et devoirs de l'homme*, apparently of 1758, but not published till after his death (*Oeuvres complètes*, 1797, vol. xxii; see especially pp. 25, 124, 265, 726.)

and Christian, view of man as the battleground between these passions, and reason, his divine part. Mably believes in Natural Law; the reasonable man will be both virtuous and happy, and reason will be the same in all times and places. The state's function, then, is to make its members contented by making them love virtue, and especially the four virtues most productive of others— temperance, diligence, love of glory, and piety; and to repress the worst of the passions, especially avarice and ambition. Without these there would be neither poverty nor riches, and wants would be few. Phocion throughout has his eye fixed upon Sparta. What made Lycurgus the supreme lawgiver (he can hardly be referred to without a parenthesis calling attention to his divine wisdom) was his psychological penetration. Consulting, not the prejudices of his contemporaries, but the voice of nature, 'il descendit dans les profondeurs tortueuses du coeur humain, et pénétra les secrets de la Prudence. Ses lois, faites pour réprimer nos passions, ne tendirent qu'à développer et affirmer les lois mêmes que L'Auteur de la Nature nous prescrit par le ministère de la Raison.'[1] He realized that *moeurs publiques* are determined by *moeurs domestiques*; as Sparta's later history showed, the best constitution is useless without private virtue. Going, as always, to the root of the matter (and thus needing very few laws), he not only abolished riches and the useless arts, but destroyed the springs of luxury by setting up his public repasts, and by preventing all *voluptés* even in marriage—love is a dangerous and disorderly passion and the politician should not try to make use of it (this is presumably directed at Helvétius). He turned the women, in most states the first source of corruption, in effect into men (elsewhere Mably says that the only alternative is to shut them up). He understood that whenever the law leaves us idle our passions will get us into mischief, and so kept the citizens busy with games, drill, and their agricultural occupations—not the degrading and unnecessary trades of the Athenians, which are fit only for helots.[2] (This Sparta, supposedly ideally happy, sounds a grim place compared with Helvétius' sensuous and artistic country, or even Rousseau's with its innocent festivities and ideal family life.)

Although Mably believed, on the grounds of the Golden Rule in ethics, and of sensationalist psychology (the philosopher

---

[1] *Oeuvres complètes* xix. i, p. 50. [2] Ibid. iii. 113 ff.

Condillac was his brother), in the equality of man, he did not believe in democratic government. He preferred to control the vices and caprices of each section of society, and to conciliate particular interests, by means of mixed government; by this he means a government combining, as he says, the advantages of each simple form, in which the legislature consists of the whole people but there is a strong senate and magistracy. Such a government, recommended by Plato and possible only in small states, did Lycurgus set up in Sparta; to this also did Rome finally attain.[1] Not so Athens, whose feeble and tumultuous government Phocion abuses. Solon's laws were superficial and inadequate; and the ambitious Pericles corrupted the Athenians further, encouraging idleness, luxury, and avarice, above all by his system of pay for office. All states must decline after, and because of, prosperity. They can sometimes be gradually reformed; but when they are content with their degradation the only hope lies in the *sainte violence* of a Lycurgus, seizing the rare opportunity for a safe revolution.[2] Mably is, with Machiavelli, one of the few laconizers who do not balk at this implication of the Lycurgus legend as they receive it from Plutarch.

In *Observations sur l'histoire de la Grèce*[3] (1776), among other things Mably treats more fully what he had already touched upon before, Sparta's foreign policy and later history. As an expert on international law and a lover of peace he is bound to look beyond the confines of the city-state. Citizens, he says, should indeed be perpetually under arms and trained to repress attacks, but wars of conquest are both the result and cause of the vices. We are not only reminded that Lycurgus ('dont on ne peut jamais assez admirer la sagesse et les lumières') forbade all but defensive wars, but assured that he began the policy of binding allies to his country by benefiting and protecting them, and that before the Persian wars Greece was a federal republic, with Sparta as its capital and model; and Lycurgus thus in a sense the legislator of the whole Greek race.[4]

[1] Ibid. ii. 80.   [2] Ibid. v. 287.

[3] Ibid. vii, Book i, pp. 16 ff. (a rewritten version of *Observations sur les Grecs*, 1749, to which there was a companion-piece *Observations sur les Romains*, 1751). Cf. *Entretiens* iv. 170 ff.

[4] In fact Sparta, it will be recalled, only set about building up a league, which never covered much more than the Peloponnese, in the middle of the sixth century.

R

Unfortunately the Spartans did not make their allies emulate their own laws, succumbing to ambition and mistakenly thinking to preserve their own superiority. (We are treated to the sermon Lycurgus should have given them.) The result was gradual corruption on both sides. Mably in fact puts Spartan decline earlier than most moralising writers do, arguing that Pausanias' ambition and the booty of Plataea began what Lysander and the Peloponnesian War completed. He is so convinced that fourth-century Sparta was worthless, and that virtue alone gives strength to a state, that he only mentions Agesilaus to blame him for suspending the punishments for cowardice after Leuctra. It was morale, not numbers, that mattered.

It may be said that such interest in Sparta is natural enough, in a work professedly dealing with Greek history, or even put in the mouth of a man like Phocion. But Mably showed it in all his political works; and when, in 1768, he came to a clash with the physiocrats, now at the height of their influence, the quarrel involved Sparta very definitely. He addressed his *Doutes proposés aux économistes sur l'ordre naturel et essentiel des sociétés*, a series of letters on the recent book of Mercier de la Rivière, to the *Éphémérides du Citoyen*, a journal that had recently become a physiocratic mouthpiece. Mably, with his traditional view of Natural Law, could not but be shocked at the new, materialistic interpretation of social and economic laws; and he was bound to regard the economists' aims largely as the encouragement of luxury and the satisfaction of the passions. He now stands revealed as a nostalgic communist, looking back wistfully to a condition which alone can preserve men's equality and thus prevent riches and so vice of every kind, but which is not now to be re-established. Nonetheless, he feels that the various types of property of which the physiocrats talk are not all necessary and natural. Societies can exist very well without *propriété foncière*; the Spartans did not own their land, they only had the usufruct of it. This view, in which Mably is almost isolated, leads him now to state that Sparta's six hundred years of prosperity only ended after private ownership of land was introduced in the fourth century, and that it was because property-owning neighbours were bound to be greedy that Lycurgus had to turn the citizens into soldiers.[1] 'Je sais que votre journal ne fait pas grand cas de cette république;

[1] *Oeuvres complètes* xxi. i, pp. 7, 14-15.

mais je prends la liberté de vous avertir que, si ce mépris est nécessaire à votre philosophie, vous dépréviendrez beaucoup de gens contre elle.' The Jesuits, too, brave these so-called laws in Paraguay (and if they oppress the Indians, as the Spartans did the helots, that is a different question). The Romans tried at least to limit landed property, but this was impossible in a conquering nation flooded with booty.

Mably then moves on to the physiocrats' political doctrines, berating them for paying magistrates and permitting a mercenary army, and refuting their idea of a despotic government subject only to the laws of 'evidence'. Such *despotisme légal* is likely, given the strength of the passions, to sink into *despotisme arbitraire*. It is only in mixed states that the laws survive and rule, and the interest of all citizens is the same. Though such governments only take us part of the way to perfect equality, and though Sparta and Rome were not without faults, they had the best laws known to man. And Sparta subsisted longer than any simple government.[1]

This is because Mably chooses not to believe in China's four thousand years of happiness. Its intensive agriculture and its populousness have seduced the physiocrats. If despotism is gentle there, it is only because it is so old, and its subjects so apathetic and uncritical (their life is spent in learning to read). In his attack on various contemporary ideas of China Mably evinces a sceptical power he never turns on classical antiquity. As his opponents realized: but their arguments, and even a work entitled *Examen historique et politique du gouvernement de Sparte; ou lettre à un ami sur la législation de Lycurgue, en réponse aux doutes proposés par M. l'Abbé de Mably contre l'ordre naturel et essentiel des sociétés politiques*, by a professor of Greek,[2] had no effect whatsoever. Sparta even recurs in the proposals for Poland that, like Rousseau, Mably was invited to make; though here he cautiously insists that Lycurgus' violent revolution was successful only owing to exceptional circumstances and the exceptional character of the legislator.[3] And in his most complete and influential political work, *De la législation* (1776), though Mably has his eyes fixed on the modern world, antiquity is only just over his shoulder. This is a

[1] Ibid., iii. 72.
[2] J. F. Vauvilliers (professor at the Collège de France and active in the Revolution as a moderate), 1769.
[3] *Du gouvernement et des loix de la Pologne, Oeuvres complètes* xv. 157; xvi. 51.

dialogue between an Englishman, a soon-converted believer in commercial principles, and a classically-minded Swede, a defender of his country's new and, as it was to prove, short-lived constitution, her Diet, her sumptuary laws, and her poverty. Milord rallies the Swede on his countrymen's Platonic politics. Are they going to offer a prize for the re-invention of black broth? With their heavy copper currency they recall 'les vénérables Spartiates'. The Swede could ask no better; the Spartans were happy, because they were just and fearless; their country, though small, was respected and feared.[1] (Later he admits that Count Fersen and the rest had not been equal to proposing truly Roman or Spartan laws—though they would have found the Swedes ready for them.) The failings, and possible prospects, of European states are discussed; and here Rome receives much space, since with her separate orders of citizens, and her complicated assemblies, she resembles modern countries, and their States-General, more closely than Sparta could do (though representation is a positive advantage and safeguard). But Sparta remains nearer the ideal, in economic and foreign policy as well as virtue, and Mably praises her with his old abandon. The long discussion on education, the direct cause of a love of the laws, and thus of happiness, results in a plan that is Platonic and Spartan in almost every point. The boys are organized in troops and under prefects; Lycurgus was very right to discourage premature foreign travel.[2] One does not however remember Plato's or Lycurgus' pupils being made to study so much history.

And shortly after the *De la législation* Mably published a work written in fact earlier, for a princely pupil of his brother's, on the value of history as a school of morals and politics. Many nations are here reviewed; but need we name the state that can never be too much studied, either for its institutions or its spirit?[3] It is the state that followed most closely the laws of nature; that lasted longest, that shows how even a small state may be made strong, that teaches innumerable other lessons and inspires all the writer's views.

Mably, always gloomy, grew more so in his old age. The *De la législation* is yet more pessimistic than the *Phocion*. He has now no

---

[1] Ibid. xvii and xviii; xvii, i, ch. 1, pp. 7, 13.   [2] Ibid. xviii; iv. i, 120.

[3] *De l'étude de l'histoire* (1778), *Oeuvres complètes* xxiii. 20, 34–5, 53, 66, 72–3, 75, 77, 84, 134, 309.

hope of *sainte violence* in a monarchy, resigning himself to wait for a Theopompus instead of a Lycurgus; and he concentrates more on repressing the vices (without communism, they cannot be extirpated) than on encouraging the virtues. And the final lessons that he makes Sparta and Rome give are very repressive. They appear in a little essay of 1784, which offered advice to the United States of America. Here they teach the Americans that it is wise to restrict popular liberty and not to allow real democracy. Neither of these two ancient states, knowing as they both did the weak and passionate nature of man, expelling as they both did unworthy poets and philosophers, would ever have allowed the freedom of the press.[1]

Long before any of these three had ceased writing it had become clear that Sparta was no longer to be ignored. Helvétius in 1758 in his résumé of the arguments *pro* and *con le luxe* implies that the hostile party depended heavily on her example. Saint-Lambert's article on the subject in the *Encyclopédie* begs his readers to put away the prejudices of both Sparta and Sybaris; his article 'Législateur'[2] shows him anxious to insert a little Spartan spirit, into large modern kingdoms; he lauds Sparta and Peru for replacing the *esprit de propriété* with the *esprit de communauté*, and linking honour with love of country, the source of every virtue. It is hard, but possible, to make a modern state on this pattern, and therefore to make it happy. A similar belief that it was possible to adopt a modicum of republican feeling, *pace* Montesquieu and Rousseau's usual arguments, could perhaps be ascribed to such educational reformers as continued to point to Sparta's recognition that education and the nation should go together; but the details of their plans are for the most part neither anti-intellectual nor egalitarian.

The *Encyclopédie*, mostly through the pen of its prolific and faithful contributor, the Chevalier de Jaucourt, poured out information on Lacedaemonian customs under various headings, but with, perhaps, a certain lack of ingenuousness—or else an excess of it. Others have inquired whether Jaucourt's article 'Xénélasie de Lacédémone'[3] might not contain some irony; could one of the

---

[1] *Observations sur le gouvernement et les loix des États-Unis d'Amérique, Oeuvres complètes* xvi. 137, 177.
[2] *Encyclopédie* (1751–65) ix. 357a–363a.
[3] Ibid. xvii. 651b–654a.

most cosmopolitan of the generally cosmopolitan *Encyclopédistes* really feel such admiration, expressed at such length, for an institution designed to prevent corruption spreading from abroad? It seems unlikely. Jaucourt, much under the influence of his revered friend Montesquieu, admitted that republics depend on virtue, but they are easily corrupted—look at the Italian republics —and have no proper separation of powers. He treats Athens fairly coldly. Solon's constitution was very well, but the Athenians soon stopped practising it and turned to aggression instead of trade. A few rather chilly remarks on Sparta too may be extracted from some of his articles on ancient history; to say her only aim was liberty, and the only advantage of that liberty was glory, does not sound very enthusiastic. But his articles specifically on Sparta are enthusiastic in the extreme; only (it does not seem to have been observed) they mostly consist of quotations from other people. In the lengthy 'Lacédémone, république de'[1] he warns us what he is doing and proceeds to pile up, unattributed, the most wildly eulogistic passages of Montesquieu, Rousseau, and Helvétius, and of older writers such as Montaigne and Guillet. Lycurgus had the sublime idea of combining the three powers into one. Then he employed the passions to 'briser tous les liens de la parenté', for otherwise, as a *beau génie* points out, all love of country must perish (this is Helvétius; there is a lot of Helvétius; he frequently ran into criticism from the other *philosophes*). There is also a sublime assumption that all money is evil, and we are treated to Rousseau's pronouncements on the Spartan games, and to the Spartan mother, the boy with the fox, and the whipping contests. Alas, corrupted by *délices*, we could not emulate these; but (echo of Montaigne) Spartan history 'est tout miracle en ce genre'. The famous deeds of heroism 'passeroient peut-être pour folles si elles n'étoient pas consacrées par l'admiration de toutes les siècles' (Helvétius again). What genius, as M. de Montesquieu observes, was needed by Lycurgus 'pour voir qu'en choquant les usages reçus, en confondant toutes les vertus, il montreroit à l'univers sa sagesse !'

Another long and effusive article, 'Sparte ou Lacédémone',[2] is

[1] Ibid. ix. 152b–160b; cf. 'Grecs' ('Histoire ancienne et littérature, vii. 912a–918b)—Sparta the capital and refuge of Greece, and thus Lycurgus in a sense the legislator of the whole country).

[2] Ibid. xv. 428b–432b. More information s.vv. 'Géronte' (vii. 649b),

primarily topographical and descriptive, but here Jaucourt seems to take the opportunity to exhibit the extravagances of ancient rather than modern writers, especially in praising the simplest household utensils of their favourites. Nor can we take him very seriously, surely, when he declares, against the commonest knowledge, that Sparta had a vast and increasing population, and proves it by detailing the enormous colonizing activity that he must have realized was quite legendary: 'elle peupla Byzance, quatre ou cinq villes d'Asie, une dans l'Afrique, cinq ou six dans la Grèce, trois ou quatre provinces d'Italie, une ville en Portugal, une autre en Espagne près de Cordoue.'

But someone closely concerned with the *Encyclopédie* seems to have disapproved of this light-hearted attitude. For the article is followed by an anonymous addition, possibly due to the editor Diderot himself in one of his most Rousseauistic moods, which attempts a more serious and coherent evaluation.[1] It is wrong to see the Spartans as a purely military people knowing only how to obey, suffer, and die.

> Peut-être faudroit-il voir dans Lycurgue celui de tous les philosophes qui a le mieux connu la nature humaine, celui, surtout qui a le mieux vu jusqu'à quel point les lois, l'éducation, la société pouvoient changer l'homme, et comment on pouvoit le rendre heureux en lui donnant des habitudes qui semblent opposées à son instinct et son nature. Il faudroit voir dans Lycurgue l'esprit le plus profond et le plus conséquent qui ait peut-être jamais été, et qui a formé le système de législation le mieux combiné, le mieux né qu'on a connu jusqu'à présent,

What he did was wise in his circumstances; for a fierce but small people, exposed to invasion, needed obedience and courage above all else. But wise in any circumstances would have been his introduction of the rule of law, his understanding of the connection between the physical and moral aspects of man, and the

---

[1] Ibid. xv. 432b–434b; J. Lough, 'The Problem of the Unsigned Articles in the Encyclopédie' (*Studies in Voltaire and the Eighteenth Century*, ed. Theodore Besterman, vol. 32, 1965, p. 327), includes it with a query among articles attributable on grounds of internal probability to Diderot, p. 380.

'Gymnopédies' (vii. 1021a–1022a, already concerned with naked girls and public education, but referring to Guillet not Rousseau as apologist), 'Lycurgées' (ix. 774a), 'Misitra' (x. 575b–577b), 'Scytale' (xiv. 847b), etc.

measures that brought true happiness by suppressing envy, rivalry, and lawsuits, which all have their root in luxury and related phenomena. The Spartans had their pleasures—dancing, poetry, the cult of wit, and the famous festivals. Essentially they were peaceful, for distant campaigns are impossible without money and Lycurgus forbade a navy. If they were, at last and inevitably, corrupted, it was Athens who set the example and forced on the famous war.

If Diderot's mind had not been so receptive to different points of view and so continually in evolution one would firmly deny that this could be his. When he wrote the article 'Grecs, philosophie des'[1] he dealt with the Greek legislators but passed over Lycurgus very briefly, ominously comparing his régime to that of a monastery and regretting that his laws were never written down. His subsequent sympathy for the economic school was not likely to increase his sympathy for Sparta; and if he became ultimately disenchanted with the economists, he became even more so with would-be enlightened despots. Nothing could be more damning than to put high praise of Sparta's government into the mouth of the imaginary military tyrant, inspired by Frederick, of the *Politique des souverains*.[2] And while he is still paying extravagant compliments to Catherine, the language in which he descants on the superiority of her Code, and her achievement, to that of Lycurgus, is entirely typical, as we shall see, of the anti-Spartan party.[3] But Diderot is rather more favourably disposed in his *Réfutation* of Helvétius' posthumous *De l'homme*, of just the same date. Here he can say 'je ne blâme point les lois de Lycurgue, je les crois seulement incompatibles avec un grand état et un état commerçant'—as Helvétius himself had admitted,

---

[1] Ibid. vii. 904b–912a; esp. 908b–909a.

[2] 1774 (*Oeuvres Politiques*, ed. P. Vernière, 1963, p. 181), civ: it was the only good government in Greece and would have finally conquered the whole country. cv: my subjects shall be helots under a more decent title.

[3] Letter to Catherine, 13 Sept. 1774 (M. Tourneaux, *Diderot et Catherine II*, 1899, p. 489), congratulating her on peace with Turkey, and repeating his prophecy that Russia would one day be visited, as Lacedaemon, Egypt, and Greece had been, but for better reasons. 'Lycurgue fit des moines armés; sa législation fut un sublime système d'atrocité. L'humanité sert de base à la vôtre. Il forma des bêtes féroces très formidables: vous travaillez à former des citoyens honnêtes et des défenseurs de la patrie qui se feront craindre dans les camps et chérir dans la société.'

they could not be safely introduced to France. In such a state he would distrust illiberal methods of preventing inequality, and, though disgusted at the use of wealth as a criterion for office and honour, would distinguish and welcome a good kind of *luxe*. And he is attached to the family and education within it. Nevertheless, though standing out against exaggerated idealization of antiquity, poverty, and the power of education, Diderot confesses that if Rousseau had not gone quite so far he would have been hard to answer. If democracy is only possible in small states, it is sad that the security of the only nation that can be happy is bound to be precarious.[1] And we shall see him in his writings on art seeking inspiration for painting in the Spartan spirit.

The result of all this was that if by the sixties there was a widely spread notion that the Spartans were a *peuple philosophe*, other writers were making newly bitter attacks upon her, appending, unlike Rollin, no list or a very brief one of *choses louables*. There are close echoes of themes we met in the first part of the century; but the bitterest attacks came from representatives of various currents of thought highly typical of the full Enlightenment. Humanitarians abused the famous *moeurs* as cruel and savage (and, they usually argued, unnatural and contrary to self-interest, which is often regarded as the base of common interest). Laconism is scarcely to be looked for among adherents of the newly sophisticated economic doctrines (the physiocrats indeed combined, as we saw, liberal economic ideas with 'legal despotism'), and many, thinking of France, continued to put their hopes in a strong though not despotic monarchy. Those who believed in progress could wholeheartedly admire no ancient state; even those who only thought progress would take place in the future could not approve one content or proud to stagnate, as they saw it. Many had a pacific and cosmopolitan outlook; many disliked fanaticism in religious even more than in political guise and were now outspoken enemies of Christianity, or at least of some manifestations of it.

To come to individuals: Voltaire's later works, not surprisingly, are spattered with occasional rude remarks about Sparta. In the *Dictionnaire philosophique* (1764) the article on 'Luxe'[2] now complains that those who oppose it cite Sparta. Why not San Marino?

---

[1] *Oeuvres complètes*, ed. J. Assézat, ii. 275 ff.
[2] *Oeuvres complètes*, ed. Moland, xx. 17.

Sparta was just as useless to her neighbours, and produced no more great men—contrast luxurious Athens. And he goes on to the savage Iroquois. Anyway, small states are no model for great (Voltaire was a relativist). In the *Essai sur les moeurs* the great deist professes to be scandalized at those *grands charlatans* the ancient legislators who used religion to cheat their peoples.[1] It is in connection with *L'Esprit des lois* that most of his animadversions upon Sparta occur. Voltaire, who laughed at Rousseau, admired Montesquieu's genius but disagreed with most of his conclusions and considered them based on the flimsiest evidence. He takes exception to Montesquieu's rhetorical remarks about Lycurgus' introduction of theft, to declare that there could be no such thing where there was no property, 'pas même celle de sa femme'; it was rather an 'éducation de Bohême'. Anyway, we really know nothing about Lycurgus, since Plutarch lived so much later—a welcome appearance by Voltaire the critical historian. He also defends the pacific Penn from the imputation of being a *véritable Lycurgue*, and hopes the Pennsylvanians won't be forced 'à devenir enfin aussi méchants que nous et que les anciens Lacédémoniens, qui firent le malheur de la Grèce' (he then moves on to attack Paraguay).[2] More fundamentally, he did not believe virtue—or, necessarily, equality—commoner in or more vital to a republic than any other state. Once, indeed, he even argues that Montesquieu was wrong in describing Sparta as such at all; it was after all a monarchy, or might, with an assertive king, at any moment become one. This is perceptive, even if inspired by the spirit of contradiction.[3]

He also put an irritated *tarare*! in the margin of his copy of *Émile* besides one of Rousseau's beloved Spartan apophthegms[4] (designed to show that the citizen has no thought of self—for Voltaire's view of *amour-propre* as necessary, pleasurable, but to be hidden, like the organ of generation, see the *Dictionnaire philosophique*). And he liberally annotated with *bravos* a tirade by Chastellux maintaining that Sparta strongly recalled a monastery —a comparison not new, but newly invidious. 'Qu'est ce donc

[1] Ibid. xi. 156.
[2] *Commentaire sur l'ésprit des lois* (1777), Ibid. xxx. 418–19.
[3] *Questions sur L'Encyclopédie* (1771), s.v. 'Lois, esprit de', *Ibid* xx. 3, 5, 10.
[4] G. R. Havens, *Voltaire's Marginalia on Rousseau* (1933), p. 77 (equally damning on Regulus, the Roman example).

que Sparte?' asked Chastellux, who had been inspired by disagreement with Mably to argue that public felicity was due to the progress of prosperity and enlightenment, not to virtue and piety. 'Une armée toujours sous les armes, si ce n'est plutôt un vaste cloître ... on se croit tantôt dans la forteresse de Spandaw, tantôt aux Camaldules. Quel coeur, à moins qu'il ne soit revêtu du triple airain de l'érudition, n'est pas saisi de terreur au récit des moeurs lacédémoniennes, comme à celui des austérités des Fakirs ou des Jammambes?'[1] Chastellux's picture of the ancient world, which he greatly despises, seems to be heavily coloured by his idea of Sparta; Voltaire, who was ready to admire many aspects of antiquity, puts queries instead of bravos on the page when Athens comes under fire, for like many of his generation, though highly critical of her fully-developed constitution, he could not but be drawn to a state where the pacific arts and philosophy (even if of too metaphysical a cast) had flourished, and where, despite the condemnation of Socrates, which they believed to have been bitterly repented, a good measure of religious toleration obtained.

One of the first and most distinguished theorists of progress was Turgot, whose *Tableau philosophique des progrès successifs de l'esprit humain* mentioned Athens' contributions (while deprecating her democracy) and ignored Sparta; conversely, in his less well-known *Discours* on the advantages brought by Christianity, he sets up Sparta as the representative of savage and ignorant antiquity. Not realizing that Nature uses individual desires for the good of all, Lycurgus destroyed all property and family ties, had even to forbid the citizens agriculture and all necessary arts, and made the helots wretched—for what? their masters were not happy. This fatal example of *esprit de système* also made change for the better impossible.[2] How much wiser was the moderate and empirical Solon (who was often used as a stick to beat the laconizers, by whom he was usually despised). All this was written as early as 1750, when Turgot was still an Abbé at the Sorbonne; but his subsequent exchange of Christianity for administration and economics is not likely to have altered his ideas on this point.

Sparta's likeness to a monastery and unwillingness to progress

---

[1] *De la félicité publique* (1772). Voltaire's notes are printed in the 1827 edition; see especially pp. 78–85.
[2] *Oeuvres*, ed. G. Schelle (1913), i. 194 ff.

away from savage and indecent habits also brought the Baron d'Holbach down against her, thus putting him on the other side of the fence from his fellow-utilitarian Helvétius, with whom he had something in common on political questions. 'Les Spartiates n'ont été que des moines armés par un fanatisme politique', he said roundly. The Romans were no better; ancient virtue in general consisted only in this military and political fanaticism, as distasteful as religious fanaticism or Christian virtue to Holbach the atheist, and incompatible with equity, reason, or humanity; humanity is the first of the virtues, and reason must control the passions and show the individual his interest. Patriotism too often means 'une haine jurée contre les autres nations' and entire sacrifice of self to an unreasonable ideal. Nonetheless there were aspects of Holbach's thought that might have led him to waver like Diderot. He denied that commerce and luxury lead to happiness, wished to reduce inequality and give land to as many as possible. He insisted on the rule of law under whatever constitution, with a national army to preserve this liberty, and believed morality to be the government's business. And, inevitably:

Si Lycurgue s'est trompé, ou n'a pas consulté les règles de la saine morale dans la formation de ses loix, on ne peut disconvenir qu'il n'ait au moins très bien senti le pouvoir d'une éducation publique. . . Si ce législateur farouche, à l'aide de l'éducation, a pu former des guerriers fanatiques qui méprisoient la douleur et la mort, pourquoi des législateurs plus humains et plus sages ne formeroient-ils pas de même des citoyens vertueux et raisonnables?

(Much the same applies to his treatment of women.)[1] With this Turgot must have agreed; his plan for public education is one of the best known of the time.

As we saw, economic and other criticism came from physiocrats and their friends. Mably was justified in complaining that the *Éphémérides du Citoyen* disliked Sparta, though at first it admitted some *choses louables* (such as education) as well as objecting to enthusiasm, interference with property, and measures contradicting the laws of nature and of self-interest.[2] After Mably's intervention the journal recurred several times to the subject.[3] It

---

[1] *Système social* (1773) i. iv, pp. 41–2; iii. ix, p. 118.

[2] 1767, Tome i, p. 113 (review of Hübner's *Essai sur l'histoire du droit naturel*, 1757, which was pro-Lycurgus).

[3] 1768, Tome vi, p. 138; vii. 205; 1769, v. 20.

insisted in particular that the miseries of slavery were an integral part of the whole Lycurgan system, and not to be swept aside as an unfortunate but irrelevant detail. And it gave a friendly review[1] to Vauvilliers' learned but hardly profound treatise, which did however succeed in proving, by reference to Aristotle, that Mably's ideas of communism in Sparta were much exaggerated. Vauvilliers also applied himself to the decline in population, regarding it as an unequivocal proof of failure and attributing it to inefficient cultivation in a state uneconomically small and employing slave labour, not to mention to infanticide, an often fatally rough upbringing, reckless fanaticism in war, and the rejection of immigrants. His horror at Spartan mothers, infanticide, the *crypteia*, whipping contests, and so forth is comprehensive. He denied that the legislator's prime duty is a moral one; but Lycurgus destroyed moral blessings as well as physical pleasures. His political views transpire in the complaint that to neglect the education of the heir to the throne was fatal; and so was the power given to the ephors, those dregs of society, since 'les contrepoids de l'autorité sont le fléau de tous les états'; for the senate's shortcomings see Aristotle. Yet Lycurgus was a great man: 'il est des erreurs qui portent le caractère du génie.' How far even Aristotle, the first man to attack the chimeras of equality and communism, was from the *systèmes lumineux* of today!

The *Éphémérides* was also provoked by Rousseau and his classicizing picture of Geneva to more cavilling; and it may be mentioned that one important contributor at least finally decided that even Solon was no good. Essentially a poet, not a thinker, his behaviour was often unworthy of a *philosophe*, his measures for the relief of debt were in fact an attack on property as dangerous as Lycurgus', and his regulation of exports showed how ignorant he was of the true doctrines of free trade and the vital importance of cereals.[2]

Finally, the historical scepticism about early Sparta, which had been so strikingly suspended, seems to have been gathering force. We have seen a trace in Voltaire, and Condorcet approvingly annotated his words: we know nothing of Sparta till the fifth

---

[1] 1770, i. 238.

[2] 1772, i. 69 (review by the Abbé Baudeau, who had been the first editor, of Savérien's *Histoire des philosophes anciens*, itself anti-Lycurgus but pro-Solon).

century, and then she was obviously 'féroce et tyrannique'[1] (he also has some particularly cutting description, in familiar vein, of the Spartiates as slave-owning monks and virtuous criminals).[2] Among more scholarly writers perhaps we should single out De Pauw, whose *Recherches philosophiques sur les Grecs*,[3] published in both Berlin and Paris in 1788, was a work of considerable fame in its time and of almost hypercritical character. De Pauw, who is not altogether unjustly contemptuous of the inadequate scholarship of Montesquieu and others, states flatly that Plutarch's *Life of Lycurgus* is fiction, and argues, often rightly, that many of the institutions attributed to the lawgiver are really either earlier or later in date, and that many had a far less glorious purpose than was usually thought. There was never real equality, money did circulate, if there were no walls it was only to prevent a royal *coup d'état*(!), and so forth. De Pauw, who was notorious for his low opinion of American Indians, compared them to the Spartans; their chiefs are 'ces caciques' (and he also made comparisons, to his mind very damaging, of their economic system to medieval feudalism). It is indeed only opponents of both who keep up the old connection of Spartan and savage, it may be remarked; primarily no doubt because admirers regarded Sparta as a rational and strongly-organized society, but also perhaps because, among admirers of savagery, the gentle Tahitian, so recently discovered, was replacing the tough Red Indian in favour.

As the seventies and eighties went on, the anti-Spartan party might, one suspects, have felt that it was winning. Even Helvétius

---

[1] In the famous Kehl edition (1785–9), xxix. 369. The ancients' belief that the Public Will can demand everything of the individual is false and fatal to progress. There are other ways than theirs, too, to deal with luxury.

[2] Op. cit. xli. 504.'C'était la législation du couvent de Saint-Claude; à cela près que les moines ne se permettaient point d'assassiner et d'assommer leurs mainmortables. L'existence de l'égalité ou de la communauté des biens suppose celle d'un peuple esclave. Les Spartiates avaient de la vertu, comme les voleurs de grand chemin, comme les inquisiteurs, comme toutes les classes d'hommes que l'habitude a familiarisé avec une espèce de crimes, au point de les commettre sans remords.' (The case of the serfs of the monastery of Saint-Claude in the Franche-Comté was one of the *causes célèbres* in which Voltaire had taken an interest.)

[3] C. de Pauw, *Recherches philosophiques sur les Grecs* (1788) ii. 232 ff. The chief object of de Pauw's polemic is Gouvey's *Histoire philosophique et politique des loix de Lycurgue* (1768), a dissertation crowned by the Académie des Inscriptions.

PLATE 4

A Spartan Mother and her Son
(L. J. F. Lagrenée the Elder, Stourhead, Wilts)

and Mably had, in their later works, been driven briefly on to the defensive, especially over the helot question. And no whole-hearted, all-round laconizer emerged to succeed them. Perhaps Rousseauesque sensibility in fact worked against the acceptance of Rousseau's favourite state. (His political works were much less read than *Émile* and the *Nouvelle Héloïse*.) The minor and less systematic writers who do stand for various kinds of simplicity and equality tend to desire a gentler kind of society. Some point out how Sparta could be improved on; Rétif de la Bretonne, in the *Découverte Australe*, a full-scale Utopia with public education, elderly magistrates, and even some community of women, said Rousseau had exaggerated in admiring a state where one class was sacrificed to the rest and idleness idealized; and though he compares the agricultural communities set up by the characters of the *Paysan perverti* to Lacedaemon as well as the States of Nature and Pennsylvania, he stresses the improvements made over all these. Charles-Robert Gosselin on the other hand praises Spartan education and social organization unreservedly[1]—but it emerges that his boys are to learn chemistry and do gardening instead of gymnastics, under partly female supervision, and that he remains loyal both to all-powerful monarchy and to Christianity.

Crete perhaps benefited from distrust of Sparta; she could never be forgotten of course among those who had been brought up on *Télémaque*, which enjoyed towards the end of the century a special revival of popularity owed perhaps partly to the increasing vogue for antiquity and for moral romances in Greek settings in particular (as well as to a misunderstanding of Fénelon's political ideas). Pechméja's *Télèphe* (1784) is also set in Crete; equal inheritances and hard work for all ensure simplicity and equality, there are few laws and few magistrates, and a patriotic education; but the arts and enlightened monarchy flourish.[2] In a similar way

---

[1] *Plan d'Éducation* (1785), especially pp. 5, 39, 123, 129.

[2] Voltaire in his tragedy *Les Lois de Minos* (1772) uses Crete as background for an attack on the aristocratic interpretation of constitutional monarchy, primarily associated with Montesquieu and the Parlements rather than with republican theory and the ancient world. He proclaims his inspiration in Frederick the Great's poem about Poland and refers to recent events in Sweden; Maupéou's *coup* against the Parlements, which Voltaire applauded, is at least as relevant. The play is a spirited plea for a strong, legally-based monarchy, personified by Teucer, who is hamstrung in his struggle to do away with the savage and superstitious laws of Minos by the fanatical populace and by the

Saint-Lambert in a fable in his *Catéchisme universel* uses Tarentum as a modified and milder Sparta.[1] Others had always insisted on limiting admiration for Sparta by combining it with admiration for Athens—one for virtue and equality and the other for arts and enlightenment; thus Mably's own brother, Condillac.[2] Some works avoid all mention of Sparta where one might have looked to find her; such is that inconsistent compilation of various philosophic ideas, not to say various philosophic hands, Raynal's *Histoire philosophique des deux Indes*.[3]

But a new and momentous development seems to be connected with that disillusion with monarchy that affected those who were already liberals in economic and moral matters and drove them towards a belief in popular sovereignty; shortly before the Revolution the first defences of Athenian democracy are expressed. In its practical application, however, this disillusion with the king, together with excitement over events in America, suggested that the only possible way out of the *impasse* was through some sort of mixed and necessarily representative government; and this often led away from antiquity altogether—though America's simplicity made her yet another modified Sparta.

But it would be wrong to end with the impression that laconism had been more than weakened; as the Revolutionary years were to show, it had some life in it yet. And on the very eve of the Revolution appeared the Abbé Barthélémy's learned piece of historical fiction, long years in the making, *Les Voyages du jeune Anacharsis*, on which generations were to be brought up in succession to Rollin. Its author, as a level-headed scholar, a humanitarian and pacifist and indeed an admirer of beneficent

[1] 1798 (but written in the eighties), ii, p. 138.
[2] *Histoire ancienne (Oeuvres,* 1798, ix, pp. 141 ff).
[3] 1770; it does say that it is not where possession is easy, as in the North American forests, but where it is hard, as in Sparta, Rome, and the ages of chivalry, that love inspires men to glory and great deeds.

---

tyrannic nobles defending their place in a system of checks and balances that results in anarchy. (Some of this could conceivably apply also to a Mablian version of the laws of Lycurgus.) Teucer points out that the Greeks are a cruel and barbaric race. Aided however by some neighbouring noble savages, whom he proposes at the end to introduce to arts and monarchy, he and enlightenment win the day.

kings, has to take account of criticisms and indeed to water his laconism a good deal; but it survives in spite of all.[1]

Closely as admiration for Spartan virtue was, especially at this period, connected with admiration for Spartan institutions, it could be detached, and now, perhaps, to some extent was. The rising admiration for antiquity in general was in part a reaction against modern society that was basically, or could easily become, political. But when Manon Phlipon, later Mme Roland, wept that she had not been born in Sparta or Rome, it was the opportunities for domestic virtue, and for bringing up sons to public spirit and heroic action, that she regretted; it was the grand deeds of Plutarch's characters that she imagined herself performing. In all this Rome had a greater place than Greece; the school education, which, if we may trust the later Revolutionaries, had such an unusual effect on those exposed to it, was still exclusively Latin. Aspiring young lawyers like Desmoulins thought longingly of the opportunities in Rome or indeed Athens.

Neoclassicism in the visual arts was of course the product of many factors: the excavations at Pompeii and Herculaneum, the publication of many hitherto little-known remains such as those of Paestum, Athens, and Spalato, the labours in the fields of ancient coins and sculpture by the antiquarians (despised as these were by the *philosophes*), and many others. But, as we know, to most eighteenth-century thinkers forms of government, economic institutions, moral habits, science, and art were inter-connected. The revolt against Rococo was inevitably also seen as a revolt against superficiality of feeling, against artifice and luxury, and against political despotism. The links are as clear to Winckelmann as to Diderot. We need not therefore be surprised at the occasional appearance of Spartan subjects in the visual arts, though the classical tradition in both these and in imaginative literature had always had different sources and a different emphasis: simplicity and nature appearing easily in Homeric or Hellenistic-pastoral guise, purity and refinement in Athenian terms, and sober grandeur in Roman ones; while the great themes of mythology kept their fascination.

In the middle of the century there were attempts to revive the serious and didactic tradition of history painting. Cochin, a friend of the *philosophes*, planned a series of decorations on the theme of

[1] 1778; see esp. chs. xli–l (vol. ii, pp. 481–603).

S

the pacific ruler, which was finally turned down by Louis XV. Among the subjects projected were Numa, Solon, and so forth, and also 'Lycurgus wounded in a sedition'. Cochin's chalk drawing on this last theme was exhibited at the Salon in 1761 and much admired. Diderot approved the forcible representation of the crowd, but as so often when faced with modern interpretations of antiquity found the word that sprang to his pen was 'petit'. The true spirit was absent. The great man was unworthily represented pointing to his damaged eye: 'un homme comme Lycurgue, qui sait se posséder dans un pareil instant, s'arrête tout court . . . toute action plus marquée serait fausse et mesquine'.[1] The drawing, as we observe, is in no sense fully neoclassical; but though the architecture of primitive Sparta is still grandiose, it shows signs of trying to be genuinely Greek. Indeed, the temple is even Doric, though a Roman version rather than the genuine archaic sort, squat and severe, that was soon to have a significant, if not perhaps consciously Spartan, vogue.

Diderot picked a similar quarrel with a picture in the Salon of 1771, by Lagrenée, entitled *Rapporte ce bouclier ou que ce bouclier te rapporte*—a more 'enthusiastic' subject, and forerunner of a number of Spartan mothers after 1790. Well painted, he thought; but added 'Quoi! c'est là un Spartiate! . . . Supprimez le bouclier et vous ne verrez plus qu'un jeune homme qui fait des protestations à une femme qui n'est pas de son âge.'[2] He was too sensitive a critic not, for the most part, to see merit wherever it was to be found. But in history painting at least he, who idolized Poussin and lived to welcome the advent of J.-L. David, longed for force, simplicity, *grand goût, âme*. 'Peindre, comme on parlait à Sparte': so, in fact, runs one of his *Pensées détachées sur la peinture*. It is unlikely that any of the other paintings shown in these years at the Salon which dealt with pseudo-historical Spartan subjects would have satisfied him. The list is a short one, shorter than that on many single traditional subjects, or modern favourites such as the death of Socrates; and the scenes chosen, with their tendency to deal with brave ladies or romantic episodes in the life of members

[1] D. Diderot, *Les Salons*, ed. J. Seznec et J. Adhémar, vol. i (1957), p. 138 and plate 63.

[2] Ibid. vi (1967), p. 172 and plate 73; pointing out that the criticism, in parentheses, is closely based on that in Daudet de Jossan's *Ombre de Raphael*, of the same year.

of the royal families, have the most tenuous relation with philosophic laconism. But the very fact that Spartan subjects do for the first time appear has its significance.[1]

In poetry and drama the connections with contemporary thought are more explicit. P. D. E. Lebrun, attempting patriotic verse that was not a mere glorification of the ruling dynasty, saw himself as a new Tyrtaeus,[2] and in all things as a leader of popular opinion on the model of the Greek poets, especially Pindar. And the ideas of the whole period are reflected rather neatly in the drama. The first half of the century has nothing to show but a tragedy on Lycurgus that reached neither the stage nor print,[3] and, in Marmontel's *Aristomène* (1749), an attack on Spartan imperialism and the unnatural and ferocious quality of her virtue that is, compared with older Messenian tragedies, newly serious. (Virtue, however, it still is, especially in the kings.) In 1754 appeared a comedy, *Les Lacédémoniennes*,[4] treating the newly topical subject with detachment. Lycurgus is the hero (and Harlequin his servant). He is regarded, vaguely, as a *philosophe*, and opposed by a prude, a *petit-maître*, and an actress. But finally by a trick he forces them all to accept his severely virtuous legislation, while he departs for ever from Sparta, accompanied by a charming *jeune veuve* in man's clothes (and slightly less devoted to the excesses of reason than her lover).

In another mediocre comedy, *Alcidonis*,[5] eighteen years later there is rather more precision; the author has obviously read his

---

[1] The catalogue for the Salons reveals, apart from the works mentioned above, only a drawing of Lycurgus giving a king to the Lacedaemonians, by Pajou (1763) like Cochin's subsequently engraved; *Agésilas jouant avec ses enfants*, Hallé, and *Othryades the Lacedaemonian*, a model in plaster (1779); *Courage des femmes de Sparte*, by Le Barbier l'aîné (Spartan women repulsing a Messenian attack on them at a festival), a sketch of Spartan women aiding their menfolk against Pyrrhus, by Perrin, and *Amour Conjugal* (Leonidas, Cleombrotus, and Chilonis) by Le Monnier (1787); *Mort d'Agis* (Monsiau), *Leonidas, Cleombrotus and Chilonis* (Fortin), 1789.

[2] The Ode 'Aux Français' (referring to defeats under Louis XV) opens
O Messène! frémis; Sparte n'est point domptée;
Il lui reste ma Lyre: elle enflamme les Coeurs.
Tu le disais: ta Lyre, ô sublime Tyrtée
Enfanta des Vainqueurs. (*Oeuvres*, 1811, i. iv. 1, p. 222.)

[3] *Lycurgue*, by F. M. C. Deschamps (1683–1747).

[4] *Les Lacédémoniennes ou Lycurgue*, Comédie en vers et en trois actes par M. Maihol . . . (1754).

[5] *Alcidonis ou la journée Lacédémonienne*, by Louvay de la Saussaye (1772).

Rousseau. We are warned at the start that the scene is the market-place at Sparta, 'qui n'est ornée que d'arbres et entourée de cabanes'—how far we have come since the magnificent inventions of Signor Burnacini!—and half the odd customs in Plutarch are dragged on to the stage. Hither a philosophic young Athenian has followed his beloved, a philosopher's widow in search of her father. And apart from a clear condemnation of harshness to slaves and over-emphasis on good birth, we are plainly meant to admire, and to contrast with all we hear of Athens, Spartan simplicity and virtue, Spartan magistrates (prompt and accessible), and Spartan education (including military training for both sexes); while we see with our own eyes, in a series of *intermèdes*, that Spartan festivals are pleasurable as well as patriotic. Even the comic slave, under his Athenian master's instruction, is more or less converted from his first terror that the lady may have taken a *passion philosophique* for the place, and that he may have to stop there and 'se stiler au service des Hilotes'.[1]

Finally, a desperately serious *Agis*.[1] The quarrel between Laignelot's hero and Léonidas is, in a crude form, just that between Rousseau and Mably and their opponents. On the one side, Lycurgus, equality, the abolition of both poverty and luxury, the replacement of wealth by virtue and civic spirit, all resulting in a (purely moral) ascendancy over Greece; on the other, charges of enthusiasm, of ignoring the rights of property, of desiring *vertus grossières* impossible in a civilized country. But the representative of this latter view, Léonidas, dependent on the rich and corrupt and on foreign troops, is not merely a despot but an absolute monster. And Laignelot, though forced by history to let Agis perish, cannot resist killing off his enemy too and producing, politically at least a happy end. Indeed the forced and naive spirit of the play presages remarkably that of the Revolutionary period; when, it is satisfactory to note, its author was in fact busy on the political stage as an extreme radical.

The play's own demerits, as well as the division in public opinion, provoked a lively burlesque,[2] which had great fun, in

---

[1] J.-F. Laignelot's *Agis* (1782) was played at Versailles in 1779, where it was understandably not much liked in spite of its monarchic hero; and in Paris in 1782, with some success, Agis' struggle against the senate being identified with that of Maupéou against the Parlements.

[2] J. F. T. Goulard *Agis, parodie d'Agis*, (1782).

particular, with Agésistrate's exaggerated Spartan-maternal sentiments and active participation in all the street-fighting, and with Agis' visionary fits and self-conscious appeals to posterity. Solemn thesis and satirical antithesis may stand for the last word of France upon the subject.

17

THE FRENCH REVOLUTION
AND ITS AFTERMATH

WARNINGS have been uttered of late against supposing that classical antiquity, far from having a significant influence upon the
course of events in the French Revolution, was even referred to,
by most of the leading figures of the time, with any great frequency or seriousness, and against giving too much political
importance to superficial classical fashions. Such warnings are
doubtless justified; but it is misleading either to take all the classical
states together, or to take them in isolation from other possible
sources of inspiration. In particular, Sparta's place in the literature
of and about the Revolution can only be understood if the history
of her reputation in the previous half-century be kept in mind.
For if many of the politicians of the time had read Livy, Cicero,
and Tacitus at school, they had not learnt much about Greece
there. The interest in Rome, indubitably the most discussed
ancient state at this as at so many periods, may have been fed in
part directly from ancient sources; but in spite of Plutarch (or for
that matter Rollin) it is clear that Sparta still appears almost
exclusively in the very individual dress given her by recent
French writers. This is not quite the case with Athens, whose
democracy gradually becomes more acceptable than ever before
in modern times.[1]

Certain ideas rooted in Montesquieu, Rousseau, and Mably,
which those thinkers had associated with Sparta, did undoubtedly
become prominent, especially in the later stages of the Revolution.
But even to these three, as we saw, Sparta had seemed a remote
and extraordinary place and certainly no direct model for France;

---

[1] H. T. Parker, *The Cult of Antiquity and the French Revolutionaries* (1937) has
been of great use to me, and I would only wish to differ from him in degree and
emphasis. With all his caution, he does not quite resist the temptation to give
Robespierre and Saint-Just a 'preference' for Sparta over Athens, and their
more 'moderate' opponents the reverse.

while other writers had gone a long way towards making her name a thoroughly invidious one. Thus even among those of the revolutionaries most convinced that a republic must be based on virtue, and virtue on a public and patriotic education, the ultimate appeal to Sparta is comparatively rare. Such an appeal was liable to provoke as many as it attracted. And thorough-going laconism was really not possible; France's size, wealth, prowess in the arts, even her new representative government were not to be altered; and with the exception of a minute band of extremists the revolutionaries were defenders of property and believers in the new liberal economic doctrines—at a time when the word 'Sparta' evoked above all else economic egalitarianism or even communism. And so, though certainly there was more discussion of Sparta by practising politicians now than at any other period, if one discounts superficial mentions of Lycurgus as a great law-giver, and of Spartan patriotism, the majority, possibly, of references are made in the course of attacks on those ideas of Rousseau and others indicated above, as at best alien and unpractical, and at worst oppressive and barbarous; and especially in declarations that Spartan institutions must all be taken together—which would involve taking slavery. Thus the ideas of the pre-Revolutionary laconophobes remained potent; and indeed, with the growth of the theory that the whole Revolution, or at least the Terror, was inspired by idealization of Sparta as well as Rome, or at the least could be fairly described as Spartan, generally in the most hostile sense, Voltaire's idea of Sparta may be said to have defeated Rousseau's.

The Revolution only gradually developed a serious interest in ancient republics. The deputies of 1789 were of course almost to a man still loyal to some kind of monarchy. And, as in America, events had placed legislative power in the hands of an assembly, not an individual—Lycurgus, even later, is not quite so prominent as recent eulogies might have seemed to portend. The enthusiasm and self-confidence of the time led to assertions that France was or would be not only unlike but far superior to any ancient state— occasionally the horrible *moeurs* of Sparta being specially picked out for contrast.

But if any part of Greece could seem relevant, it must be Athens, which had so often been treated as a symbol or a type of France, or in particular Paris. The Right and Centre made a certain amount of her democratic excesses, anything like which they were concerned to avoid by preserving a measure of power to the king. Moderates however might praise the empirical Solon, and the free-born eloquence of Demosthenes as well as Cicero.[1] More important and more radical was Camille Desmoulins, who united the admiration felt by so many *philosophes* for Athenian civil liberty, commerce, arts, and humanity with a belief in democracy, and could admire Pericles—the politician as well as the orator and intellectual—as well as Solon. After an enthusiastically classical youth, he was convinced by the example of America that large republics were practicable; and though, when taken up by Mirabeau, he worried about the effect of his patron's dinners on his republican austerity, he did not really think that the French could or need attain that quality. In summer 1789 Desmoulins was already pointing out that Sparta was the one Greek state with a privileged and an unprivileged order, and praising by contrast the egalitarian discipline of the Athenian army as a possible model for the present. He soon attacked Spartan and Platonic conceptions of liberty and equality, especially as interpreted by Mably, quite explicitly: 'C'est détruire la passion de l'amour avec un rasoir.'[2] Wine inspires more contempt for kings and nobles than Eurotas water can do. Athens proved that republican liberty was possible in a state where the government was concerned with procuring individual happiness, where commerce, luxury, and the theatre flourished, Aspasia was made welcome, religion was cheerful, every citizen equal before the law, and all careers open to talent.[3] Certainly Desmoulins, a struggling and dissipated lawyer, would have been happier there.

After September 1790, and more especially after the flight to Varennes, there was for a time growing agitation for a republic; but many of the republicans were more interested in America than any other examples of the form, and if a few mildly defend Rome or ancient states in general, arguing in particular that their short-

---

[1] As an amusing example, the extravagant Olympe de Gouges, who considered herself a supporter of constitutional monarchy, proposes in her dramatic piece *Mirabeau aux Champs Élysées* (April 1791) to send Solon down as a replacement, qualified by *douce morale* and experience of an opulent state, for the defunct statesman. The mixed reception committee in heaven does not include Demosthenes, for he has actually been reincarnated as Mirabeau.

[2] *La France libre* iv. (*Oeuvres*, ed. J. Claretie, 1874, i. 93).

[3] *Révolutions de France et de Brabant*, no. xx, p. 306 (not in Claretie).

comings had nothing to do with their republicanism, it does not seem that anyone set up Sparta as a model—or even, to anything like Desmoulins's extent, Athens either. And the Legislative Assembly (autumn 1791 to autumn 1792) was too busy with the intrigues leading to the outbreak of war to worry about the various types of possible state.

But in September 1792, largely as a result of the foreign war and the king's folly, France found herself a republic. The new Convention was faced with the urgent questions—what sort of republican constitution should France have, and how is a precarious republic to be preserved? The answer to the latter question at least had been given by Montesquieu, Rousseau, and Mably, to whom the Convention was more than once advised to turn: by the encouragement of political virtue, that is, by political education in the widest sense. Political virtue, so pacific in the palmy days of 1789, now had to be military virtue as well, and events, after the battle of Valmy, might encourage belief in the old thesis of the worth of citizen troops animated by patriotism.

These ideas are to be found in individuals from various sectors of the Convention; the republicans of 1792–3, the Montagne or Jacobins on the one hand and their opponents, among whom Brissot and the Girondin deputies were so prominent, on the other, differed less on theoretical issues than personalities and tactics, and the latter at least scarcely formed a party. In late 1792 and early 1793 the most open admiration of Sparta would seem to come from an opponent of the Montagne, the Protestant pastor Rabaut-Saint-Étienne, who wrote that his contemporaries might learn from the *Entretiens de Phocion* and the severe manners of the Spartans there displayed how a republic is constituted; he also advised them to turn to Montesquieu's discussion, based on the ancient republics, on the authority of elders.[1] Rabaut has been called a socialist, and certainly wanted increased economic equality, tentatively suggesting that there might be some sort of maximum for individual properties. In this he was not supported by his friends; but his views on education, as we shall see, found more favour.

But the name of Sparta was more often used as a stick to beat either side with. Certain Montagnards readily employed it;

---

[1] *Chronique de Paris*, no. 3, p. 11 (3 Jan. 1793); no. 124, p. 3 (4 May 1793). Cf. no. 6, p. 22 (6 Jan. 1793).

Robespierre, distrusting the authors of the new plan for public education, described it, in effect, as Spartan.[1] Desmoulins, to some of whose extravagances Brissot had taken exception, called the latter's concept of a republic Puritan, Roundhead, and—later at least—Spartan. 'Que voulez-vous avec vôtre brouet noir et vôtre liberté de Lacédémone?' he inquired with his usual verve; 'Le beau législateur que ce Lycurgue, dont la science n'a consisté qu'à inspirer des privations à ses concitoyens; qui les a rendu égaux comme la tempête rend égaux tous ceux qui ont fait naufrage.'[2]

It was true that Brissot and many of his friends piqued themselves a great deal on their own virtue and simplicity. But if they wanted classical precedents they usually found them among the heroes of Rome and Athens. And in any more serious sense Desmoulins's attacks would seem entirely unjustified. Brissot, an admirer of Rome in his youth, but soon of America, provoked Robespierre by praising, not Rousseau, but Voltaire and the other great men with whom Condorcet had been associated. Condorcet himself, in his writings on education and in the famous posthumous *Esquisse*, retains all his detached attitude to antiquity and, by implication at least, his old dislike of Sparta.[3] And if one must generalize, it is a similar philosophic current that would also seem dominant in most of the Gironde deputies (Bordeaux, it is worth observing, was a proud commercial city) and their friends.[4] At any rate, a few weeks before their fall, in the debate on the constitution, the most famous orator of the group, Vergniaud, uttered an eloquent if entirely unoriginal warning about the inapplicability to French problems of the sort of republic acclaimed by Rousseau and Montesquieu. If you do want an austere, poor,

---

[1] *Lettres à ses Commettans* (1793), 2nd series, no. 2, p. 57.

[2] *Le Vieux Cordelier*, no. vi (ed. Mathiez et Calvet, 1936, p. 191), cf. J. P. *Brissot démasqué* (Claretie, p. 261).

[3] See esp. *Sur l'instruction publique* (*Oeuvres complètes*, 1847, viii. 197 ff.) and *Esquisse d'un Tableau historique des progrès de l'esprit humain* (written in hiding in late 1793), *Oeuvres* ix.

[4] Buzot, writing in hiding and despair, attributed his friends' fall however to putting too much trust in Montesquieu, Rousseau, and Mably (that fatal trinity), and included Lycurgus, who had had his eye knocked out, among previous republican martyrs. Of Mme Roland's early wish to be a Spartan woman (for Rousseauesque, not Helvétian reasons!) no trace seems to remain by the time of the Revolution—she had no sons.

and warlike régime such as Sparta's, he said, you must be as logical as Lycurgus; divide up the land, 'brûlez même les assignats . . . déshonorez les arts'; use helots, depend on foreigners for trade. You will find you have plunged your country into famine and civil war, and turned yourselves into brutes. More briefly, he warns his hearers against Roman, Pennsylvanian, and other types of republic. But he does not deny the need for virtue and equality in some less chimerical form; and he praises, as the one speaker who has realized the need for moral institutions that will strengthen the government by making it loved, Saint-Just.[1]

Vergniaud makes it plain both that mildly 'Spartan' ideas could be combined with a horror of Sparta, and that the Montagne, and even the man who was later to be regarded as a Spartan come back to life, were not yet being identified with the place. Indeed there were all sorts of attitudes on that side too. There were men impatient with classical learning and modern theories, urging the government to get on with the war; there were those who talked, when they did talk of antiquity, of Rome and Athens in the first place—a class that includes Marat, though he was described admiringly by Robespierre's brother as living 'en Spartiate'.[2] And there was Desmoulins, confident at this time that his old friend Robespierre ('l'Aristide de la Révolution', as well as the Cato) would bring in Athenian principles. Solon's institutions could acclimatize themselves in France; Versailles and other palaces could be turned into Prytanea (where those who deserved well of the Athenian republic were fed at the public cost).[3] And even Desmoulins asserts that the eighteenth century is in most respects in advance of antiquity.

But in the autumn of 1793, after the elimination of the so-called Girondins, Desmoulins's famous journal the *Vieux Cordelier* turned to attack the extreme left-wing Hébertistes, and in effect the whole Terror, still to some extent preserving his Athenian point of reference. In Number IV he recommends the clemency of Thrasybulus, and recalls that the freest and most democratic of peoples raised an altar to Pity.[4] In Number VII—suppressed at the

---

[1] 8 May 1793 (*Réimpression de l'Ancien Moniteur*, 1847, xvi. 345).
[2] *Oeuvres complètes de Maximilien Robespierre, Lettres*, vol. iii (1926); clxxviii, p. 174.
[3] *Histoire secrète de la Révolution*, 1793 (Claretie, p. 351).
[4] Mathiez et Calvet, pp. 122, 124.

time—his interlocutor, the *Vieux Cordelier* of the title, calls Athens the one republican and democratic state of antiquity, closely resembling France today except in its possession of perfect freedom of speech. Solon, in spite of his penchant for wine, women, and poetry, was a model legislator.[1] Camille in his own person throws a little cold water, but the eloquent description of Athenian *sansculottes* remains with us. But this time the object of attack is not described as Spartan; it was under the form of the Terror at Rome under Tiberius that Desmoulins so memorably depicted the present. And indeed Tacitus and imperial history were soon put under frequent contribution for the same purpose.

For a time Desmoulins was supported by Robespierre; but the latter with great skill succeeded in ridding himself both of the extreme left wing and of those who were described as moderates or Indulgents; and with Danton and the latter group Desmoulins went down. From the spring of 1794 Robespierre and Saint-Just, though not alone, were supreme. These are the men whose beliefs and policies—and, in the latter case, character—have so often been described as Spartan. But, as ever, only very hesitant explicit praise of Sparta is to be found, and the statues of Solon and Demosthenes, which stood with those of Lycurgus and Plato and other great men in the new hall of the Convention, had no need to be out of countenance. Robespierre himself was that *rara avis*, a real follower of Rousseau in politics as in religion from the beginning of the Revolution; though he long professed indifference as to whether the popular state he wanted was nominally a monarchy or not, though he at first opposed the foreign war, and though he never, in spite of pressure, entirely abandoned liberal and moderate economic principles. He was perhaps the most theoretically minded of the Revolutionary leaders and certainly the most devoted to the idea of the virtuous republic.

One gets the impression that he would originally have liked to appeal to Sparta. Indeed he regarded himself and his colleagues of the Constituent Assembly as emulating Lycurgus in declaring themselves ineligible for re-election. A German observer shows him, in the early period of the Revolution, attacking the representative principle at private gatherings and replying, when asked what he would prefer, 'the Lycurgan system'—till he was laughed

[1] Ibid., pp. 201 ff, 230 ff.

out of it.[1] His journalistic writings in the summer of 1792 show him deprecating too easy comparisons between recent events and the sublimities of antiquity and especially Sparta; and also, significantly, praising the Greek-descended Marseillais for uniting 'l'industrie d'Athènes à l'héroïsme de Sparte'.[2] Early in 1793 he includes Agis among revolutionary martyrs (a list that was usually heavily Athenian, since that notoriously ungrateful republic had exiled or put to death most of her great men) and praised the ancient legislators' prudent regard for the religious prejudices of their day[3] (the more Voltairean tended to congratulate themselves on appealing, unlike the ancients, only to the authority of reason). But in his discussion of the educational proposals, already referred to, he refuses contemptuously to 'produire . . . un moment d'illusion, en vous présentant le fantôme de quelques institutions lacédémoniennes, étrangères à nôtre situation actuelle'.[4] Before the republic is instructed, it must be preserved and constituted. He elsewhere expresses (in a note) a strong condemnation of Solon for moderation—he was a *feuillant* whose policies led straight to the tyranny of Peisistratus. But the context with its approving parallels between the Montagnards and Athenian democrats suggests that Pericles rather than Lycurgus might be set up as Solon's rival and superior. And (over the question of the appeal to the people on the fate of the king) he accuses Brissot and others of unreal and more than classical notions of democracy.

Such were the useful weapons of party struggle. When Robespierre and his friends were in the ascendant, he was revealed as very ready to support public education and patriotic fêtes; but, as we shall see, over the latter he preferred to evoke other Greek memories and over the former he said nothing about Sparta. And, in his favourite scheme, the introduction of a political religion, he refers to Sparta and Athens together; deism, the true social and republican religion, was that of Socrates and Leonidas and the great Roman Stoic heroes.[5] But such references are infrequent and

---

[1] K. E. Oelsner (*Robespierre vu par ses contemporains*, ed. L. Jacob, 1938, p. 78).

[2] *Le Défenseur de la constitution* (*Oeuvres*, vol. iv, 1939, ed. G. Laurent, p. 126, no. 4; p. 336, no. 11).

[3] *Lettres à ses Commettans*, 1st series, no. 7, p. 334; no. 8, p. 342.

[4] *Lettres à ses Commettans* (1743), 2nd series, no. 2, pp. 49 ff.; no. 1, p. 23, n. 1.

[5] Dubious, most particularly in the case of Leonidas! though we will not

unimportant. And if he had come to believe that in a still imperfectly regenerate republic fear must take a place beside virtue as a principle of preservation, let it be remembered that this idea was not in the laconizing tradition of the time.

Saint-Just is a little bolder than Robespierre. In 1791 he subscribed to the usual belief that Lycurgus' all-demanding state, and its economic egalitarianism, were quite unsuited to France. He admires the great man, but by dint of regarding him as a sort of Solon in his regard for the passions and limitations of his people; and though 'à Dieu ne plaise que je veuille établir le gymnastique parmi nous', he frankly regrets that this and other ancient institutions should appear so strange to our corrupt minds.[1] His speeches in the Convention have a few approving references to Lycurgus—usually linked with Solon.[2] As time passed he became more and more convinced of the need for forcible regeneration through public institutions; but though, almost alone, he can refer to Lycurgus when recommending severity, as well as include him among the martyrs of the republican ideal, it is thus that in well-known words he sums up his government's policy in 1794: 'nous vous offrîmes le bonheur de Sparte et celui d'Athènes dans ses beaux jours; nous vous offrîmes le bonheur de la vertu, celui de l'aisance et de la médiocrité.'[3] Instead of criticizing Desmoulins' Athens he attacks his ideas as those of Persepolis.

And the *Fragments sur les institutions républicaines*,[4] jotted down in the last months of his life, scarcely mention Sparta save to shudder at her method of dealing with excess population, while it is Rome and Athens that are cited to show the value of having many institutions rather than many laws, and a somewhat adapted censorship that is regarded as the most important of the institutions proposed. But some—by no means all—of the others do very strongly recall the *Life of Lycurgus*. In particular many aspects of the educational system, where boys live by companies in boarding

---

[1] *Esprit de la Révolution et de la Constitution de France*, 1791 (*Oeuvres Complètes*, ed. C. Vellay, (Vol. 1)) ii. 2, p. 265, ii. 3, p. 266, iii. 2, p. 282 (referring to Lycurgus), iii. 6, p. 287.

[2] Especially his speech on the Constitution, 23 April 1793, *Oeuvres Complètes*, 1,419 ff.

[3] Speech of 14 March, 1794, op. cit., ii. 267.   [4] Op. cit., ii. 492 ff.

quarrel with his subsequent words, that 'il y a loin de Socrate à Charmette et de Léonidas au Père Duchesne', the opponents of all religion.

schools; the curious institutionalizing of friendship;[1] the penalties
for cowardice; possibly even the barring of gold and silver
(though not for purposes of coinage). *Le laconisme du langage* is, as it
had long been, one of Saint-Just's demands. And a certain anti-
intellectual bias, like the belief in enthusiasm, the praise of agricultural and military life, and the huge demands of the state on the
individual, are among the features that doubtless contributed, after
the work was published in 1800, to the picture of Saint-Just as a
Spartan. Certainly his Lycurgus, at the time of his death, had
become less careful than the pseudo-Solon of 1791; 'il est des
hommes', he wrote in his never-delivered final speech, meaning
Billaud-Varennes and his fellow-plotters, 'que Lycurgue eût
chassés de Lacédémone sur le sinistre caractère et la pâleur de leur
front.'[2]

Billaud, however, deserves a word. One of the most sanguinary
among the colleagues of Robespierre and Saint-Just, who finally
helped overthrow them on the 9th Thermidor, he shared their
interest in first principles, being another fervent believer in
regeneration, and also, this time, in considerable economic
equality. No wonder then that he can use Sparta as the great
example of a regenerated state, and praise especially her education
and, in very Rousseau-like terms, the noble influence of her
women. He can also, as well as dismissing Solon as a time-server,
approve Lycurgus for his severity.[3] But he recognized that the
reform of *moeurs* is difficult to carry through successfully—as
Lycurgus and Agis, as well as Solon and the Gracchi, had found.
Nor could equality in France possibly be attained by Spartan
methods, which—short of all Frenchmen becoming agricultural
labourers—required slaves. Not agrarian laws, fear of which
haunted many people in these years, but strict regulation of
inheritances was the solution.[4] And even Billaud is more than
once found praising Athens as well as Sparta—for its admission,
for example, of public as opposed to private *luxe*.[5] And he was
happy to see contemporary history in Athenian terms—finally

---

[1] Cf. *Réimpression de l'Ancien Moniteur* xvi. 464: 'il ne faut pas diviser les amis,
dit Lycurgue'—more significant in the context of the *Fragments* than its own,
perhaps.

[2] *Oeuvres Complètes*, ii. 487.

[3] *Les Élemens du républicanisme*, (1793), pp. 41, 78, 122.

[4] Ibid., pp. 97, 101, 119.   [5] Ibid., pp. 4, 82.

describing Robespierre as the tyrant Peisistratus (this became a popular designation) and himself and Collot d'Herbois as, heaven save the mark, Harmodius and Aristogeiton.[1]

More than once, in this account, the subject of education has cropped up. This is the field in which theorists were out in force and in which praise of Sparta is commonest. But the pattern that we have already found emerges here too: the keenest laconizers are only individuals, and individuals associated with various political groups; reference to Sparta is still most commonly unfriendly. And the Robespierrist régime did not, ultimately, in this any more than other fields, see itself as Spartan, nor was it, by contemporary opponents, at least, so seen.

The volume of discussion of all problems of education was far too great in these years to be dealt with here at all fully. We have seen how almost every leading critic of the *ancien régime* had advocated a national education, and how great the faith in its transforming power often was. The Constituent Assembly planned the constitutional establishment of *instruction publique* for all, and the Legislative Assembly set up a Committee to deal with the matter—for, as the Revolution progressed, it became urgent to take the young out of the hands of the ever more hostile clergy. At first, reference to Sparta is vague or adverse. The most important of the plans produced in the early years, that published under the name and after the death of Mirabeau, that of Talleyrand (with one degree of free and voluntary public education and thereafter a scholarship system, anyone being free to open a school), and above all that of Condorcet, produced before the Legislative Assembly by the Committee in April 1792 (it had five degrees of voluntary public education for both sexes, and no state control over teachers or curriculum), were all anxiously liberal, and their authors all rejected, explicitly or implicitly, antique or Spartan precedent; though Rousseau and ultimately Sparta may lie hidden behind favourable references to gymnastic exercises and national fêtes.

Late in 1792 the Committee of Public Instruction put before the Convention suggestions, especially for primary schools, still based on Condorcet's plan. Now that the republic was in being, the education of antiquity was intimately involved in the resulting burst of argument. And antiquity, here alone, means primarily

---

[1] *Mémoires*, ed. A. Degis (1893), pp. 423–4 and 451 (cf. p. 401 for further praise of Spartan education and Spartan heroism).

not Roman but Spartan (though the Committee manifested hopeful interest in a monograph on Athenian education).[1] Durand-Maillane, himself a member of the Committee, criticized the plan for giving too much power to the teachers, who would form a powerful private interest; and he wished to see primary education alone in the hands of the state—did Rome or Athens organize higher instruction?[2] Durand-Maillane, an independent, was attacked for anti-intellectualism, but deputies of various political tendencies shared his view that public virtue was the one aspect of education with which the state needed to concern itself. Ducos,[3] who fell with the Girondins the next year, and Leclerc[4] insisted that since that was the business of primary schools they must be compulsory for everybody, as at Sparta. The latter also proposed that, as in that place, the father who did not put his children through the state education should lose his civic rights.

Such devotees of public virtue, if they were ready to cut down the state's part in intellectual or vocational training, were anxious that national education should be understood as something covering man's life from cradle to grave. For this purpose the most powerful weapon was of course the patriotic festival, as elaborated by Rousseau with close reference to classical antiquity. Patriotic fêtes of a sort, centred at first on the *féderations* of the National Guard, with their oaths of loyalty, had sprung up spontaneously in the last months of 1789, and the first national *Fédération* was held in Paris in July 1790 on the anniversary of the fall of the Bastille. The habit spread to the rest of the populace. As Christian influence became less and less welcome or available, the fêtes tended to take somewhat classical forms. But the really Spartan festival seems to be a rare exception. Such however was one that is often picked out; on 14 July 1791 Boulogne-sur-Mer saw a festival 'worthy of the fairest days of Lacedaemon', where all elders except 'selfish celibates' took part in a public dinner, to which at the end a troop of children were introduced.[5] Dinners and reverence for elders were not uncommon features; but the exclusion of bachelors and arrival of the children are surely straight from the *Life of Lycurgus*.

[1] *Procès-Verbaux du Comité d'Instruction Publique de la Convention Nationale*, ed. J. Guillaume, vol. i (1891), p. 298.
[2] Ibid. i. 127.
[3] Ibid. i. 191 (cf. p. 189).
[4] Ibid. i. 192 ff., especially p. 197.
[5] Gorsas, *Courrier* xxvi. 317.

T

The early plans on education all proposed that these spontaneous phenomena should be taken up and organized, and the Constituent Assembly before it broke up voted unanimously in this sense. As it became clear that the Revolutionary Church was a broken reed in the encouragement of Revolutionary sentiment, and above all after the institution of the republic, the matter began to seem urgent. In December 1792 Rabaut-Saint-Étienne, with whose cast of mind we have already become acquainted, criticized the Committee's proposals in this context. He distinguished *instruction publique* from *éducation nationale*, the wider and more important—antiquity, he believed, showed the extent to which it could unify the nation. 'Personne n'ignore quel était à cet égard l'éducation des Crétois, des autres peuples grecs, et surtout de ces Spartiates qui passaient leurs jours dans une société continuelle, et dont toute la vie était une apprentissage et un exercice de toutes les vertus.' It was hard to create such an education today, but France might at least adopt national festivals. Rabaut proposed that Sunday services according to the new national Church should be followed in fine weather by military and gymnastic competitions. All the children are to be dressed alike; elders over sixty are to sit and censure their behaviour, and a senate elected among them is to give prizes.[1] The speech was so much admired that Rabaut was put on the Committee—Robespierre therefore had some basis for his complaint about its Spartan notions; but among those who repeated Rabaut's arguments, Spartan references and all, was the Jacobin Jeanbon-Saint-André,[2] later Robespierre's colleague on the famous Committee of Public Safety, and, though he was less close an associate, Marie-Joseph Chénier (far more prominent at this time even as a poet than his unfortunate brother André). 'A Lacédémone', said the latter in April, in a debate on the constitution, 'l'éducation ne se bornait point à la jeunesse: le législateur l'avait étendue à tous les âges, et il était vrai de dire que la vie d'un Lacédémonien était une éducation perpetuelle. Législateurs philosophiques, imitez cette république célèbre.'[3]

---

[1] Guillaume, op. cit. i. 231 (*Projet d'Education Nationale* par J. P. Rabaut, published version of his speech to the Convention). Cf. p. 230, his indebtedness to Bancal and his *Nouvel Ordre Social*.

[2] Ibid. i. 272 (*Sur l'education nationale*, published June 1793 but written earlier). He also approves Durand-Mallane: ancient states had *éducation nationale* but not, strictly, *instruction publique*.

[3] Ibid. i. 419–20 (from report in *Journal des débats et des décrets*, no. 218).

With the disappearance of the so-called Girondins, including Condorcet, education went back into the melting-pot, and there was a new burst of discussion. The Committee put forward a plan by Sieyès, which did only involve one grade of public education; those who wanted more, repeated a supporter, ought not to cite Greece and Rome.[1] But the triumphant Jacobins distrusted Sieyès and various features of his plan, which was rejected. Festivals were prominent among his proposals; but, with competitions in poetry and oratory, and more stress on *gloire* than *patrie*, if they recall Greece at all it is Athens or Olympia.

Among the various pamphlets appearing at this time, one might deprecate any real public education as illiberal and describe almost all the ideas associated with it as ridiculously Spartan: 'L'égalité de l'éducation n'est qu'une chimère dans une République immense ... où l'inégalité de fortune et d'état est nécessaire pour le bonheur commun. Ne vous donnez pas le ridicule de vous calquer sur Sparte. Vous n'avez pas d'ilotes ... Quel pays d'ailleurs! les anciens Spartiates ne sont bons à citer que pour amuser les enfants.' Physical education? 'Nous voilà encore dans la Grèce'; children will be put off for good if it is compulsory. Military training? Civil wars will result. But Sparta was quite right in teaching religion.[2] On the other extreme, a brochure could continue to praise the simple, patriotic education of Sparta and its amazing influence. But as so often the detailed proposals appended are not very Spartan, and indeed the education received by Solon is described as all that could be desired.[3]

In July Robespierre, bypassing the Committee, appeared as the backer of an educational scheme worked out at the end of the preceding year, a legacy of the republican martyr Lepeletier. Like others, Lepeletier accepted the Condorcet plans for higher 'instruction'; it was 'éducation' he worried about—the primary schools were not egalitarian enough for a republic. In their place he would institute *maisons d'éducation nationale*, removing children from the age of five to that of twelve entirely from their parents' care—a totally new provision among the plans that had been seriously discussed. But though he expressed admiration for

---

[1] Ibid. i. 581 (P. C. F. Daunou, *Essai sur l'instruction publique*).

[2] Ibid. i, Appendix iv, p. 624 (*Courtes réflexions sur l'instruction publique*, P. J. D. G. Faure).

[3] Ibid. i, Appendix v, p. 630 (*Sur l'éducation publique*, C. Duval).

Sparta and Plato's *Republic*, Lepeletier regarded a communal education prolonged till adulthood as a *beau songe*; adolescence must be devoted to specialized training, and France needed farmers, merchants, and craftsmen as well as the soldiers created by Lycurgus or the philosophers of Plato. And he put comparatively little stress on the direct inculcation of patriotism, or on physical education.[1] His plan therefore was in some respects much less Spartan than were the fanciful proposals, also published at this time, of Rousseau's friend and pupil Deleyre (who had been associated with the enemies of the Montagne).[2]

Nonetheless Lepeletier's plan was greeted by a torrent of objections that it was impossibly classical: 'il ne suffit pas qu'un système se présente escorté de noms illustres, qu'il ait pour patrons Minos, Platon, Lycurgue, et Lepeletier', the Convention was told; consider the differences between France and Sparta, and the financial, practical, and moral difficulties of the scheme.[3] One objector felt children should be brought up in society, not shut up 'dans l'enceinte d'une petite communauté, pas même dans celle de Lycurgue'.[4] Another agreed that children might live at public expense in such a manner in Sparta or perhaps Lucca or San Marino, but never in France. Here there were schools, such as that of the Chevalier Paulet, which gave a severe and economical education and would produce a generation superior in all respects to the Spartans.[5] A supporter of Sieyès' project gave a warning that *pensionnats* are hard to run without abuse, and insisted like so many others that Sparta's institutions must be taken together or not at all. A small state, without industry, that sacrificed civil

---

[1] Ibid. ii. 35.

[2] *Idées sur l'éducation nationale* (extracts only in Guillaume i, App. vii, p. 645). All children would finally attend his voluntary boarding schools from seven to eighteen. They would lead *la vie fraternelle des Spartiates*, with many possessions in common. Some of their occupations (gardening, nursery-school visiting) may be Rousseauesque but are not Spartan; but there is much military exercise and dancing, and reading of Plutarch to appropriate background music (e.g. the *Life of Lycurgus* to military strains). The Spartan motto *s'abstenir et ignorer* is to be the guiding principle, the education of girls is to be, as at Sparta, partially similar to that of boys. Further references to Plato, Bacon, Montaigne.

[3] H. Grégoire (Guillaume iii. 173; cf. 178, quoting Grégoire's *Mémoires* i. 344).

[4] *Observations sur les différents projets de l'instruction publique*, J. M. Coupe (Guillaume ii. 134).

[5] C. L. Masuyer (Guillaume i. 148)—a speech revised and printed at this point.

rights to political liberty might adopt both slavery and *pensionnats*; neither would do for France.[1] Lepeletier's plan had already been watered down, largely on grounds of expense, when it passed the Convention in August. Communal education was to start in a small way, voluntary and for boys only. But it was found in the autumn that the plan was creating doubts in the most patriotic breasts—even on the score of parental rights. Now, at the start of the dechristianization campaign, there was a traditional comparison that might appear especially telling: 'on nous a proposé l'éducation commune, comme à Sparte. Mais Sparte était un couvent, une abbaye de moines'.[2]

Henceforth in the practical discussions on education the fatal name is scarcely mentioned—though the provision that primary schools are to be compulsory was attacked as one of the unworkable 'contraintes prétendues lacédémoniennes' recently advocated. But this is not, of course, to say that ideas of *éducation nationale* and the need for *institutions politiques* were out; far from it. The fêtes, however, leave Sparta behind them. The autumn of 1793 saw M.-J. Chénier presenting a report on the subject (the only sort of thing he was good for, Mme Roland had thought), but he had revised his views on the propriety of imitating that celebrated republic, or Crete either, and spoke contemptuously of 'des romans politiques, faiblement échafaudés d'après la république de Platon ou d'après les romans historiques composés sur Lacédémone', and praised the great men produced by the republican institutions of Athens.[3] But fêtes were now mostly to be tied to the new Revolutionary calendar, and they were tending to develop their own forms. In the spring of 1794 Robespierre helped to replace the cult of Reason by the cult of the *Être Suprême*; the famous festivals organized in its service by the painter David were thoroughly eclectic; and it may be added that ultimately public dinners were stigmatized as aristocratic, and even as having been subsidized by Pitt.

After Thermidor, however, among those who regarded the fall of Robespierre and his allies as merely the removal of a dictatorship, not as an attack on the principles of the Revolution, Sparta occasionally bobs up again. Chénier produced more of his reports

---

[1] *Essai sur l'instruction publique*, P. C. F. Daunou (Guillaume i. 581).
[2] P. J. Duhem (Guillaume ii. 674).   [3] Guillaume ii. 756, 759.

on fêtes, general and particular, arguing for forms he regarded as
more truly classical than David's interminable processions and
allegories. At last France should get gymnastic exercises, as
practised in Athens and Sparta (executed, indeed, on one occasion
by 'cette colonie de Spartiates', the pupils of the recently founded
École de Mars), and, if and when it became possible, the banquets
Lycurgus had considered so vital.[1] There was an enormous
amount of discussion on how to celebrate the *fêtes décadaires* that
replaced Sunday in the Revolutionary calendar. Among the many
projects we cannot but single out that of Eschassériaux. He complained to the Convention that recent proposals were neither
republican nor emotionally satisfying enough. He wanted to keep
well clear of any sort of religion whatsoever: 'ce n'est point
l'oeuvre de Moïse que vous avez à faire: c'est celui de Lycurgue.'
The latter's was both strictly political and supremely *touchant*:
'voyez quel amour, quel charme, le génie de Lycurgue avait
imprimé à ces fêtes données sous le ciel, sous les regards de la loi
et de la vertu, à tous les citoyens de tout âge et de tout sexe, à ces
fêtes où ils célébraient ensemble la douce égalité, la fraternité et
la patrie.' Eschassériaux went on to read his proposals. They
included hymns sung antiphonally by different age-groups,
plenty of dancing and military exercises, and occasional (frugal
and decent) banquets, all under the censorship of elderly citizens.[2]
Since he also presented the Committee's next report, it is not
surprising that it opens with praise of Greek institutions and the
attendrissant character of Spartan fêtes; but the proposals have been
slightly modified, and the *Être Suprême* has reappeared.[3] Argument
continued. But the mass of the people had always been loyal to
their old beliefs. The pacification of the rebel areas soon involved
concessions to the Church, and the *fêtes décadaires* were doomed.
Gradually the whole idea of national festivals faded.

Away from the context we have been exploring, Sparta aroused
very little interest. But she does occasionally resume one of her
best roles, recently played much more in England than in France—

---

[1] Guillaume v. 93, cf. 100.

[2] Guillaume v. 414 (*Réflexions et projet de décret sur les fêtes décadaires*, par
Eschassériaux l'ainé, 23 nivôse l'An III).

[3] Guillaume v. 463 ff., headed by a quotation from Rousseau about raising the
level of men's souls to that of *les âmes antiques*; and proving, by explicit references, the Spartan origin of the antiphonal choirs.

that of the foe of foreign despots. From the outbreak of the war in 1792 references to the Persian wars were common. Dumouriez, holding his forest passes before Valmy, said that he was in the Thermopylae of France, but intended to do better than Leonidas. In autumn 1793, during the dechristianization movement, the town of Saint-Marcellin (Isère) renamed itself Thermopyles (much less famous than the new Marathon, however, which was meant to commemorate Marat as well as the battle). Babies called Léonidas are hard to find, however, though there were a few Lycurguses and even a Spartiate. Ostentatious republican rectitude led more often to Aristide or even Phocion, and Brutus was far and away the commonest classical name. In July 1794 the theatre, regarded as an important method of national education, and now heavily subsidized and controlled, produced its first Spartan show—there had been plenty with other classical backgrounds. This was a *Combat de Thermopyles*, in which Léonidas, no monarch now but a democratic general, prophesies a happy and kingless future for mankind. The battle is a smashing if dearly-won victory, directly causing the Persian retirement from Greece;[1] but none of these inaccuracies will have worried the popular audience.

Politicians with an eye on such useful productions were apt to congratulate the public on the appearance, or forthcoming appearance, of a new Tyrtaeus, or even a school of Tyrtaeuses. The name stood in verse for all that Demosthenes represented in prose. Poets and musicians were both dubbed, or dubbed themselves, with the coveted title. Lebrun seized an opportunity he had long been waiting for; Gossec led the musical claimants. But Rouget de l'Isle, author of the Marseillaise, was thought to qualify particularly well by fighting for the republic (against the rebels of the Vendée) as well as hymning it. It is perhaps owing to the popularity of the comparison now that nationalist struggles all over Europe in the next generations produce so many aspirants to the title of the new Tyrtaeus—forgetting no doubt that what Tyrtaeus had in fact urged his countrymen to do was to crush the Messenians' independence and reduce them to slavery.

But the Tyrtaeuses of 1793 or 1794 talked very little of Sparta. One pointed out that in both Sparta and Rome

[1] *Combat de Thermopyles ou l'école des guerriers, fait historique en trois actes et en prose, par Loaisel* [de Tréogate] l'an iii.

Ils n'étaient pas tous enfans,
Pas tous enfans de la patrie[1]

and another, in an *Élan Patriotique*, compared Mably to Demosthenes on the tribune at Athens, inspiring his people with hatred
for kings.[2] Since Demosthenes was Phocion's great opponent,
Mably should have been turning in his grave. In almost every
field Athens was able at last to trump her rival's cards. She could
resist the Persian monarch as well as Sparta could, and the Macedonian better—Demosthenes is not a mere orator now. She had
better tyrannicides, better republican martyrs (Lycurgus and Agis
are rare, and Cleomenes is even harder to find; royal birth and
extreme economic programmes presumably explain that). Even
those women who formed clubs and agitated for rights left
Sparta alone, unlike many earlier and later advocates of female
emancipation; perhaps they were wise, since Spartan women had
recently been regarded as either purely domestic or else excessively
immodest. They contented themselves with Brutus' wife and the
mother of the Gracchi, and a statue was erected to Phocion's wife,
whose virtues are reported by Plutarch.

On the other hand the catalogues for the Salon show an increasing fondness for Spartan themes. For a time these are those established over the previous decades. Lycurgus still presents his infant
nephew as king to the people in 1791, and even, under a more
tactful title, in 1793. This year no less than six Lacedaemonian
works were shown, of which two concern female heroism, and
two the life of Agis, with markedly revolutionary captions. In
1795 there were as many as four Spartan mothers, one the work of
a *citoyenne*. Thereafter the occasional Spartan subject tends to be
domestic or military (or both—javelin-throwing at a *fête domes-
tique* in 1798), but there is no Leonidas till 1810. A fairly consistent
time-lag, in short.

We need not, therefore, be surprised at the tendency, during
and immediately after the reign of the Jacobins, to find them
popularly associated with Athens rather than Sparta.

Ces Solons nés d'hiers, enfans réformateurs,

they are called in a play that rashly appeared on the boards early in

---

[1] *Couplets*, par Delattre de Metz, in *Les Concerts républicains*, ed. C. F. X.
Mercier (1795), p. 174.
[2] C. F. X. Mercier, *Le Despotisme et autres poésies patriotiques* (1795), p. 29.

PLATE 5

Leonidas at Thermopylae
(J.-L. David, Musée du Louvre)

1793, to cause uproar.[1] And in the comedies which, after Robespierre's fall, display comic figures who have taken classical names, it is easier, as it had been in fact, to find Aristides and Solon (and lots of Romans) than a single Spartan name. Robespierre himself was put on the stage under various tragic classical disguises, including every possible Athenian tyrant, not Peisistratus alone (also Catiline, Appius Claudius, and Nero). He does, it is true, also appear as Pausanias—necessarily, however, as an un-Spartan Spartan therefore. The preface to the published version of Trouvé's tragedy explains that the subject is the ninth of Thermidor and the main character its chief victim: 'la seule différence, c'est que ce dernier fut un lâche et vil scélérat, au lieu que Pausanias avait l'énergie du crime et mêlait de l'éclat à ses vices.' Robespierre had been accused often enough of aiming at a tyranny, and Pausanias' helots do rather nicely as *sans-culottes*, but in the interests of his parallel the author abandons ancient history to show Pausanias exercising his monstrous rule in the city itself and using a corrupt and sanguinary tribunal to destroy his crowds of victims, including a heroic girl and many members of the senate. It is this body that gathers courage to bring about his fall—the ephors are not mentioned. Trouvé however cannot forbear to introduce Pausanias' mother, who draws the moral.

> Bourreau de ton pays
> Tu veux par la Terreur étouffer l'énergie
> De quiconque oserait braver la tyrannie!
> Tu crois pour commander à des républicains
> Que toujours dans le sang il faut plonger ses mains . . .
> Mais le tien à ton tour expiera tant de crimes
> Et ton supplice ira consoler tes victimes.[2]

After Thermidor the republican temper grew less heroic, and apart from certain survivors of the previous period interest in the political examples of antiquity shifted or declined—though taste in many respects was as classical, and as Greek, as ever. Gradually there asserted itself the belief, occasionally put forward during the Revolution itself, that half-baked admiration for antiquity, and more especially Rome and Sparta, was largely responsible for the Revolution and above all the Terror—a belief that slides into and

---

[1] J. L. Laya, *L'Ami des loix.*
[2] C.-J. Trouvé, *Pausanias,* 1810 (produced 1795).

is nourished by the mere description of it as Spartan. Perhaps it is not clear which path Lakanal is taking when, shortly after Thermidor, he shows the new tendency to paint Robespierre and all his crew as idolaters of war and ignorance, and says (primarily, but perhaps only primarily, of education) 'j'admire autant qu'un autre l'austérité des Spartiates, auxquels on prétendait nous assimiler', but how much better it is to develop, rather than repress, and so forth.[1]

At any rate, the myth appears full-grown next year, when Volney employed his *Leçons d'Histoire* at the École Normale to point out the dangers of inaccurate historical knowledge to the half-educated. The learned Volney began his intellectual career in Holbach's Salon, was a prominent deputy in 1789, under suspicion in 1793, a close ally of the First Consul but a disillusioned opponent first of the emperor and then of Louis XVIII—a perfect link between two ages. He has all the contempt of many of the *philosophes* for antiquity, their fear of enthusiasm, their international and pacific outlook, all strengthened by his own experience, which included life abroad and membership of the society of the *Amis des Noirs*. Just when superstition seemed to be declining,

une tempête nouvelle emportant les esprits dans un extrême contraire, a renversé l'édifice naissant de la raison et nous a fourni un nouvel exemple de l'influence de l'histoire, et de l'abus de ses comparaisons. Vous sentez que je veux parler de cette manie de citations et d'imitations grecques et romaines, qui, dans ce dernier temps, nous ont comme frappés de vertige. Noms, surnoms, vêtemens, usages, lois, tout a voulu être spartiate ou romain.[2]

In his anxiety to exculpate modern thought Volney puts it all down to classical education (though he also attacks Rousseau and calls recent persecutors his disciples). He does not spare Athens, equally aggressive and equally tarred with political and civil inequality; but it is the governments of Sparta and Rome which he likens to that of the Mamelukes or the Dey of Algiers (not to

---

[1] Parker, *The Cult of Antiquity and the French Revolutionaries*, p. 2 quotes a conservative journalist, Regnaud de St. Angély, who put republican agitation down to a thoughtless admiration for Sparta and Rome as early as summer 1791 (*Observations, Postillon par Calais*, no. 519, p. 2). Desmoulins, not alone, believed in the influence of school education on himself and on others.

[2] *Leçons d'Histoire*, 1803 (*Oeuvres Complètes de Volney*, 1860, especially pp. 592-3).

mention Huns, Vandals, and wild beasts). The Spartans in particular had followed 'une vraie règle de la Trappe', and after his visit to America Volney described them as savage enough to be the Iroquois of the ancient world. All familiar language, with a new edge to it—for recent politicians had been *de modernes Lycurgues*; echoed, too, by various historical or pseudo-historical studies on the ancient world.

Such a belief could only have found sustenance in the abortive Babeuf plot of 1796. This was not simply because Babeuf's economic theories, which sprang directly from the Utopian communism of the pre-Revolutionary period, could be seen as the logical development of Jacobin egalitarianism. In addition, though Babeuf himself had finally repudiated Robespierre, some of his friends had not, and many of his followers in 1796 were not true communists at all, but the democrats of 1793, alarmed at the progress of reaction and the increasing grip of the new plutocracy.

As the name he chose suggests, Gaius Gracchus Babeuf's main point of reference in antiquity was the struggles of the Roman tribunes to impose limitations on the possession of land. But here at last was someone with no reason to be nervous of Sparta or interested in Athens (the writings of the conspirators betray a contempt for intellect and the arts). Babeuf had always insisted that a republic without equal division of land was imperfect, and associated such a programme with Lycurgus and Agis, as well as Camillus and the Gracchi, believing it only possible to introduce in such crises as France was now undergoing. Commerce, as at present organized, was disastrous; so that he could even sympathize with Lycurgus' abolition of it.[1] In 1793 he at least considered Lycurgus and Agis proper names to consider taking (it would be interesting to know how many of the few who did take them were socialists or communists). Furthermore, the *Égaux* (the name was perhaps, or perhaps not, directly inspired by the *homoioi*?) were taught by a colleague to look back regretfully to

> vous, Lycurgues des Français
> O Marat! Saint-Just! Robespierre![2]

We might perhaps add that our old friend Laignelot, the author of

[1] *Pages choisies de Babeuf*, ed. Dommanget (1935), p. 129 (letter to J. M. Coupé, 10 Sept. 1791); p. 207 (to Ch. Germain, 28 July 1793).

[2] P. Buonarroti, *Conspiration pour l'égalité . . .* (1828), p. 239.

Agis, after an active career as a Montagnard and a Robespierrist narrowly escaped implication in the plot.

Nothing, however, could interrupt the triumphal course of Sparta's patriotic armies. The poet Fontanes, very far from an extremist, had embarked on a vast and never completed epic on the Persian wars, inspired by *Anacharsis*. He read parts of the Thermopylae episode in public in 1797, to great applause. It aims at lofty serenity in its portrait of Leonidas, and attains traditional heartless heroism in that of his wife. But the feeling for Greek myth, shown in Hercules' appearance to Leonidas and the latter's apotheosis, and the trace of lyrical melancholy show why this friend of Chateaubriand's is regarded as a precursor of the Romantics. The Thermopylae episode, however, if a favourite of its creator's, was meant to be subordinate; we begin at the Olympic games, and Themistocles and Athens were to have been the main heroes of the epic.[1] Meanwhile, the government looked with a friendly eye on *Léonidas ou le départ des Spartiates*, a *tableau lyrique* by young Guilbert (de Pixérécourt, the prolific melodramatist), produced in 1799 but conceived some years earlier.[2]

Napoleon, an Italian and the conqueror of Italy, tended to see himself in Roman, not Greek terms—except that at the time of his eastern adventures he was pleased to dwell upon the exploits of Alexander as well as Caesar. The war with England had from the start been compared with Rome's struggle against the commercial, maritime, and perfidious Carthage. Virgils were thus in more demand than Tyrtaeuses. But Napoleon's eastern ambitions were not without relevance, as we shall soon see, to the cult of Thermopylae; and during his reign the most famous of all paintings on a Spartan subject was being painted—David's *Léonidas*. Napoleon went to visit it; but his comment—why paint the vanquished?—does not suggest that he saw himself in the rôle.

Having got going on Sparta, painters seem to have found it hard to relinquish. There are a number of titles in the Salon catalogue now, almost without exception military or military-domestic; Spartan mothers, wives, and fathers part from or receive home

---

[1] *La Grèce sauvée* (*Oeuvres de M. de Fontanes*, 1859, p. 269; especially Chant ii, pp. 291 ff.).

[2] Unpublished. Presented to the Opéra in 1795 and recommended in the official report of 6 pluviôse l'An VII (H. Welschinger, *Le Théâtre de la Révolution*, 1880, p. 130).

The painting was first exhibited in 1814. 'Tous les Spartiates

members of their family. The politicians, Lycurgus and Agis, have at last receded. David's painting was on the easel for many years. This remarkable composition, depicting nude youths and helmeted warriors, is dominated by the figure of Leonidas, seated and gazing gravely at us (or at his impending doom) from the centre of the canvas. David regarded the work as his masterpiece.

His pupils, set to produce ideas on the subject, came up with battle-scenes. But 'je veux donner à cette scène quelque chose de plus grave, de plus réfléchi, de plus religieux. Je veux peindre un général et ses soldats se préparant au combat comme de véritables Lacédémoniens, sachants bien qu'ils ne s'échapperont pas . . . je ne veux ni mouvement, ni expression passionnés . . . je veux caractériser ce sentiment profond, grand et religieux qu'inspire l'amour de la patrie.' And so, in the end, the spirit of 1793 was embodied in a Spartan work after all. For one can hardly doubt that it was of his political as well as his artistic career that David was thinking when, at the very end of his life, he recalled his ideas and intentions about the picture and said proudly 'sais-tu bien qu'il n'y avait que David qui pût peindre Léonidas?'

The painting was first exhibited in 1814. 'Tous les Spartiates avaient été exterminés dans la campagne de Russie et dans la guerre de l'invasion. On montrait les Thermopyles à des vaincus.'[1] So wrote the old Terrorist Barère—who, however, after Waterloo and as a member of the Assembly active in the brief attempt to unite Napoleonic and liberal support against the foreigner, proposed to address the army as Spartiates and remind them that Thermopylae was fought both for the monarch and for the country and its holy laws.[2]

The attempt was unsuccessful. But after the Restoration classical sympathies were common among the liberal opposition, while Romanticism, with its emphasis on religion and the Middle Ages, was at first identified with reaction.

> Vive Aristote, Rome et Sparte . . .
> Je suis classique et libéral![3]

Sparta, however, could surely only mean Thermopylae to anyone calling himself a liberal.

But now we are, as well, in the era of philhellenism. Europe had

---

[1] *Mémoires de B. Barère* (1843) iv. 174. [2] Ibid. iii. 222.
[3] Émile Deschamps, *Oeuvres complètes* (1872) ii. 108.

long found it easy to see any struggle in the Mediterranean against the Turk in terms of the Greek, and especially the Spartan, struggle against Persia. In the late eighteenth century this became truer than ever. Not only were the French and English, at least, particularly up for their own purposes in Spartan history; it was now plain that, though the modern Greeks might possess some Spartan characteristics, they could lay claim to few Athenian qualities, apart from trickery and cunning. Furthermore, it became generally known that the inhabitants of the part of Greece proper that bore perhaps the most prominent part in all resistance to the Turk were supposed to be descended from the ancient Spartiates.

The fierce inhabitants of the Mani—Cape Matapan, the ancient Cape Taenarum at the south-western extremity of Laconia—were in effect still independent, in their mountain retreats, of Turkish control. Ignorant and wild as they were, some realized, or were supposed to have realized, that they were regarded by Byzantine[1] and later scholars as the remnant of the ancient Spartiates. Their manners, including the warlike character of their women, said the French historian Rulhière, who talks like the friend of Rousseau and Mably that he was, 'les a rendu sinon dignes de cette gloire, au moins dignes d'y prétendre'.[2] He tells us that for three centuries their councils of elders had called themselves in all their dealings the senate of Lacedaemon (which one may take leave to doubt); and that when, in 1770, the Maniotes rebelled in support of the unfortunate Russian attempt to raise Greece, they sent a 'Spartiate delegation' to Fyodor Orloff, who was in Italy preparing the expedition. Orloff, who certainly had a penchant for the classics, organized the heterogeneous troops at his disposal in Greece into two 'Spartiate legions', and when one of these took Mistra the Russian bulletins, falling into a still common topographical error, made play with the liberation of Sparta. Voltaire's correspondence with Catherine shows him watching the progress of 'ces braves Spartiates' with an interest in which he was certainly not alone.[3]

---

[1] Constantine Porphyrogenitus in the tenth century endorsed their descent from 'ancient Romans', i.e. Greeks.

[2] C. C. de Rulhière, *Histoire des révolutions de Pologne* (1778–90) xi. viii (vol. iii, p. 101). The laconophobe and mythicidal de Pauw proves all connection impossible and grumbles about the fuss, op. cit., vol. ii, p. 414.

[3] *Documents of Catherine the Great . . .*, ed. W. F. Reddaway (1931); letters

By the end of the century French ideas were filtering into Greece, strengthening both the desire for a revolt that should not be dependent on Russia or even the Orthodox Church, and also a classical revival in thought and art. Of course this was not exclusively Spartan; but Spartan themes, in particular the fatal number three hundred, run through much of the popular patriotic verse of the succeeding period. The first and best known of the new Tyrtaeuses, as they were inevitably hailed, was Rhigas, who produced a patriotic hymn inspired by the Marseillaise complete with apostrophe to Leonidas.[1]

Napoleon's eastern plans aroused great expectations, and the arrival of French troops in the Ionian islands in 1797 was welcomed. Napoleon reminded their commander to make propaganda about Marathon and Thermopylae. He also sent an embassy to the Maniotes, 'ces dignes descendants de Sparte, le seul peuple de l'ancienne Grèce qui ait su conserver sa liberté'. His envoys were members of the curious Maniote colony in Corsica, and, if we may believe the somewhat fanciful account published, the occasion was one for an orgy of Spartiate sentiment on both sides.[2]

Can one really also believe that the Maniotes at some point adopted as the device on their banners the famous phrase 'with your shield or on it'?[3] What at any rate is certain is that when in 1821 the Greek revolution proper broke out the Maniotes were among the first to rise. Their leader Petros Mavromichalis, known as Petrobey, immediately addressed an appeal for support to the powers of Europe, dated from the camp of the Spartiate forces and referring to himself as the Spartiate leader—and as such he naturally often appears in foreign accounts.[4]

[1] C. Rhigas, Ὕμνος πατριωτικός (1798).

[2] *Voyage de D. et N. Stephanopoli en Grèce pendant les années 1797 et 1798 . . .* (1800).

[3] So says G. Isambert, *L'Indépendance Grecque et l'Europe* (1900), p. 54, perhaps rhetorically. Contrast G. Finlay, *History of the Greek Revolution* (1877) iv. 33: 'The inhabitants of Maina have lost all memory of the very names of Laconia and Sparta.'

[4] S. Tricoupis, Ἱστορία τῆς Ἑλληνικῆς Ἐπαναστάσεως (1853–7) i. 368. He may be said in a sense to have stuck to his role; see Julius Millingen, *Memoires of the Affairs of Greece . . .* (1831), p. 28. He was declared to have

xlii, xliv, xlviii, lviii, lxi, lxii, cxi. Catherine excuses her action in making peace by saying the Spartiates have much degenerated since antiquity.

In other parts of Greece other ancient memories were evoked, and the naval operations of the next years gave Athenian history a considerable place. But all over Europe the flood of literature provoked by the struggle tends to give pride of place to Leonidas. Liberals—for it was among liberals that Greece obtained most support—forgot, as Voltaire had done, that they really disliked Sparta. In France at least the movement was more literary than political, and finally conquered all but the most reactionary circles. Chateaubriand, visiting Sparta some years before, had as we should expect shown no great enthusiasm for her *moeurs*, nor for considering the pirates of Taygetus the heirs of Lacedaemonian liberty. He preferred, he said, the memory of Helen and the poet Alcman to that of black broth and the *crypteia*; but he despised neither glory nor liberty, and was moved to cry aloud the name Leonidas, to which no echo replied, and to seek his tomb, in vain.[1] Now in his influential plea for the support of Greece he asserted the necessity of liberating 'la patrie de Léonidas'.[2]

While liberals and royalists, classics and romantics united in literary activity, Thermopylae made an unprecedented number of poetic appearances.[3] The culmination came with the enthusiastic reception accorded to Michel Pichat's tragedy *Léonidas*, with Talma in the main role, late in 1825. Chateaubriand intervened with the censorship in its favour, and indeed royalists could praise, with Hugo, its portrait of a *roi libérateur*. Romantics hailed it somewhat prematurely as a triumph for the new Romantic drama (though generally they preferred exotic present-day Greece as a setting). 'On applaudissait', said the author in his preface to

[1] *Itinéraire de Paris à Jérusalem* (1811) i. 103, 107, 112, 115.

[2] *Note sur la Grèce* (1825).

[3] See Eugène Asse, *L'Indépendance de la Grèce et les poètes de la Restauration* (1898). In his lists of titles we may notice for 1825 J. Barbey, *Aux héros de Thermopyles*; for 1827 C. Gouverne, *Léonidas aux Thermopyles*; Elisa Mercoeur, *Le Songe ou les Thermopyles*; A. Debay, *L'Ombre de Léonidas à Fabvier* (who fought in Greece). N.b. also in 1820 Gaspard de Pons, *Othryadas*, the Spartan who returned from Thermopylae only to die at Plataea, having been rejected, here, by his (dying) mother. Casimir Delavigne includes *Tyrtée aux Grecs* in his *Trois nouvelles Messéniennes* (1822).

offered to deliver the Peloponnese to the Pasha of Egypt, and the Greeks 'compared his conduct to that of Pausanias, and would willingly have made his end the same'.

the published work, 'dans le Léonidas, le Léonidas nouveau, ce Marcos Botzaris, dont la mort si héroïquement méditée a re-suscité l'héroïsme des Thermopyles' (the comparison had been popularized by Byron). There were frequent contemporary references in the play, culminating in a great prophecy by Léoni-das about the influence of Sparta's memory. Otherwise we may remark that the Spartan mother is still indispensable, and even the renegade King Demaratus displays Spartan virtue by returning to the right side in the nick of time.

Philhellenism perhaps helped to keep up the number of pictures on Spartan themes exhibited at the Salon from 1815 to 1830. They are even more innocuously sentimental and military than before, and perhaps largely derived from a self-perpetuating tradition of suitable subjects for history painting—though, even in this restricted area, it is as clear as it is in England that pure history painting is giving way to genre and landscape.

In spite of this all but general infatuation, it was largely, it seems, the continued identification of the principles of the Revolution and of Sparta that determined serious French apprecia-tion of the latter far into the nineteenth century. Barère, and he was not alone in protesting, complained that from 1795 to 1832 each wave of reaction had blamed the Convention for imitating Sparta and Rome, whereas that body had in fact known perfectly well how different France's character and problems were, and it was only the virtue of the ancients it imitated.[1] But a connection, even if not strictly a causal one, was on many lips. The liberal Benjamin Constant, faced with the German philosopher Fichte's political theories, wrote that the authors of 'ces idées Spartiates . . . recommençeraient Robespierre avec les meilleures intentions du monde'.[2] Victor Hugo declared that the impious *sagesse* of Voltaire had attempted forcibly to set

> Le casque étroit de Sparte au front du vieux Paris

and indeed was so besotted with past times 'mal lus et mal compris' that

> Par ses embrassements réveillé sous la terre
> Lycurgue qu'elle épouse enfante Robespierre.[3]

---

[1] Fragment quoted in H. Carnot's preface to *Mémoires de Barère* i. 102.
[2] *Journal intime*, ed. Mistler (1945), p. 183 (May 1804).
[3] 'A Alphonse Rabbe' (1835).

(Poor Voltaire!) Sparta's reign was short, however, for, as Hugo wrote elsewhere of his own birth in 1802,

> Ce siècle avait deux ans! Rome remplaçait Sparte.
> Déjà Napoléon perçait sous Bonaparte.[1]

And indeed Rome might well be detached to stand for the empire, leaving her Greek ally to represent the Revolution alone.

Even surviving revolutionaries contributed to the process. Barère, in spite of the protest quoted above, speaks as casually as anyone of the constitution of 1793 as 'trop parfaite, trop sévère, trop Spartiate', of the 'députés Spartiates du côté gauche', and, in a much quoted passage, of Saint-Just as their perfect representative: 'S'il eut vécu dans le temps des républiques grecques il aurait été Spartiate. Ses fragments prouvent qu'il aurait choisi les institutions de Lycurgue. Il a eu le sort d'Agis et de Cléomène ... son style était laconique, son caractère était austère, ses moeurs politiques sévères'.[2] This portrait was elaborated in the memoirs, untrustworthy but eloquent, of Charles Nodier.[3]

Saint-Just and his colleagues indeed were sometimes contrasted with their chief opponents. When Buonarroti undertook to vindicate the memory of Babeuf, he prefaced his work with an analysis of the Revolution proper, in which the Robespierrists' enemies all appear as selfish aristocrats, and his supporters as the sole disinterested and democratic group. 'Ceux-là [the Girondins and Indulgents] soupiraient après les richesses, les superfluités et l'éclat d'Athènes; ceux-ci voulaient la frugalité, la simplicité et la modestie des beaux jours de Sparte.' He adds that such classical comparisons are not altogether adequate and illuminating. But his own economic theories still involve the names of Minos, Lycurgus, Plato, More, Mably and all (and defending the Terror by various ancient examples he claims that no one blamed Lycurgus for putting a few Lacedaemonian aristocrats out of the way).[4] Such language was however already out of date. The new socialist generation, in France as elsewhere, dealing with the problems of a

[1] *Les Feuilles d'automne* i (1830). In a philhellenic context, however, Hugo like anyone else could appeal to Leonidas.

[2] Ibid. ii. 108; ii. 60; iv. 408.

[3] Charles Nodier, *Souvenirs* (1850) i. 1. Cf. his introduction to Saint-Just's *Institutions* (1831).

[4] P. Buonarroti, *Conspiration pour l'égalité, dite de Babeuf* (1828), pp. 5–6, 9, 50 n.

modern and increasingly industrialized society, has little time for antiquity.

This notion that Robespierrists and Indulgents could be described as Spartans and Athenians was more or less supported by a survivor of the latter party, who repeatedly stressed his admiration for a Periclean republic *à la* Desmoulins—*lois*, but also *luxe*—as opposed to Lycurgan despotism. Indeed at one point he wrote an epitaph for himself as REPUBLICANUS PERICLIDIS MORE— meaning, presumably, a republican after the fashion of Pericles, but the Latin is very revolutionary.[1]

Leading historians of the Revolution, after the middle of the century, generally have their eyes fixed primarily on other sources of influence, and other comparisons, than the classical ones. But Taine for one accepted the picture of a Spartan and an Athenian party—though with up-to-date, German-influenced scholarship he reproached the former for not seeing that it was Dorian tradition, not Lycurgus, that made the country what it was. And if, after the end of the century, protests began to be uttered against regarding Sparta and Rome as powerful influences, it seems likely that a very large proportion of those who have written on the period have somewhere used the description 'Spartan' for individuals or groups. So much is doubtless justifiable—or it would be, if 'Spartan' itself were not so slippery a term, and if its use as a compendious summing-up were not so easily mistaken for an assertion, at the least, that those so described expressed great admiration for that state, to the exclusion of others, in particular Athens.

Closely related to the exaggeration of Sparta's place in the Revolution, though less deeply rooted, perhaps, was the exaggeration of Sparta's influence on, or the Spartan character of, Rousseau's thought; Taine is again guilty here. It tends in the same way to mean excessive stress on any totalitarian or repressive aspects. Rousseau himself has by now been rescued from this interpretation. But has the whole tradition that we have been discussing left some trace on the apparently still widespread belief that the *philosophes* in general, or most of them, were admirers of Sparta?

Meanwhile, as in other parts of Europe, Athens was entering on

[1] M.–A. Baudot, *Notes historiques*, ed. Mme E. Quinet (1893), p. 210; cf. pp. 15, 122, 127, 165, 166 (written in the twenties or thirties).

her long-delayed inheritance. At first she sometimes still suffers
from being regarded as another, if minor, model for the revolutionaries, but soon these are being reproached by historians for
ignoring 'true' antiquity, that of Athens. France had here, as we
have seen, her own tradition of admiration for, and indeed of
association with, Athens on grounds of polish and culture. But the
German idealization of Greece and Athens now had its effect
across the Rhine (some admiration for the vigorous Dorians
resulted from the inevitable translation of K. O. Müller's famous
book, but these seem, in France, to take specifically Spartan shape
remarkably seldom). Two pro-Athenian English scholars,
Thirlwall, whose work Flaubert took to Greece with him, and
of course Grote, were also influential. The leading French
historian of antiquity in the middle of the century, Victor Duruy,
condemns Lycurgus' aims as impracticable, inflexible, and often
immoral (and refers to the equally paradoxical Rousseau).[1]
Fustel de Coulanges, a little later, is no more enthusiastic, whether
in his well-known book *La Cité Antique* or in a special work on
Spartan property institutions confuting revived theories about
primitive communism.[2]

The revival of interest in antiquity, and especially Greek
antiquity, that began to mark many aspects of French taste from
the 1840s has been much written on. It might turn to the charming simplicities of the archaic period, and it soon discovered the
sophisticated luxuries and the subtle religious strivings of the late
classical period; but in so far as it did draw inspiration from a
particular age, rather than from Greek mythology and life in
general, it was the age of Pericles and Pheidias. There was a love-
affair with its refined and delicate taste and intelligence, sometimes
also with its generous devotion to country and liberty; all virtues
that the prosaic modern age, and, especially, to some, the Second
Empire, lacked. 'Le haut génie de la Grèce est tout dans Pallas
Athéné', says Michelet in his rhapsodic *Bible de l'humanité*;[3] the
Athenians only proved their generous magnanimity by their
childish admiration for the *moeurs* of Sparta, barbaric and
Machiavellian at once, and oppressive of the true Greek liveliness,
joy, and freedom. It is well known how to Renan Athens was the

---

[1] *Histoire de la Grèce*, (1846 etc.) p. 185.
[2] *Études sur la propriété à Sparte*, (1888).
[3] *Bible de l'humanité*, (1864) pp. 181 ff.

representative of *le miracle Grec*, all reason and serenity, while Sparta, in a brief aside, was but the dead and done with *maîtresse d'erreurs sombres*.[1] The long list of atticizers, as the Greeks would have called them, need not here be detailed; but the striking lack of interest which poetry and the visual arts show in Sparta is worth noticing.

Nothing could be more detached from old traditions than the treatment which Hugo, late in life, gave to the Three Hundred. 'Les Trois Cents' evokes a sinister and exotic Asia, and the arrogance of Xerxes, which culminates in his traditional order to give three hundred stripes to the unruly Hellespont. But from these stripes Neptune creates three hundred soldiers,

> Et Xercès les trouva debout aux Thermopyles.[2]

The mass of verse by poets of the generation after Hugo which is inspired by Greek themes seems hardly ever to turn to Sparta at all. But, as so often in France, the theatre has a neat comment to make. No one familiar with the authors of *l'Ilote*,[3] Charles Monselet, famous in his day as a gourmet, and the better-remembered Paul Arène, would expect any sort of laconism in their little comedy. No indeed; stupid Spartiate uncle seeks to keep half-Athenian nephew to the straight and narrow by displaying a helot *abruti par l'orgie*. But the helot concerned turns out to be an exiled Athenian in borrowed garments (Alcibiades' *valet*, to be precise) getting drunk the only way available. His ironic harangues convert all the other characters to the joys of life as known in Athens.

In the visual arts subjects from ancient history made way for a new repertory from the Middle Ages and modern literature, and later were almost exclusively taken from contemporary life. Delacroix' great decorative schemes, however, remained fairly traditional in subject-matter. He more than once painted Lycurgus consulting the Pythian oracle; but this is simply a lovely and mysterious scene of sacrifice before an enthroned priestess. Better known, perhaps, is his drawing of Spartan girls wrestling. It has been pointed out that this is one of the rare subjects that permit the Romantic painter to treat the female nude in violent action.

[1] *Prière sur l'Acropole* (1876; reprinted in *Souvenirs d'enfance*, 1883).
[2] In *La Légende des siècles*; 'Les Trois Cents' dates from 1873.
[3] 1875.

Degas' early but famous painting of *Jeunes filles Spartiates* leaves the philosophic, and indeed the Romantic, tradition even further behind. It is simply a study of naked youth in action or preparing for action. There is no moral to be drawn from these awkward young bodies and this bare landscape, both as un-Greek as could be. But its ancestry goes back to a group of pictures on the same theme exhibited in the Salons of 1817 and 1819, and thus, indirectly, to the first French painter to choose a Spartan subject, Cochin, the friend of Diderot and other *philosophes*.

One of the few French writers who protested against what he regarded as the modern undervaluation of Sparta was Louis Ménard, republican, democrat, and defender of polytheism. But even he, though placing the free and intelligent Spartan above the brutal Roman as a type of courage and patriotism, neither places them on an equality with the Athenians he adored nor considers them as in any way a model for the present.[1] However, it was to Ménard that Maurice Barrès turned when, early in this century, his *Voyage de Sparte* revealed his reaction against the Athenian ideals of the previous generation, of Taine, Renan, and the archaeologists of the French School at Athens. He can admire, he cannot feel for these ideals. He is most at home contemplating the remains of the Frankish occupation of Greece. But Mistra is not the only place in the Eurotas valley to inspire his enthusiasm. The whole landscape, with heroic Taygetus dominating the sensuous plain, breathes magnanimity and evokes Leonidas and Helen in equilibrium and due balance. Modern Greece should send her children here to learn to be Greeks, to revive the 'traditions doriennes, graves et vigoureuses'. It is not the artificial Sparta of Plutarch and David but a vital, even brutal place of Dorian lance and lyre. 'Je sais tout ce qu'on a dit sur la dureté orgueilleuse de Sparte. Ces critiques sentent l'esprit subalterne.' And 'Quant à moi, j'admire dans Sparte un prodigeux haras.' But Barrès, who does not recur elsewhere in his work to Sparta, was perhaps, as has been suggested, aiming at little more than a provocative *jeu d'esprit*; his friend and fellow-nationalist Maurras, incidentally, was so fascinated by his visit to Athens that he never got to to the rest of Greece at all. It is in Germany that a Sparta closely related to that of Barrès was to be taken seriously; so seriously as to become sinister.

[1] *La Morale avant les philosophes*, (1860).

18

ITALY IN THE EIGHTEENTH CENTURY

VICO and the theatre between them earn Italy a chapter to herself here, even if a short one. As so often in more important matters, Vico's attitude to Athens and Sparta is remarkably original and pregnant for the future, though it also bears some resemblance to much enlightened thought of the early eighteenth century. In the *Scienza Nuova*[1] he relegates Sparta firmly to a primitive stage in human progress. Upon the primeval theocracies, he argues, followed the heroic aristocracies. For these, early Rome above all, but also Sparta, provide the material—with a glance at the 'revived barbarism' of the Middle Ages, from which Venice is a survival. Heroic, in fact, is virtually a synonym of barbaric. In heroic states only the heroes possessed land or civil rights—thus Sparta. They controlled religion—thus most clearly Rome—even believing themselves divine or of divine descent. Heroic education was cruel, 'as in the case of the unlettered Lacedaemonians, who were the heroes of Greece' and subjected their unloved children to the whipping contests. The unwalled nature of heroic cities would seem perhaps chiefly inspired by Sparta. The heroes were arrogant and violent, and oppressed the poor. Laws and magistrates protect the freedom only of the few; for example, it was the ephors who had poor King Agis (rather a favourite of Vico's) strangled for attempting to pass popular measures affecting debt and inheritance. Plato and Aristotle both judged Sparta's laws to be savage and cruel.

Vico insists that it has been a great error to regard Lycurgus and other early lawgivers as supremely wise. *Omne ignotum pro magnifico*; crude, obscure, and small origins tend to be exaggerated and we also tend to judge by what is familiar to us. In fact, primitive peoples are unable in their laws even to formulate universal rules, but only concern themselves with particular

[1] G. B. Vico, *Scienza Nuova* (3rd ed., 1744) ii.

commands and prohibitions (the revolutionary belief that the historian must appeal to the philologist is here most interestingly put into practice). The third and final stage in history is marked by the fully human state, where the law is dictated not by force but by developed human reason. To this class belonged Athens, the most humane of all states, after Solon's legislation; so, ultimately, did Rome. Here the free people is sovereign. The government may, however, be entrusted to an aristocracy, and in the end, to avoid faction, the ideal form, that of popular monarchy, must be established. Civil rights are equal for all, the laws are well understood, the priesthood open to everyone, the powerful are prevented from oppressing the weak, and sufficient property is ensured to the poor.

The greatest Italian thinker of the century was little read outside his native Naples until the Romantic period. In Naples, the first home of 'political economy', thinkers congregated. Here, as in other intellectual centres in Italy, there was acquiescence in enlightened monarchy, interest in economic and penal questions, and pride in the arts and sciences. References to Sparta fall under various influences, perhaps mostly French, but rarely involving approval of more than one or two aspects—most often that of public education.

Since the Italians themselves regarded their theatrical achievements as their main contribution to European civilization at this period, it would be unkind not to treat here one of the few partly successful works of art that this book can mention, even though its chief creator was not Italian at all. Supposedly Lacedaemonian opera librettos continued to be written, or re-set, throughout the eighteenth century, but in 1770 we come on one that is out of the ordinary. The last fruit of Gluck's collaboration with the poet Calsabigi, who always claimed to be largely responsible for the operatic reforms associated with their names and with ideas of truth, nature, and Greek simplicity, was *Paride ed Elena*. It treats of Paris' arrival in Laconia and his wooing of Helen; and, taking his cue from the Ovidian *Heroides*, Calsabigi gave mythological Sparta characteristics from the historical period. In the preface to the score, Gluck (or perhaps Calsabigi for him) explains how he sought to enrich the somewhat thin plot by recalling the traditional contrast of Phrygian and Spartan (particularly obvious to a musician, on account of the fame of the Phrygian and Dorian modes). Thus while Paris' airs are exquisite and languorous, Gluck admits to sacrificing everything to dramatic value in the music of the Spartans, and in the *nativa rozzezza* of that given to the naturally proud and modest Queen Helen, here represented as unmarried. A newly-serious exploitation of national contrasts inspired Gluck elsewhere, and his efforts here are considered by qualified judges as not unsuccessful. The choral and balletic aspects of opera, developed and integrated by Gluck, here issue inevitably in a Spartan festival with choruses to Apollo and martially gymnastic dances. Probably the French interest in Spartan fêtes is relevant, innocent of political ideas though the work is.

Unlike the next one on our list. It seems suitable that Alfieri, in whose mental progress beyond the level of the ordinary young Piedmontese nobleman Plutarch played a considerable part, should have left us, among other and mostly Roman tragedies from that source, one on King Agis. It emerges from the *Parere* appended to the play that he saw Sparta as a mixed government, conformably with his admiration for the classics, Machiavelli, and England, rather than with his admiration for Montesquieu. His specifically political writings do not treat in detail of Sparta, although it is worth noting that he approves Rousseau's enthusiasm, if not his theories, and would admit some redistribution of wealth; and also that 'the people' he cares for consists of the 'solid citizens', not the plebeians. *Il principe e le lettere*, however, reveals an enthusiasm for Lycurgus, who was far above other princes (mainly through not wanting to be a prince at all). This work, with its thesis that literature only flourishes in free states, might seem unwise to remind us of Sparta, but Alfieri's curious identification of the good writer with the good citizen bears him through. In all essentials Lycurgus *was* a great writer, and *veri letterati* were unnecessary, false ones impossible, where virtue alone reigned. Nonetheless, poets did exist in Sparta, enthusiastic and efficacious encomiasts of virtue, and so did orators of admirable pith and brevity; while the lack of scientists was a matter of no importance.

Although Alfieri's compact, energetic, and nervous style might appear suitably laconic, *Agide* (1786) is not one of his best works. He himself thought that, even if the idea of liberty as the inspiration of a king rather than a private citizen was new and interesting, such a figure would be thought mad by a modern audience; he would have to wait for sympathy until Italy again provided a republic such as Rome's. It is true that none of the other plays on the subject can rival the passionate expression of Agis' grief at the corruption of a once mighty nation and his longing to restore her to her rightful place. If he can effect a regeneration that shall be (as Italy's needed to be) military as well as moral, and a political liberation amounting to thorough republicanism, he is ready to lose not only his throne and his life, but to allow his reputation to be maligned—a note that strikes freshly after the rows of Spartans as smugly conscious of the *exemplum* they are providing as of their country's welfare. The play's construction, too, is unusually compressed and effective; it does not lack dramatic scenes—even the final suicide of Agis and his mother, thus cheating their enemies, may be accounted such. But the actual purport of Agis', or Lycurgus', laws is vague; Alfieri's moral approach makes him sound naive here, and superficial, while as usual his personages are mere mouthpieces for his own ideas, and the brevity of his language is nearer the rhetorical artificiality of Silver Latin than vigorously natural laconism. Alfieri was always prone to strain and exaggeration; and these are certainly faults in the last tragedy by a writer of any distinction set in a scene which seems often to have encouraged these qualities in art.[1] It would be rash to say that Spartan themes were not, to use Alfieri's word, *tragediabili*; doubtless there are very few satisfactory tragedies on any subject, and very few indeed, for a complicated set of reasons, from the periods and places where interest in Sparta was highest. The analogous myth of republican Rome has been, as a subject, less fatal, though dangerous enough. But perhaps the noble Roman was never so inhumanly single-minded as the noble Spartiate; and his tongue, his surroundings, his whole tradition, have been a nearer, richer,

---

[1] Almost contemporary was another *Agide*, by Cosimo Giotti of Florence, whose editor claims that (by not introducing suicide) it is as superior morally as it is aesthetically inferior to Alfieri's. This much safer affair progresses via melodrama and bathos to the pious conclusion that Heaven backs those who revenge betrayed kings and oppressed innocence. We are told that it gained the author grand-ducal favour; also that here for the first time heroes appeared on the public stage without powder and plumes on their heads and spangles and embroidery on their coats—'troppo disdicevoli in ispecial agli Spartani' (*Teatro Moderno: Anno Teatrale* i (1804), tom. xi, cf. the life appended to Giotti's *Gusmano d'Almeida* in tom. v).

and more living reality to Rome's heirs in Europe. It is true, indeed, that Greek history proper, at least of the classical period and as opposed, of course, to Greek mythology, has produced few works of art in any fields to compare with those inspired by Roman history.

The Jacobin theatre in Italy annexed Alfieri's 'tragedies of liberty', to the fury of their author, now disgusted by the French Revolution; it is also said to have produced an *Agide* itself, by the versatile scribbler Michele Mallio. At this time, in obedience above all to the impulsion given first to republicanism and then, in reaction, to nationalism by the French and their invasions, touches of laconism can be found in various quarters. In Naples, at the time of the short-lived Parthenopean republic, Vincenzo Russo produced an egalitarian socialist Utopia with incidental reference to Sparta; the more moderate Pagano sketched a constitution roughly based on the French *Constitution de l'An III*, adorned with classical terms and an *eforato*, a not particularly Spartan council for preserving the laws; but he much preferred Athens. The highly intelligent historian and publicist Vincenzo Cuoco criticized this project as empty and abstract, and could not think Spartans and Romans anything but a disastrous direct model for Neapolitans and Milanese. He himself admired Napoleonic monarchy, popular and orderly, with enlightened views on the economy and legal reform, and strong military power. He gave his ideas classical dress in *Platone in Italia*, and says little of Sparta directly. But he did admire her education and public spirit, and felt that the revival of Italy demanded, as well as military recovery, a similar sense of citizenship. He even criticizes his admired Vico for praising the disorderly Athenians as civilized and employing the word '*barbari*' to cover the virtuous Spartans and courageous Samnites.

In others, laconism, which was never general, might be diluted by a pessimism natural in this unhappy period, rather than by historical sense. The hero of Foscolo's *Jacopo Ortis*, fleeing from Venice to his native village, sits under a plane-tree reading the lives of Lycurgus and Timoleon to his humble friends, but he has in truth despaired of Plutarch, antiquity, and mankind in general. All nations must be cruel conquerors; so were the Spartans. Elsewhere, too, Foscolo seems to feel that disappointment with Sparta, where he had hoped to find natural equality and justice, is disappointment with humanity itself.

19

SPARTA IN GERMANY

FOR all the mass of works dealing with German thought and German writers in their relation to *die Antike*, there seems to be no special study of the German attitude to Sparta[1]—perhaps because the Spartans are here so often concealed under the more general rubric of Dorians, or even of Greeks. But the story is of some interest. It could only be properly told by someone very familiar with the intellectual history of Germany during the past two centuries; but the following pages may provide a basis for further investigation.

The complex developments may, in simplified form, be stated thus: according to a long-supreme tradition, Sparta appeared as a relatively unimportant, even sometimes as an un-Greek, element in the Hellenic world—over-harsh and, as compared with other states (usually Athens in particular), lacking in respect for the individual and for his full mental and spiritual unfolding. This, somewhat adapted, is still the view of Hegel, even though the power of the state now balances the importance of the individual; and, adapted in a different direction, of Nietzsche, despite his rejection of so much in the traditional German picture of Greece. There was a second tradition, however, according to which the Dorians, and thus especially the Spartans, were the most truly and typically Hellenic of all the Greeks. It found its inspiration in Pindar, and Sparta's literary and artistic achievements (and therefore concentrated on a very early period); but it also approved more or less strongly of her political system. This second tradition has roots almost as old as the first—it was originally formulated by Friedrich von Schlegel—but only became dominant in the present century; the two interact—Nietzsche, indeed, contributed with some effect to the picture of the Dorians. The leading personages

---

[1] But G. Billeter, *Die Anschauungen vom Wesen des Griechentums* (1911) is a quarry from which much relevant material can be extracted; while for some evidence concerning more recent classical scholarship, see P. Janni, *La Cultura di Sparta Arcaica: Ricerche I* (1965), ch. i.

in the story are not, with some exceptions, either strictly political theorists or professional classical scholars; they usually belong to that class in which Germany has been so rich, the philosophers of history. To their mediation, to their habits of generalization, and to their tendency even to treat the past, on occasion, symbolically rather than historically, is due the fact that Sparta, and the ancient world in general, could be made to appear in such dramatically different yet always immediately relevant roles; and this in an age of profound and careful historical scholarship, when the contrasts between the ancient and modern world were well understood.

Taking up the outline of the tale in the early eighteenth century, we find that, before the Greek revival got under way, Spartan figures received an occasional mention in literature under first French and then English influence. German, like almost every other language, has its eighteenth-century tragedy on Agis. This is *Agis König zu Sparta*,[1] produced by Gottsched in his attempt to provide his countrymen with a proper theatrical repertory on the classical, or more accurately the French classical, model. This cramped and chilly work crowds the multifarious events of Plutarch's *Life* into the inevitable unities by means of an unconscionable series of messenger-speeches reporting meetings in the senate. It is too dependent on its source to leave much room for personal interpretation, but Agiatis (not a very forcefully Spartan female), who speaks Agis' epitaph, praises his concern with true glory and thus with his people's well-being, and also his moderation and *bürgerlich* simplicity:

> Die edle Mässigkeit, der sich sein Herz ergeben,
> Hiess ihn als König doch nach Art der Bürger leben.

But all attempts, whether engineered by his partisans or his enemies, to try, exile, or execute a king or otherwise attack absolutism arouse the author's horror. It is also made plain that Lycurgus had been a thorough cosmopolitan, especially in artistic matters. The work had less success than Gottsched's *Cato*, and indeed its author's literary dictatorship was soon to suffer a swift collapse.

---

[1] J. C. Gottsched, *Der Deutsche Schaubühne*, vol. vi. (1745). The play was probably written earlier. The Dutch and Hungarian representatives of the class (*Agis Koning van Lacedemonien*, 1701, and György Bessenyei's *Agis*, 1772) I cannot discuss.

During the subsequent enthusiasm for English literature,
J. A. Ebert, contributor to the famous *Bremer Beyträge* and translator of Young's *Night Thoughts*, was also responsible in 1749 for a
prose version of Glover's *Leonidas*, and it seems, from various
indications, that this work was widely read for many years in
Germany, though perhaps not only for its political message.[1]
Original novels and poems with classical settings continued to be
largely Rococo. But as, during the *Aufklärung*, feeling against the
rulers and their frequent misgovernment developed, political
thought began, if still feebly, to stir. Its weakness finds explanation
in the social and economic peculiarities of Germany, and the
tendency of the nobility and the still small middle class to be
directly dependent on the princes. However, both academic
republicanism, often with French roots, and admiration for the
English constitution did exist. The better-known publicists and
historians have little special interest in Sparta, and fall under
diverse influences in what they do say of her; but in 1762 an
obscure and anonymous work, describing itself as *Political and
Moral Considerations on the Spartan Legislation*[2] and drawing con-
fusedly on Montesquieu, Rousseau, and the English tradition to
express its hatred of despotism, deprecates the idea that the famous
Greek constitutions could never be revived, and proves, with
truly Germanic thoroughness, that England is an exact or indeed
perfected reproduction of Sparta.

Meanwhile, the great Greek revival was in the making. This
reaction against a narrow Christian pietism and an equally
narrow rationalism had resemblances, indeed links, with developments in France and elsewhere. But against Montesquieu or
Rousseau there stand, as its first major prophets, Winckelmann

[1] English editions were published in Breslau and Leipzig; in 1776 the German translation appeared in Zürich, with a fiery preface warning the *Eyds-
genossischen Jugend* against oligarchic as well as princely oppression. (Note also
a French prose translation, Geneva, 1738.)

[2] *Politische und Moralische Betrachtungen über die Spartanische Gesez-Gebung
des Lykurgus*, Frankfurt and Leipzig, 1762 (see esp. chapter xxi). Rome and
Carthage were tyrannic, Switzerland resembled more closely the Achaean
League. But France is England's Persia, the base Irish are her natural helots,
Scotland is a happier Messenia; English naval wars with Holland recall Sparta's
with Athens; the admittedly less impressive Alfred was her Lycurgus, Cromwell
her Nabis, etc., etc. Or should she be compared to a colony of Sparta, perhaps
Tarentum, where the same race, spirit, and laws subsisted in a more natural
environment?

and Lessing; it grew out of a revival of Greek studies in schools and universities, and its most vital controversies concern, not social or economic questions, but art, poetry, and mythology. And thus Greece came to mean first and foremost early and classical Greece, and especially Athens, while Rome was given but an inferior and secondary place. Either she was merely the modern world's gateway to Greece, the preserver of her sublime traditions; or she was regarded as tainted like her daughter France with artificiality and aridity.

Winckelmann, writing in 1755, derives the excellence of Greek art from that of Greek life. In a kind climate and untrammelled society Nature created human beings free and perfect in mind and body. Though the artist was thus enabled to rise beyond even perfect natural beauty to the ideal, the Greeks themselves partook to a great degree of the sublime qualities of Greek art (he means, and knows, chiefly sculpture)—above all, of the famous *edle Einfalt und stille Grosse*, noble simplicity and quiet grandeur of both form and spirit. Explaining why the Greeks were physically so beautiful, Winckelmann turns to Sparta—one could almost think he believed her institutions directed entirely to that end. He describes the Spartan youth, descended from heroes, undeformed by swaddling clothes, brought up to sleep on the ground, to swim and wrestle; and how they had to attend naked every tenth day before the ephors, who ordered them to diet if they were getting fat. No wonder they acquired their grand *Contour* (a leading characteristic of Greek sculpture). Youths and girls 'followed Nature' in their dress (stays were unknown); and both, by appearing naked in public, provided the artist with models incomparably finer than those available today. Here is perhaps one germ of a tendency to see the Spartans as an art-loving and art-inspiring people that has formed an element in most German admiration of Sparta. But Winckelmann gives his highest approval to the Athenians of the age opening with the fall of the tyrants—in fact, therefore, the period of rising democracy. Yet his complete lack of political interests is clear. To him this is the age in which the state protected and encouraged art, and art inspired a whole people; while the Greek character, cheerful, gentle, and soft-hearted, was seen to the best advantage.[1]

[1] J. J. Winckelmann, *Gedanken über die Nachahmung der Griechischen Werke in Malerei und Bildhauerkunst*, 1755.

Lessing was not so anxious for formal imitation of the Greeks and reminded his contemporaries that they had been only human, and in fact inferior to the men of the present in pure thought. But he revered their art and literature, regarding the latter as characterized not so much by beauty, like the former, as by truth, especially truth to feeling and thus to Nature again. He, too, turned to fifth-century Athens, where among other things society produced not only dramatists but the kind of audience that he himself, in the weakness of public and community spirit, found lacking. He too saw the Greeks as primarily gentle and tender.[1]

The influence of both these men was visible in Herder.[2] Herder was of course far from a mere Hellenist; he is often considered not only as the philosopher of *Sturm und Drang*, a movement that saw early Greek literature, especially Homer, as but one manifestation of the natural and passionate creative spirit of the *Urmensch*, but also as a precursor of romanticism, with its revival of the Middle Ages, and even of nineteenth-century nationalism. Nonetheless his vision of Greece deeply affected the full classicism of Weimar. Herder saw nations and their civilizations more consciously as individual wholes than his predecessors had done; likewise the history of each people is regarded organically. Since language and religion are for him the main forces shaping a nation, he naturally thinks primarily of the Greeks and the Germans in general, rather than of the various component entities. Though upon the whole he believed in progress, if not uninterrupted progress, and though he thought every nation formed by peculiar influences that made successful imitation of another impossible, the Greeks, who represent the youth of the world, remain close to his heart. He still observes them primarily through their language and literature, art and mythology. Their geographic position, and their climate (which he overestimates), first ensured movement, reciprocal influences, variety. Their institutions encouraged emulation between states, the games in particular contributing to the development of the arts (and in art they alone, with the sensuous imagination created by their religion and their conditions of life, reached perfect beauty). It is for their vitality, many-sidedness, freedom, and spontaneity that Herder's

---

[1] G. E. Lessing, *Laokoon* (1766); *Hamburgische Dramaturgie* (1767–9).

[2] J. G. von Herder, *Ideen zur Philosophie der Geschichte der Menschheit* (1784–91).

Greeks are to be admired. They followed no rules, but rather, without restraint, their inner urges. They did not know the fearful split between feeling and thought, desire and duty: they were whole, harmonious, and balanced. Such is in a nutshell the doctrine of classical German Hellenism, whether its adherents regarded their own people as hopelessly inferior to the Greeks, as fast catching up with them, or as potentially or even actually superior owing to a higher aim and greater strictly intellectual powers.

In spite of the limitations of the Greek outlook, in spite of the frequent errors natural to youth, Athens did more for the enlightenment of its citizens than any other state, Herder believes. In its service, yet in free choice, men could put forth all their various gifts. There was a moment in which Greece reached the height of human possibilities.

The Spartans would appear to have contributed little to this picture of Greece, unless in Herder's tendency, bequeathed to others, to treat them welcomingly as one of the various elements making up the lively whole of Greek culture. His most definite political idea, his hatred of despotism, appears in the praise given to Lycurgus and other lawgivers for declining supreme power. But Lycurgus' refusal to accept change and growth, his attempt to put the clock back to the rough heroic age, are against all Herder's principles. His pleasure in the Greek republics, which treat men as of age and encourage their capacities, is united with vagueness as to the best form of government, and suspicion of the (one day perhaps dispensable) state. Perhaps Sparta is in his mind when he criticizes Greek republics for demanding too much of their citizens; the state should encourage and stimulate, not check and form. At the same time he admires Greek devotion to the community, though he thinks it unfortunate that Sparta practised it in the frame of such *harte patrizier-Gesetze*. Nonetheless he can describe the principle of Thermopylae and that of Athens, in other words, patriotism and enlightened citizenship, as the two eternal poles of human development.

This is an area where Herder's thought is notoriously confused. His real influence, as far as we are concerned, lies in his justification of the tendency to hypostatize a whole people, and in his eloquent account of 'the Greeks' which results from it.

Up to the great dividing line formed by the French Revolution professional classical scholars were also somewhat uncertain in

x

their treatment of Sparta. As far as Greek history was concerned the middle of the century had fed on dry compilations, or fluent adaptations of Rollin; but a burst of original scholarship soon followed. Heyne, who may almost be regarded as the fourth great prophet of Hellenism, so great was his influence on a series of famous pupils, whom he taught to see each period as a whole, using every sort of surviving evidence, actually wrote an essay on the proper valuation of Sparta. In this he takes a line above the French mêlée[1] (elsewhere he takes a similarly lofty attitude to Phocion, congratulating his own countrymen on living in a non-political age, in which they can and should pursue only private virtue and happiness). He rightly reproaches Sparta's most recent assailant, de Pauw (whose work we may remember was published in Berlin as well as Paris, and whose contempt for antiquity was not unshared in enlightened Germany), for his cavalier treatment of dates and sources. On the other hand Heyne can discount, because he can explain, the excesses of ancient idealization. Typically, he deprecates Sparta's inability to adapt to changing circumstances and increasing civilization without, though he recognizes that she was well adapted for survival in a barbaric age. He deplores the constitutional weaknesses that encouraged aggressive war, and has a horror of the power finally attained by the ephors, since it was not only tyrannical but democratic. On the other hand, he thought there was much to be said for public education (the drawbacks of home teaching and the private tutor were a live issue at the time), at least in a smallish state, and at bottom he still likes the traditional mixed constitution of three, or even two, parts. This last could be said of a number of writers, especially those connected like Heyne with the leading German university, Göttingen in Hanover, where English influence was strong.

In this politically confused and somewhat naive state of affairs the conclusion of Wilhelm Heinse's well-known novel *Ardinghello*[2] is comprehensible. The individualistic and undisciplined, not to say licentious, hero, a sixteenth-century painter but very much of the *Sturm und Drang*, founds a Graeco-Italian colony in the Aegean, to which French Utopian novelists as well as political

---

[1] C. G. Heyne, *De Spartana Republica Iudicium*. *Soc. Regiae scient. Gott. Comm.* ix (1787–8). Cf. *Opuscula Academica* ii. x (1787) and iii. xx (1788).

[2] J. J. W. Heinse, *Ardinghello* (1787).

thinkers, the new German Hellenism and a foretaste of political philhellenism all contribute something. It goes without saying that *das alte Athen unter dem Pericles schien wieder aufzuleben* in the new community; yet at the same time it was supposed to be founded on the premises of Plato and Lycurgus, especially as to communism, free love, and the acceptance of war as a stimulus to noble characters.

The seventeen-nineties saw both the great age of Hellenism and of Weimar. At the same time the French Revolution gave a strong impulse to political thought, which took various directions but, largely owing to the influence of Kant, usually remained primarily ethical and idealistic in approach. In many of the chief hellenizing writers disgust with the Revolution, which so disappointed almost everyone who had welcomed it, would seem even to have strengthened their distrust of politics. They remained strong individualists, and were mostly desirous of limiting the power of the state. Though none were democrats, dislike of the princes, now almost all extreme reactionaries, encouraged a form of republicanism.

In this situation Schiller, for one, saw that Sparta really would not do. It has even been said that the clearest exposition of his political ideas is that to be found in the little essay of 1790 on Lycurgus and Solon.[1] Historically speaking it is uncritical compared with Heyne's work; its form and some of its language suggests acquaintance with the French controversy, but its conception is German, and partly Kantian. Its lesson is simple. Remarkable as Lycurgus' achievement was, in regard to his own purpose of creating an isolated, self-sufficient, and unchanging state, yet in the light of the proper end of mankind, the *Zweck der Menschheit*, it is to be condemned. This end is the progressive development of all man's capacities; the state should be but a means to this end, never an end in itself. Since Lycurgus sacrificed all other qualities to patriotism, the perdurability of his institutions simply prevented progress and called a halt at immaturity and imperfection. Solon of course forms a contrast. Though he dangerously extended the scope of his laws to deal with customs and manners, and was rather too democratic, yet he made the state serve man, and enabled the citizen to attain true virtue, which is

---

[1] F. von Schiller, *Die Gesetzgebung des Lykurgus und Solon* (*Historische Aufsätze aus der Thalia*).

the pursuit of duty in free will.[1] Nor had Schiller forgotten this picture of Solon's Athens when he came to embody his conclusions on ethics and aesthetics in the famous essay *Über Anmut und Würde*. He views with distaste Kant's demand that duty should conquer inclination, spirit overcome matter. For him, sense and will must co-operate, the will desiring only the morally good, which is also the beautiful. For the free man laws must be internal, not external. The Greeks understood this, and sometimes achieved it, in their art at least. It was the ideal of the Athenians.

Hölderlin, too, perceived that Sparta was in some sense incompatible with the Greece he longed to recreate. This is one of the themes of his novel *Hyperion*, set in modern Greece.[2] The Hellas that Hyperion desires to see reborn is fundamentally Athenian; his visit to the ruined city and his lecture on the causes of her now departed perfection form the heart of the book. Hyperion concludes that the Athenians not only shared with the other Greeks the influence of a most beneficent land and climate (how clear it is that none of these writers had been to Greece!) but that, more than the rest, they were able to develop at their own pace, in perfect freedom and isolated from outside stimulus, through an undisturbed childhood to a natural maturity. Of his own will King Theseus gave up to them most of his power. As a result, *schön an Leib und Seele*, they could develop their love for art and religion, those offspring of Freedom—freedom not only from arbitrary despotism but also from the despotism of law, typical of the sterile, rational north with its distrust of the free life of nature— and also of perfect human nature or *vollendete Menschennatur*.

But Sparta, Hyperion thought, was precocious in its development, and only saved from chaos by the external discipline of Lycurgus. All her virtues thereafter were the result of conscious effort and struggle. Discipline is ever fatal to those unripe for it; the state that had no true childhood could never, when the time for school was past, regain the perfect naturalness of maturity.

'Die Spartaner bleiben eine Fragment; denn wer nicht ein vollkommenes Kind war, der wird schwerlich ein vollkommener Mann.'

---

[1] Schiller's old teacher J. J. H. Nast uses almost identical language of Lycurgus in a lecture of 1792 (see his *Gelegenheitsschriften*, 1820). This was given before the Duke of Württemberg and ends by congratulating so many modern princes on realizing what the *Zweck der Menschheit* is. There would seem to be a close relation between the two works.　　　　[2] Hölderlin, *Hyperion* (1797–9).

Sparta, moreover, is associated with Hyperion's vain attempt to recreate Greece by armed rebellion. To his Diotima, who now professes herself an admirer of sublime Spartan femininity, he speaks of Agis and Cleomenes as demigods in their struggle against the fate of their city and of Greece. It is Sparta that he and his insurgent bands besiege, that is the scene of their defeat and demoralization and of his despair of Greece. The historic events of 1770 offer support to the symbolism; Greece cannot be rediscovered by this road.[1]

Plenty of other writers continued to adhere to a conception of 'the Greeks' to which the second state in Greece contributed little or nothing, and if they found occasion to mention her it was usually with more or less condemnation. Pious hellenizers included scholars such as Wolf, the pupil of Heyne and friend of Wilhelm von Humboldt, together with Humboldt himself, some of the romantics like Schlegel, at least for a time, and even the philosopher Hegel in youth. Bartholdy actually got to Greece, to marvel that rich and pleasant Laconia, and the cruel and almost barren rocks of Attica, produced in each case men of a contrary nature.[2] Indeed, it was against all their principles.

Humboldt was the most extreme of individualists, whose early *Ideen zu einem Versuch, die Grenzen der Wirksamkeit des Staates zu bestimmen*[3] shows fear of state activity in education as in other fields as a possible threat to *Bildung*, conceived as the development of all one's powers, the true purpose of life. Of such development the Greeks, as could be seen above all in their peculiarly natural and original literature, were a prime example, through their combination of nature with culture, their energy, receptiveness, and power of *Phantasie* rather than reflection. Their rich language, full of images, was their portrait. As late as 1807, by which time he thought that the present might well outstrip antiquity by uniting modern reflective content with Greek perfection of form, he still saw the Greeks as too *edle, zart, fein und humane*, even in their decline, to limit their freedom by adopting the kind of constitu-

---

[1] Sparta can still stand for Greece in action; cf. *Der Archipelagus* 271

        dann, dann, o ihr Freuden Athens! ihr Taten in Sparta!

[2] L. S. Bartholdy, *Bruchstücke zur nähern Kenntniss des heutigen Griechenlands* (1805), esp. p. 249.

[3] See also *Geschichte des Verfalls u. Untergangen der Griechische Freistaaten* (1807-8); *Latium und Hellas*, (1806), both first published 1896.

tion that would sink the Man in the Citizen and give strength to resist Rome. He also saw them as lacking in class hostility and excessive respect for birth and wealth. Athens fell into frivolity and demagoguery; but the republics did encourage the whole man to take part in public life, though they had no proper constitutions. Humboldt does speak with admiration of Thermopylae, for he thought war could be a valuable part of *Bildung*; otherwise, almost his only reference to Sparta is a logical but casual expression of contempt.

As for Goethe, the greatest and for a time almost the most wholehearted hellenizer of all, he was the least interested in purely political or constitutional matters; to our story he contributes nothing, except the significant fact that the Sparta of *Faust* Part II is simply the home of Helen, who stands for the spirit of Greece or ideal beauty. Even one who came into conflict with his distinguished contemporaries, and especially Schiller, on their exaggerated enthusiasm for antiquity and on other subjects, could not really differ from them on Sparta. Manso was a judicious historian, a link between eighteenth-century enlightenment and nineteenth-century liberalism, whose two volumes on Sparta deserve the name of the first modern history of the subject and can still be read with respect.[1] He points to the cruelty, faction, and superstition of the Greeks in general; he doubts the all-ennobling power of art, and scoffs at Schiller as a superficial student of Kantian abstractions. He places Lycurgus firmly in his primitive environment, pouring scorn on recent estimates of his sublime wisdom (for these surely the Germans were not responsible). He even doubts the Spartans' courage, though not their crude freedom and equality. Nonetheless, Manso's ability to treat a distant period in its own terms and through all its manifestations marks him as of his period; and indeed he shares many of its categories of thought. Since man's aim is the harmonious development of all his potentialities, Athens (though horribly oligarchic like all Greek cities) is far preferable to her opponent; and the Spartans fail to be complete men. They treated the Man, where he stood in the way of the Citizen, with hateful coldness, they ignored the finer feelings, neglected the arts and sciences, and remain *ein lehrendes und warnendes Beyspiel* of heroic virtue and its limitations.

The nineteenth century, however, was to rehabilitate the state.

[1] J. F. K. Manso, *Sparta* (1800–5).

And what, it may be asked, of the thinker who stands at the very beginning of this development, and is well known to have advocated at one time an ephorate and at another a strictly isolated state with valueless coinage and a closed, tripartite class structure? Yet Fichte differs from the majority of his contemporaries in his care for equality and material well-being, and also in the revolutionary sources of his youthful thought. And at neither of the above-mentioned stages does he have any direct preoccupation with Sparta. He did not look back; the purely rational state was yet to come. In the *Grundlage des Naturrechts* (1796-7), in which he still sees the state as only set up to ensure the individual's rights and freedom (defined by Kant as the power to act in accordance with reason), the ephors are certainly elected to check the government in the name of the sovereign people. They are, however, as he points out, very different from those of Sparta (or, one may add, of the Calvinist tradition) in that they lack not only executive but even judicial powers; they can only pronounce an interdict and convene the sovereign people to give judgement on the offending government—monarch or magistrates—by universal referendum. A few other features of this last great contribution to the tradition of Natural Law sound familiar to us; the permanent, because perfectly rational, constitution and the brief and simple laws (indeed Fichte believes the state will wither away) are thoroughly Utopian.

Der Geschlossene Handelstaat of 1800 criticizes the recent flight from the state, however, and it may be under Jacobin or even Babouviste influence, for Fichte was slower than his contemporaries in turning against the Revolution. At first sight the new state looks Lacedaemonian enough, and Constant as we saw took strong exception to 'ces idées Spartiates'. But that is the Frenchman speaking. Fichte's curious construction is built chiefly on the conception of property as a right to act upon, rather than possess, objects. His three classes, producers, manufacturers, and traders, follow from this idea; and the closing of the state to outside economic influences, the token currency, and other severe regulatory measures are necessary to ensure the smooth inter-working of the three classes and preserve their equality. In all other respects men are free to live and think as they like. The state is merely there, not to protect property, as had been so often stated, but to provide each man with his fair share of it. Even Plato, let alone

Sparta, would seem far from Fichte's mind. And indeed political thought in Germany was not likely at this period to measure itself against the ancient world. The Romantics were on the whole against finding wisdom in foreign models; and when it became clear that a powerful state could not be created by the revival of feudalism, industrialization and other new developments were upon the country.

But meanwhile the framework within which first scholars and then a wider circle of writers were to revalue Sparta had been created. Friedrich von Schlegel, though he later turned to Catholicism, the Middle Ages, and reaction, was in youth the most enthusiastic of Hellenists. He had at that time the idea of dividing Greek poetry into schools, according to the local civilizations that gave them birth, or the branches and subdivisions of the Greek peoples.[1] Of these *Stämme* (there is no precisely equivalent English word) the Ionians and Dorians are the most prominent, clearly differentiated at least by dialect and mythological tradition, to which so much attention was now directed. Schlegel realized that this idea of his was new and fruitful; it was indeed one of the expressions of the great German effort to reach understanding through generalization to which in spite of all excesses we are so much indebted. He owed something to the language of art-history and to Winckelmann; something, too, to Herder and his interest in the variousness of the Greek genius.

At first, in 1794, Schlegel described epic as Ionian, lyric as Dorian, and drama as Athenian; Alexandrian poetry formed a fourth school. But this crude schema had to be further elaborated, with lyric being subdivided into Ionian, Aeolian, and Dorian styles, the last regarded as its culmination. Each school (or as he later preferred to put it, period or style) expresses itself in art, manners and customs, and political forms, as in everything else. But just as it is clear that the account of the Ionians as clever, quick, and receptive is largely based on the impression Schlegel received of the narrative and objective style of Homeric epic, so the root of the description of the Dorians is plainly in the aristocratic grandeur and moral seriousness of Pindar, who wrote in Doric dialect. From the start, however, language reminiscent

---

[1] *Von den Schulen der Griechischen Poesie* (1794). Cf. *Bruchstücke zur Geschichte der lyrischen Dichtkunst* (*Vorarbeiten zur Geschichte der Verschiedenen Schulen und Epochen der lyrischen Dichtkunst bey den Hellenen*), (1795).

of Winckelmann on the Greeks in general is used of the Dorians; we are told of their *milde Grossheit* and, indeed, that in contrast with the easily orientalized Ionians they form the older, purer, and more truly Hellenic branch, chiefly responsible for the development of those two essential products of the Greek spirit, music and gymnastic. Schlegel filled out the picture of the Dorians by assuming that their *Sitten und Verfassungen* can be discovered by studying Sparta, where they survived most purely and flourished most strongly (an assumption based largely on Pindar, especially the First Pythian), and also the not dissimilar society created by Pythagoras (an Ionian working in and for a state not all Schlegel's arguments can prove Dorian: he gives up the attempt later); while both of these were transmuted into philosophic terms by Plato. He recalls that the Spartans were the first to exercise naked, as Herodotus tells us, and so to develop that Dorian idea of the beautiful, later extended to all Greece; that women partook in the Dorian education, and were nobler and more highly regarded than elsewhere in Greece (and more particularly Ionia, where nature encouraged luxury and education was merely intellectual).[1] He believes, however, that a chaste and idealized *Männerliebe* also marked the purest Dorian states. He stresses the reverent conservatism of the Dorians, and, unlike Schiller, gives a positive value to their feeling for law as well as freedom. He insists however that their whole way of life sprang from love and enthusiasm for the beautiful, not for law as such, though the beautiful to them was always defined by laws or rules; for devotion to beauty required leisure, which their political system was designed to ensure. Schlegel recounts all that was known in his time of Spartan music and poetry, and of the schools of art, especially sculpture, flourishing in Dorian towns of the Peloponnese; but he also points to the Dorians' power of organizing themselves in communities bound by law, unlike the Ionians, who soon lost their freedom and wavered between tyranny and anarchy. And in his later *History of Literature* he has become especially strong on the Dorians' hostility to the destructive spirit of democracy and to the sophists.

Here are almost all the themes of twentieth-century German laconism already expressed. But it should be remembered that, to Schlegel, Ionian, Dorian, and so forth are primarily styles, that can

[1] See also *Über die Diotima* (1795).

be adopted by persons of different origin,[1] or even historical periods, developing one from another; his theories are not yet to any great extent racial or national ones. It should also be remembered that Athens produced, for the young Schlegel, a civilization surpassing the Dorian and uniting Dorian and Ionian characteristics, as its tragedy unites epic and lyric elements; a civilization more exact and richer, and also more 'ideal', than the Dorian, though with all its nobility and grandeur; and far more 'ideal' than the Ionian. It also produced in Solon the wisest and most humane of legislators. Schlegel is perfectly willing to concede that Athenian civilization, like the Athenian population, was perhaps less purely Greek than the Dorian.

It is also of significance for the future that the Dorian style or period is essentially an early one, culminating in Pindar and before the Attic tragedians. And thus, while Schlegel admits that the Dorians were always intellectually and spiritually limited and politically often oppressive, he can throw out as corrupt and decadent everything that is repulsive in Spartan history from the Peloponnesian War onwards and can regard Athenian and other later laconizers as creating an exaggerated and artificial idea of the Dorian. And finally, let us notice what is something of a paradox: though this picture of Sparta lays more stress on her artistic achievements than almost any previous one, it is even less suited to provoke art in others. For it passes over all individual figures and episodes.[2] Lycurgus disappears in the general Dorian heritage while Agesilaus, Agis, or such picturesque figures as the Spartan mother are relegated to the period of decadence.

At any rate, for this as for more general reasons, some of which we have seen, poems or paintings on Spartan subjects are rare in Germany. Even in philhellenic literature, of which there was a flood, Leonidas is a great deal harder to find than he was in France and England.[3] Such literature inherited on the one hand

---

[1] Tyrtaeus, whom Schlegel accepts as an Athenian and who wrote in Ionic dialect and elegiac not lyric measures, counts as an Ionian; similarly Solon, though he is described as doing much to create an essentially Athenian and therefore partly Dorian civilization.

[2] Brasidas however is among the heroes neglected by Plutarch whose life Schlegel would like to write; *Briefe an seinem Brüder A. W. Schlegel*, ed. O. Walzel, no. 56.

[3] R. F. Arnold, *Der Deutsche Philhellenismus, Euphorion, Ergänzungsheft* ii (1896) 165 ff. collects the titles of many scattered philhellenic poems. Only

from the classical writers of Germany the theme of the lament on the ruins of Athens; but the younger generation, seeking an outlet for the patriotic feelings suppressed since 1813, and now fully in the Romantic stream, was particularly drawn to the modern Greek setting, exotic and Christian at once. The ghosts of antiquity may haunt this world, however, sometimes successfully to inspire, sometimes to be hopelessly yearned after; as they do in W. Müller's popular *Lieder der Griechen*,[1] which were to some extent modelled on modern Greek verse-forms. The *Waldhornist* is here forcing somewhat artificially martial strains from his instrument, and the ghosts do include a few Spartans. Leonidas appears to Alexander Ypsilanti in his Austrian prison to announce a success on the site of Thermopylae:

> Da erwacht der Fürst vom Schlummer, ruft entzückt: Leonidas!

Another poem records an engagement on that holy spot under the very eyes of the king's spirit:

> Da kreist er mit dem Flammenschwert als Wächter um den Pass
> Den er mit seinem Blut gefeit, der Held Leonidas.

Further, not only is Byron Tyrtaeus resurrected, but the Spartan mother appears, easily recognizable to every educated reader, in the up-to-date garb of a Maniote woman. As far as other authors are concerned one gets the impression that Sparta would have got no look-in at all had it not been for the Maniotes. For example, in Waiblinger's youthful novel *Phaethon*, heavily reminiscent of Hölderlin's *Hyperion*, the heroine's mysterious father in his German *Schloss* turns out to be a *Nachkomme der alten Spartaner*, son of a *wilder Maniate*, and a patriot who in his youth collected the local populace, trained it by the Eurotas in classical contests,

---

[1] *Lieder der Griechen* (1821), *Neue Lieder der Griechen* (1823), and *Neueste Lieder der Griechen* (1824); all in *Lieder der Griechen* (1844), where see esp. p. 34 'Alexander Ypsilanti auf Munkács'; p. 73, 'Thermopylä; p. 137, 'Byron'; and p. 11, 'Die Mainottin'—congratulating herself that her seven sons have gone to war against the Turk and that Spartan blood flows in their veins, she proposes to the other *Mutter der Mainoten* to collect stones from Sparta's ruins to use against any men returning alive but defeated. Cf. also p. 46 'Der Mainottin Unterricht' and p. 55 'Der Mainotte'.

---

one bears the title 'die Thermopylen'; nor are there others promising Spartan subjects.

and took a vain part in the revolt of 1770.[1] (But to his idea of 'the Greeks' the Spartans still contribute nothing; indeed he can blithely apply elements of Thucydides' description of the Athenians to them all.)

But at this very time Schlegel's ideas were being taken up by a number of scholars.[2] Though the discovery of the Aegina marbles seemed to give striking embodiment to all that had been said of Dorian sculpture, the field of discussion widened most significantly to include political history; cohesion within and rivalry between the *Stämme* was traced in every possible and many impossible places.[3] And soon Carl Otfried Müller popularized and reinterpreted the Dorians in accordance with some of the new political feelings of his period. He wrote to a friend that he could not emulate Friedrich Schlegel and Schleiermacher, who had given insight into the deepest springs of the Dorian soul; but he would investigate its workings in the middle ground of history.[4]

This he did, first in a dissertation on Aegina, and then in his famous work on *Die Dorier*, published in 1824—the main surviving part of a projected history of all the Greek *Stämme*, which had perhaps the more influence for remaining uncompleted and without the balance that a full discussion of the Athenians might have provided.[5] Of these he says little, but seems to consider them as basically Ionian though with certain peculiarities, perhaps to their advantage. Müller protests against such oversimplified generalizations as that of the 'subjectivity' of the Dorians as opposed to the 'objectivity' of the Ionians; but he has no doubts as to the reality of national personalities, and his aim is to provide a full and unprejudiced study of one such. Circumstances may modify or even ultimately extinguish this character, he thinks; but it is preexistent to circumstances.

Müller believed that the political forms of the Dorians were

---

[1] F. W. Waiblinger, *Phaethon* (1823); for more Maniotes, Harro-Harring's play *Die Mainotten* (1825).

[2] Above all August Boeckh, *Enzyk.*, pp. 281 ff., *Kl. Schr.* iv. 39.

[3] E.g. J. F. C. Kortüm, *Zur Geschichte Hellenischer Verfassungen* (1821); the Peloponnesian League a Dorian League—decisively refuted by Grote and others.

[4] C. O. Müller, *Briefe aus einem Gelehrtenleben*, 1797–1840; ed. S. Reiter (1950), i. 36 (to L. Tieck).

[5] *Geschichte Hellenischer Stämme und Städte*, 1820–4. Vol. i, *Orchomenos und die Minyer*; vols. ii and iii, *die Dorier*.

originally everywhere in Greece much what they remained in Sparta and Crete. He realized that Lycurgus has many of the features of a mythological personage, and also that Sparta's peculiarities were likely to be the result of many adjustments— based however, he supposed, on Dorian tradition and on the behest of the oracle of Apollo at Delphi in particular (he attempted to show that it was the Dorians who introduced the religion of Apollo to Greece, as well as developing lyric in his service). Platonic and other accounts of the Dorian mode in music; what is traditionally called Doric architecture; the newly-found sculpture from Dorian areas; and a philosophic approach still partly identi- fied with Pythagoreanism also contribute to the final picture, which is that of a people gifted in the orderly subordination of individual elements to a whole. The desire to preserve unity, once achieved, led to a feeling for stability and respect for tradition. And from the same roots sprang self-restraint and obedience. This character was thoroughly masculine in its self-sufficiency, its need neither to impart to others nor to receive from them, and also in its warlike readiness for self-defence. (Though he mentions its respect for women, Müller is here some way from Schlegel, who in his essay *Über die Diotima* suggested that the Dorian, lyric, inspiration was feminine, in contrast to the masculine, dramatic spirit of Athens.) Müller's Ionians are of course curious about external reality, receptive to external interests and impressions, and thus condemned to foreign contamination and premature dissolution. And so the Dorians (having annexed Apollo, Pytha- goras, and other most doubtfully Dorian elements) can easily stand for the true Greeks and their *reine und klare Harmonie*: which places man at the centre of vision, flees mystery and the dark, is content with the here and now, and confident in the gods; and loves beauty—a beauty of proportion and form, not of superficial decoration—indeed prefers, unlike the moderns, *Darstellen* to *Wirken und Schaffen*, and turns man himself into a work of art.

Sparta, *der Dorische Normalstaat*, and thus by implication the pattern state of all Greece, is above all representative of the Greek realization, claims Müller, that the state is not merely an institu- tion for the defence of persons and property, as the modern heresy holds, but a single moral agent created by its components' possession of the same opinions, principles, and aims; something possible only where natural affinity binds a *Volk*, or smaller

Stamm, together. In his admiration Müller glosses over the disagreeable sides of early Sparta; the helots were better off than the slaves of the commercial states, the *Crypteia* must really have been the mild institution introduced under that name in Plato's *Laws*. But perfect unity cannot be maintained against internal change and external pressure for ever, though the state that has had it will stand, in a petrified condition, long after the receptive, individualistic ones have dissolved for ever. That, in rather exaggerated form, as Müller admits, describes the fate of Sparta and Athens.

We must beware, however, of supposing that such praise of Sparta imposed itself generally, either in the scholarly world or outside it. It is fascinating to see Hegel adapting the main stream of German Hellenism to his own ideas and the growing feeling for the state, so that Athens can still remain in the forefront.[1] After his early Hellenomania, when he was a friend of Hölderlin, Hegel came to believe that Christianity provided a higher synthesis than paganism and that the present marked an advance on either the classical or medieval past. But he retained a deep hankering for Greece. His ideas of Greek art and religion were still rooted in Winckelmann and his successors. But he saw the Greek social ethos as relevant to his visions of freedom as being at home in one's environment, or perfectly adjusted to one's place in the scheme of things; a basically unpolitical notion of freedom descended from Kant's definition of it as subservience to reason. Hegel supposed that the Greeks, and more particularly the Athenians, after they had defeated the oriental under-emphasis on the individual and at the same time had acquired a national consciousness, lived in a society that was on the whole at home in the world around it. Its existence was essentially directed to realizing the beautiful (explaining the external by means of the imagination) and its behaviour was determined by *Sittlichkeit*, traditional morality, rather than *Moralität*, individual critical judgement. For this view of Athens Hegel was drawing heavily on his reading of Aeschylus and Sophocles. Its democracy was the expression of the objective will, not of individual wills (and its small scale and slave basis further remove it from modern democracy), and encouraged the formation of great political characters like Pericles, whose devotion to the public good left him without any

[1] G. W. F. Hegel, *Vorlesungen über die Philosophie der Geschichte* (2nd posthumous ed., 1840) ii. ii. 3–4.

private life. Individual freedom and the considerable measure of equality allowed all the citizens to develop their peculiar capacities. Hostile criticism is only applicable after the outbreak of the Peloponnesian War, when the delicate balance was upset by the rise of critical thought and the individualism fatal to Greece. True freedom however can only be attained by the synthesis of these two ways of life—by the individual's rational comprehension of and choice of a life devoted to the state. An age in which this is attained, even if it surpasses Athens in power of thought, will probably be its inferior in art, which will no longer be an adequate means of expression. The more thoughtful return to the perfect adjustment of Greek life was an old German theme, though Hegel integrates it into his whole dialectical process.

It should now be clear what an inferior place Hegel gave Sparta. Here the activity and freedom of the individual were kept entirely in the background, the forced equality in land was a failure, destroying family life and the liberty to dispose of one's property. Though the institutions were framed for the sake of the state, their object was a lifeless equality. The Spartans practised an inhuman severity, especially on their helots. They had no intellectual culture, and were despised by the other Greeks, with whom they had little in common (this in flat contradiction to the Schlegel-C.O. Müller tradition; Hegel only refers to the latter on a minor point, to condemn Sparta's lack of written law). To sum up, Athens and Sparta were both inspired by the idea of political virtue, but only in the former did it develop into the *Kunstwerk freier Individualität*, or did *Sittlichkeit* involve the active pursuit of beauty, even of truth. In the age of disintegration the new *Moralität* issued at Athens in *offener Leichtsinn*, but in Sparta as *Privatverderben*, and the Athenians remained amiable, even noble, while the Spartans' vulgar greed led to vulgar ruin. It may well be thought today that Hegel's idea of early fifth-century Athens as a place where community feeling was still strong is much nearer the truth than that previously current; he can make good use of Pericles' Funeral Oration here.[1]

---

[1] Schopenhauer, who was ultimately an extreme individualist, is revealed incidentally as a traditional philathenian. Differentiating *Reproduktionskraft*, the vegetable impulse, *Irritabilität*, typical of animals, and *Sensibilität*, the truly human, he associates these with, or symbolizes them by, the Boeotians, Spartans, and Athenians respectively (*Über den Willen in der Natur*: *Physiologie und*

If we turn to the great classical historians, whose influence spread beyond learned circles and beyond their own country, we shall find no special enthusiasm for Sparta here either, though she received all the attention that the problems of her development deserved. True, in spite of the scholarly suspicion of much Romantic philology, and of Schlegel in particular, that developed, the doctrine of the different characters of the *Stämme* was usually accepted, though often in modified form: the differences were not so great, or they were largely or wholly due to external factors, or there were exceptions to the rule. But the superiority, or the supremely Greek nature, of the Dorians was little favoured. For one thing, the development of oriental studies drew attention to the part played by eastern influence in the making of Greek civilization,[1] and thus even led, as with Müller's own pupil E. Curtius, whose history of Greece was elegantly written and widely read, to admiration of the Ionians (for whom Curtius re-annexed Apollo).[2] Curtius held, however, that the greatest achievements of Greek civilization were panhellenic ones. These did indeed include the Spartan state; for the broad-minded Heraclid Lycurgus was probably no Dorian, and his task was to weld together different racial elements. However, if this was a brilliant work of *Staatsordnender Klugheit*, that was not what the 'natural Ionian' Curtius most cared for. The old fascination of Athens remained, and her civilization was what was often seen as the most truly Greek, to which all the other *Stämme* had contributed. It may be observed that the impact of Grote (whose work was actually excerpted as propaganda by a German democrat) might help by reaction to motivate arguments against the radical democracy of the late fifth century and the sophists; but neither, it seems, against the Athens of the previous age, nor in favour of Sparta. It would also be a mistake to suppose that Sparta aroused special interest in historians in Prussia (where Hegel's influence was greatest); a tentative comparison between Sparta's attempt to unite Greece and Prussia's to unite Germany

[1] E.g. in M. Duncker, *Geschichte des Alterthums* (1852–7).
[2] E. Curtius, *Griechische Geschichte* (1857).

Pathologie). He also thought women should be kept down, and quotes Aristotle for the damage their materialistic vanity did in Sparta, where they were too free (*Kleine Philosophische Schriften xxvii*: *über die Weiber*).

may be made in the 1870s,[1] but the comparison with Macedon is much more important; prefigured by eighteenth-century comparisons of Philip and Frederick the Great, temporarily reversed by Niebuhr's burning defence of Demosthenes (Stein) against Philip (Napoleon),[2] it was finally developed by Droysen, the historian of Alexander as well as of Prussia.[3] Macedon had the advantage of a single king, a more normal aristocratic social system, and ultimate success in uniting the nation.

The majestic procession of historians continued through the century. Busolt's history of Greece is primarily a work of erudition, and his special study of Sparta's League was mainly inspired by the contemporary interest in, and growth of knowledge about, that of Athens; it is cool in tone, though it reflects contemporary political terminology, with 'liberal' Athens, 'conservative' Sparta, and the contrasts of *grosslakedaemonisch* and *kleinlakedaemonisch* foreign policy; he still found Sparta, with its prevention of the free intellectual and moral development of the individual, one-sided.[4] The popular and sensible Holm,[5] more liberal than many, steers a moderate course between Athens and (impressive but narrow) Sparta and minimizes the innate differences between the *Stämme*. What the more original and brilliant Beloch[6] valued the Greeks for was rationalism and the scientific approach; he despised all their political achievements, condemning not only

[1] G. Busolt, *Die Lakedaemonier und ihre Bundesgenossen* (1878), p. 248, draws a rough comparison between Germany before the Franco-Prussian War and Greece before 480; in both a groping towards unity was at first expressed only in rare festive meetings—Panhellenic games, or 'Schützen, Turner und Sängerfesten'. In both, a military state—Prussia, Sparta—then forcibly imposed a federal system over a considerable area, and a foreign danger, successfully resisted, strengthened it; but less in Greece than in Germany.

[2] For Niebuhr on the Spartans, see *Vorträge über alter Geschichte* (1847, but from lectures of 1826 and 1829–30)—unscrupulous, and attempting to spread by force of arms barbarism and an out-dated, alien, and thus unnatural constitution. Although post-Periclean democracy is censured, the Athenians appear in traditional guise: noble, generous, sensitive, and the happiest of nations, because it was that which lived most intensely.

[3] J. G. Droysen, *Alexander* (2nd ed., 1877); and taken up often thereafter. Athenian democracy suffers in this comparison, too, of course; Demosthenes indeed has only recently been rehabilitated.

[4] G. Busolt, *Griechische Geschichte* (1885–1904). *Die Lakedaemonier und ihre Bundesgenossen* (1878).

[5] A. Holm, *Griechische Geschichte* (1886–1894).

[6] K. J. Beloch, *Griechische Geschichte* (1893–1904).

Y

democracy but the particularism and individualism persistent everywhere (disenchantment was often reinforced by closer acquaintance with modern Greece and its uneasy state under its German kings, and many scholars despised the political achievements of ancient Greece for diverse reasons). Beloch also for a time went so far as to deny a separate Dorian invasion, and he was highly sceptical of early Spartan history. Eduard Meyer sometimes defends Spartan policy against such charges as selfishness; but he delivered a particularly crushing rebuke against the whole doctrine of the *Stämme*, which found some echo in the early twentieth century. In 1919, as rector of Berlin University, he saw defeated Prussia as Athens at the end of the Peloponnesian War.[1]

The influence of Schlegel and Müller is better sought among those who were not primarily historians. One of the greatest of all Greek scholars, Wilamowitz, pronounced, admittedly when very young, a highly Prussian and patriotic oration (on the emperor's birthday) defending Athen's empire as a true *Bundestaat*, unlike Sparta's weak, uncultured, mere *Staatenbund*. He confessed that the thesis was paradoxical, and later added a note regretting he had been unfair to the Dorians: 'I did not yet know Pindar.' Though he continued to regard these as dealing, unlike the Athenians, with problems remote from the modern world, he came to give a glowing account of Dorian virtue as expressed in the legend of Heracles. Later still he recanted; it wasn't a Dorian legend at all. But his latest works show a continuing sympathy for early Sparta; he insisted that Spartiate life was not that of a mere *Offizierkorps*, and that if there was reverence for *nomos* there was also reverence for the superior individual. Though he wrote very coolly, like Schlegel, of the Sparta of the laconizers, and of poor Agesilaus and his epoch, he confessed that they provided a corrective for the feeble and exhausted age of democracy and the

---

[1] E. Meyer, *Geschichte des Alterthums* ii (1893) p. 583 ('Man abstrahiertse it K.O. Müller das Doriertum aus den Spartanern, das Ionertum aus den Ionien des 6. und 5. Jahrhunderts, verallgemeinert die historisch gewordenen Unterschiede, ganz unbekummert darum, dass zum Beispiel Argos, Korinth, Korkyra, Syrakus in das Dorische Schema absolut nicht hineinpassen, und datiert sie in der Urzeit Zurück'); *Preussen und Athen* (1919).

Pauly-Wissowa, the great classical encyclopedia, has no truck with the idea of *Doriertum* either, whether under Dorians vol. x, 1905, article by J. Miller) or under Sparta (vol. iii, *Zweite Reihe*, 1929, article on Spartan history by V. Ehrenberg, whose views were later increasingly vilified).

sophists.[1] Interest in early Sparta, it may be observed, was justifiably stimulated first by the discovery of fragments of Alcman's verse in papyrus, and early in the twentieth century by the English excavations on the site of the city, and by new approaches to the study of primitive societies. Much work was done on the peculiar cults of Laconia; and squeamish admirers of the Dorians were given a shock by a famous article devoted to Dorian pederasty, which adduced startling ethnographical parallels.[2] But it was not the professional classical scholars who did most to advance the concept of Dorianism, or to give it a relevance to modern life.

A renegade professor of Greek, who declared that philology must be transformed into philosophy, and a famous historian who was not a qualified classical scholar between them did much to transform the general German view of the Greeks around the turn of the century; neither was an admirer of Sparta, but they added a good deal to the current idea of the Dorians, and to discussions of the relation of culture and the state in Greece. Nietzsche's first original work, the *Geburt der Tragoedie*, expounds his famous conception of the interaction of the contrasting Apolline and Dionysian impulses. The first, a flight from the horror of life, is associated with dreams and the world of appearances, and is expressed in the visual arts, in a spirit of measure and calm, and in the individual principle. The second is an acceptance of the truth that underlies reality and a breaking of the barriers that divide men, as in the frenzy of wine or Dionysian exultation, and it is primarily expressed in music. The cult of Dionysus was at this time thought to be an oriental, even barbaric import later than the time of the sublimely Apolline Homer, in whose epic poetry Dionysus is barely mentioned; though the Dionysian is of course something within each man, as well as an imported cult. To

---

[1] U. von Wilamowitz-Moellendorf, *Reden und Vorträge2*; *Euripides Herakles* (1889); *Staat und Gesellschaft der Griechen* (1910 and 1922); in the latter, esp. i, B. iv and v, pp. 83–99. Note his description of the Sparta-legend 'which drove Immermann's schoolmaster mad, and attracts so many other schoolmasters'. The reference is to Agesel, the old schoolteacher in Immermann's satiric novel *Münchhausen* (1838), who was driven insane by a new work on linguistic science, decided his family must be descended from Agesilaus, and took to living in a Spartan manner on a hill he called Taygetus—a pleasing figure, though not one who has much to do with our general picture.

[2] E. Bethe, 'Dorische Knabenliebe', *Rheinische Museum* lxii (1907).

Nietzsche the Dorians stand for resistance to the new spirit. The Dorian state, cruel and relentless, with its harsh education, could only have lasted so long as part of this stubborn struggle; Dorian art reached in it a certain rigid majesty, a *trotzig-spröde starre Majestät*. This argument would involve among other dubious steps going back to Müller's belief that Apollo was an exclusively Dorian god, an unsound idea by now generally given up, and excluding from strictly 'Dorian art' the lyric poetry, including Pindar, which had formed the original basis of the whole idea; also ignoring as far as Sparta is concerned her whole fame as a centre of musical culture. For Nietzsche goes on to describe and praise the Greek acceptance and modification of the Dionysian, and its reconciliation with the Apolline, in lyric poetry and above all in Aeschylean tragedy.

That did not mean that he worshipped Athens—though he mocked at complacent contemporary attempts to see Germany as Periclean. Indeed he thought the dominance of Athens after Salamis fatal to Greek civilization, as bringing about the victory of a narrowly rational, ethical spirit, the spirit of Socrates, hostile to instinct, art, myth, and true philosophy. The Greece he loves is the Greece of the sixth and early fifth centuries, naive and spontaneous, productive of great aristocratic individuals—the lyric poets, the early philosophers. But while Pericles and even Alcibiades can appear in the list of great men, no Spartan is mentioned. In *Wir Philologen*,[1] written about 1874, Sparta is condemned as a caricature of a *polis*, a corruptor of Hellenism, where there was nothing great to justify the mindless brutality of the state. He also pours scorn on Otfried Müller's criteria of Greek nationality; language, he observes, may be forced by conquerors on any people, and the truly Greek was in fact largely created by the adoption of foreign, and especially Phoenician, elements (we may remember Nietzsche's dislike of anti-semitism). Nor does any stage in his winding intellectual journey ever bring him back to Sparta; neither the doctrine of supermen, nor that of evolution and recurrence, nor, certainly, his increasingly exclusive admiration for the (much extended) Dionysiac element.

Burckhardt's Greece is in some relation to Nietzsche's (they were in Basle at the same time). Especially as described in his early essays it is a place full not only of tension and strife but

[1] *Wir Philologen*, p. 128.

cruelty and savagery.[1] Culture and the individual are dependent on slavery as well as encouraged by competition and war; protected, yet ultimately menaced by religion and above all by the state. Burckhardt too admires the honourable and cultivated aristocrat of archaic Greece, and loathes democracy as likely to strangle liberalism. But Sparta appears to his pessimistic view as in a sense the most typical, because the most oppressive, of Greek *poleis*. Its foundation cost the subject peoples particularly dear, though no state can be founded without cost; and the price was not worth paying, since this state had no aim beyond that of asserting itself, and did nothing for the culture that is the state's only real justification. Burckhardt does not question Sparta's Dorian nature, and indeed identifies her decline with the decline of her Dorian aristocracy, but the *Stämme* are not very important to him.[2]

[1] J. Burckhardt, *Griechische Kulturgeschichte* (1898-1902, but delivered in lecture-form in Basle from 1872), esp. 1. 98-148.

[2] Meanwhile, it might be noted, some socialists were showing an interest in Sparta that has different roots and a different character and might repay investigation. The old admiration, which seemed to have become irrelevant in an age of industrialism, creeps in again via the far-reaching historical theories of Marx. The pure milk of his gospel flows in Engels' *Ursprung der Familie, des Privateigentums und des Staates* (1884), worked out with the aid of notes left by Marx, who had been impressed with the researches of the American anthropologist Lewis Morgan into the society of the North American Indians. The book accepts such a pre-civilized stage common to all races. In it, society is founded on the *gens* or kinship group, based in its original form on *Mutterrecht*, descent being reckoned through the female line. There is communism in property, no money, and equality not only between all men in the group, but between men and women. There are no destitute, and no state. This in many ways ideal state of affairs, Engels explains, was subverted by the rise of property, caused by advancing prosperity. In order to hold on to his property and pass it on to his children, man instituted monogamy and *Vaterrecht*. The family was consequently now based not on natural but on economic conditions; the first class-opposition, and class-oppression, was the resulting antagonism between man and woman. Thus opened the period in which every development was founded on the suffering of others. Engels ends by prophesying that in a higher form the gentile state, signalized by man's control of his means of production, will yet return.
  The Greeks were the first to abandon the gentile state and advance into civilization, with all its contradictions and troubles; but Sparta retained vestiges of the earlier period. (It should be pointed out that the Swiss scholar Bachofen wrongly thought that he had established the persistence of *Mutterrecht* into historical times at Sparta.) There were free "pairing marriages", and hints of the yet earlier group marriage. Since there was no domestic slavery, women were

From about 1900 Nietzsche and in a smaller way Burckhardt had much influence, though they cut little ice with classical scholars, except in helping to direct their attention to the darker and more primitive sides of Greece. But they contributed much to the contemporary break with the traditional German way of looking at the Greeks, and, among imaginative writers, to a far freer and more symbolic use of antiquity. Increased sympathy with Sparta was to come, however, chiefly from another direction; from those who combined a belief that Greeks and Germans were racially closely connected with a mystical idea of the virtue of the *Volk*, and the need for the individual to return from his artificial, urban, existence to his roots, living in mysterious and reverent community with his landscape and his ancestors. This last is an

---

still highly honoured. This point was also stressed by August Bebel, the organizer of German socialism, in *Die Frau und der Sozialismus*, a famous plea for emancipation, arguing that the status of women and of the workers is similar and indeed historically connected. Following Engels closely, he vaunts the virtues of Spartan women; both roundly condemn the Athenian system.

And, to Engels, Athens provides the clearest example of the rise of the state established to defend private property and perpetuate class distinctions. Ch. V stresses the economic exploitation of the poor before Solon, and the mass of slaves employed after him—it was this last that ruined Athens (singularly inadequate explanation).

Well into the present century admiration for the Spartan revolutionary leaders Agis and Cleomenes is to be traced among historians of socialism (e.g. R. von Pöhlmann, *Geschichte der sozialen Frage, und des Sozialismus in der alten Welt* (1912); or Max Beer, *Allgemeine Geschichte des Sozialismus*, rather more prudent). Socialism is a word still openly used in a well-known scholarly article of 1925 (Bux. 'Zwei Sozialistische Novellen bei Plutarch'—i.e. the Lives of the two kings—*Klio*, 1925) which claims that Agis and Cleomenes are only understandable now that the terminology of modern social democracy can be used to analyse the social movements of Hellenistic Greece. We meet capitalists and proletariat. In open relation to the failure of German social democracy in 1918, Agis' action is described as a theorist's attempt to put into practice a doctrine—Stoic socialism—that had lost touch with reality. Cleomenes' welcome from the poor in other Peloponnesian states is made much of. Historians have since tried to explode the notion of Stoic socialism, which was widely accepted for a time, stressing the conservative aspects of Stoicism and playing down its influence on Cleomenes (and the Gracchi). They have also shown the impossibility of exporting the Spartan ideas to the rest of the peninsula, though there can be no doubt that the rich did fear Cleomenes' example. And in the last generation or so Marxist historians, in Russia and elsewhere, seem to have transferred most of their interest, and even a good deal of their sympathy, to Athens.

outlook that has its origins far back in the last century, but that gathered force early in this one, and, above all in the unhappy years after the first World War, took a bewildering variety of forms and permeated most of the German Right. When also united, as it was not always, with a liking for a strong state as well as *Volk*, and a reaction against the Dionysian, a remarkable identification of Sparta and Germany might result.

The early nineteenth century had discovered the links that connect the various languages described as Indo-European, among them Sanskrit, Greek, Latin, and the Germanic and Celtic tongues; and some scholars thence deduced the substantial racial unity either of all who spoke them or at least of élites able to impose their speech on their subjects. Even more rash, but the inevitable result of contemporary modes of thought, particularly in Germany, was the belief in a consequent inherited similarity of character, outlook, and social and political institutions among all these élites, described as Aryans, later often as Europeans, Nordics, or just Germans.

It was natural that a family of peoples who could thus be made entirely, or largely, responsible for the triumphs of classical antiquity as well as modern western civilization (not to mention the newly rediscovered cultures of ancient India and Persia) should appear the salt of the earth. The doctrine of a conquering race, superior in all or most respects to the ruled, appealed particularly, in internal politics, to opponents of democracy anxious to preserve power to those they regarded as genuine descendants of this original aristocracy, and, in foreign affairs, to hopeful imperialists. In Germany at least the popularity of the theory was to be further both a cause and a result of anti-semitism.

Its first prominent representative was the Frenchman Comte J. A. de Gobineau, who had little immediate influence in his own country but, chiefly via Richard Wagner, ultimately a good deal in Germany. He certainly contributed to the outlook of Houston Stewart Chamberlain, another habitué of Wagner's circle and perhaps the chief popularizer of the belief in German racial superiority. But the details of Gobineau's argument soon seemed unscientific. His single white race, pouring down from the Hindu Kush, was replaced by a varying number of distinct white or near-white races, distinguished by apparently objective physical or 'somatological' characteristics; the chosen people, whatever name it was given, was always fair, blue-eyed, and long-headed. The lengthy argument as to its provenance seemed to be resolved by a majority vote in favour of northern Europe, perhaps even Scandinavia or Germany itself; hence the name Nordic. Gobineau's fanciful notions of how his white race got diluted by his black and yellow races were replaced, under the influence of Darwin and modern biology, by more subtle theories of heredity and selection. It was thought that conscious application of the new knowledge to the future of the race, by means of what Galton called the science of eugenics, made Gobineau's pessimistic vision of the world's future unnecessary. To many people the whole of human history now seemed flooded with new light. In opposition to those who stressed such factors as environment, they saw all, or the highest, civilization as the creation of members of the Aryan or Nordic race, and its decline as always owing to their extinction or submergence by the subject population. The fall of Rome was analysed at particular length in these terms. But Greece was forced into the pattern too. Passages of ancient authors mentioning fair hair and blue eyes were collected and supposed to become rarer as time went on; the few surviving skulls were diligently measured, with apparently satisfactory results.

Now Gobineau himself had been distinctly chilly in his estimate of Sparta. He regarded all post-Homeric Greeks, at least those south of Thebes, as heavily semitized (his Semites are already mixed, black with white). And though in his *Inegalité des races humaines* he suggests that the Dorians succumbed more slowly to contamination, and that Spartan egalitarianism, limited monarchy and attitude to inferior races, and the proud bearing of their warriors and women, were all Aryan, he also sees post-Lycurgan Sparta as incorporating the semitized idea of the state, in contrast to the Aryan conception of individual liberty.[1] He is even more firmly anti-Spartan in the *Histoire des Perses* (the Persians are his real love). Here it is chiefly their lack of a feudal system that he criticizes. He is unexpectedly tender to the usually unpopular Lysander, who was on good terms with the Persians; conversely, Pausanias and Agesilaus, who fought them, come out badly.[2]

The French Darwinist, too, Vacher de Lapouge,[3] like Gobineau

---

[1] J. A. de Gobineau, *Inegalité des races humaines* (1853–5), esp. ii. iv. 3 and 5.
[2] Id., *Histoire des Perses* (1869), esp. ii. iv. 10 and 13.
[3] G. Vacher de Lapouge, *Les Selections sociales* (1896), p. 228; *L'Aryen . . . son*

finally more popular in Germany than at home, was unable to praise them wholeheartedly. He was a good deal of a pacifist, as well as an individualist, and felt that though the Spartans tried to preserve the purest Hellenic elements their constitution was odd and oppressive and their foreign policy scandalous. Though doubtless the most Aryan of Greek peoples, their institutions paralysed their aptitudes, and they were merely incomparable soldiers. Had they survived to unite Greece and obtain a period of *détente*, they might have done great things by uniting Roman tenacity with Greek artistic genius.

Even in Germany, Houston Stewart Chamberlain, whose *Grundlagen des XIX Jahrhunderts*[1] was especially influential in disseminating racial and *Volk*-inspired views, still took little interest in the Spartans. He revered Greece as the best example of a Culture, as opposed to a more mechanical and less creative Civilization—an old distinction in German thought. For man's very definition lay in his creative individuality, his artistic powers in the broadest sense. Even the political systems of Greece were works of art rather than of intellectual comprehension. Thus Lycurgus and Solon were both dilettantes, great as was the former's achievement in uniting a people so difficult of unification. The *Stämme* are not very important in his picture of Greece. Most of her great men were, he thought, Ionians, and the struggle of east and west, Europe and Asia in this period meant little to him.

But other writers were inevitably drawn to the Dorians.[2] The Greek peoples were of course now all Nordic in origin, so great innate differences between the *Stämme* could not be sustained. There was however plenty of basis for interpreting them in terms of relative purity from and contamination by preceding or surrounding non-Nordic peoples. The chief characteristic of the Ionians since Schlegel had been susceptibility to oriental influence. The Dorians were late-arrived and supposedly exclusive, both politically and intellectually. And so Sparta became the most purely Nordic state in Greece, and those who had once been

[1] H. S. Chamberlain, *Die Grundlagen des XIX Jahrhunderts* (1900).
[2] Early in the century H. Driesmans, *Rasse und Milieu* (1902); and at more length the better-known Ludwig Woltmann, *Politische Anthropologie* (1903).

rôle social (1899), pp. 355–6; 295. Their psychic type was that of the Anglo-Saxons, exaggerated and incomplete.

described as children of Abraham were now praised for their exceptional freedom from Semitic blood and influence. In works of this tendency the chief historical authority referred to is the brilliant but unsound (and by then nearly a century old) Otfried Müller.

Sparta had other attractions. She really seemed to fit the Aryan theory, or some versions of it, so well. Her constitution appeared so obviously as the work of a conquering military aristocracy, marking itself off as a caste; a moderate example of that Aryan characteristic of which the rigid caste-system of India was seen as forming one extreme, and the more or less open aristocracies of modern Europe the other. Her decline was past all dispute connected with the decline in numbers of her ruling class. Her laws concerning marriage and children seemed to reveal a striking interest in eugenics—rashly supposed to amount to a conscious desire for racial purity. Spartan women, like German women since Tacitus' day, were honoured in typically Aryan fashion.

Beyond this, there is no unanimity concerning the characteristics of Aryans or Nordics. But whether these were seen as lovers of freedom or discipline, a strong state or a limited monarchy, physical beauty or sexual asceticism, the Spartans could be made to fit the bill. If Sparta was uncivilized compared with the rest of Greece, the feeling that barbarian youth and freshness had more to offer than the tired old age of civilization was gaining ground. If she was cruel, Christian ethics were sometimes rejected as effete and Semitic (while eugenic theory condemned pity and aid for the weak as disastrous folly). In these last respects, Nietzsche's influence was after his own death significant. His own not very prominent remarks about Sparta could be ignored.

The flowering of civilization in other parts of Greece had of course to be explained; either by allowing the non-Nordic peoples, or the crossed strain, some, especially artistic, ability (certain writers even preferred mixtures) or else by arguing desperately that the great Athenians, anyway, were still pretty pure in blood. Plato in particular (though he had usually been treated by Nietzsche as one of his bugbears), who had sprung from the oldest aristocracy and been an opponent of the 'oriental–democratic' tendencies of his day, is much in favour for his Nordic purity.

The flood of racial and *volkisch* writing gathers force after the first World War, and we may single out the work of the prolific and popular H. F. K. Günther who in a special work dedicated to the *Rassengeschichte des Hellenischen und des Römischen Volkes* (1929) analyses Spartan decline in some detail. He claims that the Spartan state shows the racial structure of Greece as a whole with particular clarity, and that the military discipline of its rulers, like the freedom of their women, was a truly Nordic characteristic. His favourite ancient sources for Sparta are such as we are hardly accustomed to: passages from the poets Alcman and Bacchylides, now resurrected in papyrus, describing golden-haired Spartan women.[1] Sparta's fall, like that of all civilizations, was a process of denordicization—owed to 'enlightenment', losses in war, and the fatal law permitting the sale of land, by which many pure-blooded Spartans came to lose the citizenship; for an aristocracy is maintained by maintaining its land. The decline of discipline is illustrated by Agesilaus' father's selfish marriage, and his son's nonetheless successful claim to the throne. Agis IV is a hero who attempts to revive the Nordic element.[2] Plato gets high marks for his political views and his racial purity; and with the Spartans he is exonerated from all taint of pederasty, which spread from pre-Nordic Crete. Günther was incidentally doubtful about the extent of Nordic influence in republican Rome, which had been commonly thought predominant.

The Dorians are also in favour with various writers who were not primarily interested in racial matters. Spengler's *Decline of the West*, one of the most influential of the philosophies of history, works out in detail a cyclic theory of civilization. In the Dorian or Gothic spring-time, according to his schema, life centres on the countryside, the traditions of the soil, on natural religion and aristocratic society (we may recall the description of Sparta as a group of villages and her purely agricultural economy). But the country is fated to be defeated by the town, by fifth-century Athens or eighteenth-century Paris; and later still by the great city.

[1] Alcman, *Partheneion* 11; Bacchylides, *Idas* (written for the Spartans) 20, C19. Fair colouring becomes a conventional attribute of beauty in Greek literature, and may be particularly applied to Spartan women in allusion to Helen.

[2] 'Es ist vielleicht kein Zufall, dass der so vorwiegend nordische Dichter Graf Alfieri diesen Stoff zu einem Trauerspiel verwendet hat' (p. 41, n. 2). Presumably Günther was unaware of all the other authors of plays about King Agis, or are they all as Nordic as the Piedmontese Count?

This stage was reached in antiquity with Rome's conquest of the known world, and was being reached again as Spengler wrote, as he thought; it marks the passing of Culture into Civilization, Soul into Intellect, State into Society, irreligious, materialistic, and imperialist. Fortunately Germany, as Spengler and others believed, was still a young country.

To Spengler all the Greeks were Apolline, not Dionysiac. Certainly, what had been the new way of looking at Greece had come to seem out of date, and there was in some circles a desire for the Apolline from which the Dorians benefited. It was a desire for the positive and stable. Perhaps it should also be linked with the revived sun-cults of Germanic lore, and with the cult of the beautiful Nordic body and even nudism. Its connection with racial theory can certainly be seen in a work by a classical scholar[1] who tries to draw a contrast between the masculine, day-lit, balanced Nordic cult of Apollo and the Muses, of the Olympian gods whose home is heaven or the mountain tops, and on the other hand the enthusiastic mysteries of the 'Pelasgic' substratum of the population, practised especially by women and slaves, associated with night and earth, running to extremes of sensuality or asceticism, concerned with the beyond rather than the here and now. This indicates a return, in some degree, to the definitions of early German Hellenism, even if they are now seen as applicable only to an aristocratic minority of Greeks. Sparta is not discussed at length, but all higher art and learning are associated with a simplicity of life like hers, and the Nordic quality of 'laconic' speech is pointed out: compare the very silent, very Nordic Westphalians (the *Niederdeutsche* was a frequent recipient of Nordic enthusiasm). The myth of Heracles is considered aggressively anti-Pelasgian.

A more personal and striking synthesis of past traditions was provided by the poet Gottfried Benn's return to the Apolline. His essay, *Dorische Welt*,[2] published in 1934, is an investigation into the relations of culture and the state, employing the categories of Nietzsche and Burckhardt. He considers that the Greeks expressed

[1] K. Kynast, *Apollon und Dionysos* (1927).
[2] G. Benn, *Gesammelte Werke* i (1959) 262. Benn remarked in an earlier edition of his essays (1950) that the piece was inspired by the composer Kaminski's *Dorische Musik* of 1933. F. Wodtke, *Die Antike im Werk Gottfried Benns* also sees the influence of Taine and Spengler.

themselves in both. Both are the creation of a shaping and forming will, but the state must come first, moulding the individual till
he becomes *Kunstfähig* or capable of art. Though Benn stresses the
dark side of the state, and quotes Burckhardt on the painful
creation of Sparta, he does not follow him in considering Sparta
unjustified, because cultureless. To him she was not only a *Macht*,
harsh to her slaves, with leaders often corrupt, and kings the very
embodiment of war; a *Soldatenstaat*, a *Männerlager* in essence. She
was also the creator of Greek art; of the 'orchestra', where physical
exercise was united with music, and whence all lyric and tragedy
sprang (and here he goes back to Schlegel rather than Nietzsche).
But the *Spartanisch-Apollinisches* is still more significantly expressed
in sculpture, also created with and from the introduction of public
gymnastics, and in architecture. Its forms were carried all over
Greece by the Spartan armies. An Apolline *Dorismus* lies behind all
Greek values; masculine, ordering, and intellectual, it overcame
the primitive and Dionysiac. Sparta is 'der Ausgangspunkt, die
Keimzelle des griechischen Geistes'; and 'zwischen Rausch und
Kunst muss Sparta treten, Apollo, die grosse Züchtende Kraft'.
Aeschylus and Sophocles—not Euripides—are Dorian; Plato is the
last great Dorian, the mouthpiece of the camp by the Eurotas.
The liberal period could not appreciate the place; but the new
Anthropologische Prinzipienlehre could do so. Benn is, even more
obviously than Nietzsche, using the past to make poetic symbols;
although it is not quite clear how far he is aware of the radically
unhistorical nature of his remarks.

Benn's insistence on the autonomy of art, once created, with its
own laws of development, its ability to express itself alone, indicates one aspect of his opposition to Nazism; and of course it
would be very wrong to think that all the writers or scholars,
many of them distinguished, who, after the first World War,
accepted a definition of *Dorismus* in whole or part, and showed
interest in or even admiration for Sparta, were to become Nazi
sympathizers. But among some works that were much favoured
by the Nazis, certainly, a usually crude approval of Sparta can
be found. Günther was put into a professorial chair in spite of
academic disgust.

Among 'philosophies of history' A. Rosenberg's notorious
Mythus der 20. Jahrhundert (1930) stands out. Its pseudo-historical
introduction—was the origin of the Aryan race perhaps Atlantis?

—briefly resumes the usual view, indeed shows a certain moderation by refusing to jettison Jesus Christ and insisting that he must have been Nordic. Before the rise of Germany, 'am schönsten getraümt wurde der Traum des nordischen Menschentums in Hellas'. The precious strain was already strong in Mycenean Greece, but was strengthened by later invaders with aristocratic constitutions preventing *Blutmischung*: 'die Dorer, dann die Mazedonier, schützten das schöpferische blonde Blut.'

Fuller discussion of Sparta was to appear in another approved work, and to concern her agrarian system. *Volk* and countryside made up a whole; the true German had long been seen as a farmer, and the Indo-Germans or Aryans as peasants as well as, or rather than, warriors. In 1928 Walther Darré published a cranky book, *Das Bauerntum als Lebensquelle der nordischen Rasse*, in which he proclaimed the latter view. In the dearth of evidence for this remote period, and because as he says the Spartiates were so often adduced as the perfect example of a purely military Aryan aristocracy, Darré leans heavily on Spartan history. He finds that the population declined less by losses in war, intermarriage, and so forth than by a combination of 'economic and biological' causes. Changing circumstances and rising costs led the citizens in the fifth century to limit their families, to change the law in order to pile up properties, and often to live away from their land, which encouraged rebellion from below. Had they preserved the 'old-Nordic' laws of inheritance, by which one specially chosen son (not necessarily the eldest) took everything, and had they also introduced a rational money economy, all would have been well. Cleomenes, trying to restore the situation, unfortunately ignored the racial principle and gave land-lots to inferior persons. Not so Horthy in Hungary.

Darré, with frequent horticultural and veterinary comparisons, discusses the whole question of breeding, as it is relevant to hereditary law, marriage and artificial selection through exposure at birth, harsh education, and the extirpation of criminals. He suggests that instead of exposing the unfit we could sterilize them; Himmler was an admirer of his. Sparta appears several times here, as well as early Rome and Germany, especially in connection with the Nordic attitude to the father as representative of state and society and of their claims to interest in all these matters, rather than as an independent patriarch. Darré, of course, soon became directly responsible for the agricultural policy of the Third Reich; the *Lebensgesetz der Verbundenheit von Blut und Boden* was recognized, and the state established control over peasant properties, limiting size and the right of sale, establishing the principle of one owner one farm, and seeing to the owner's racial purity.

There were many admirers of the new Germany who considered it as closely related to Greece, in character as well as blood. This so-called Third Humanism, which grafted newer 'Dorian' ideas on to a Hellenism derived from the great eighteenth-century masters, laid stress on a strong *Staatsgedanke*, on patriotic and paramilitary education, on the love of sport, on *Diesseitigkeit* or living in the real world; on *sinnliche Denken und Fühlen* and the combination of *hartester Realismus mit reinstem Idealismus*, all of which Greeks and Germans were thought to share. Certainly to many, especially the more pacific and less anti-intellectual, early classical Athens was Nordic enough, and they could see Sparta's contribution as Plato saw it, as valuable but one-sided. It is true, too, that novels, plays, and poems concentrated on aspects of German history rather than the classical world (sculpture and architecture on the other hand showed distinct Greek influence, and the Doric order had a definite vogue for its strength, simplicity, and 'organic' form—though nothing could be more un-Spartan than the Nazi obsession with leaving grandiose monuments to posterity). Yet there undoubtedly were people who saw the present not merely in Greek but in Spartan terms, especially when discussing education and the role of youth. It is only necessary to turn to the academic historians still active, the best of whom, while accepting the orthodox picture of Sparta in its outlines, and bearing witness, and indeed contributing, to increased interest in the subject, feel it necessary to protest against gross inaccuracies. This is the burden of Helmut Berve's little book of 1937, aimed at a general audience; and even more enlightening is a later scholarly review of his, discussing four more new books.[1] The three German ones, two of which are written for a fairly popular audience, mark, as he says, the present relevance of the subject-matter. Two of them are specially concerned with the problems of Spartan land-tenure. The author of the main work, an admirer of Darré, puts much stress on the *rassisch-biologisch* factor (so much, indeed, that his reviewer was

[1] H. Berve, *Sparta* (1937); and in *Gnomon* (1941).

moved to protest). He holds that because Sparta was never sufficiently aware of its importance her state soon became an empty,
rationalistic, and moralistic Utopia. Her fate has more to teach us
than her forms; for example, her history proves that it is not
enough to keep the race pure, but the claim to *Lebensrecht* must be
hardened by repeated *Aüsserung des biologischen Lebenswillens*.
This seems to mean that the greatest episode in Spartan history was
her unprovoked conquest of Messenia.

As for the French work in the quartet, Berve feels that it lacks
'tiefe innere Anteilnahme an Lakedaemon', and that in general the
French have little interest in and feeling for Sparta's way of life in
contrast to German sympathy and enthusiasm. Not surprisingly,
it is this work which has been reprinted and, though slight, holds
its place today.

The progressive coarsening, and final taking-off into complete
fantasy, of twentieth-century German laconism seem very
properly to be epitomized by Hitler. He prided himself on an
admiration for Greece, especially Greek art, and remarked that the
ancestors who counted were the Greeks, rather than the ancient
Germans so enthusiastically pursued by many of his own followers.
If a belief in racial conservation and the survival of the fittest, and a
preoccupation with power over others, were the two poles of his
thought, it is fitting that he should single out the Spartans'
courageous decision to destroy inferior children (rather than adopt
the unnatural method of birth control, which allows all those born,
however feeble, to survive) as the reason for their capacity to rule
over 350,000 helots, though themselves only 6,000 in number. By
this systematic policy of race preservation Sparta became the first
volkisch state.[1]

If we may trust the *Table Talk* of the war years, Hitler repeated
these highly dubious numbers with ever cruder stress on the
naked power of the Spartans. The 6,000 entered Laconia as conquerors, and took everything; they proved their greatness by the
miraculous achievement of ruling for several centuries 340,000
helots, Asia Minor, and Sicily.[2] He also had a great admiration for
the spirit of Thermopylae, attributing it to the German troops in
the first World War and later to the Sixth Army cut off in
Stalingrad; who met indeed a similar fate.

[1] *Hitler's Zweites Buch* ii. 17.
[2] *Hitler's Table Talk*, ed. Trevor-Roper, § 63 and § 140.

Finally, Hitler seems to have had a notion that a *Volk* preserved its cooking more faithfully than its language, and that the peasants' soup in Schleswig-Holstein probably bore a close resemblance to Spartan broth. If this suggestion, unlike most of his ideas, is Hitler's own, as he appears to imply, it entitles him to a high place among laconomaniacs.[1]

All such excesses have naturally disappeared today; and indeed classical studies continue to owe new light on Sparta to German scholars. It is hardly surprising, however, if these have not thrown off every trace of conceptions of 'the Dorians' and of Sparta herself which go back so far in their intellectual tradition that the fragility of their basis is hard to recognize.

[1] Ibid., § 4 and § 148.

20

ENGLAND: FROM THE WHIGS TO THE LIBERALS

IN THE early eighteenth century the dominant political belief of first the Whigs and then the Tories too was that of the sublime wisdom of the constitution of 1688. From Liberty as enshrined therein every blessing flowed—virtue, prosperity, excellence in the arts and sciences. Like Romans and Venetians before them, the English considered their version superior to all its prototypes—sometimes because of the fully equal share of the king, sometimes because, with representation and limited suffrage, the democratic element was not really democratic at all. The enormous literature in prose and verse celebrating English liberty does however often continue to consider English history and origins; while, as Voltaire observed, the English of the Augustan age liked to see themselves in Roman dress (though many people at this time believed antiquity had nothing really to teach the present age). But for a time Spartan precedents are rarely and briefly recorded. King Theopompus, incidentally, owing to the new stress on the king's share in the constitution, can turn up in a surprising context. In 1719 Steele, opposing the Peerage Bill that threatened to deprive the king of the power to create new peers, was one of those who argued that this would destroy the famous equilibrium in favour of aristocracy, and he points out that Theopompus, gracious and moderate as he was, made a disastrous mistake in giving power to the ephors. 'This unwary step prov'd fatal both to the Crown and the People, and ended in the ruin of the Constitution.'[1]

But though, by the time of George I, there was little disagreement on fundamental issues, there was plenty of antagonism to

[1] Sir Richard Steele, *The Plebeian*, no. 1; cf. no. 2. Addison in the *Old Whig* complained of historical parallels *ad conflandam invidiam*. Steele maintained he had a serious purpose and quoted his authorities, the scholars Cragius and Emmius.

Sir Robert Walpole's ministry. Tories and dissident Whigs combined in opposition, and Bolingbroke conceived his *Idea of a Patriot King*, as devoted to his subjects' liberties as he was independent of favourites. It was held by some that Frederick Prince of Wales was cut out for the part. The 'patriots' thought that the causes of corruption were private and party interest, and wealth misapplied as luxury; they also attacked Walpole's peaceful foreign policy. In these circumstances Sparta—consistently, if not often—again functioned as a good example. Even her censorship of music might provide a lesson for a society spoiling its taste with Italian opera.[1] But above all her kings were a model (wicked ministers had to be Athenian or Roman).

The popular *Grecian History* of Temple Stanyan dealt with Sparta very much in this spirit; Lycurgus' work ensured virtue and liberty, left no room for 'private Debates and Animosities', and, though with some defects, notably overindulgence to 'Adultery, Theft and, in some cases, to Murder itself', it still excelled that of Solon and occasionally even overtook Christian morality. At about the same date, Richard Glover's epic *Leonidas*[2] was a tremendous success with the circle of the Prince of Wales and all opponents of the court party. It was even thought that Glover's generally prosaic and jerky—probably consciously laconic—verse put him on a level with Pope. 'Leonidas' Glover, as he was known, was emboldened to enter political life. His hero, repeatedly described as a patriot, fills the part of the public-spirited and freedom-loving king to perfection. The Spartans' 'rigid virtue' is contrasted with the faction and corruption to which some of the Greeks have succumbed, and above all with the mostly luxurious and servile followers of Xerxes, under

The absolute controulment of their King,

who does not believe that heaven can desert the cause of monarchy.

[1] *The Craftsman*, no. 29 (Feb. 1727). This famous paper liked historical hints, but rarely refers to Sparta. Eustace Budgell *A Letter to Cleomenes King of Sparta*, (1731) praises the lack of avarice, also female patriotism, careful education, and the just employment of talent (places not sold or given to relatives); but he draws as many lessons from Rome and Athens.

[2] 1737; the dedicatee, Lord Cobham, the distinguished opposition Whig, had a bust of Lycurgus—with those of Socrates, Homer, and Epaminondas—in his Temple of Ancient Virtue at Stowe. It had a suitable inscription dealing with *libertas* and the prevention of *corruptela*.

In case we missed the obvious lesson, we may read it in a poetic epistle to Glover by George Lyttelton, one of the leaders of the opposition to Walpole, who laments that

> No longer we to Sparta's fame aspire,
> What Sparta scorn'd instructed to admire,
> Nursed in the love of wealth, and form'd to bend
> Our narrow thoughts to that inglorious end.

and warns us that

> Lo! France, as Persia once, o'er ev'ry land
> Prepares to stretch her all-oppressing hand.[1]

Glover's Spartans, however, seem notably domesticated and gentle in their tastes, and Glover's other chief poems, on commerce and science, show how limited in scope laconism still was. Poets at least nonetheless show regular signs of it. Thomson's *Liberty* (dedicated to poor Fred) in ploughing through her history lectures arrives at Sparta, to commend her for mixed government, resistance to Persia, and the absence of faction that springs from the lack of wealth and therefore of corruption.[2] (Athens here and elsewhere does well too, in spite of her liability to faction.) And among the mighty Greek dead on whom he meditates in *Winter* appear Lycurgus, 'severely wise' in controlling the passions, Leonidas, and Agis, who tried and failed to save a 'rotten state'.[3] There are brief Spartan references in several other poets. Collins, opening his 'Ode to Liberty' a few years later with the words

> Who shall awake the *Spartan* Fife
> And call in solemn Sounds to Life
> The Youths, whose Locks divinely spreading
> Like vernal hyacinths in sullen Hue
> At once the Breath of Fear and Virtue shedding
> Applauding Freedom loved of old to view?

[1] 'To Mr. Glover on his poem Leonidas' (*Poetical works of Lyttelton*, 1785, p. 61).

[2] 1735–6. Part ii, lines 109–35, especially the last:
> There too, by rooting thence still treacherous self
> The public and the private grew the same.
> The children of the nursing public all,
> And at its table fed—for that they toiled,
> For that they lived entire, and even for that
> The tender mother urged her son to die.

[3] *The Seasons: Winter* i. 453 ff. (in the expanded, 1744, version).

PLATE 6

Leonidas taking leave of his family

(from Glover's *Leonidas*, 1804 edition)

is politically vaguer though poetically perhaps happier.[1] About this time Garrick was turning down the Reverend John Home's first tragedy, *Agis*, 'which some of the best judges such as the Duke of Argyle, Sir George Lyttleton, Mr. Pitt, very much approved of', as David Hume, who did not himself much admire it, observed.[2] It was produced, however, in 1758. 'I cry to think it should be by the author of *Douglas*: Why, it is all modern Greek' wrote Gray[3]; but 'by dint of good acting and powerful support' it ran for some time.[4] It was doubtless in part for its familiar political tone that Lyttelton and others praised it, and Home's patron Lord Bute twice took the future George III to see it. Here is the patriot king again, this one struggling to restore virtue and preserve liberty against plots to set up a sole monarch on the oriental pattern. The people is loyal—it is corrupt rulers and nobles who have done the damage.

> Equal and free, our happy fathers knew
> No interest but the interest of the State.

Understandably, however, all mention of dividing estates and abolishing debts is suppressed. And Spartan virtue, in the person of Agis' friend (this was Garrick's part), does not exclude study in Athens, and a love for an Athenian lady which temporarily overcomes his sense of duty; while the semi-happy end is brought about by some imaginary Thracian mercenaries, not the Spartans at all. (We are a long way from Rousseau still.) Perhaps the only new touch is a hint that the foreign-inspired party is irreligious as well as tyrannical. The prologue draws political and military lessons for the whole audience, including the female part, which is to urge its menfolk on to the war with France. And the public appears willingly to have made contemporary application of various martial passages.[5]

---

[1] *Odes on Several Descriptive and Allegoric Subjects* (1747).

[2] *Letters of David Hume*, ed. Greig, i. 204.

[3] *Correspondence of Thomas Gray*, ed. Toynbee and Whibley, ii. 560. Gray's early-deceased friend Richard West left a fragment of a tragedy on *Pausanias*, which might well have appeared as in some sense a continuation of the epic *Leonidas* of Glover, who was his cousin. It is printed in *The Correspondence of Gray, Walpole, West and Ashton*, ed. Toynbee, ii, Appendix B vii.

[4] Genest, *Some Account of the English Stage* (1832) iv. 515.

[5] See especially *The Story of the Tragedy of Agis with Observations on the Play, the Performance and the Reception*, prefixed to the play (1758). Who was the author of the prologue?

Though Walpole had been dead some years now, doubts about the state of the nation persisted, and were summed up in the successful *Estimate of the Manners and Principles of the Times* (1757) by a disgruntled clergyman, John Brown, who had studied Montesquieu. In his *Thoughts on Civil Liberty* (1765) he suggested a remedy. Since laws and institutions are insufficient in themselves, he embarked on a consideration of the manners and principles of the Spartans, the Athenians (he decides they had none), and the Romans (who only had a sadly mixed lot). As for the first,[1] their institutions, which involved prostitution, adultery, thieving, and assassination, were thoroughly barbaric—but the way they were preserved and maintained was beyond praise. Not only were the great principles of religion and honour harnessed to the task, but the unified, national education created the spirit of patriotism and prevented the division some writers had so wrongly thought necessary in a free state. The lack of such an education was the chief fault of Athens and Rome; its introduction is the prime remedy for England's ills. Brown also hankered after the restriction of trade and luxury, though he knew such a proposal would run him into trouble. Almost more corrupting was the Grand Tour:[2] 'the Writer would not willingly be thought chimerically to adopt all the Rigours of the *Spartan* State: But could wish to see a Law enacted, parallel to That of LACEDAEMON, by which their raw and inexperienced Youth were prohibited from bringing Home the new Follies and Vices of foreign Countries, picked up in a premature and too early Travel.'[3]

---

[1] Sect. vii, pp. 42–61.

[2] Sect. xxv, p. 153.

[3] There had been strikingly similar things in *Reflections on the Rise and Fall of the Antient Republicks adapted to the Present State of Great Britain* (1759) by Edward Wortley Montagu, Lady Mary's erratic offspring. In recent controversies, he thinks, 'historical facts have either been misrepresented or ascribed to wrong principles'. He too sees faction and corruption as causing decay in the past and threatening it now; he too fears impiety, both 'the atheistical doctrine of Epicurus' and modern deism. His first and in some respects most approved ancient republic is Sparta. Lycurgus' original design was almost identical with that of the creators of the modern English constitution; the ephorate later destroyed the balance of power, but Sparta long retained public virtue and rational and manly happiness. Like Brown, Montagu would adopt her unified education; he fears luxury and trade and would even approve some egalitarianism ('a landed interest diffused through a whole people' is the safeguard of a free country). Fortunately England has at last a militia. As for Athens,

By this time, however, England had emerged from the doldrums into the great age of the elder Pitt, and such desperate remedies recommended themselves very little. The new period, with growing knowledge of contemporary French thought and increasing interest in everything Greek, is well aware of Sparta. It judges her variously according to English or French criteria.

The writers of the Scottish Enlightenment were particularly likely to consider her in the course of their investigations into man and society. Like their contemporaries across the Channel, their views on her are determined by their views on such subjects as progress, or the laws of economics; on whether they preferred 'cultivated' to 'rude' ages, or feared the growth of 'opulence'.

Adam Ferguson, as a close follower of Montesquieu, admired Sparta, but not as a model for his own day.[1] He has a long consideration of 'this singular people', and considers Lycurgus and Solon 'the heroes of political society'. Sparta (like Israel and Crete) is a democracy, because wealth is equally distributed; and in Sparta alone was 'the moderation and equality of the citizen' achieved, and the desire for riches stifled. There is no point in comparing forms of constitution, and indeed Sparta's forms were imperfect. It was her spirit, her public practice of virtue, as Xenophon put it, that was so admirable. But 'we must be content to draw our freedom from a different source'—from legal safeguards, not the virtue of our citizens. Ferguson is still more explicit than Montesquieu in contrasting the state where virtue, and that where law, rules. He also gets nearer than almost anyone else in Britain in the eighteenth century to the idea of Spartans as noble savages rather than citizens under a sophisticated constitution when he claims that here the manners 'prevailing among simple nations before the establishment of property' had largely survived, and that Lycurgus would have found the American Indians admirable material.

---

[1] *Essay on the History of Civil Society* (1767) iii. vi ('Of Civil Liberty'), especially pp. 237–51.

democracies are supremely factious; our manners are all too much like hers— our Shakespearemania recalls her passion for the stage. But in some ways we are more like Carthage, which combined a good constitution with opulence and commerce, and whose errors were the same as ours—continental entanglements, neglect of her fleet, and use of mercenary forces. He warmly defends the Carthaginian character from Roman libels.

To Hume (who had no opinion of his book) Ferguson wrote 'I know that you are an admirer of the Athenians as well as Mrs. Montagu, and if I were to plead the cause of Sparta against her I must appeal elsewhere.'[1] If so, Hume's ideas had perhaps hardened a little since his earlier days. In two of his *Essays*, written some years before (and before the French arguments over Sparta and Athens had been formulated), he had shown little disposition to admire any of the ancient republics. They were 'extremely fond of liberty; but seem not to have understood it very well'; they were quarrelsome, lacked 'humanity and moderation'. Even in Athens property was precarious and trade undeveloped, while her assemblies were marked by 'licence and disorder'. Sparta's exclusion of commerce and luxury, to which we could never return, is certainly 'violent and unnatural'. But the following remarks are fairly neutral: 'It is well known with what peculiar laws SPARTA was governed, and what a prodigy that republic is justly esteemed by everyone, who has considered human nature, as it has displayed itself in other nations, and in other ages. Were the testimony of history less positive and circumstantial, such a government would appear a more philosophical whim or fiction, and impossible ever to be reduced to practice.' Perfect equality, however, he argues elsewhere, certainly is impossible. And would be pernicious, for it would have to be enforced by a tyrannic power.[2]

With the victory of Adam Smith's economic doctrines, foreshadowed by Hume, the idea that Sparta was, as a society, peculiar and irrelevant, even 'unnatural', gained in authority. (Smith himself once has kind words for the empirical Solon, and once links Spartans with savages and Stoics.) Several Scottish writers of the second rank seem to try to steer a middle course in their judgement; but their praise tends to be general and conventional, and their criticism particular and devastating.[3]

---

[1] Hume MSS. in the possession of the Royal Society of Edinburgh, v. 25: letter of 17 April 1767, quoted by G. Giarrizzo, *David Hume Politico e Storico* (1962), p. 44, n. 64.

[2] *Essay on the Populousness of Ancient Nations; Of the Original Contract; Of Commerce*: from *Political Discourses*, 1752 (ed. Green and Grose, 1875, vol. iii, especially pp. 291, 408, 410, 449).

[3] The eccentric Lord Monboddo (best remembered now for including the Orang-outang among primitive men) breaks most of the rules. He was a great admirer of antiquity, though usually preferring the Egyptian to the Greek forms of government as less popular. He believed profoundly in the

In England too, a closer look at the famous manners often excited disgust. There is much that is similar in French and British abuse of them at this period. But though the rarely infidel British make less of monk-like Spartans and their worse than Christian fanaticism, they make even more of their interference with property and family life, their treatment of children and especially of slaves (Hume and Smith were among the opponents of slavery). Frequent reference is made to contemporary slavery. It seems to be at this period, too, that the word 'helot' begins to be used for any particularly oppressed population, as the well-known *Letters of an Irish Helot* indicate.[1]

Furthermore, even some admirers of the constitution, seeing Sparta now in Rousseauistic terms as a democracy and a republic, were quite prepared to give her up. Delolme,[2] the Genevan exile whose panegyric of the English system was received with enthusiasm here, argues that to think the whole people must have the suffrage is to be deceived by word-play, and claims that the Romans and Spartans, who spent their whole lives fighting or in the forum, were far from happy; if one looks beyond mere form one finds that in Athens alone did the people enjoy real liberty,

---

[1] William Drennan, *Letters of Orellana or an Irish Helot*, 1785 (Drennan was also the Tyrtaeus of the United Irishmen, however). The O.E.D. quotes nothing before 1823, but then *Blackwood's Magazine* on the 'helotism of Ireland' (and Byron's *Age of Bronze* on South America's). See also *The Helot's Defence of himself, O'Connell, and Catholic Emancipation* (1834).

[2] *The Constitution of England* (1775), pp. 221, 259.

---

importance of heredity, and therefore in the hereditary monarchy of superior families—Sparta's royal houses were truly such, inheriting their virtues from Heracles. The heroic monarchy of Homeric times, and the monarchies of Sparta, Rome, the American Indians, and even Britain, had something in common. They all were or would be ruined by wealth, which Lycurgus was very right to forbid; or which, as he says elsewhere, only governments like those of Egypt and Sparta, based on religion and philosophy, can prevent. Elsewhere again he remarks that 'the last stage of civil society, in which the progression ends, is that most perfect form of polity', which regulates every aspect of education and private life; as in Sparta and the states of Plato and other philosophers. See, for this curious mixture of monarchy, Rousseauism, and other components, especially *The Origin and Progress of Language* (6 vols., 1774–9), vol. i. ii. iv, p. 243; vol. iv. i. viii, p. 185; iv. i. x, p. 213; iv. i. xi, p. 222; v. i. vi, p. 39; v. iii. ii, p. 186; cf. *Antient Metaphysics* (6 vols., 1779–99), vol. v. ii. ii, p. 67.

though it was highly imperfect in the absence of representation, an independent executive and judiciary, and so on.

Thus, too, the cantankerous Dean of Gloucester, Josiah Tucker,[1] trying to wipe the floor with all the dangerous doctrines of Rousseau and his English admirers. He opposed a practical, not to say crude, common sense to all idealization of primitive life or antiquity (in which he is not unlike Dr. Johnson). 'I have now, I think', he says complacently, after making hay with Sparta, Athens, and Rome, 'cleared off a great deal of those vast Heaps of Rubbish, which lay in my Way.' First, such states were not, as their eulogists claimed, democracies. Second, their inhabitants had not more but less liberty than other people. Third, life there was very disagreeable. Tucker was always anxious that England should spend less energy on war and more on commerce. This helped to put him out of sympathy with the Spartans, who also used their helots 'much worse, and with more *wanton* cruelty than the Planters do the Negroes in the *West-Indies*. And that is saying a great deal. Now I ask are these measures proper to be adopted in *Great Britain*? And is this the plan of a Republic, which some future patriotic congress is to set up, in order to correct the Evils of our present unhappy Constitution?'

The Dean lambasts Athens just as vigorously. But on the other hand many of the most advanced thinkers of the time, and those most anxious for reforms, turn firmly to her as they abandon Sparta. Dr. Priestley, the distinguished scientist and utilitarian, who was one of Tucker's bugbears, had very promptly taken up the cudgels against Brown's national education.[2] Individual virtue and happiness are the object of education (which he would have largely religious and scientific in content). 'The great excellence of human nature consists in the variety of which it is capable', and to curb variety is to crush talent. 'The various character of the Athenians was certainly preferable to the uniform character of the Spartans, or to any uniform national character whatever.' Happiness and virtue spring largely from the domestic relations, and a man must be free to choose his wife and educate his children

---

[1] *Treatise Concerning Civil Government* (1781), pp. 217–19.

[2] *Remarks on a Code of Education proposed by Dr. Brown*, printed with *An Essay on a course of Liberal Education* ... (London, 1765). See especially pp. 137 ff. The arguments are repeated more briefly in *An Essay on the First Principles of Government* ... (1768).

as he pleases. A society which, like Sparta, requires for its survival the sacrifice of this freedom must be a bad one, 'and had better be utterly abolished'. Priestley for one would get out of it at once. In addition, he believes passionately in progress; thus to try and fix institutions is fatal. All Sparta got thereby was 'the continuance of what I should not scruple to call the worst government in the world', one that 'continued nearest to her pristine barbarity'. Had we too been educated in an invincible attachment to our institutions, 'we like the old Spartans or the sons of bigotry in Spain and Portugal at present, might have been hugging our chains and have been proud of them'.

This idea was often expressed, if less picturesquely. Nor was Priestley odd in his preference for education under a tutor and the guidance of the parent; since Locke, discontent with existing schools and colleges had often taken this form (a great contrast to France). But, as with many radical figures of the time, a dissenting background doubtless helped to make him even more suspicious of governmental interference than members of the established Church were likely to be. (It is perhaps worth noting, as we trace the rising laconophobia, that nonconformists often also had a background in trade.)

The great step of actually praising Athenian democracy is taken at the time of the French Revolution by Tom Paine (in the wake of increasing mockery by Bentham, for one, of classically-inspired ideas, and mixed constitutions and the notion that England had or ought to have one in particular, as well as of increasing pressure for franchise reform). Though Paine does not mention Sparta by name, the *Rights of Man* shows clearly what he thought of her.[1] 'Though the ancient governments present to us a miserable picture of the condition of man, there is one which above all others exempts itself from the general description. I mean the democracy of the Athenians. We see more to admire, and less to condemn, in that great, extraordinary people, than in anything which history affords.' For any government involving the principle of heredity is not only irrational and incompetent (the mixed constitution is thus a supreme illogicality) but likely to crush the talents given free play in a democracy. True, these are used to still better advantage under a representative system. 'Athens, by representation, would have outrivalled her own democracy.'

[1] 1791–2.

Adopting it, as a large nation must, 'what Athens was in minia-
ture, America will be in magnitude'. Paine's advocacy for a
variety of religious beliefs and against 'what are called national
religions' also links him with nonconformists like Priestley and
Price and shows the liberal current of English radicalism.

But it is not so simple as that. If there is little real political
Rousseauism there is sentimental and educational Rousseauism.
In the remarkable Thomas Day's *Sandford and Merton* Harry tells
Tommy all about the brave and hardy little Spartan boys, and
how 'if they committed any faults they were severely whipped',
and about Agesilaus' simplicity, while Mr. Barlow tells them both
the story of Leonidas.[1] Here new and traditional ideas on suitable
fodder for the young meet.[2] And one suspects it would be found
that many minds were in a thoroughly confused state. At any rate
John Thelwall, the reforming leader of the nineties, combines
poetical and other apostrophes to Athens strongly flavoured by
Paine with praise of Sparta derived from France and from seventeenth-century English republicans (he seems to have got most of
his ideas on ancient history from Moyle)—though he too is given
pause by the helots, as one so hostile to slavery and sympathetic to
the hungry English labourer might well be. As for William
Godwin (another ex-dissenter by religion), though in many
respects nothing could be less Spartan than his individualistic, not
to say anarchic, creed, with its inspiration in progress or 'per-
fectibility', as well as defending Athenian democracy he has a
definite tenderness for Lycurgus, whom he is anxious to vindicate
from Rousseau's belief that he used the authority of religion rather
than that of reason to recommend his laws. Above all, Godwin's
extreme doctrines on property lead him to a sympathetic consideration of Sparta; though he assures us that Matter, by which
he means mechanical inventions, 'will be the Helots of the period
we are contemplating. We shall end in this respect, oh immortal
legislator! at the point from which you began!'[3] It is left to an
opponent to argue that, shorn of chimeras and put into practice,

---

[1] 1783–9; i. 85; ii. 125, 139; iii. 123.

[2] For the latter *The Spartan Manual*, 1785 (a collection of largely Spartan
apophthegms), which could almost have been produced in the Renaissance.

[3] *Political Justice* (1793) i. 92, 361; ii. 505, 804–5, 842, 845–6. All these remarks
survive in the revised edition. In the children's *History of Greece* Godwin
published in 1811 under the pseudonym Edwin Baldwin he is still pro-Spartan,
proclaiming his inspiration in Rollin.

Godwin's system would prove identical with and as despotic as that of Lycurgus, which in spite of pious dislike of all utilitarian morality he paints in terms strongly reminiscent of Priestley's.[1] One will also find a good round condemnation of Sparta, on familiar individualistic, progressive, and pacific principles, in Malthus' great work.[2]

Throughout, conventional and Whiggish admiration persisted, if often on a not very serious level. The poets continue to talk about Lacedaemonian freedom; the laureate, Thomas Warton, discovers a new model king in Pindar's Hiero of Syracuse, who

train'd obedient realms to Spartan laws.[3]

A number of works of art on Spartan subjects were exhibited at the Royal Academy in the seventies and eighties; headed by Benjamin West's *Leonidas and Cleombrotus* of 1770 (this is the third-century Leonidas, of course). England was in the van of the neoclassical movement in art, and in the revival of history painting. These works prove little but a familiarity with Plutarch, Glover's *Leonidas*, several times quoted in the catalogue, and perhaps recent plays. They tend to be moral (*A Spartan Youth convicted of Intemperance*) or even domestic (*Leonidas leaving his wife and children*, a scene of Glover's).

Many people in these years got their knowledge of Greece from the histories of Rollin, in original or translation, and his not much more than epitomator Oliver Goldsmith.[4] To this, not to any English obsession with foxes, is perhaps largely due the primacy that the Spartan boy and the fox begins to gain over the hundreds of ancient anecdotes of similar type. The prologue to Mrs. Cowley's tragedy *The Fate of Sparta or the Rival Kings* (1787) shows that what the public is now expected to know about Sparta is the fox story. This play, after much frankly invented intrigue, ends with Chelonice (Plutarch's Chilonis again, still devoted both to husband and father—also, more important, Mrs. Siddons) inheriting the throne of Sparta. Genest described it

---

[1] W. C. Proby, *Modern Philosophy and Barbarism: or a comparison between the theory of Godwin and the practice of Lycurgus . . .*, London, n.d. (1798?).

[2] T. R. Malthus, *An Essay on the Principle of Population* (2nd ed., 1803) i. 5. 63–4.

[3] *Ode for His Majesty's Birthday* (1786). His inspiration is obviously Pindaric, see above, p. 57.

[4] *The Grecian History* (1774).

as 'so egregiously absurd that no excuse can be made for Mrs. Cowley on the score of her being a woman'.[1] Finally, as proof of general interest in the place, I cannot forbear to mention the officer serving in the American War of Independence who, halting under heavy fire and hearing talking in the ranks, 'harangued the men upon the discipline of the Lacedaemonians and their mode of marching to the attack in perfect silence. This circumstance gained the regiment the sobriquet of the Lacedaemonians.'[2]

And in some quarters Sparta benefited by the horror of democracy, and consequently of Athens, aroused by first the American and then, still more, the French revolutions. (Here, again, is a striking contrast with the French themselves; the damning thing, with them, came to be to call the revolutionaries Spartan.) This horror is visible in two works that have been described as disputing the honour of being the first serious political histories of Greece, those of John Gillies and William Mitford. The former, who became Royal Historiographer for Scotland, reveals his principles in his dedication to George III. 'Sir, the History of Greece exposes the dangerous Turbulence of Democracy and arraigns the Despotism of Tyrants. By describing the incurable evils inherent in every form of Republican policy, it evinces the inestimable benefits ... of well-regulated monarchy.' Open comparisons between America and Athens are made. But Gillies approves a surprising amount of Sparta's social as well as political system: 'such a constitution of society seems the highest elevation and grandeur to which human nature can aspire.'[3]

Mitford was colonel of the Hampshire militia at the time of Gibbon's service in it, and later a Member of Parliament. His history, even more successful than that of Gillies, appeared at intervals between 1784 and 1810 and became notorious for its anti-Jacobinism. The first volume discussed approvingly both limited monarchy and the possible mixtures of constitutions as they appeared in both Greece and England. But Mitford was also, like Gillies, remarkably ready to admire Sparta's social institutions, even if primarily from a distance and as a 'wonderful phenomenon', and with exception made for the treatment of the helots.

---

[1] Genest, op. cit. vi. 473–5.

[2] *History of the Markham Family* (1854), p. 57. The regiment was the 46th.

[3] *History of Ancient Greece* (1786). Cf. his earlier work *The Orations of Lysias and Isocrates*, 1778 (esp. p. 63 for Athens and America).

'The law required that every Lacedaemonian should be, in the strictest sense of the modern term, a gentleman', he held. He even quotes Rousseau on Lycurgus with approval, and contemplates Spartan ideas on theft, and on the breeding of men as well as dogs and horses, with much equanimity.[1] The later volumes were increasingly reactionary in sentiment and open about their author's revulsion from events in America and France.

Such developments were not confined to professed scholars. Even Burke, who generally despises classical parallels, points out that Europe was now for the first time divided on a secular, political issue, just as Greece had been at the time of the Peloponnesian War; and that France, like Athens then, was 'the head and ally of all democratic factions, wherever they existed.'[2] A moderate, and of course only temporary, defender of the French, Sir James Mackintosh, scarcely dared to defend Athens as well, and tried to prove that, because of representation and the separation of powers, France did not resemble her at all.[3] It is understandable therefore that in the eighteen-thirties the historian Connop Thirlwall[4] could complain of "all the attempts, which for the last forty years have been systematically made in our own literature—the periodical as well as the more permanent, for political and other purposes, to vilify the Athenians'.[5]

During the Napoleonic Wars the old identification of French with Persian tyranny gave a last kick, or so in particular the revival

---

[1] *History of Greece*, i. v.2 especially.   [2] *Thoughts on French Affairs* (1791).
[3] *Vindiciae Gallicae* (1791), esp. p. 103.   [4] *History of Greece* (1835–44).
[5] In an artistic and intellectual context Athenian prestige naturally remained high throughout. 'It was about this time' (*c.* 1815—wrote Henry Cockburn in *Memorials of his Time*, 1856) "that the foolish phrase 'The Modern Athens' began to be applied to the capital of Scotland; a sarcasm, or a piece of affected flattery, when used in a moral sense; but just enough if meant only as a comparison of the physical features of the two places." By 1825 an English writer had published a long and mainly satirical account of what he persisted in calling 'the Athens' at the time of George IV's visit; and Peacock's demolition of the notion in *Crotchet Castle* (1831) has capital fun with Scottish deficiencies in Greek scholarship and the drama, for which political economy is no substitute. If he demotes the Edinburghians to the status of Boeotians, 'whose redeeming virtue was in fish', another analogy suggested itself when the term Doric came to be applied particularly to the Scots dialect. Englishmen disliking both Scots claims and the Spartans have pointed out that a devotion to haggis, reminiscent of that to black broth, is only one of the regrettably Lacedaemonian features of the supposed Athens of the north.

of interest in Glover's *Leonidas* would suggest. An expanded version of 1770 had had little success (like a sequel, the *Athenaid*, in the eighties), but now several new editions came out, that of 1804 with engravings by well-known artists. A broadsheet of 1803 entitled *The Briton's Prayer* consists of sentiments extracted from the poem, some suitably 'varied' (Xerxes is varied to Buono). And a weak dramatic 'enlargement' of 1792 made print, though not the London stage, in 1814[1]—the last act was enlarged with funeral games, a martial ballet, and Handel's Coronation Anthem to the words 'Jove save the King'. The occasional Spartan works of art shown at the Academy in these years include two representations of Leonidas at Thermopylae (the last quotation from Glover in the catalogue occurs as late as 1837).

But here we are doubtless slipping into genuine philhellenism. Sympathy for Greece took the same form as elsewhere in Europe, with Turks often seen as Persians and Maniotes as Spartiates. Among Philhellenic poets Byron takes of right first place, and among various references to Lacedaemon we can hardly ignore, hackneyed as it is,

> Of the three hundred give but three,
> To make a new Thermopylae.[2]

But he was far from isolated—for example, rather earlier there was Haygarth, who wrote of the Three Hundred that

> still their spirit walks the earth,
> Their martial sounds are heard from Maina's rocks.[3]

Most of the philhellenes were liberals, and couple Athens with Sparta often enough. But, it would seem, Shelley's radicalism went too deep even for this compromise. In his *Hellas* Athens stands alone as the representative of Greek freedom—a record, perhaps, in philhellenic verse.

The themes of this, as of eighteenth-century patriotic poetry, could be adapted to the circumstances of other countries enslaved by foreign tyranny. Italy, in particular:

[1] *Thermopylae, or Repulsed Invasion*, by J. P. Roberdeau, *New British Theatre* ii.

[2] 'The Isles of Greece' (*Don Juan*, Canto iii, Stanza 86).

[3] William Haygarth, *Greece, A Poem* (1814).

> better be
> Where the extinguished Spartans still are free
> In their proud charnel of Thermopylae
> Than stagnate in our marsh,

wrote Byron in the *Ode to Venice*. But the full flood of pro-Risorgimento English poetry comes from a rather later date, when the course of English laconism was run.

In the age of franchise reform and the influence of German thought it soon proved to be run. As elsewhere in Europe, we have now to move further away from the main stream of political argument towards the restricted, though not yet minute, world of classical scholarship to trace our argument.

The excessively narrow views of Mitford aroused considerable disgust. A very early essay of Macaulay's, from 1824, combats his views at some length, in particular the 'eccentric taste' for Lacedaemon rather than Athens, which he may have disseminated[1] (eccentric already?). The distinguished scholars from among the philosophic radicals had not, of course, even Macaulay's slight hesitations about democratic Athens. The *Westminster Review* asserted its low opinion of modern histories of Greece. In 1830, when Müller's work on the Dorians was translated by Henry Tufnell and Sir George Cornewall Lewis, they explicitly dissociated themselves from their author's political views. In 1841 there began to appear Grote's great history of Greece, so famous for its passionate but reasoned defence of Athenian democracy as government in the interests of the whole state and as the safeguard of liberty. The successors of Pericles, like the sophists, are reconsidered; Grote remains to this day the best apologist of Cleon. His picture of Sparta is scholarly and understanding but unenthusiastic, and minimizes intellectual and other achievements there. It rightly denies the equal division of land. John Stuart Mill reviewed several volumes of the work at length in the *Edinburgh Review* for 1846 and 1853, and echoed its judgements on the Spartans, whom he calls 'those hereditary Tories and Conservatives of Greece; objects of exaggerated admiration to the moralists and philosophers of the far nobler as well as greater and wiser Athens'; their state did nothing for progress, it was petty in its policy and

[1] 'On Mitford's History of Greece' (*Knight's Quarterly Magazine*, 1824). Cf. 'History' (*Edinburgh Review*, 1828); both in collected editions of Macaulay's *Essays*.

AA

ineffective in controlling its members (who could be magnanimous in their way) when beyond its boundaries. Mill's review also agreed on the Athenians, who in spite of all errors are wrongly accused of fickleness; they were by Greek standards remarkably free from faction and violence, and in tolerating individualism and variety were superior to modern democracies. Their empire, if strictly to be deprecated, was beneficial in its effects; would it had lasted longer. Like Grote, he turns to Thucydides' Funeral Oration for his praise of Athens.[1]

Grote's great history more or less superseded the fine and very recent work of Connop Thirlwall of Cambridge, published between 1835 and 1844, which shared some of its presuppositions. Thirlwall was a broad-minded churchman, and like Grote an admirer of German scholarship. We have had a hint already of his views on Athens; he could admire Pericles, if not his successors, and had little tenderness for Sparta. His book helped to pave the way for Grote, whose ultimate triumph was backed by hitherto unparalleled learning and critical judgement. Lengthy and scholarly as the work was, it was widely read. An inferior historian, Cox, was a disciple of Grote's. And the German histories translated in Victorian times, those of Duncker, Curtius, and later Holm, were among those most moderate in criticism of Athens.

A serious defence of Sparta, or even much interest in her, seems hard to find in Victorian England. Carlyle picks up the comparison with Frederick William's Prussia; beer soup and drill at court, but also training in frugality and hardihood, and, apparently, veracity—just slightly more serious and favourable than Voltaire had been, therefore.[2] Visitors to Greece are not inspired to paroxysms of horror or delight when they reach Laconia. Artists, to judge from the Academy catalogue, give her up. In literature it is easiest to come upon a few incidental hits against her in the course of a narrative dealing primarily with Athens. There is, however, Bulwer Lytton's unfinished (not to say, to the modern reader, unfinishable) novel, *Pausanias the Spartan*,[3] which makes

---

[1] Reprinted in *Dissertations and Discussions* ii. 283 ff. and 510 ff. The feminist Mill excludes from his condemnation the Spartan treatment of women. The first review is still sniping at Mitford's prejudices.

[2] *Frederick the Great* (1858ff.), especially vol. iv, ch. viii.

[3] Posthumous publication 1876. Lytton also wrote a history of Athens, pre-Thirlwall, and wisely left it unfinished.

that ambiguous hero sufficiently attractive to the reader, and palliates his treachery to Sparta, by endowing him with sympathy for the helots and disgust at the limitations of his countrymen's intellectual and political outlook. Grote with a dash of Müller (in the sense of a belief in the different qualities of the *Stämme*), a slight hankering for the gentlemanly Spartans of the Whigs and the patriotic ones of both Whigs and philhellenes, make up the only slightly ambivalent attitude of this author, and of many later writers. Thorough liberals did not waver in aversion. Though Acton's history of liberty was never written, he gave a lecture on the 'History of Freedom in Antiquity' in 1877.[1] It discusses Athens at some length, with a panegyric on Pericles and reservations on the position of minorities and the tyrannic possibilities of democracy. But it virtually fails to mention Sparta—an omission no previous century could have comprehended.

Several objections to such generalizations will immediately spring to mind. How can a general disdain for Sparta be squared with the devotion to Plato so conspicuously shown by intellectual Victorians? Grote and Arnold, Newman and Jowett, Ruskin and Pater—the many-sided genius of Plato meant different things to such very different men, but to almost all of them Plato's concern with political and social reform was one of his chief attractions. The *Republic* was one of his best-admired works; it became staple study in the new and influential Greats school at Oxford.

The answer would seem to be that Plato's ideal state was usually seen primarily as an emanation, if a critical one, of Athenian society—as to a great extent it is. The Victorian interest in fifth-century Athens and the real if limited similarities between the two ages have often been pointed out—a triumph over foreign despotism followed by commercial and imperial expansion, an extended franchise but the only gradual erosion of the power of the upper classes, and the collapse of many old religious and other certainties. In this setting Plato's ideas, above all on political education and leadership, sometimes also on social welfare and egalitarianism, seemed as relevant as Thucydides' analysis of Athenian democracy and imperialism.[2]

[1] Reprinted in *The History of Freedom and other Essays* (1907), p. 1.
[2] Some interesting quotations in R. Ogilvie, *Latin and Greek* (1964), pp. 91 ff.

Grote[1] and Mill,[2] his faithful reviewer, openly regretted Plato's progression from (as the former, drawing on a phrase of Plutarch, put it) the Socratic to the Lycurgan stand-point—from negative *elenchus* to dogmatic revelation. What they felt most sympathy for in the *Republic* was not only the stress on proper training for politicians but the serious treatment of population problems. But Grote resembles later writers in minimizing the contacts with Sparta (greater, he admits, in the *Laws*, which received, as ever, less attention). The important academic introductions and commentaries to the *Republic* also stress the differences as much as the similarities. Nor did the rising influence of Hegel on political philosophy and views of the state affect this situation; Hegel, it will be remembered, admired Athens.

To all this the chief exception is Pater, who was led under German influence to what he admitted to be a 'day-dream' of Sparta, sympathetically Platonic perhaps in intention but fantastically aesthetic in effect.[3] He calls up the narrow winding lanes of the picturesque villages that made up Sparta, with their ancient remains of a 'hieratic and religious' Dorian architecture; the great tranquil plane trees, the quiet, spacious, half-rustic houses, the countryside itself, alternately severe and luxuriant from the alternation of mountain and valley, the purity and vigour of life in the highland atmosphere. Above all he admires the Spartan youth, and the 'half-military, half-monastic spirit, which prevailed in this gravely beautiful place', providing 'a spectacle, aesthetically at least, very interesting, like some perfect instrument shaping to what they visibly were, the most beautiful of all people, in Greece, in the world'. It was the unity, as of a work of art, the patience, discipline, restraint, as of an artist, that drew Pater. But he also saw the place as something like a venerable English public school in an ancient ecclesiastical city where past and present intertwine. He speaks of 'public school slang', would like to hear the 'school singing'. (The identical rather cloying taste recurs, with, briefly, the explicit comparison, in *Emerald*

---

[1] Grote, *Plato and the other Companions of Socrates*, (186).

[2] Mill, op. cit. iii. 275 ff.

[3] *Plato and Platonism* (1893), ch. viii. He even suggests that it was often for excessive beauty that outstanding helots were killed; though often the touching devotion of the helot to his noble young master will have formed a lovely and natural relationship (!)

Uthwart, where that modest hero's schooldays in the shadow of Canterbury cathedral are described.) And yet, asks Pater, to what purpose is all this discipline and self-sacrifice? Simply the fashioning of oneself into a perfect work of art? The Christian student has another and better justification. 'It is because they make us ask that question; puzzle us by a paradoxical idealism in life; are thus distinguished from their neighbours; that like some of our old English places of education though we might not care to live always at school there, it is good to visit them on occasion.'

The Platonic and educational contexts are naturally related, and here too Pater is an exception. The now notorious comparison of public school and Spartan ways of life seems elsewhere hard to find until we reach the liberal opponents of both in quite recent years. The leading educationalists of the period do not, I think, turn to Sparta for precedent, though to Plato they may. The features since regarded as so similar were of course natural growths, either of an earlier date, like fagging and the prefect system, or of the later part of the nineteenth century: the athleticism that developed from the fifties on was to a great extent a muscular Christian invention, and the patriotic and military outlook, like an all too frequent neglect of intellectual and artistic values, was largely the product of the new schools for the new ruling class of the great age of imperialism.

If we go back to the great Dr. Arnold, indeed, we find that he felt no temptation to over-praise Sparta. She was notoriously an oligarchy, or aristocracy, if a curious one, and he pointed out, very rightly, that Greek nobles bore little resemblance to Christian gentlemen.[1] He was explaining, in what was still the era of Mitford, his preference—nourished on Thirlwall and the Cambridge school, on German literature and on Vico—for the admittedly over-democratic Athenians. And much later his son uses the name 'Lycurgus House' in attacking not the public schools, on which he is also severe, but the inadequate would-be practical education served up in private academies to the materialistic and narrow, though energetic, middle class—the Philistines for whose enlightenment Matthew Arnold was always concerned. 'You are not to suppose from the name of Lycurgus that any Greek or

[1] *Thucydides*, ed. Arnold (1830–5), i, Appendix iii, p. 669. Cf. a letter quoted in A. P. Stanley's *Life and Correspondence of Thomas Arnold* (1844), p. 415, asking what the Swiss and Spartans made of the liberty they defended so heroically.

Latin was taught in the establishment; the name only indicated the moral discipline, and the strenuous earnest character, imparted there.' As to the instruction, that consisted of futile pseudo-scientific experiments and left the mind ('*qua* mind') entirely untouched.[1]

With the extension of the public school system just at this time something of the spirit of Lycurgus House no doubt crept into some of these institutions. But if they were called Spartan occasionally, it seems to have been mostly in the simple sense of uncomfortable[2]—in which superficial meaning the word was, it seems, becoming more frequent, an indication perhaps that it aroused no profound passions. At the lowest educational level, as ever, outworn ideas persisted, and from such histories as those of Goldsmith or Godwin, reprinted far into the century, children might learn to admire Spartan virtue and the boy with the fox.

In two other currents of thought it might appear worth while to look for references to Sparta. One is that of socialism and social reform: but England was less historically and theoretically-minded than Germany, and one doubts if much would be found, at least after a splendid pamphlet of 1840 called *Lycurgus and the Spartans historically considered*.[3] The author believes that Sparta proves 'the doctrine of socialism respecting the formation of character', that is, that education and environment are of first importance. So let us introduce the system of 'the benevolent Owen', of which the results would be even more 'delightful', helots and military outlook being omitted. The scholarship paraded is old-fashioned—Rollin, Gillies, and Mitford would have been appalled at the use they are put to. In the same way, though racial ideas had a good deal of popularity for a time, the English tended to be wary of world-historical perspectives. Certainly Mr. Phoebus in Disraeli's *Lothair* (1870), who is a devotee of everything Aryan, is led by his admiration for Greek art and the Greek feeling for the body to approve of Spartan eugenics; but he is a foreigner (and scarcely the mouthpiece of Disraeli's own ideas). In accordance

[1] *Friendship's Garland* (1871).

[2] O.E.D. quotes *Athenaeum*, 19 July 1884, 'the hardy but squalid Spartanism of our older public schools'.

[3] J. N. Bailey, *The Social Reformer's Cabinet Library of Short Treatises on Important Subjects, Historical Series*, no. 1 (Leeds, 1840).

with the pro-Athenian mood of the time, Galton singled out the Athenians as the most gifted people ever seen,[1] and declared Sparta's eugenic measures 'so alien and repulsive to modern feelings that it is useless to say anything about them', while in our present ignorance any attempt to emulate them might do more harm than good. The cautious and liberal Galton did write a eugenic Utopia, a naively innocuous work that takes an English university as its model and operates a marking system chiefly sanctioned by public opinion; but even so he suppressed it.[2]

The twentieth century brought, it would seem, only a hardening of older attitudes to Sparta, especially from the thirties on. The reaction against German and other racialism and totalitarianism helped to turn careless contempt into active distrust or even horror. Socialists might join the liberal camp; the strain they could feel may be illustrated from Naomi Mitchison's historical fiction. In *Black Sparta* (1928) the stories more than once turn on young Spartiates, proud of and devoted to their state, coming face to face with the realities of helot life on which it is based, while in *The Corn King and the Spring Queen* (1931) she deals with the revolution of Cleomenes, always the last refuge of left-wing would-be admirers of Sparta, exaggerating its pro-helot aspect and still not stifling her doubts.

The Nazi interest in Sparta was made known, for example by Richard Crossman in *Plato Today*, which like some other works on Plato of about the same time draws attention to, and even overstates, the totalitarian and 'fascist' elements in his political thought. Indeed, it is noteworthy that Plato's assailants, in the controversy that arose on this issue, tended to use Sparta, whose repulsiveness was well-established in this country, as a cudgel to beat Plato with, and that they exaggerated his, and the *Republic's*, laconism.[3]

Similarly such a critic of the public schools as T. C. Worsley lumps them with Sparta and Nazi Germany, while Gilbert Murray for one compared the second World War with the Peloponnesian War, England of course playing the role of

---

[1] F. Galton, *Hereditary Genius* (1869).
[2] Id., *Enquiries into Human Faculty* (1883).
[3] E.g. Bertrand Russell, 'Philosophy and Politics' in *Unpopular Essays* (1950), p. 12, and above all K. R. Popper, *The Open Society and its Enemies* (1945 and 1952).

liberal and democratic Athens.[1] Of late, professional ancient historians have shown interest in, and, at least when addressing a wider public, distinct animosity to, Sparta. Even our one constructor of philosophies of history, Professor Toynbee, condemns the place firmly both in *A Study of History* and his more recent book on *Hellenism*, though on different grounds. In the first, it is primarily Sparta's over-specialization, her over-adaptation to peculiar circumstances, resulting in the atrophy of the power of rational choice, and thus in a society relying on instinct, like a swarm of ants or bees. In the second he sees her as the extreme case of the Greek worship of Man, and consequently of the State, which to the religious mind constitutes *hubris*.

It is Athens, today, to which reaction is often anxious and ambiguous—largely because Athens was an imperial as well as a democratic power. It has sometimes seemed in recent years that scholars of left-wing tendencies have been trying to defend her by stressing the solidarity of the *demos* in the subject states with that of Athens, and minimizing her economic dependence on allies and slaves. On the other extreme, only a few years ago there appeared an astonishing survival of the Oxford-Hegelian, Plato-and-Thucydides attitude, which attacked imperialist democracy both in Britain and Athens and rashly idealized the aristocratic opposition to Pericles (who was compared to Lord Rosebery).

As usual, we oversimplify. There are, it seems, a few laconizers yet, though the admiration expressed by Dr. Kurt Hahn, the founder of Gordonstoun, in one breath for Plato, the public schools, and the Spartan virtues is doubtless representative of a conservative German tradition. But at an unsophisticated level laconism of a primarily moral kind has never died out, and perhaps will not while the traces of puritanism remain. The partly outraged correspondence in the *Listener* provoked a few years ago by a fairly hostile broadcast on Sparta would bear this out; so would commercial willingness to use 'Spartan' as a brand name.

But as personal experiences will show, among educated people in England the reaction to Sparta is almost invariably hostile. Her contemporary embodiment is usually found in South Africa, and the press is still able to denounce her Spartan system and to refer to the victims of apartheid as helots.

After a journey in which we have seen a single people pass, in

[1] G. Murray, *Greece and England*, 1941 (in *Greek Studies*, 1946).

the imagination of posterity, through so many transformations, and inspire so many contradictory conclusions, we may be excused from trying to draw one more. Perhaps we should not even conclude, with Valéry, that the study of history is the most dangerous and misleading of all studies, for Sparta is an exceptionally remote and ill-documented subject. Given the comparatively sophisticated attitude towards history to which we have attained, and the widening gulf between modern life and that of the past, it is improbable in the extreme that she will ever regain an important place as exemplar to the present; while the extraordinary circumstances that led to the German belief in a close blood-relationship, as well as a spiritual affinity, are not likely to be repeated. Nevertheless, it seems certain that her name will remain with us for some time yet, to symbolize in dramatic fashion some of the social and political possibilities always before us. It is, in fact, inappropriate to draw any conclusion from the history of the Spartan tradition, for the reason that it has surely not yet come to an end.

APPENDIX

NOTE ON THE UNITED STATES

ONE does not get the impression that references by American writers to Sparta, considered apart from other ancient states, have ever been very prominent or formed a clear pattern. The agitation leading up to the Declaration of Independence concerned itself either with the colonists' rights within the established order or ultimately with their natural rights; and subsequent euphoria reinforced the feeling that antiquity had been left far behind. Nor, representation being so much admired, was a single lawgiver in demand. Even the comparatively conservative John Adams, an admirer of Montesquieu and the English tradition, thinks a few political advances have been made since Lycurgus' day, while disliking Spartan manners (except for the military exercises incorporated in education).[1] The debates at the time of the Federal Convention in 1787, which was to reform and strengthen the federal government, occasionally seek ancient precedent; usually in the Greek leagues, and in these Sparta's role had been most often objectionably dominant or disruptive. The smaller states could find confirmation in this of their fear that even equal voting powers for all, irrespective of size, in the central councils would not be sufficient protection. Supporters of the new constitution retorted that it was not Sparta's large size but her intrigues that did the damage, or else that it was her inadequately republican system that prevented co-operation with the Greek democracies. The *Federalist*, recommending the constitution, does advert to the stability which a senate gave Rome, Sparta, and Carthage; Hamilton appeals to ephors and tribunes to show that the people could trust even a smallish body of representatives. But any division of the executive powers, as in Rome or Sparta, was deprecated, and Sparta's 'habits and manners' were considered particularly irrelevant to America.

The subsequent movement towards democracy was suspicious of centralized government and strongly individualistic. The French Revolution helped to strengthen the vogue of antiquity, but not of Sparta in particular, while the more conservative and anglicized party, at least, was possibly confirmed in mistrust of her. But there were certainly Americans who were named Leonidas, and a number of

[1] John Adams, *Defence of the Constitutions of Government of the United States of America against the attack of M. Turgot* (1787), Letter xl.

Spartas appeared on the map; just as more than one small town intending to set up a college called itself Athens.[1]

As time went on, however, the appeal to antiquity became strongest
in the increasingly conservative Southern states. At first, perhaps, this
was because intellectual fashions lagged behind Europe and the Southern
gentleman required a classical education. Soon the reasons were more
particular, and no other society in the nineteenth century appealed so
seriously to Greek precedent. The doubt whether slavery and republicanism were compatible was early raised (the federal constitution not
only involved a natural rights clause but guaranteed all states a republican constitution) and answered: 'the purest sons of freedom in the
Grecian Republics, the citizens of Athens and Lacedaemon, all held
slaves.'[2] In the debates on the admission of Missouri to the Union in
1820 Southerners praised Rome, Athens, and Sparta in turn for combining liberty, even democracy, with slavery.

After 1830 the South became yet bolder in its defence of slavery and
of its own rights against possible interference by the federal government. John C. Calhoun's fear of such majority despotism led him to
his doctrine of the 'concurrent majority', by which each interest in a
free state has the power of nullification or veto. For this he found
precedent primarily in England, Rome, and Sparta; and he further
advocated a plural executive as another check on the central power.
This is the mixed constitution in a new form, with the old exemplars.
And his positive advocacy of slavery led him, and later Southern
theorists, to build directly on Aristotle (not to mention the Bible and
Sir Robert Filmer) in creating an organic theory of the state.

But if Southern society was Greek democracy revived, as was very
widely held, the democracy specified was often that of Athens, for the
South boasted of its refinement and was devoted to oratory (possibly
of a style too florid to deserve the name of Attic, but Demosthenes was
a name to conjure with). Post-Periclean Athens was finally seen to bear
a suspicious resemblance to Yankee society, over-democratic, restless,
and commercialized; but some authors, including the scholarly Hugh
Swinton Legaré, were equally averse from the Spartans and anxious to
dissociate the latter's tyranny over 'their subjugated brethren', owned
by the state, from the paternal and personal relationship with the
irrevocably inferior Negro. It was the white wage-slaves of Europe and
the North who were the modern helots. And then, Sparta had inspired

---

[1] As for a later Laconia in Washington state, 'Laconia on account of its location at the summit was named after what I thought was Laconia in Switzerland
... but in looking over the Swiss map this morning I am unable to find a place
of that name there'.

[2] *Annals of Congress*: 1st Congress, 2nd session, p. 1242 (Jackson of Georgia).

the *Republic*, the direct progenitor of socialism and all other disastrous *isms*. (Aristotle is in, and Plato out.)

On the other hand Sparta is sometimes considered acceptable. The lively and provocative George Fitzhugh, reviewing Carlyle's *Frederick the Great*, spoke of Prussia, Sparta, and the South as all well run. He could recommend the slave state as a better form of socialism, and was able to return by this road to admire Lycurgus. As war approached, the spirit of Thermopylae was sometimes summoned up.

Outsiders have occasionally been ready to accept the comparison of the American South with Sparta, or, under the ultimate influence of German scholarship, to speak of a Dorian mentality; this is significant as being very much of the same pattern as the common present-day comparison with South Africa. One sees why it is tempting. The Southern way of life was believed to encourage the spirit of liberty, and to reconcile the idea of democracy (dear to the small farmers of the hills) with that of aristocracy (for which the rich planters hankered). It performed this miracle by binding into an aristocracy of equals all whites, who, according to a current myth, were sometimes all regarded as of gentle descent. The Southern system was also thought to prevent great inequalities of wealth, to ensure leisure, a sense of unity, stability, and permanency. The intellectual primacy of the North was finally admitted, but often regarded as of less importance than the South's political and social superiority, while cultural nationalism and a powerful censorship formed a barrier against its influence. There was a strong suspicion of a society based on great cities, industry was often (not always) despised *vis-à-vis* agriculture, a great regard for legal rights was professed, and society became increasingly military-minded, as the ubiquity of military titles and a liking for the education of the military academies shows.

INDEX OF NAMES

Price, Richard, 354
Priestley, Dr. Joseph, 352–3, 354, 355
Proby, W. C., 353 n.
Procopius of Gaza, 118
Prodicus, 18 n.
Propertius, 108
Protagoras, 199
Prussia, 225, 326–7, 328, 370
Pseudo-Archytas, 84, 153
Pseudo-Xenophon, 27 n.
Purcell, Henry, 217 n.
Ptolemy of Lucca, 127–8
Pylos, 26, 113
Pyrrhus of Epirus, 88, 92, 218, 265 n.
Pythagoras, Pythagoreans, 57, 58, 63, 83, 84, 96, 97, 99, 100, 104, 110, 319, 323
Pythagoras, a Spartan, 104
Pythian Oracle (*see* Delphi), 299

Quinault, Philippe, 212–13, 214
Quintilian, 130

Rabaut-Saint-Etienne, Jean Paul, 271, 280
Raleigh, Sir Walter, 187
Ramsey, Chevalier Andrew, 221, 224
Raynal, Abbé, 262
Regnaud de St. Angély, J. de, 288 n.
Regulus, 256 n.
Remus, 141
Renan, Ernest, 298, 300
Rétif de la Bretonne, N. A. E., 261
Rhigas, Constantine, 293
Richelieu, Cardinal, 211
Roberdeau, J. P., 358
Robespierre, Augustin, 273
Robespierre, Maximilien, 268 n., 272, 273, 274, 275, 276, 277, 278, 280, 281, 283, 287, 288, 289, 260, 295, 296, 297
Roland, Mme (Manon Phlipon), 263, 272 n., 283
Rollin, Charles, 222, 224, 255, 262, 268, 312, 354 n., 355, 364
Rome, Romans
as democracy, 151, 153, 189
as empire, emperors, 1, 114, 134,

146, 156, 160, 274, 296, 334, 345
as mixed constitution, 100–3, 120, 140, 144, 150, 151, 187–8, 247, 344, 369
as monarchy, 161, 194, 351
as republic, 1, 137, 139, 141, 142, 144, 146, 148, 153–4, 157–8, 165, 170, 184, 192–3, 200, 201 n., 210, 228, 231, 233, 238–40, 244, 251, 258, 263–4, 268–9, 270, 272–3, 276, 285, 287–8, 290–1, 295, 300–5, 309, 316, 344, 348–9, 351–2, 368–9
mentioned, 2, 101–5, 113, 117, 119, 126, 130, 133, 142, 149–55, 162–3, 193, 197, 199, 201 n., 225, 229, 237, 240 n., 249, 279, 289
Romulus, 103, 104, 105, 141, 143, 144, 145
Rosebery, Lord, 366
Rosenberg, Alfred, 339–40
Rossaeus, G. G., 162
Rouget de l'Isle, C. J., 285
Rousseau, Jean-Jacques, 1, 142, 145, 227, 229, 231–41, 243–6, 247, 251–3, 255–6, 259, 261, 266, 268–9, 271–2, 274, 277–9, 282, 284 n., 288, 292, 297–8, 308, 347, 351–2, 354, 357
Rulhière, C. C. de, 292
Ruskin, John, 361
Russell, Bertrand, 365 n.
Russia, Russians, 292, 293, 332 n.
Russo, Vincenzo, 305

Sabines, 99, 122, 219
Sabus, 99
Sagalassus, 109 n.
Saint-Just, A. L. L. de R. de, 268 n., 273, 274, 276–7, 277, 288, 296
Saint-Lambert, J. F. de, 251, 262
St. Pierre, Abbé de, 225
Salamis, battle of, 15, 113, 330
Samians, Samos, 20 n.
Samnites, 99, 305
San Marino, 175, 255, 282
Sannazaro, Jacopo, 124 n.
Savérien, A., 259 n.

INDEX OF SUBJECTS